SERIAL KILLERS

The Minds, Methods, and Mayhem of History's Most Notorious Murderers

Richard Estep

ABOUT THE AUTHOR

Richard Estep is the author of twenty books, most of them in the field of paranormal nonfiction, including *The Haunting of Asylum 49: Chilling Tales of Aggressive Spirits, Phantom Doctors, and the Secret of Room 666*. He is a regular columnist for *Haunted Magazine* and has also written for the *Journal of Emergency Medical Services*. His lifelong fascination with ghosts has led him to investigate haunted locations around the world for the past 25 years. Estep appears regularly on the TV shows *Haunted Case Files*, *Haunted Hospitals*, *Paranormal 911*, and *Paranormal Night Shift*. British by birth, Estep now makes his home a few miles north of Denver, Colorado, where he serves as a paramedic and lives with his wife and a menagerie of adopted animals.

SERIAL KILLERS

The Minds, Methods, and Mayhem of History's Most Notorious Murderers

Richard Estep

ALSO FROM VISIBLE INK PRESS

Real Ghosts, Restless Spirits, and Haunted Places, 2nd edition
by Brad Steiger
ISBN: 978-1-57859-401-6

Real Miracles, Divine Intervention, and Feats of Incredible Survival
by Brad Steiger and Sherry Hansen Steiger
ISBN: 978-1-57859-214-2

Real Monsters, Gruesome Critters, and Beasts from the Darkside
by Brad Steiger and Sherry Hansen Steiger
ISBN: 978-1-57859-220-3

Real Vampires, Night Stalkers, and Creatures from the Darkside
by Brad Steiger
ISBN: 978-1-57859-255-5

Real Zombies, the Living Dead, and Creatures of the Apocalypse
by Brad Steiger
ISBN: 978-1-57859-296-8

The Sci-Fi Movie Guide: The Universe of Film from Alien to Zardoz
By Chris Barsanti
ISBN: 978-1-57859-503-7

Secret History: Conspiracies from Ancient Aliens to the New World Order
by Nick Redfern
ISBN: 978-1-57859-479-5

Secret Societies: The Complete Guide to Histories, Rites, and Rituals
by Nick Redfern
ISBN: 978-1-57859-483-2

The Spirit Book: The Encyclopedia of Clairvoyance, Channeling, and Spirit Communication
by Raymond Buckland
ISBN: 978-1-57859-172-5

Supernatural Gods: Spiritual Mysteries, Psychic Experiences, and Scientific Truths
by Jim Willis
ISBN: 978-1-57859-660-7

UFO Dossier: 100 Years of Government Secrets, Conspiracies, and Cover-Ups
By Kevin D. Randle
ISBN: 978-1-57859-564-8

Unexplained! Strange Sightings, Incredible Occurrences, and Puzzling Physical Phenomena, 3rd edition
by Jerome Clark
ISBN: 978-1-57859-344-6

The Vampire Book: The Encyclopedia of the Undead, 3rd edition
by J. Gordon Melton
ISBN: 978-1-57859-281-4

The Werewolf Book: The Encyclopedia of Shape-Shifting Beings, 2nd edition
by Brad Steiger
ISBN: 978-1-57859-367-5

The Witch Book: The Encyclopedia of Witchcraft, Wicca, and Neo-Paganism
by Raymond Buckland
ISBN: 978-1-57859-114-5

The Zombie Book: The Encyclopedia of the Living Dead
With Brad Steiger
ISBN: 978-1-57859-504-4

"REAL NIGHTMARES" E-BOOKS BY BRAD STEIGER

Book 1: *True and Truly Scary Unexplained Phenomenon*

Book 2: *The Unexplained Phenomena and Tales of the Unknown*

Book 3: *Things That Go Bump in the Night*

Book 4: *Things That Prowl and Growl in the Night*

Book 5: *Fiends That Want Your Blood*

Book 6: *Unexpected Visitors and Unwanted Guests*

Book 7: *Dark and Deadly Demons*

Book 8: *Phantoms, Apparitions, and Ghosts*

Book 9: *Alien Strangers and Foreign Worlds*

Book 10: *Ghastly and Grisly Spooks*

Book 11: *Secret Schemes and Conspiring Cabals*

Book 12: *Freaks, Fiends, and Evil Spirits*

PLEASE VISIT US AT VISIBLEINKPRESS.COM

SERIAL KILLERS

Visible Ink Press®
43311 Joy Rd., #414
Canton, MI 48187-2075

Visible Ink Press is a registered trademark of Visible Ink Press LLC.

Most Visible Ink Press books are available at special quantity discounts when purchased in bulk by corporations, organizations, or groups. Customized printings, special imprints, messages, and excerpts can be produced to meet your needs. For more information, contact Special Markets Director, Visible Ink Press, www.visibleink.com, or 734-667-3211.

Managing Editor: Kevin S. Hile
Cover Design: Graphikitchen
Page Design: Cinelli Design
Typesetting: Marco Divita
Proofreaders: Larry Baker and Christa Gainor
Indexer: Shoshana Hurwitz
Cover images: (Front) Shutterstock; (back) Milwaukee County Sheriff's Department.

ISBN: 978-1-57859-707-9

Cataloging-in-Publication data is on file at the Library of Congress.

Printed in the United States of America.

10 9 8 7 6 5 4 3

CONTENTS

PHOTO SOURCES

ABC Television: p. 196.

Algr (Wikicommons): p. 357.

Americasroof (Wikicommons): p. 110.

Associated Press: pp. 7, 155, 166, 204.

John Atherton: p. 277.

Jonathan Billinger / Great Moorcourt Farm / CC BY-SA 2.0: p. 2.

California Department of Corrections and Rehabilitation: p. 143.

City of London [England] Police archives: p. 311.

Cuyahoga County Sheriff's Office: p. 254.

Daily Telegraph (London, England): p. 40.

Des Plaines Police Department: p. 19.

El Dorado Police Department: p. 260.

Elkman (Wikicommons): p. 105.

Gregg M. Erickson: p. 53.

Richard Estep: pp. 24, 26, 29, 31.

ExecutedToday.com: p. 236.

Executive Office of the President of the United States: pp. 16, 353.

Federal Bureau of Investigation: pp. 68, 272, 276.

Florida Department of Corrections: p. 119.

Florida Memory Project, State Archive of Florida: pp. 63, 65.

Dual Freq: p. 181.

Full Sutton Prison: p. 79.

Geograph Britain and Ireland: pp. 45, 47.

Greyloch (Wikicommons): p. 58.

Indianapolis Police Department: p. 28.

JetPhotos.com: p. 325.

Library of Congress: p. 241.

Los Angeles Police Department: pp. 85, 229.

Milwaukee Police Department: p. 180.

Larry D. Moore: p. 329.

Mtaylor848 (Wikicommons): p. 150.

Nonexyst (Wikicommons): pp. 212, 214.

The Orchid Club: p. 17.

Puck magazine: p. 306.

Rept0n1x (Wikicommons): p. 95.

Revere Senior High School, Richfield, Ohio: p. 170.

Rostov (Russia) Police Department: p. 216.

RustyClark (hottnfunkyradio.com): p. 126.

Salt Lake County Sherrif's Department: p. 61.

San Francisco Chronicle: p. 192.

San Francisco Police Department: p. 191.

San Quentin State Prison: pp. 92, 201.

Santa Cruz County Sheriff's Office: p. 137.

David Shankbone: p. 84.

Shutterstock: pp. 5, 9, 18, 37, 74, 83, 88, 90, 99, 100, 107, 112, 121, 124, 129, 132, 139, 147, 149, 153, 163, 164, 172, 176, 188, 230, 262, 266, 279, 282, 289, 292, 303, 316, 319, 340, 344, 347, 349, 356.

Ian Smith: p. 11.

Howard Sounes: p. 4.

Spacemountainmike (Wikicommons): p. 327.

St. Louis County Jail: p. 247.

Tulsa Police Department: p. 207.

United Kingdom government: p. 294.

University of Texas: p. 336.

U.S. Army: p. 314.

U.S. Department of Justice: p. 111.

Vidor (Wikicommons): p. 57.

Wakefield Prison: p. 94.

Chris Whippet / *Cranley Gardens, Muswell Hill* / CC BY-SA 2.0: p. 77.

Wise County Police Department: p. 270.

Public domain: pp. 20, 34, 35, 42, 52, 187, 190, 220, 224, 225, 234, 238, 240, 300, 307, 308, 310, 323.

Acknowledgments

It takes many people to make a book this size a success, and I would like to take this opportunity to extend my sincere gratitude and appreciation to the following:

First and foremost, I'd like to thank Roger Jänecke for giving me the opportunity to undertake this project in the first place. Roger, you were a pleasure to work with, and I am very appreciative of the support and latitude that you afforded me throughout the entire process.

Editing is an underappreciated but crucial part of the publishing process, and thanks are due to Kevin Hile for the time and effort he spent making this a better book.

I'd also like to thank my wife, Laura, for not only reading (and correcting) the manuscript from start to finish but offering thoughts and suggestions along the way.

Thanks also go out to my test readers for taking the time to read the manuscript in its early stages and letting me know what worked and didn't work for them. Thank you, Cami Andersen, GinnyRyan Andersen, Linda Fellon, and Jennifer Hirzel.

Last but by no means least, my heartfelt thanks to you, the reader, for spending your hard-earned money on my writing. I appreciate each and every one of you.

INTRODUCTION

Few things in life seem to fascinate us as much as the phenomenon of the serial killer. One only has to look at the proliferation of movies, television shows, podcasts, and books on the subject to see that. Although the serial killer has always been with us in one form or another, the explosion of interest in serial killer pop culture is relatively new.

Although media coverage of killers such as Ted Bundy and John Wayne Gacy garnered a lot of attention, many attribute the real genesis of this fascination to the release of the 1991 movie *The Silence of the Lambs*, starring Sir Anthony Hopkins as the quintessential Hollywood serial killer Dr. Hannibal "The Cannibal" Lecter. Hopkins' genuinely creepy and utterly compelling performance in the role catapulted the fictional serial killer into the mainstream, and almost 30 years later that interest shows no sign of waning; if anything, there is a bigger appetite for knowledge and understanding of serial killers than ever before.

Why is this? I think that the root of our fascination lies in the fact that when it comes to the serial killer, we truly are dealing with a monster—evil in its purest and rawest form. Yet, with the exception of a small handful, such as the gleeful Charles Manson, most of them look no different than the rest of us. Indeed, they could easily pass for one of us. They don't have horns or a forked tail. Serial killers look like doctors, waiters, teachers, and construction workers—even game show contestants. Indeed, serial killers have held all these positions and many more besides. They are found in all walks of life and at all levels of society.

They are also not easy to identify. They could be the person sitting in the seat next to you on a flight, or one of the diners at the table behind you in a restaurant, or the person bringing you your food. For all you know, the mechanic working on your car or the nurse giving you a healthcare checkup could be hiding a dark secret, and you would never suspect them until it was too late.

If this sounds like a case of scaremongering on my part then perhaps a little reassurance is in order. Yes, serial killers live and walk among us, often hiding in plain sight, but they are relatively few and far between. Serial killers generally tend to target those who are relative strangers, although there are some exceptions. We are ten times more likely to be killed by a family member or a friend, statistics show, than by a predatory stranger. This is one of the reasons why, when somebody disappears without a trace, suspicion usually first falls upon their significant other or a parent when police start an investigation.

Each serial murderer is different, but many share commonalities. In the same way that a doctor can diagnose the nature of a specific disease or ailment by understanding which physical signs and symptoms make it distinct and unique, so too can we gain a better understanding of the serial killer by comparing and contrasting them, looking at the common features that they share and also those that set them apart.

My main reason for writing this book was to attempt to understand serial killers better, to try and figure out just what it is that makes them do the awful things that they do. Are they simply bad people who are evil and irredeemable? It would be easy to jump to that conclusion and to not explore the issue any further. After all, we are talking about people who rape, torture, and murder whenever they feel the urge—is it even fair to call them *people* at all? What kind of person could do such monstrous acts? And yet, things are a little more complex than that. The guards at Auschwitz, for example, were ordinary men, many of them married with children. Most had never harmed anyone or anything in their lives before, yet somehow they ended up being willing participants in the extermination of millions of innocent human beings.

I spent many hours poring over newspaper articles, legal documents, books, and video footage to write *Serial Killers*. Wherever possible, I looked at images of the criminals I was researching at various different stages of their lives. Browsing through the childhood pictures, I was struck by just how unremarkable they had all looked when they were kids. No evil glares or stares, no resemblance to the character of Damien from the movie *The Omen*. They were just kids. But, at some point in their lives, something changed. Had it taken root in their childhood and grown along with them, or had there been some kind of precipitating event, some sort of physical or emotional trauma, that had sent their lives along a different path—sending them down a road to murder?

You will not be surprised to learn that there were no easy or simple answers, but there *were* answers, and we'll highlight them as we make our way through the pages of this book. Here are a few examples to get us started.

Most serial killers are white, but we'll look at several exceptions, including Maury Travis, Lonnie Franklin, and Tsutomu Miyazaki. In addition, the majority of them tend to target victims within their own ethnic group. African Americans tend to kill other African Americans, and Caucasians tend to kill other Caucasians. Once again, this is more of a guideline than a rule; some serial killers crossed those boundaries and killed a demographically diverse range of people.

It's also true that the great majority of serial killers tend to be male, but once again we'll look at some of exceptions such as Nannie "The Giggling Granny" Doss and the infamous murderess Aileen Wuornos, who had her own Hollywood motion picture in the form of *Monster,* starring (and produced by) Charlize Theron.

Another repeating pattern was that many serial predators stalked and killed those who lived on the fringes of society, deliberately targeting sex workers, drug addicts, alcoholics, and the homeless—people who were vulnerable, open to easy manipulation, and, above all, would not be missed when they disappeared. That's often how the serial killer evades detection for so long: They avoid potential targets whose sudden, unexplained absence would raise questions and make it more likely the police would diligently pursue them.

Surprisingly, there turns out to be an apparent link between homicidal behavior and significant trauma to the head. A number of the murderers who are studied within these pages sustained a closed injury to the head or a concussion at some point in their lives, after which they began to show some telltale signs of criminal behavior: torturing animals or sudden, unexplained outbursts of rage, to name just two.

"The serial killer daily observes people throwing their entire lives away on repetitive jobs, territorial obsessions, promotions to a particular desk, key to the executive toilets," said the Moors Murderer Ian Brady in his book *The Gates of Janus*. "To his eyes, this is insanity. He craves excitement. Vibrant meaning. Purpose. But it never seems to come."

Before we dive into the murky waters of our subject, a word about what this book is not. It isn't a ranked list of serial killers, a sort of *Who's Who* of the worst (whatever that means), those with the biggest body count, or a "best of." Its aim is to provide a representative sampling of the overall serial killer corpus, examining them on a case-by-case basis.

In each instance, I have endeavored to follow the subject from childhood into adulthood, identifying any factors that might have contributed to (or been a telltale sign of) deviant behavior. I have attempted to paint a picture of the life, and in many cases the death, of each killer. Sometimes this was a fairly simple and straightforward process, resulting in a relatively short chapter; in others, such as the infamous Ted Bundy, I go into considerably more depth and detail, which means that those sections of the book run significantly longer.

The subjects are a mixture of the well-known and the relatively obscure. While everybody has heard of Jack the Ripper, Tsytomu Miyazaki is mostly unknown, particularly in the Western world. The same is true of Andrei Chikatilo, a household name in Russia but somebody who is almost unheard of elsewhere. I have endeavored to cast a wide net when it came to selecting my subjects, which includes going back in time to the days of Scotland's infamous "Resurrection Men," the body-snatchers Burke and Hare. There is even some debate among historians about whether one of the subjects, the notorious Sawney Bean cannibal clan, ever existed at all.

The research process behind the writing of this book was extensive and took me to some pretty dark places, both figuratively and literally. The manner in which the book came about was a strange one. I am perhaps best known for writing on the subject of ghosts, and for my appearances on the TV shows *Paranormal 911*, *Haunted Hospitals*, *Haunted Case Files*, and *Paranormal Night Shift*. Over the course of 2018 and 2019, I had cause to investigate three separate cases of alleged hauntings that were each said to be connected with a different serial killer.

In the small, sleepy town of Auburn, Illinois, there stands an old movie theater known simply as "the R." I visited the R myself to research claims that it was haunted by the spirit of John Wayne Gacy, who was said to be attached to a piece of furniture there—a wooden armoire—that had once contained a number of Gacy's paintings. The research I carried out into Gacy's background, including his childhood, term of imprisonment, working life, and the murders he committed, both fascinated and repulsed me in equal measure.

Going back to the early days of the twentieth century, I had the questionable good fortune to spend several nights investigating the infamous Villisca Axe Murder House in Iowa. On the night of June 10, 1912, a person (or persons—theories abound) unknown walked from room to room inside the small wooden home of Josiah Moore. Using Mr. Moore's own axe, which he had taken from the woodpile outside, the killer smashed in the skull of every single person in the house. Along with Mr. Moore and his wife, Sarah, all four of the Moore family's children (Herman, 11; Mary, 10; Arthur, 7; and Paul, 5) were killed, as were two friends of the family who were staying for the night after a church function: Ina Mae (8) and Lena (12).

Eight lives were snuffed out in the space of just a few short minutes, and the town of Villisca was torn apart. To some extent, the shockwaves of that night are still felt today, for the crime is certainly the one thing for which Villisca is still best known. In the aftermath of the killings, as the bodies of the Moore family and their two young guests still lay lifeless in blood-soaked beds, it seemed as though anybody who wanted to could parade through the house, checking out the grisly sight for themselves.

There were several different suspects for the atrocity, but even today, almost 90 years after the crime, the murderer or murderers have never been definitively identified. The Villisca murders are still listed as officially unsolved. The most common belief was that the perpetrator was a local, possibly even a resident of the town itself. Because of this, the entire town was in a state of shock that took months to dissipate. For weeks afterward, fathers would stay awake at night and stand watch, keeping a shotgun or pistol close by in the expectation that the killer might return to murder their own family next. Families began sharing the same house in order for the head of the household to get a little rest, keeping watch in shifts and alternating with his neighbor.

Yet there is another theory, one altogether darker and more disturbing—a theory that I find to be both more compelling and more believable. It is known as the "Man from the Train" theory after the book *The Man from the Train: The Solving of a Century-Old Serial Killer Mystery* by Bill James and Rachel McCarthy James. The authors postulate that, far from being an isolated incident conducted by a local resident of the town, the Villisca axe murders were just a single part of a much wider pattern of axe murders conducted by a serial killer, who was riding the rails across the United States, killing entire families in their beds as he went.

Based upon their extensive research, the authors listed a number of unsolved axe murders that fit a similar pattern to those which took place at Villisca. The commonalities are striking, almost to the point of eeriness. For example, a young woman or older female child always seemed to be the object of sexual attention from the killer, who entered by a downstairs window much of the time, usually after the family had gone to bed for the night. The killer used the family's own axe, rather than bring one himself, and made sure that all of the windows, mirrors, and other reflective glass surfaces inside the house were draped, perhaps in order to avoid catching sight of himself while he was carrying out the murders and molestation. It is equally telling that all of the murder scenes were located close to railroad tracks, giving the killer easy access to and from the location by means of a train.

Police at the time failed to recognize the possibility that a serial killer might be responsible for this string of murders, and with the benefit of hindsight it is easy to see why. The Villisca crime was so heinous that it knocked the then-recent sinking of the RMS *Titanic* off the front page of the newspapers. The other murders took place at varying intervals of time and did not generate quite the same amount of newspaper column inches in as those in Villisca did. Nobody was looking for a pattern at the national level, and, therefore, nobody noticed one.

If the so-called Man from the Train was truly guilty of as many murders as the authors contend, then the sheer volume of deaths he was responsible for would have made Jack the Ripper look positively insignificant by comparison.

I walked into the Villisca Axe Murder House (or, to call it by its less sensationalistic name, the Josiah and Sarah Moore residence) on a warm summer's day. Standing directly adjacent to it is a barn. Police officers at the time of the murders speculated that the killer might have waited patiently inside the family barn until night fell, watching the house through a knot hole in the wooden wall. Once the Moores turned out the lights, he went to the woodpile, took their axe, and quietly forced entry into the house.

Even on a bright and sunny day, it is dark and gloomy in the house itself. There is a definite atmosphere inside the place, a heaviness that is hard to put into words. It looks very much as it must have looked in 1910. There is no television, no wi-fi network, no microwave, or any of the modern technological conveniences we all take for granted. In fact, there is no electrical wiring inside the house at all. A pot-bellied stove takes a prominent place in the living room alongside a piano. Behind it is a small bedroom, where two of the girls were killed.

After walking around the ground floor, I went upstairs. The staircase is narrow, steep, and noisy. Each step creaks, even if one steps on the outer edges. At the very top of the staircase is the master bedroom, where Josiah and Sarah Moore were sleeping. Some experts on the case have said that the Moores were killed first. It would have made sense; after all, the adults in the house would have constituted the greatest threat, particularly Mr. Moore. As I went downstairs and then crept back up as quietly as I possibly could, I could not help but wonder how the killer could have broken into the ground floor of the house and made it up to the second floor without waking one or both of the Moores.

One possible answer to that question may be found a few feet away from the master bedroom, a little farther along the hallway on the left. I had to crouch to make my way into the attic, the doorway of which is extremely low and narrow. There are two windows looking out onto the street outside and an equally low ceiling from which quite a few rusty iron nails poke through. It has been posited that rather than break into the house after the Moores went to bed, the killer instead might have entered while they were still at church and hidden himself in the attic. When the family was asleep, he would then have sneaked out, killed the closest victims—Mr. and Mrs. Moore—first, and then murdered the six slumbering children at his leisure.

My final stop was in the upstairs back bedroom, where the remaining children had all slept together. Many visitors have left toys here over the years, presumably as a kind of offering. Knowing what had taken place there made me feel nauseated. As I returned to the master bedroom, intending to go back downstairs, something caught my eye, a detail that I had not noticed before. There were several nicks and gouges in the ceiling above the bed: they had been made by the backswing of the murder weapon on that awful night in 1910.

It finally dawned on me that I was most likely standing in the footsteps of a serial killer.

My third and final personal experience with the world of the serial killer occurred in Indiana at a place called Fox Hollow Farm. To the uninitiated, this beautiful, faux-Tudor manor and horse ranch is a place of beauty and tranquility. Its perfectly manicured lawns and meticulously kept stable block speak of happily galloping horses and lazy days drinking iced tea in the sun.

But there is a dark side to Fox Hollow Farm, one that you will read about in greater detail in this book, for it was once the home of a serial killer named Herbert Baumeister—the "I-70 Strangler." Everybody in the local community of Westfield believed that Herb was a respectable business owner and family man. None of them could possibly have imagined that he also led a secret life, going out to gay bars in the city of Indianapolis and picking up young men when his wife and children were away. Baumeister would bring them back to Fox Hollow Farm, drug them, and have sex with them before murdering them during an act of autoerotic asphyxiation.

The murders usually took place in the basement, which housed a heated swimming pool. I was given a guided tour by the owner and was even permitted to take a dip in the pool myself. Villisca had affected me emotionally, but it was nothing compared to the impact that Fox Hollow Farm would have. The Moore family had died in 1910, more than a century before I ever set foot in their home, but the Fox Hollow murders occurred during the 1990s, well within living memory. The beds and most of the furniture in the Villisca Axe Murder House were not original to the property, but almost everything at Fox Hollow was. In fact, I was handed a length of plastic pool hose that the owner told me was the same one used by Herb Baumeister to strangle his victims—an honest-to-goodness murder weapon.

Access to the pool is gained by a staircase that leads down from the kitchen. On leaving the pool room, I stood at the bottom and looked up, thinking of just how many poor young men had made a one-way trip down that staircase, led by a stone-cold serial killer who promised them drinks, drugs, and a good time, only to choke the life out of them once they had been rendered helpless.

After their deaths, Baumeister disposed of their bodies in the woods behind Fox Hollow Farm. He used two major sites for this purpose, which were informally referred to as "mulch piles," each of them set just a few feet back from the house and inside the treeline. I had reviewed video footage taken by TV news crews, footage hat showed police officers and forensic experts carefully sifting through the mulch piles for evidence of human remains. Then I went out there myself to visit each one. Deer trails run through the woods, and the birds sing quite happily there. It would be a pleasant place to pitch a tent and camp, as long as you were completely oblivious to what had taken place in those woods 25 years before.

Returning to the house, I was given the chance to see Baumeister's bedroom and private bathroom. The house library still contained a number of his books, some of them annotated with his own handwriting, and a desk at which he had once sat to write and operate his business.

It was an intimate look into the private world of a serial killer, one that not many people are privileged to be given. As I walked around his house, it slowly dawned on me that I wanted to learn more about the man himself—and not just him, but those who did the same things that he did. Was there a sickness to all of them? A complete lack of conscience? An animalistic drive to kill? Or something else?

Shortly afterward, in a serendipitous turn of events, the good people at Visible Ink Press allowed me the opportunity to find out. The book you now hold in your hands is my attempt to answer that question.

Let's go.

—Richard Estep
Longmont, Colorado
March 2020

THE CROMWELL STREET HOUSE OF HORRORS: FRED AND ROSEMARY

Many serial killers are lone wolves. They tend to be solitary individuals, often antisocial and with few friends, who kill because they like it or they wish to feed a compulsion and are unwilling to share the experience with anybody else. If they are family men, such as Herb Baumeister or Dennis Rader (both serial stranglers), they usually lead a double life, successfully managing to pull the wool over the eyes of their spouse and children for years, sometimes decades. When their crimes are finally discovered, the murderer's wife is usually as shocked as everybody else, if not more so.

Some serial killers have willing accomplices, however, and those accomplices sometimes turn out to be girlfriends and wives. After all, who else could be trusted with keeping such a monstrous secret? Couples who abduct victims and kill them together are rare, but they do exist. One of the worst examples of just such a pair is Fred and Rosemary (Rose) West. Although Fred was believed to be the driving force behind the murders of many young women, his wife, Rose, aided and abetted many of his crimes—and some believe that she was actually the more twisted of the two.

The Wests lived in Gloucestershire, one of the most beautiful and picturesque counties in the southwest of England. The city of Gloucester itself has a long and fascinating history, stretching back to its origin in Roman times, and it is unfortunate that British people now associate the Wests' so-called House of Horrors with it.

In February 1994, the Gloucester police began excavating the cellar and backyard of an unassuming house on Cromwell Street. There, they found nine bodies, all of them young women that the Wests had subjected to horrific sexual assaults, viciously tortured—sometimes for days—and then murdered in cold blood.

As the story of what had happened behind the walls of 25 Cromwell Street finally began to emerge, the British public was horrified. Not since the trial of Ian Brady and Myra Hindley, the reviled Moors Murderers, had a murder case touched a nerve so deeply.

There were parallels with the John Wayne Gacy case, which we will delve into later. Although having a reputation for being a little odd, the Wests were known for keeping an open house. People—usually teenagers and younger adults—would drift in and out of number 25 on a regular basis. Sometimes they left and came back. Sometimes they simply disappeared. What nobody realized at the time was that they were being killed and then buried underneath the house, victims of Fred and Rose's lust. One of the victims was their own teenage daughter, Heather.

Fred West was born on September 29, 1941, in the rural hamlet of Much Marcle. When he was arrested and questioned by the police for the final time, West spun a dramatic tale about his having been sexually abused on a regular basis by both his parents, which included forcing the young Fred to have sexual relations with animals—or so he claimed. While it's true that some of those who commit acts of sexual abuse were, in turn, similarly abused during their own childhoods, it is also important to understand that Fred West

Fred West grew up here, on Moorcourt Farm, Much Marcle, in the bucolic Herefordshire, England. After his arrest, West claimed his parents sexually abused him here, but there is some doubt as to the veracity of these claims.

was a pathological liar. Detectives caught him in lie after lie—all attempts to generate sympathy from his captors—and when it suited his purpose, Fred was never beyond claiming a lapse in memory. Any stories of molestation pertaining to his childhood must be treated with a very liberal dose of skepticism.

As a teenager, Fred was involved in a serious motorcycle accident in which he suffered a number of broken bones and some head trauma, after hitting the road hard enough to fracture his skull. He had not worn a helmet. There are many instances on record of such an injury causing major personality changes and severe mood swings. It may well be that the bursts of explosive rage that Fred West was prone to during his adult life date back to this accident.

Young Fred was never academically gifted, or even capable of reading and writing to a reasonable standard. He was regarded by his classmates as being somewhat "slow," something for which he was teased mercilessly. He did not dress well, was far from meticulous with his personal hygiene, and had a reputation for being lazy. Nor was he handsome. Fred had an ape-like, almost cartoonish face, which he could not help. Children can be very cruel about such things, and as a result his childhood was often less than idyllic. It was obvious that Fred was never going to earn a living with his brain, which was absolutely fine with him. Traditionally, the Wests had always worked with their hands, and Fred would be no exception. He was also something of a mother's boy, another common characteristic among serial murderers.

Following the crash, and, later, a second head injury sustained after falling from a fire escape, Fred's behavior began to veer toward the criminal. Attempted theft and then groping a girl at a local youth club were just the start of a life spent breaking the law in one form or another. In November 1961, aged 19, he got a 13-year-old girl pregnant, which made him a sex offender in the eyes of the law. Using the supposed aftereffects of brain damage as an excuse, Fred managed to avoid going to prison for the crime. He was aided by the fact that the traumatized young girl was unwilling to take the stand and testify. Howard Sounes, author of the book *Fred and Rose: The Full Story of Fred and Rose West and the Gloucester House of Horrors*, discovered that the girl was Fred's own sister, Kitty. The incestuous pregnancy was not seen through to completion. Kitty's life was never the same again, making her the first of many victims to suffer at the hands of Fred West.

Around 1960, Fred had intermittently dated a girl named Rena Costello. She drifted in and out of his life and had gone back to her native Scotland, where she had worked as a prostitute, and had become pregnant with the baby of an Asian man. In 1960s Britain, being a single mother was frowned upon, as was having a child of mixed-race descent. Rena went back to the Much Marcle area in 1962 and immediately fell back in with Fred.

Despite his strange ways and odd appearance, Fred could be a charmer when he wanted to be. He managed to talk the pregnant Rena into marrying

Journalist and author Howard Sounes (pictured) revealed in his *Fred and Rose* that Fred West got his sister, Kitty, pregnant when she was just 13 years old.

him in November 1962. It would prove to be the worst mistake of Rena's life. Soon after the ceremony, the newlyweds went back to Scotland. It didn't take long for Rena to see her new husband's true colors. She discovered that Fred was a sexual deviant. He liked to inflict physical pain on her during intercourse and cared for nothing other than satisfying his own needs at the expense of Rena's.

This sexually motivated violence spilled over into their everyday married life. Fred was a perpetually angry man, prone to becoming enraged at even the most minor thing. He thought nothing of slapping, punching, and kicking his wife whenever he felt like doing so, for transgressions both real and imagined.

Needing to bring in some money, Fred started to run an ice cream van around the housing estates of Glasgow. He may have been all smiles when children approached him with money for a lollipop or a cone, but when Rena's daughter, Charmaine, was born, Fred's treatment of her was every bit as abusive as the way he treated her mother. He forced the child to spend hours on end in a bed that he had converted into a form of cage, keeping her confined like a prison inmate or an animal.

The marriage was now falling apart. Both Fred and Rena were unfaithful, and the infidelity was the cause of increasingly violent arguments. Things reached their breaking point when Fred, always a careless and erratic driver, struck a young boy while driving his ice cream van. The boy died of his injuries. Fred was already on the wrong side of the locals. There were rumors about him being a little too friendly with some of the young girls he met on his rounds, and he was suspected of being a pedophile. Law enforcement was now the least of Fred's worries; the true threat for him was the street gangs that dispensed on-the-spot, vigilante justice for so-called kiddy fiddlers. Afraid for his life, he dragged Rena back to Gloucester.

Still needing a source of income, Fred then took a job in a slaughterhouse. Some have speculated that this was where he attained the skills necessary for cutting up bodies, practicing on the butchered carcasses of pigs and sheep. It would certainly have helped knock any sense of squeamishness out of him—assuming that he had been born with such a thing in the first place.

After the birth of the Wests' daughter, Anna Marie, they moved into a caravan with Isa McNeill, a makeshift nanny, and a mutual friend named

Anna McFall, with whom Fred soon began an affair. Rather than prevent his violent attacks on Rena, the presence of the other women and Fred's stepdaughter and daughter only seemed to spur him on. Finally deciding that enough was enough, Rena and Isa fled, returning to Scotland for a time with Rena's lover, while the children stayed with Fred. Tragically, Rena would go back to Fred once again, despite the fact that he was now openly sleeping with Anna, who, unbeknownst to Rena, was pregnant with his child.

Fred had a decision to make. If Rena found out about Anna's pregnancy, it would cause him a world of trouble. But how could he keep Anna quiet—permanently?

In July 1967, matters came to a head. Anna demanded that Fred leave Rena. He responded by murdering her and burying her

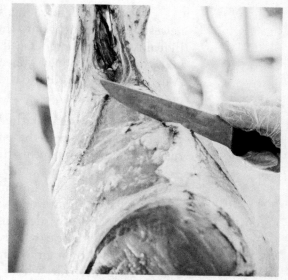

Fred West got a job at a slaughterhouse, and it was there, some speculate, that he may have honed his skills with a knife.

remains in a field. They would not be found until 1994, minus the fingers and toes, which Fred had removed and kept as souvenirs. Lying alongside her in the grave was the tiny skeleton of the unborn baby she had conceived with Fred.

Anna McFall's disappearance went largely unnoticed. If Rena ever wondered about her whereabouts, she could not have pried too deeply into the matter, perhaps not wanting to question her apparent good fortune at the unexpected loss of a love rival. She had no idea that a much greater threat was hiding just around the corner.

Rosemary Letts, nicknamed "Dozy Rosie" during her childhood because of her lack of intellect, came from a background that was both physically and emotionally abusive. Her father was a violent man, viciously beating Rosemary's mother for the slightest perceived infraction of his ultrastringent house rules. There were whispered accusations that he had been sexually molesting Rose from an early age.

Despite—or perhaps because of—this upbringing, young Rose was extremely free with her sexual favors. She was 19 years old when she first encountered Fred, who was some eight years her senior, at a bus stop in 1969. The older man immediately launched a charm offensive, flattering Rose at every opportunity and lavishing gifts upon her, doing everything he possibly could to get her into bed.

It worked. Before long, she was being passed off as the West children's newest nanny, brought onto the scene because Rena had once again left Fred. In reality, Fred had encouraged Rose to go "on the game," as he put it—having sex with men for money. When her father found out, he exploded with anger. A defiant Rose moved into the caravan with Fred. Shortly afterward, she was pregnant with his baby.

The following year, the Wests moved into a flat at 25 Midland Road in Gloucester. To support the family in their new home, Fred had once more turned to petty crime, primarily theft. Never a particularly intelligent criminal, he soon found himself caught and spending nine months in jail. Left alone to care for three children, Rose's inner tyrant came out in full force. She battered the children mercilessly, demonstrating particular viciousness toward Charmaine, who could never do anything right in her eyes. The poor girl seemed to take the constant stream of abuse in her stride, which only enraged Rose further and goaded her to perform even more vicious beatings.

> Left alone to care for three children, Rose's inner tyrant came out in full force. She battered the children mercilessly ...

Sometime in June 1971 (the precise date remains unclear), Rose murdered Charmaine, presumably during one of her violent rages, at a time and place that is unknown to this day. During the period of Fred's incarceration, the girl simply disappeared. Her body later turned up underneath Cromwell Street. Fred could not have done it because he was in jail at the time. When Fred returned to the flat after being released from jail, Rose admitted what she had done. Fred most likely told her that he had also committed murder. The two of them now shared a shocking secret, one that would incriminate them both if it ever got out, and so Fred and Rose entered into a murderous pact that would see one of them support the other in crime after ghastly crime.

Fred knew that he had to act quickly lest somebody should miss Charmaine. He buried the little girl's body in the garden behind the flat. Just as he had done with Anna McFall, he removed a number of her bones as keepsakes. The official story that Fred and Rose told the world was that Charmaine had returned to her mother, and they had both gone to live far away. They would never be heard from again.

This lie returned to haunt the Wests one year later when Rena came back and demanded to know where her daughter was. Fred played dumb, making weak excuses that Rena saw straight through. With her persistent demands for answers, Rena had now become a threat to their shared lie, and Fred had absolutely no qualms at all about removing that threat permanently.

Of course he would give Charmaine back, Fred told Rena earnestly. He just wanted to go for a quick drink with Rena first. Failing to sense the danger she was in, Rena accompanied him to a nearby pub. Fred bought her drink after drink, making sure to keep enough control over his own drinking to leave him sober enough to carry out what he meant to do next. By the time he got her back to his car, Rena was too drunk to put up much of a fight when Fred strangled her to death. With the deed done, he cut up the body and buried it in a field close to where he had buried the remains of Anna McFall.

Fred and Rose got married, formalizing their common-law relationship, and now it was Rose's turn to become pregnant. When she gave birth to Heather, her first daughter by Fred, the family moved again, upgrading from a flat to a house of their own. The property at 25 Cromwell Street would one day become infamous as Gloucester's so-called House of Horrors.

Whether Fred and Rose actually loved one another—indeed, whether either of them was even *capable* of such an emotion—will never be known, but their sexual appetites were about as far from the act of making love as it is possible to get. Their shared peccadillos invariably involved violence, pain, and torture.

Rose preferred having sex with women to men, and she engaged in numerous lesbian relationships and one-night stands while married to Fred. Sometimes, she allowed him to watch or even participate. For his part, Fred gained little pleasure from the act of sex unless it incorporated a strong streak of sadism. After moving in, he wasted no time in putting his construction skills to good use in turning the basement of 25 Cromwell Street into his own private dungeon, outfitting it with everything necessary to inflict pain and humiliation on the victims he took down there. Many of those victims would ultimately be tortured to death. Rose West was no mere onlooker; she was a more-than-willing participant, often taking turns with her husband to abuse and degrade women and young girls in the basement dungeon. Sometimes, this even included her own daughters. She and Fred raped their children repeatedly, then set their sights further afield.

On the outside, Fred and Rose West looked like an ordinary, happy couple. The ugly secret appetites for violence and sex that they shared, however, were the stuff of nightmares.

The Wests targeted girls who would not be missed, usually runaways who had broken ties with their families and struck out on their own. Some were hitchhikers, passing through

Gloucester on their way to some other destination. Others gravitated to 25 Cromwell Street because it was known as a party house, the kind of place where you could go to drink, watch porn, and even have sex with Rose, who was well known for being insatiable. Some were willing; a number of male lodgers slept with Rose and treated it like a perk. Others wanted nothing to do with the Wests' depraved sexual practices. At least one of those who tried to turn Rose down, a girl named Caroline Owens, was brutally raped and beaten by each of the Wests in turn. She was lucky to escape with her life and would later testify that Fred and Rose had threatened to murder her and bury her body under the house.

The Wests targeted girls who would not be missed, usually runaways who had broken ties with their families and struck out on their own.

A terrified Owens went to the police and pressed charges. She was so shaken up by the horrific ordeal she had suffered at 25 Cromwell Street that she could not bring herself to appear in court as a witness for the prosecution. While this reaction is completely understandable, it had one very unfortunate consequence: despite being charged with multiple offenses of a sexual and violent nature, the Wests were able to plead the charges down significantly, walking out of court with just a small fine. They were free to abduct, rape, and kill again.

With Caroline Owens now gone and effectively untouchable, Fred and Rose turned their attention to other vulnerable girls. Their next target was Lynda Gough, a free-spirited, 19-year-old girl who had caught their eye after having flings with a number of the male lodgers at 25 Cromwell Street. After gaining Lynda's confidence, the Wests finally convinced Lynda to move in (ostensibly to care for their children) in April 1973. They killed her that same month, burying her dismembered remains beneath the garage. Lynda's mouth had been taped shut and breathing tubes inserted into her nostrils, allowing her to keep breathing while Fred and Rose hung her from the cellar ceiling and tortured her. It would have been a prolonged and excruciating death.

It did not take long for the Wests to become overconfident and begin making mistakes. When Fred dismembered the body of a victim, he liked to retain small pieces, usually bones; now it was Rose's turn to keep trophies, in the form of clothing that had belonged to Lynda Gough. While they had started out targeting girls they thought would not be missed, Fred and Rose had made a mistake in choosing Lynda Gough, whose mother missed her and soon began to have suspicions when she went to visit 25 Cromwell Street unannounced. Walking around to the back of the house, she found the washing line on which the West family laundry was drying. There, flapping in the breeze, were clothes that she recognized—clothes that belonged to her daughter.

Gloucester, England, with its well-known cathedral and beautiful surroundings, seems an unlikely place for the horrors that occurred there at 25 Cromwell Street.

Pounding on the front door, she confronted Rose, demanding to know the whereabouts of her daughter. Rose played dumb, spinning a vague story of Lynda having long since moved out of town. This tale might have been more convincing had Rose not been wearing Lynda Gough's slippers while she told it, a fact that was not lost on the missing girl's mother.

The Wests' next victim was just 15 years old. Carol Ann Cooper was killed roughly seven months later. There is no way of knowing the exact circumstances of how she fell into the clutches of Fred and Rose; all that can be said for certain is that her body ended up buried beneath 25 Cromwell Street, bound and gagged in a very similar way to that of Lynda Gough. She, too, had been suspended from the ceiling and tortured to death.

A month afterward came 21-year-old Lucy Partington, who was a niece of the renowned novelist Kingsley Amis. Lucy came from a traditional background and had a stable upbringing, which meant that she would almost certainly not have willingly bought into the Wests' lifestyle of sex and sadomasochism. She disappeared from a bus stop, presumably either lured into the car with promises of a free ride by Fred and Rose, or forcibly abducted. Whichever is correct, she was tied up, raped, tortured, and killed like the other girls had been.

Therese Siegenthaler, also 21, was a foreign exchange student traveling across the country when the Wests picked her up. Much like Lucy, she was an intelligent and well-educated young woman who was also trained in the martial arts. Unfortunately, that was no defense against Fred and Rose, who bound, raped, murdered, and decapitated her dead body back at 25 Cromwell Street.

Still more victims followed, all of them young girls who had attracted the vile attention of the Wests. With each new abduction and rape, the pair grew increasingly brazen and contemptuous of the authorities, even running a prostitution business out of number 25 with their own daughter being involved.

> With each new abduction and rape, the pair grew increasingly brazen and contemptuous of the authorities, even running a prostitution business....

Lodger Shirley Hubbard had become enamored of Fred and pregnant with his baby. Jealous to the point of insanity, Rose knew this potential threat to her and Fred's marriage had to go .... and go she did—murdered and chopped up, before being buried in the back garden, as the cellar of 25 Cromwell Street had now been filled up with body parts.

The Wests even murdered their own 16-year-old daughter, Heather, in 1987 after she spurned Fred's incestuous sexual advances. Heather was not shy about discussing the awful acts of abuse that were taking place at home (although she is not thought to have known about the murders), and word was beginning to get around that Fred and Rosemary West were far from the fun, happy-go-lucky party people they liked to portray themselves as. In order to shut her up, the Wests killed Heather and buried her remains in the back garden, after having tortured her and ripped her fingernails off one by one. Fred subsequently built a patio on top of her dirt grave, and the family would sometimes sit on it and picnic, just feet above the remains of the dead girl. For many years afterward, the surviving West children were told that they had better behave, lest they end up "buried under the patio like Heather."

With the coming of a new decade, time was finally beginning to run out for the Wests. The beginning of the end took place in 1992, when police received a tip-off that Fred was molesting young girls. A police investigation was duly opened, and in an incredible coincidence, the detective assigned to look into the case already knew the name Fred West—Detective Hazel Savage had known Rena many years before and had heard firsthand reports of her husband's cruelty.

A search warrant was duly issued, and police officers at number 25 turned up a hoard of pornographic material and sex toys. When questioned gently by detectives, the West children spoke of the extensive abuse they had all endured at the hands of their parents. They were immediately taken into the care of social services. Fred was arrested and kept in custody while he awaited trial for rape. Rose made parole, for it had not yet become apparent that she was every bit as culpable in the physical abuse as her husband—if not more so.

None of the children whom the Wests had abused were willing to testify against Fred in court, leaving the prosecution no option but to drop the rape case against him. This apparent victory was short-lived, however, because the interviews had alerted detectives to the question of several disappearances: where exactly had Rena, Charmaine, and Heather gone? It seemed that nobody knew their whereabouts, and Hazel Savage refused to give up. The running "joke" about Heather being underneath the patio turned out to be horrifyingly true when police officers finally dug it up in 1994. Knowing that the game was up at last, Fred confessed to having killed Heather, but, still incapable of telling the truth even then, he tried to pass it off as being accidental. Nobody believed him.

More digging revealed even more remains. Fred admitted to another nine murders, taking all of the blame upon himself and insisting that Rose knew nothing. He told police that they were buried underneath the house. Not believing his claims, officers arrested Rose, and the Wests were charged jointly.

Rose staunchly maintained her innocence throughout her trial, claiming that she had absolutely no knowledge of the murders, which had all been committed entirely by Fred. Nobody believed this patently ridiculous assertion, but belief doesn't necessarily ensure a conviction. There was a significant flaw in Rose's protestation, however—Charmaine's death had occurred while Fred was locked away behind bars. There was no way that he could possibly have been responsible for her murder. Charmaine had been entirely in Rose's care at that time.

Rose broke off all contact with Fred, leaving him to fend for himself. He took the rejection hard. In retaliation, Fred recanted his confession and now took the line that Rose had been a fully involved party to the murders too. On New Year's Day of 1995, Fred rigged an improvised noose from the door handle of his cell and strangled himself to death.

The jury found Rose West guilty on ten counts of murder and sentenced her to life in prison without the possibility of parole.

Analyzing the case today, we are forced to wonder whether the 12 confirmed West murders are just the tip of the iceberg. Before his suicide, Fred cryptically alluded to there being up to 18 other victims, whose bodies

Actor Dominic West (no relation) played Fred West in the 2011 British television movie *Appropriate Adult* about the Wests' killing spree.

had never been discovered because they were not buried at 25 Cromwell Street. To date, no tangible evidence to back up his claims has been found, and it should be borne in mind that he was a pathological liar. Nonetheless, the possibility exists that Fred and Rose may, between them, have committed approximately 30 murders. The true number will never be known for sure.

The Gloucester City Council purchased 25 Cromwell Street in 1996 and promptly demolished it. For good measure, all of the house contents were destroyed, ensuring that nobody could profit from the buying and selling of the Wests' personal effects or those of any of their victims. If you walk past the site today, you would be forgiven for not knowing its significance. No plaques or flowers adorn the vacant lot, nothing to mark the passing of the poor unfortunates who died there at the hands of two of the most evil human beings ever to walk the Earth. The lot on which number 25 once stood is now a paved walkway with a line of black posts running along its center and strips of neatly trimmed grass bordering it on either side.

> Before his suicide, Fred cryptically alluded to there being up to 18 other victims, whose bodies had never been discovered.

The people of Gloucester have done their best to put the Wests' twisted legacy behind them. Where possible, the Wests are not spoken about publicly. The couple are now considered nothing more than a dark stain on Gloucester's past, something best left in the past, where they belong. While it is impossible to forget what went on there, demolishing the property at 25 Cromwell Street has at least removed the visible reminder of the Wests' House of Horrors. Yet for the families of their victims and the people of Gloucester, the psychological scars shall always remain.

Nor did the surviving West children escape their ordeal unscathed. While the younger children were placed into foster care, receiving a new last name and a fresh start (if such a thing was truly possible, considering the horrors to which they had been subjected), their older siblings were left to deal with the consequences of their parents' actions.

Anne Marie threw herself from Gloucester's Westgate Bridge, attempting to drown herself in the river. Rescuers pulled her out of the water and administered medical care. She had been unable to hold down a job because of her physical resemblance to her infamous mother. Stephen West encountered the same problem and also tried to take his own life by attempting to hang himself. It is understandably difficult to go through life looking eerily like one of the world's most notorious serial killers.

In an attempt to exorcize the demons of her past, Mae West wrote a memoir (*Love as Always, Mum xxx: The True and Terrible Story of Surviving a Childhood with Fred and Rose West*). Rose had continued to write to Mae while she was in prison, and the letters show that she kept up her manipulative ways to the very end. Mae believes that her parents killed many more victims than they were convicted of murdering—up to 30 more, in her opinion.

At the time of writing, Rosemary West continues to serve her life sentence without possibility of parole. A 2018 article published in Britain's *Daily Express* newspaper stated that she was slowly going blind due to irreversible glaucoma and had threatened to kill herself if she ever lost her sight completely. Rosemary West will one day die behind bars, the closest thing to justice that she will ever face.

CLOWNS CAN GET AWAY WITH MURDER: JOHN WAYNE GACY

On the surface, John Wayne Gacy was seen as a pillar of the community. He was a successful small business owner, running his own construction contracting business in Cook County, Illinois, during the 1970s. Throwing neighborhood parties and being involved with at least one committee, he was socially active, and he also also dabbled in local politics.

Creating an alter ego (a clown named, by turns, Pogo or Patches), Gacy helped with fundraisers, attended parties, and visited sick children in hospital. A staunch Democrat, Gacy was even photographed with President Jimmy Carter's wife, Rosalynn, in 1978. The First Lady of the United States hadn't the slightest idea that the man with whom she was posing for a picture was responsible for the brutal murders of numerous young men.

Looking beyond the superficial, there were a number of clues in Gacy's past that could, with hindsight, be recognized as signs of the monster he would ultimately become. As with many serial killers, he suffered at the hands of an alcoholic, abusive father, who belittled and demeaned his son on a constant basis. Gacy Sr. would drink heavily and then batter his wife and, when he felt like it, his children.

For the young John Gacy, emotional trauma set in at an early age. He was a physically weak, socially awkward kid who was made to feel like a failure, one incapable of pleasing his father, no matter what he did or how hard he tried.

As he grew, he developed a narcissistic streak that was compounded with cruel and sadistic tendencies. A pervasive sense of worthlessness and helplessness may have been a root cause, which would manifest as an intense desire to have power over others in later life.

First Lady Rosalyn Carter had no idea who Gacy was when this photo was taken in 1978.

Despite being married with children, the 25-year-old John Gacy's homosexual tendencies landed him in trouble with the law when he sexually molested a 15-year-old boy in 1967.

Gacy underwent a court-ordered psychological evaluation at the State University of Iowa (more commonly known as the University of Iowa). This included a 17-day observational stay, in which doctors noted that he liked to cast himself in the role of the persecuted victim, was highly defensive, and always had a ready excuse for anything that he may have done wrong.

Despite his best efforts, there was no talking his way out of what he had done. Gacy found himself convicted of the crime of sodomy and spent ten years in prison, where he ingratiated himself with the guards and landed himself a cushy job in the kitchen.

Due to his good behavior, Gacy was granted early release and went to Chicago to move in with his mother. While he was incarcerated, his wife had divorced him, taking the children and all of their possessions. A string of homosexual encounters took place, and Gacy showed an interest in handcuffing and physically abusing the young men he picked up, laying the groundwork for what was soon to come.

Although he remarried, Gacy didn't let it detract from his interest in men. Unfortunately, he wouldn't be satisfied with sadistic sex for long.

On January 3, 1972, Gacy picked up a 15-year-old boy at the bus station. The murder of Timothy Jack McCoy, his first victim, was unique; Gacy killed all of his other victims by strangulation, but McCoy was stabbed to death in Gacy's bedroom.

Gacy found himself standing over the lifeless body, blood-slicked knife in hand. After he had composed himself, he realized that the body would need to be disposed of. The solution seemed obvious, particularly to somebody who renovated houses, as he did. Going down to the crawl space that ran underneath the house, Gacy dug a shallow grave and dragged Timothy McCoy's remains into it.

When the grave had been covered over and the blood had been cleaned up, it suddenly struck him: he had quite literally gotten away with murder. And John Wayne Gacy liked it.

"I've got this trick. Do you want to see it?" John Wayne Gacy dangled a set of handcuffs in front of his unsuspecting soon-to-be-victim. Snapping them securely in place over the young man's wrists, he smirked, "The trick is, you've got to have the key to get out of them."

Whether impaired by drugs, drunk on liquor, or simply seduced by the charismatic Gacy's charm and flattery, the end result was always the same: what had started out as apparently harmless fun and games was suddenly twisted into a nightmare of torture and murder.

Gacy had a type: he liked young males—the more handsome, the better. He was all smiles and sweetness at first, but once the cuffs were on, the beast came out. Gacy derived great pleasure from inflicting pain on his victims, and the fact that they were restrained and utterly helpless only served to excite him more.

No matter how he managed to get them there, once they were handcuffed, the victims were usually as good as dead. Gacy would rape them, spend some time toying with them, and finally wrap a rope or ligature around their neck and slowly tighten it until they were dead.

At first, Gacy had to wait until his wife and children were out of the house before engaging in his illicit activities. An 18-year-old employee of his named John Butkovich got on Gacy's bad side after challenging Gacy about wages he was owed. Gacy responded by strangling him. Although the young man's body was buried beneath the property, Gacy's wife had no idea what her husband had been up to during her absence. Theirs was not a happy marriage, however, and it finally broke up in 1976.

After his divorce, Gacy was left with an empty house. No longer having a wife to answer to, he was now free to murder at will. The number of bodies buried in the crawl space of Gacy's house grew. So much new space was needed, in fact, that Gacy ordered his employees to dig additional trenches down there, followed by the scattering of lime to mask the stench of decomposing bodies.

A painting by Gacy of his clown character, Pogo.

Now a free man, John Wayne Gacy was abducting, torturing, raping, and killing with growing abandon. Most of his victims were between 15 and 20 years old, and they fell victim to Gacy's charming manner and empty promises. They endured prolonged sessions of torture and sexual molestation before being strangled to death and buried in shallow graves beneath the home of their killer.

Not every intended victim died. David Cram, 22, who had worked for Gacy's contracting company, also lived with the killer for a few months in 1976. Arriving home one night, he was confronted by his boss and landlord wearing full clown regalia, including face paint.

As it was Cram's birthday, Gacy slyly offered to show him his handcuff trick. Once the unsuspecting young man's wrists were cuffed, the encounter suddenly turned menacing. "I'm going to rape you," snarled the clown, grabbing him. Cram fought back, kicking and striking.

A few weeks later, Gacy attacked him a second time. Once again, Cram fought him off. Deciding that enough was enough, he moved out. Only later would David Cram realize just how close he had come to being yet another corpse buried beneath the crawl space at 8213 West Summerdale Avenue.

The killings continued. The ground beneath the house became so packed full of bodies that Gacy was forced to dispose of some of them off-site,

Gacy would dispose of his victims' bodies in the crawl space under his house. This was easier to do after his divorce left him alone in the home.

using the Des Plaines River as a dumping ground. Gacy threw at least four of them off a bridge late at night.

As with many serial killers, the downfall of John Wayne Gacy came about because of his complacency. In March 1978, Gacy abducted yet another victim, 26-year-old Jeffrey Rignall. His drug of choice was chloroform, which weakened Rignall enough for Gacy to take him back to 8213 West Summerdale Avenue. Here, Rignall was subjected to a series of savage rapes, each one of which left him with multiple traumatic injuries.

Bizarrely, the brutal assault did not end in murder this time. Gacy drove the halfway-comatose Rignall to a park and shoved him out of his car. Disoriented and semiconscious, the survivor nevertheless managed to remember one key feature about his assailant: his car. He recalled the man having driven a black vehicle. Determined to find him, a still-recovering Rignall staked out the highway until he saw Gacy's car pass by. The vehicle led police right back to Gacy.

Although Gacy was arrested and a court date was set, the police had no idea that they had taken a serial killer into custody—albeit briefly. It was only months later, in December of that same year, that Gacy made what would turn out to be his fatal mistake. He enticed a young pharmacy clerk named Robert Piest back to his house, where he assaulted and murdered him. Piest's family immediately alerted the police to his disappearance, refusing to believe that he had simply run off without a word.

Gacy had been witnessed speaking with Piest, and a background check soon revealed the former's incarceration for sodomy and his pending court case for the battery of Jeffrey Rignall. John Wayne Gacy looked like a prime suspect, and a search warrant was obtained for the house on West Summerdale Avenue.

Police found a pile of suspicious items inside Gacy's home, ranging from gay pornography and a wooden board with holes in it (this was used to restrain the hands of Gacy's victims) to jewelry and driver's licenses belonging to a number of young men, most of whom had disappeared under mysterious circumstances.

What the police officers found down in the crawl space beneath the house horrified them.

Gacy's mug shot after his 1978 arrest.

After a lengthy investigation, twenty-nine more bodies would be found on Gacy's property. The river yielded more. In total, at the time of his prosecution, thirty-three sets of human remains had been discovered, all in various stages of decomposition.

There may still be more out there.

Despite overwhelming evidence of his guilt, the cunning and manipulative Gacy adamantly refused to accept responsibility. It was a behavioral pattern that had repeated itself throughout his lifetime.

For Gacy, the nature of his sexuality was a hot button. When it was implied that he might be gay, Gacy took great pains to point out that he was, in fact, bisexual, and made it known that he had a hatred for "those fucking queers." Here were shades of his father, who regularly taunted Gacy by referring to him as a "sissy."

Gacy was also a pathologic liar. When confronted by detectives, Gacy insisted that he had never physically attacked anybody. He was too weak to overpower anybody, the result of having a debilitating heart condition. In fact, the very idea that he had murdered all those people was ridiculous. He had, Gacy insisted, been framed by his employees. *They* were the guilty ones.

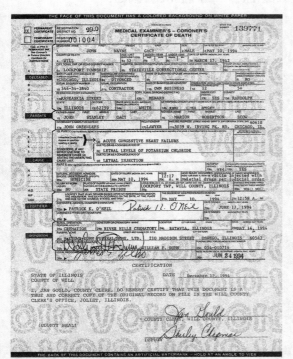

John Wayne Gacy's death certificate. Gacy was defiant to the end. His last words were, "Kiss my ass."

As picnics went, it wasn't a bad one. He had provided his jailers with a very specific list of requests: several pieces of Kentucky Fried Chicken, a side of fries, strawberries, and a large diet Coke to wash it all down with. Prisoners at Illinois's Stateville Correctional Center usually didn't eat this well, but today was an exception. The condemned man was about to eat his final meal. Prayers came next. One can only wonder how easy it was for the priest to offer absolution, knowing that the man had been sentenced to death for the vicious murders of 33 victims.

After 14 years on death row, John Wayne Gacy was about to meet his maker. It was not exactly plain sailing in the execution chamber. It normally took about ten minutes to end the life of a prisoner, but in Gacy's case, it would take almost twice that long. Gacy was strapped down onto a gurney and a needle inserted into his arm. When the order to carry out sentencing was given, the lethal injection machine was switched on.

Once the IV line was opened up, three drugs would be used to end Gacy's life. The first, sodium pentothal, put him into a coma from which he would never wake up. So far, so good. The problem came when the second drug, pancuronium, was infused. It began to solidify inside the IV tubing, turning into a kind of sludge. Officials were forced to switch out the tubing for a fresh set, allowing the medication to flow once more and paralyze Gacy's muscles, including those used for breathing.

Seconds after Gacy took his last breath, a large bolus of potassium stopped his heart from beating, finally ending the life of a man who had cut short those of so many others. His final words were, "Kiss my ass."

THE I-70 STRANGLER: HERBERT BAUMEISTER

All married couples have their secrets. For some, they are relatively minor vices and indiscretions—the tendency to spend a little too much money on a credit card, for example, or surfing pornographic websites when one's spouse isn't around. But some people take it to an entirely different level.

Herbert "Herb" Baumeister's secret was a terrible thing: he was a serial killer, responsible for cutting the lives of many young men tragically short. By their very nature, all serial killers lead a secret life. Being naturally charming and charismatic, many of them slip in and out of the facade of normal, everyday living with great ease. On the surface, all seems normal—sometimes perfect. But lurking beneath the surface is something altogether evil.

To all outward appearances, the Baumeisters looked like the perfect American family. Herb and his wife, Julie, made a prosperous living operating a small chain of thrift stores in the Indianapolis area. Business was good enough that they were able to buy a large house in rural Westfield, Indiana, nestled in the heart of a sprawling 18-acre estate. The property was known as Fox Hollow Farm, a name that would soon become infamous because of the nightmarish events that took place there during the 1990s.

Despite being married, Herb had a penchant for other men—preferably those who were younger than him. On those nights and weekends when his wife and children were away, leaving him with the grand old house all to himself, Herb's real self was allowed to come out. These were the nights when his alter ego was given free rein.

Herb's MO was well established. Down in the basement of Fox Hollow Farm was a swimming pool, completely self-contained in its own huge room with

The basement of Fox Hollow Farm sported an inviting swimming pool. It was not hard for Baumeister to lure his victims into its warm waters.

an adjoining space for the pump machinery. Adjacent to the pool was a second room, containing a wet bar, a couch, and a kitchenette.

On a distinctly creepy note, the kind of mannequins that appear in storefront windows ringed the pool on all sides. A mannequin bartender also stood behind the bar, posed as though serving drinks to invisible customers. Each figure was dressed in beach clothing and had been carefully positioned to give the impression that some kind of party was taking place in the basement of Fox Hollow Farm. According to a witness who knew Herb Baumeister personally, each mannequin had been given its own name and backstory.

Before hitting the town, Herb would crank the pool cover into place, completely sealing it off. Then he would turn up the heat as high as it would go, turning the swimming pool into something like a cooking pot.

It may have been Herb Baumeister that left Fox Hollow Farm each night, but it was a man named Brian Smart who stepped out of his car and entered one of the Indianapolis gay bars later that same evening. Sharply dressed in a jacket and tie, in stark contrast to some of the scruffier patrons, Herb's alias, Brian, would position himself in a carefully chosen spot, which would allow him to observe the entire room.

He was looking for a specific type of mark: a younger man, preferably one with no family or loved ones to miss him. The sort of man who could simply disappear from the face of the earth without too many eyebrows being raised. And he found no shortage of them while prowling the Indy gay scene. Men disappeared from those bars all the time. Most people simply assumed that they had moved on to another city, possibly out of state. It was only when the number of missing men became too great to ignore that the rumors began to start. Missing posters—*HAVE YOU SEEN THIS MAN?*—started to appear on the walls and bathroom stalls.

Herb liked a particular type of man: generally young, slender, and preferably easily manipulated. A number of his victims would turn out to have been arrested before on charges of prostitution. Shy and soft spoken, the dapper Brian Smart would tell them that he worked in construction, and his current project was a big house out in the sticks. The kicker was that it had a swimming pool installed down in the basement. Would the young man care to come back with him and party?

Many men took him up on his offer. Even when the word started to get around that gay men were disappearing without explanation, Herb still had takers. He and his intended victim would head out into the darkness, heading for Fox Hollow Farm—where the pool was waiting.

Herb and his companion, who would have been completely unaware of what awaited him down there, descended the staircase that led from the kitchen down into the basement. The first doorway on the left led into the pool room. Beneath the thick rolling cover, the water was now warm, bordering upon hot.

After fixing them both drinks, one of which was usually spiked, Herb slowly retracted the pool cover. Then he opened up the doors to the outside world, letting in the cool night air. When the heat rising from the surface of the pool met the cold draft of air, it quickly turned to steam.

The pool room began to fill with mist. Occasionally, a pocket of clear air would reveal the presence of a mannequin staring out over the water with lifeless eyes. Those mannequins would be the only witnesses to what happened next.

> While he waited for the alcohol and illicit drugs to circulate through his victim's bloodstream Herb liked to engage in a few minutes of mutual masturbation.

Once they had undressed, the two men slipped into the water. While he waited for the alcohol and illicit drugs to circulate through his victim's bloodstream Herb liked to engage in a few minutes of mutual masturbation. In addition to the chemical stimulants, the warm water acted as a vasodilator, expanding the vessels that supplied blood to the brain. This made the victim light-headed and dizzy, an effect that was worsened by the disorientating environment, a miasma of swirling steam populated with nothing but life-sized dolls—and Herb himself. When he judged his victim to be sufficiently docile, the serial killer would make his move.

"I know this neat trick," Herb liked to say, climbing out of the pool and disappearing into the mist. He returned a few moments later, holding a length of plastic pool hose coiled in his hands. Slipping the hose over the young man's neck, Herb whispered that if one used it to cut off the blood supply to the brain during sex, it could cause the most intense orgasm imaginable. This bears comparison with John Wayne Gacy's so-called handcuff trick and was performed with the same end result in mind—rendering the victim completely helpless.

Already mentally impaired and rendered susceptible to suggestion, the young man put up little or no resistance as Herb gripped the hose firmly in both hands and drew it tightly around his victim's neck.

By the time the man realized what was going on, it was too late. Herb kept on increasing the pressure, tightening the hose until both the carotid arteries and jugular veins were completely compressed. Deprived of its blood flow, it took just seconds for the oxygen-starved brain to completely shut down, sending the young man into first respiratory and then cardiac arrest. It was only when he was totally sure that his victim was dead that Herb Baumeister released his grip, allowing the body to float face-down in the water.

Some have theorized that the first time he tried autoerotic asphyxiation on a partner, Herb went too far without meaning to, resulting in the young man's accidental death rather than intentional death. While we will never know the truth for certain, later discoveries would make this seem unlikely.

Before his wife and kids came home, Herb knew that he had to dispose of the body. After dragging it out into the woods at the back of the house, he went to one of two disposal sites, or "burn piles." There, the corpse would be doused with gasoline and set on fire in an attempt to destroy the evidence. Some would be dismembered, either partially or completely. He experimented with several ways of concealing his grisly crime.

Many serial killers like to bury their victims, the ultimate example of "out of sight, out of mind." Baumeister was unusual in this respect. His laissez-faire approach of leaving the bodies out in the open to decompose, exposed to the elements and the various critters that roamed the Fox Hollow Farm estate, would make life infinitely harder for the detectives once his crimes were finally uncovered.

The pool hose that was used to strangle the victims still hangs on the basement wall at Fox Hollow Farm.

Outside appearances to the contrary, all was not well within the Baumeister family. Herb and his wife were drifting further and further apart. The more often Julie went away for the weekend, taking the kids to their property on Lake Wawasee and leaving her husband alone in the house, the more opportunities Herb Baumeister had to indulge in his grisly obsession.

Today, the residents of Fox Hollow Farm can see most of the neighboring houses when they are standing on the lawn. Back in the early 1990s, however, the neighborhood was sparsely populated. Trees came all the way up to the rear of the house, cutting off visibility by masking the house from view. Fox Hollow Farm was so isolated that Herb could quite literally get away with murder.

As his already delicate emotional state continued to unravel, Herb's sloppy mistakes began to stack up. If he had taken the time to bury the corpses and hide the evidence, he may well have evaded detection for months, if not years, longer. Had he simply gotten complacent, taking it for granted that nobody would ever venture out into the trees behind the house? Or did he have a subconscious desire to be caught, in order to bring the massive charade he was living to an end?

No matter what the answer, events were beginning to spiral far out of his control. Making a clumsy mistake, Herb had allowed one of his victims, a man with the pseudonym of Tony Harris, to live. Harris subsequently fled from Fox Hollow and went to the authorities, claiming that he had been in the presence of a murderer, narrowly escaping with his life.

Where once he had gone to great lengths to target only those men whose absence might escape notice, Herb's usually keen sense of judgment misfired on at least one occasion. He murdered a victim who had a mother who cared greatly for him—so much so, in fact, that she went to a private investigator named Virgil Vandagriff in the hope of tracking down her missing son. Vandagriff, a retired law enforcement officer with many years of experience, soon caught on to the fact that many men had disappeared without a trace from the Indianapolis gay community. The missing men looked similar and had various lifestyle factors in common. The private investigator began to suspect that their deaths might be the work of a serial killer.

> **V**andagriff, a retired law enforcement officer ..., soon caught on to the fact that many men had disappeared without a trace from the Indianapolis gay community.

When Vandagriff and Harris finally met, two significant pieces of the jigsaw puzzle came together. Vandagriff patiently listened to the escapee's story, making notes as the man talked. Slowly, a picture of a man named Brian Smart began to emerge.

Vandagriff's ears pricked up when Harris claimed to have been driven to an estate that went by the name of "something something farm," which he had noticed flash by on a custom-made wooden sign at the end of a very long drive. At the end of a sex game, Harris claimed, Smart had choked him to the point of near-total asphyxiation. He had only survived by temporarily playing dead, allowing his body to go limp until Smart had eased up the pressure on his neck.

At the end of a long and disturbing evening, Harris claims that he somehow managed to talk Smart into driving him home again. Assuming this is true, Tony Harris may well be the only man to ever escape the clutches of the serial killer who would come to be known as the I-70 Strangler.

There was no equivalent of Google Earth or any similar kind of mapping software available at that time, so Harris hit the road, driving along the highways and rural lanes. All that he had to go on was a dim recollection of the general area to which Smart had taken him—somewhere north of the city—and the carved wooden sign. Vandagriff did much the same thing, determined to get to the bottom of what looked increasingly like a series of connected murders.

Meanwhile, the police department sprang into action as well. Under the supervision of Detective Mary Wilson, undercover officers were posted to various gay bars and hangouts throughout Indianapolis. Yet months went by without a sign of anybody fitting the description of Brian Smart.

Finally, their patience was rewarded. Smart turned up at the same gay club as Tony Harris one evening. The two men chatted amicably, but Harris did not end up leaving with him. But he was able to obtain Brian Smart's license plate number.

It was just the break that Detective Wilson had been waiting for. The license plate was soon traced to one Herbert Richard Baumeister, whose primary place of residence was in Westfield, north of Indianapolis. Its name was Fox Hollow Farm. Just like that, the Brian Smart cover identity faded away.

When Detective Wilson approached him, Herb Baumeister was less than cooperative. No, he would *not* permit the police to search his house for any sign of the missing men they were looking for—not without a warrant, at any rate. Neither Herb nor his wife, Julie, would allow law enforcement officers access to Fox Hollow Farm. No warrant was forthcoming, leaving the investigation temporarily stymied.

Yet Julie Baumeister had good reason to doubt her husband's glib attempts to reassure her that everything was going to be fine. She had never been able to forget a strange incident that had taken place the year before, when her son had found what appeared to be a human skull in the woods behind their home. After venturing out there to see for herself, she was shocked to discover more bones scattered haphazardly across the ground.

As soon as her husband returned home, she wasted no time in confronting him. Rather than confess to any wrongdoing, Herb blithely dismissed the macabre find, claiming that it was nothing more than his father's old training skeleton from his days at medical school. It was certainly nothing worth worry-

The unassuming-looking Baumeister often hid his identity, pretending to be Brian Smart. He was later identified with the help of a license plate number.

ing about, he said. She remembered this now that the police wanted to search her house.

Over the space of the next six months, Herb's emotional state deteriorated, and with it, so did the Baumeister marriage. Sensing that the net was closing in on him, Herb became increasingly desperate and unpredictable. Finally, Julie had a change of heart and decided to allow detectives unfettered access to Fox Hollow Farm. What they found there was nothing short of horrifying.

Just a few feet into the tree line at the back of the house, they found the first bones. Mary Wilson and her colleagues could tell immediately that these were no animal bones. They were human. Many were fragmentary in nature, broken up and chipped. Most showed charring and other signs of having been burned and crushed. By the look of things, the killer had made at least a half-hearted attempt to dispose of the evidence, but the fact remained that the further back the police officers went, the more the woods began to look like a charnel house. As the search went on, one of the police officers tripped over what turned out to be a dismembered human foot.

Forensic experts were brought in to confirm what Detective Wilson and her fellow officer, Sergeant Ken Whisman, already suspected: they had finally stumbled upon the remains of the missing men. There were so many bones and associated fragments, in fact, that a small army of first responders had to be brought in to collect them all. By the time they were done, thousands had been gathered, ranging from tiny pieces smaller than a fingernail up to fully intact bones.

Gathering them all would take weeks of backbreaking, painstaking work. Just when they thought the job was done, another horrifying discovery was made. The boundary between Fox Hollow and a neighboring estate was marked by a water-logged drainage ditch. It, too, was littered with bones. They ran all the way down the side of the ditch. Only now did investigators begin to comprehend the true extent of the crimes that had been committed at Fox Hollow Farm. Along with the bones themselves, the searchers also found pairs of handcuffs. All of the evidence pointed squarely to one man: Herb Baumeister.

Fully aware of what the police would find when they finally set foot in the woods upon his property, Herb had no choice but to accept that the game was finally up. Taking

I explored the backyard at Fox Hollow Farm, where Baumeister would bury his victims. The sites were called simply the "mulch piles."

minimal belongings with him, he fled for the Canadian border. After a long day and night of driving, Herb stopped his car underneath a bridge to take a nap. He was woken up by the sound of a police officer tapping on the window.

Claims have been made that Herb liked to videotape his sexual escapades and the subsequent murders that followed. While this has never been definitively proven, when the Canadian police officer looked in the back seat of Herb's car, she saw a box of VHS tapes. To this day, however, those tapes have never been found. Although many video cassettes were found in the basement of Fox Hollow Farm and taken into evidence by the police department, after reviewing hundreds of hours of footage, detectives found nothing incriminating upon them. Herb was something of a soap opera junkie, and most contained episode after episode of shows such as *Dallas* and *Dynasty*.

> Due to the scouring of the bones by wind, weather, and critters, there was no way for DNA evidence to conclusively prove his guilt.

Herb spent the next day driving, looking for the perfect spot. When he found it, an isolated beach on the shore of Lake Huron, he made himself what would turn out to be his last supper: one of his favorite foods, a peanut butter sandwich. Then he penned a suicide note. A coward to the last, he accepted no responsibility whatsoever for the Fox Hollow Farm murders, instead blaming the decision to take his own life on his crumbling marriage and precarious financial situation. Yet there was one single nod of acceptance to his future notoriety. The letter was signed "*the* Herbert Baumeister."

Finally, all out of options, he placed the muzzle of his revolver up to his head and shot himself. His reign of terror was over, but the full extent of his crimes had not yet come to light.

Herbert Baumeister was never convicted for the Fox Hollow murders. Due to the scouring of the bones by wind, weather, and critters, there was no way for DNA evidence to conclusively prove his guilt. It is entirely possible that, if he had chosen to remain alive and brazen it out, he might never have been found guilty at all. Herb could have claimed total ignorance of exactly how those bodies ended up on his property. Even the testimony of Tony Harris might not have been enough to put him behind bars.

Some have questioned how it was possible for Herb's spouse to have been so oblivious to the horrific things that were going on at Fox Hollow Farm, so unaware of the kind of man her husband really was. It's true that there were clues, if one looked hard enough. She had seen her husband naked just a handful of times over the course of their marriage and said that they had no real sex life to speak of. Herb had made a point of keeping his body covered up, perhaps ashamed of his relatively scrawny physique. Many people grow suspicious of their spouse, it is true, but usually such suspicions extend to matters of infidelity—not murder.

The attractive, faux-Tudor style of Fox Hollow Farm belies the horrors that occurred within the peaceful setting.

As word of the grisly discovery at Fox Hollow Farm got out, law enforcement began to scrutinize some of their unsolved cold cases. Of particular interest was an earlier series of murders that took place along the Interstate-70 corridor in Ohio during the late 1980s. The bodies of nine young men were dumped in streams, usually naked or at least partially undressed. Subsequent investigation revealed that the corpses appeared at the same time Herb Baumeister was traveling to or from Ohio on a "business trip." Although it has never been definitively proven, if Baumeister was indeed the culprit, then he was responsible for twice as many killings as the authorities first believed.

This also meant that Herb's first murder was not an accident, no "sex game taken too far" in the pool at Fox Hollow Farm. The I-70 Strangler most likely killed his victims on lonely stretches of road, somewhere along the more rural parts of the interstate. Assuming that Herb was behind the killings, he was taking the opportunity to indulge in gay sex culminating in murder while he was away from the prying eyes of his wife.

Killing in public is a risky proposition. No matter how carefully the murderer prepares, no matter how many precautions he takes, there is always the chance of discovery. Yet many serial killers feel a compulsion to do what they do, no matter how great the risk. Many prefer to lure their victims back to a safe haven, somewhere they have prepared in advance so that they can kill at their leisure.

The I-70 murders stopped just as suddenly as they had begun—just a few short months before the Baumeister family took up residence at Fox Hollow Farm.

THE MOORS MURDERERS: IAN BRADY AND MYRA HINDLEY

Whereas Fred and Rosemary West, owners of the notorious Cromwell Street "House of Horrors," are arguably the most evil and twisted killer couple on record, Ian Brady and Myra Hindley—the so-called Moors Murderers—come in a very close second.

All murder is reprehensible, but there is something particularly twisted and repugnant about the murder of children. They are true innocents, which only makes it all the more heinous when a child falls into the clutches of a serial killer, or a pair of serial killers working together.

In just a little over two years, the Moors Murderers lured five children into isolated locations, then tortured and killed them. Even today, several years after their deaths, just the mere mention of the names of Brady and Hindley evoke strong feelings of revulsion and hatred among the people of the United Kingdom. Indeed, Myra Hindley was even dubbed "the most evil woman in Britain."

Ian Stewart (not yet Brady) was a bastard in both senses of the word. Born fatherless to a waitress in Glasgow, Scotland, in 1938, the infant boy wasn't with his mother for very long. Struggling to support him on a limited income, Brady's mother gave him to a local couple named the Sloans to raise. She would visit him on a regular basis throughout his formative years, but it was the Sloans who gave him the closest thing possible to a normal family upbringing, and he happily took on their name. They were by all accounts a warm, decent, and loving family. There is no evidence of Ian Sloan having suffered physical or emotional abuse during his childhood, suggesting that the acts of depravity he would later commit were more likely caused by nature rather than by nurture.

Stories abound of the young Sloan torturing animals, a red flag present in the upbringing of many serial killers. Frank Flanagan, one of the youth's neighbors, claims that Brady threw a live cat out of an upstairs window and buried another alive in order to see how long it would survive before it asphyxiated. (Mercifully, Flanagan claims to have released the cat before it suffered harm). Brady himself refutes this and other animal cruelty tales in Alan Keightley's book *Ian Brady: The Untold Story of the Moors Murders*. Keightley was Brady's closest confidante during the later years of his life, sharing many conversations with him while the latter was imprisoned. Although the claims Brady makes in the book offer us significant insight into his state of mind, it must be remembered that Brady was more than capable of telling barefaced lies when it suited his purposes. He was also a master manipulator, and one gets the feeling that he was attempting to portray himself in a very specific way when Keightley interviewed him.

A lover of horror movies, young Brady visited the cinema to see them so often that he earned the nickname "Dracula" from those who knew him. Yet this doesn't tell the whole story; although it doesn't fit the classic serial killer stereotype, Brady enjoyed more than horror movies and violent thrillers. He was a self-professed lover of all different types of films and was just as likely to see a classic such as *Casablanca* as he was to buy a ticket for something more lurid.

Brady's mother had married a man named Patrick Brady, whose surname Ian adopted. Neither she nor his adopted father suspected just what it was that their son was turning into.

As Brady neared adulthood, he also developed an interest in the philosophies of German Friedrich Nietzsche and, to a lesser extent, some aspects of Nazism—not the ideology of the belief system itself but rather Adolf Hitler's ability to captivate and mesmerize an audience. Ian Brady was no idiot—in fact, he possessed an above-normal level of intelligence—but it was already apparent that he was twisted, and before the age of sixteen, he was already immersed in the world of petty thievery. Breaking into homes and burgling them was one of his favorite pastimes.

Burglary may not be a violent crime, but it wasn't long before the teenage Brady displayed a tendency toward aggression. His

The young Brady was interested in the ideas of German philosopher Friedrich Nietzsche, as well as Hitler, and the concepts of a superior man, nihilism, and the will to power.

group of friends were really an informal gang, and they sometimes clashed with other rival gangs. The Gorbals, the part of Glasgow in which they sometimes liked to hang out, could be a tough and unforgiving place. One such confrontation resulted in Brady smashing a rival youth in the face with a type of bludgeon known as a cosh. Brady found the violence to be intoxicating, a source of excitement and exhilaration rather than disgust. He rarely left the house without there being a weapon concealed somewhere on his person.

His violent tendencies were not limited to other boys. After hearing that a casual girlfriend of his had gone out on a date with another boy, an angry Brady confronted her and threatened her with a switchblade.

Years later, Ian Brady would claim that the death of the family dog was a big factor in pushing him over the edge and along the road to darkness. The experience, he said, helped instill in him the absolute conviction that God did not exist. Coupled with his interest in the philosophies of Nietzsche, it soon becomes apparent where his nihilistic belief system first originated.

Much of his reading time came after he was sentenced to serve time in a Borstal for his larcenous offenses. A Borstal was essentially a prison for those boys who were too young to be incarcerated with adults. Rather than use it as an opportunity to clean up his act and go straight, Brady smuggled in whiskey and got drunk on more than one occasion. After one such incident, which came to the attention of the prison governor and got him transferred to an institution with a higher level of security, he finally changed tack and began to spend the lion's share of his spare time studying philosophy and reading literature. He developed a fascination with the works of Russian writer Fyodor Dostoevsky, with particular emphasis on the author's musings on incarceration and injustice. When Brady wasn't pondering the big questions of life, he was also reading up on accountancy and bookkeeping.

On his release from the Borstal, Brady went straight back to his life of petty crime. One of the conditions of his parole was that he find legitimate employment in order to keep his freedom. While he hated the idea of working a nine-to-five job, there was no other choice. Living with his mother and stepfather in Manchester, Brady tried his hand at a number of manual jobs, loathing each and every minute spent working at them.

Russian author Fyodor Dostoevsky, famous for such novels as *Crime and Punishment* and *The Brothers Karamazov*, held a fascination for Brady during his time in prison.

He finally took a job at a chemical company called Millwards, where he would be using his bookkeeping skills to earn a steady living—and perhaps, more importantly, to keep his parole officer off his back. This led to a fateful encounter with one of the typists, a young woman named Myra Hindley—his future accomplice in the Moors Murders.

Unlike Brady, who had spent his formative years in Scotland, Hindley grew up in the blue-collar regions of Manchester. The family was poor, and like many men of the World War II generation, Hindley's father—a member of the elite Parachute Regiment—was more than willing to settle disputes with his fists. He indoctrinated his daughter with the same propensity for violence. Myra Hindley was more than capable of fighting if pushed, and sometimes even if she wasn't.

While it might not have been love at first sight, it didn't take long for the 18-year-old Hindley to develop a crush on Ian Brady shortly after she was hired at Millwards. Quiet and somewhat mysterious, but with an angry streak that would rear its head from time to time, the enigmatic Brady was able to charm her without even trying. The fact that he was four years her senior only made him seem more worldly and mature to her.

It took her more than six months to pluck up the courage to finally approach him, just to break the ice and say hello. Six months after that, during the Christmas holiday season of 1961, Brady took Hindley out on their first date, a night at the movies.

As their courtship continued, she began to fall increasingly under Brady's spell. Hindley had been raised Catholic, and rather than rebel against it or simply pay the beliefs lip service as some children do, she appears to have been a genuine believer; yet it took just a few months for Brady, an avowed atheist who scorned all forms of organized religion, to completely subvert her long-held beliefs. The "new Myra" bleached her hair blonde and began wearing short skirts, low-cut tops, and knee-high leather boots. She hung on Brady's every word, completely obsessed with everything he said and did. She professed to no longer believe in a God at all. If she had still held any sort of genuine Christian beliefs, one wonders how she could ever have stomached the atrocities that she and Brady were soon to commit.

Guns were more commonly seen on British streets during the 1960s than they are today. Some of those who had served in the military had hung on to their service revolvers, for example, and there was no shortage of rifle and gun clubs to be found. Hindley joined one of each, managing to procure herself a rifle and two handguns in the process. She and Brady talked of committing armed robberies together, perhaps fancying themselves as becoming the British equivalent of Bonnie and Clyde.

All their talk of robbing banks and armored cars ultimately came to nothing, but Brady and Hindley soon developed a fascination with something darker: they fantasized about committing murder and getting away with it. On July 12, 1963, the sick fantasy became a reality. The pair set out to hunt for "the perfect victim," with Brady cruising the streets of Gorton on a motorcycle while Myra drove around in an anonymous-looking van that her lover had borrowed for the evening.

They had arranged a signal prior to setting out. Riding along behind the van, Brady would flash the motorbike's headlight when he spotted somebody that he thought would fit the bill. The somebody in question turned out to be a 16-year-old girl named Pauline Reade. Myra knew Pauline as a friend of her sister, which would help allay any fears that might be brought on by "stranger danger" when the van pulled up alongside her and the driver cheerfully offered her a ride.

Saddleworth Moor is a huge, barren stretch of wilderness, frequented only by hikers and people walking their dogs. It is a lonely, bleak, and windswept place. One could easily commit a murder there without being seen. As she drove in that direction, Myra began to spin a tale about having lost one of her gloves somewhere on the moor. Would Pauline be kind enough to help her look for it? The light was fading, and they would have to move quickly,

Saddleworth Moor, which borders West Yorkshire in England, was scoped out by Hinley and Brady as an ideal desolate location for their murderous designs.

she insisted, but once the glove was found, she would drive Pauline to wherever she wanted to go.

Pauline had no reason to be suspicious. She had been on her way to a disco, but what harm was there in repaying one act of kindness with another? Hindley drove to an isolated section of the moor and parked. A short while later, Brady pulled up alongside the van on his motorbike. Hindley allayed Pauline's concerns by telling her that he was her boyfriend and had come along to help them find her missing glove.

It is here that Brady and Hindley's accounts of the murder diverge. Hindley claims that Brady led Pauline Reade away and killed her, coming back thirty minutes later and escorting Hindley to the scene of the crime. Pauline was not yet dead, and Hindley said that she stood over her body while she died, bleeding to death from a pair of very deep wounds to her throat. Brady then buried her, telling Hindley in an emotionless tone that he had raped Pauline before she had died.

Ian Brady's story, on the other hand, held that Myra was an active and willing participant in both the rape and the murder. Of the two stories, Brady's is the more plausible. In an effort to garner sympathy from both the jury and the court of public opinion, Myra Hindley would attempt to paint herself as an impartial observer, rather than a willing accomplice, hovering on the periphery and not getting her hands dirty. Yet how likely was it that Pauline Reade would have willingly accompanied a stranger out onto the moor while Myra remained behind in the van? If Hindley truly was as much under Brady's thrall as she claimed to have been, then why would she have stopped short of murder, particularly after the couple had spent so much time discussing and planning their "perfect crime"?

When Reade's body was finally discovered, the coroner found that she had been savagely beaten about the head, which both Brady and Hindley were capable of doing based upon their former track records, and then had her throat cut so violently that the spinal cord itself was severed. This takes a significant amount of force, as the cord is protected by bony vertebrae that are capable of withstanding a great deal of damage. Hindley was no weakling, so once again, she and Brady were both physically capable of committing this act.

According to a letter of appeal that she would later write to the home secretary in a vain attempt to secure her freedom, Hindley insisted that Brady had threatened her in the minutes leading up to the murder, claiming that if she backed out, she would end up dead and buried next to Pauline Reade on Saddleworth Moor.

Pauline's body was buried in a shallow grave just one meter deep, with a shovel that Ian Brady had hidden near the spot for just that purpose. It would not be discovered for more than twenty years. It is impossible to know for sure exactly what cruelties were inflicted upon the poor girl in the minutes leading up to her death. Forensic science was limited in what it could ascertain from a body that had lain unprotected in the ground for so long, and the only witnesses to the crime, Brady and Hindley, were both pathological liars.

Bearing this in mind, we must also take Hindley's account of what happened next with a huge grain of salt. Supposedly, Brady took her back to her grandmother's house, where the couple were now living together in a single room, and choked her into unconsciousness as a warning about what would happen to her if she ever spoke about the murder they had just committed.

> **P**auline's body was buried in a shallow grave just one meter deep, with a shovel that Ian Brady had hidden near the spot for just that purpose.

> I used to ask him why he was strangling me so much, so many times…. This was before the offenses took place—and he told me he was "practicing" on me. I said one of these days, he would go too far and kill me, but he just laughed and said he wouldn't—he needed me.

Four months later, the pair decided to kill again. They picked up 12-year-old John Kilbride at a market, in a car that they had rented for that specific purpose. The young lad was making a little pocket money by helping market traders load and unload their stalls when a blonde woman approached him and asked if he would help her put some boxes into the back of her Ford Anglia. If he did, she would give him a ride back to his house. Having nothing better to do now that the market day was coming to an end, John agreed.

It was November 23, 1963. In British schools, cinemas, and televisions, a government-backed ad campaign called "Say No to Strangers!" was in full swing. Its aim was to prevent children from being enticed into accepting rides from people they didn't know, even if said stranger did promise to show them some puppies, give them a present, or claim to be a friend of their parents.

Unfortunately, John was taken in by Hindley and Brady's pleasant and charming affect, and he got into their car after one of them promised to give him a bottle of sherry. When the eager boy was belted into the back seat, Brady told him that the sherry was back at his house, and they needed to go and pick it up—but wait a minute, he had an idea! Myra had lost one of her gloves on Saddleworth Moor. Perhaps all three of them could find it if they went up there to look for it.

The pair sexually assaulted John Kilbride before cutting his throat, just as they had done with Pauline Reade, and then strangled him. His body was also buried in a shallow grave. By eight o'clock that evening, the Kilbride family were concerned enough to call the police. When a week had passed with no sign of the missing boy, a large-scale search was organized, with 2,000 volun-

Brady and Hindley managed to lure their victims by being pleasant, charming, and apparently harmless.

teers coming forward to help look for John. Patches of wasteland and old, abandoned buildings—essentially anywhere that an adventurous young lad might choose to go and play—were all combed for signs of him, but to no avail.

Another six months passed before Brady and Hindley struck for the third time. Their next victim was another 12-year-old boy, named Keith Bennett. Photos of Keith show him to have been a cheerful lad with a toothy grin. He encountered the Moors Murderers while walking to his grandmother's house on the evening of June 16, 1964. Bundled into the back of Myra Hindley's minivan, where Ian Brady was lying in wait, Keith was taken onto Saddleworth Moor, sexually molested, and then strangled to death.

By now, the couple's pattern of committing a murder approximately once every six months had been established. They set out to do so again on December 26, 1964, selecting ten-year-old Lesley Ann Downey as their next victim. Rather than prowling the streets, Brady and Hindley instead chose a fairground as their hunting ground. Walking past carousels, ghost trains, and other amusements, they kept a close eye on the crowds, on the lookout for something very specific—a child unaccompanied by an adult.

Lesley Ann was dark-haired, good-natured, and, unfortunately, a little too trusting. Wanting to be helpful, she said yes when Brady and Hindley asked if she would assist them in carrying some shopping to their car. They took her to the house of Hindley's grandmother, where she was made to strip naked, then tied up and tortured.

Brady recorded the sound of the poor girl begging for her life, while the Christmas song "The Little Drummer Boy" played in the background. The tape, which was sixteen excruciating minutes long, emotionally scarred everybody who heard it afterward. The tape was played during Brady and Hindley's trial. When a sobbing Lesley Ann was heard to say that she could not breathe and that her neck hurt as she was being slowly strangled, members of the jury broke down in tears and covered their ears with their hands. Police chief John Stalker, a seasoned homicide detective who listened to the tape as part of the investigation, was haunted by it forever afterward.

"I first heard the tape when I was a detective sergeant investigating the Moors Murders," Stalker later said during an interview. "When the 16-minute tape was played at the police station before the trial, I saw senior police officers and legendary crime reporters—hard men who had been through the war and seen terrible things—break down into tears.

"Anybody unfortunate enough to have to listen to her harrowing, last desperate moments could not fail to conclude that Hindley was evil and an equal partner with Brady in the crimes."

Before they killed her, Lesley Ann Downey was forced to remove all of her clothes and assume different positions while her tormentors took degrading photographs. After she finally succumbed to asphyxia, her dead body remained in the bedroom overnight. There was little chance of her being discovered; Myra Hindley's grandmother had gone to stay with relatives for the evening, celebrating the British tradition of Boxing Day (the day after Christmas). Brady and Hindley got up early the following morning in order to bury their fourth victim on Saddleworth Moor, tossing the dead girl's clothes into the shallow grave alongside her.

In the new year, the couple began to spend time socializing with Myra's younger sister, Maureen, and her husband, David Smith. Smith and Brady shared a similar criminal background, one of petty larceny with a streak of violence. Smith looked up to Brady, seemingly as susceptible to his charm as his sister-in-law was. For her part, Myra felt threatened by Smith's encroachment on her relationship with Brady and didn't like the idea of Smith getting too close to them. Although she could not have known it at the time, her concerns would turn out to be well founded.

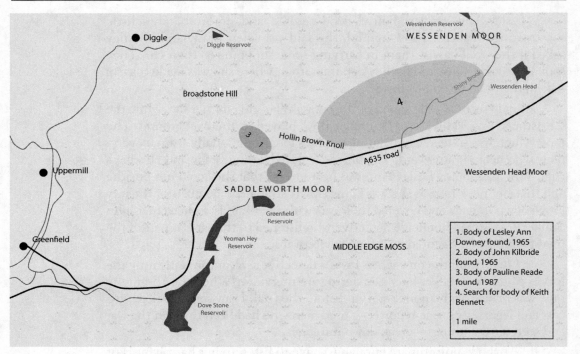

This map shows where several of the murder victims' bodies were found by police.

It would be another ten months before Brady and Hindley felt the compulsion to kill again. On October 6, 1965, they set out to find a potential victim. This time, they posed as brother and sister, and rather than use the tried-and-tested missing-glove fabrication, they simply picked up a young man with the promise of taking him home for a few drinks.

At 17, Edward Evans was older than their other four victims. If his suspicions were aroused, the machine operator trainee would also have been far more capable of fighting back. Perhaps after having preyed upon helpless children during the earlier murders, Brady simply wanted a bigger challenge this time. Whatever the reason, Brady called in David Smith to witness events that day. It would ultimately lead to his undoing.

Hindley went to fetch her brother-in-law, and when the two of them came back to the house, Brady and Evans were drinking and chatting amicably together. Brady had Smith wait in another room, out of sight but still within earshot. A few minutes later, the sound of panicked screaming from the living room brought Smith running. Despite his rough background, nothing could have prepared him for the sight of Ian Brady standing over Edward Evans's body, battering the youth about the head with an axe. According to statements he would later make, Brady claimed he intended to kill his victim with a single blow, but Evans had turned his head away just a split second before impact.

Brady struck him again and again. Despite his best efforts to protect himself with his hands, the brutal assault went on until his skull finally fractured and Evans stopped moving. The autopsy showed fourteen separate wounds on his skull. In order to make sure that he was dead, Brady then strangled him.

The body of Edward Evans was tied up in a bundle and carried to the vacant bedroom, where it was left for the night. Ten months before, the room had been used to store the body of Lesley Ann Downey. This time, Myra's grandmother was at home when the murder took place, but despite the screams echoing throughout the house, she did not come to investigate their source. So much blood had been spilled in the living room that it took three hours for Brady, Hindley, and Smith to scrub it clean.

Ian Brady and Myra Hindley may not have possessed a conscience, but at least David Smith did. The savagery he had witnessed preyed on his mind when he returned home after the murder. He immediately told Maureen, and together they went to a call box and phoned the police to report what had just happened. When officers searched the house later that same day, before Brady and Hindley got up to go to work, they found the bundle containing Edward's body locked up in the spare room. Brady tried to pass the murder off as having been an argument between two friends that had gotten badly out of hand, but Detective Bob Talbot wasn't buying any of it.

> **B**rady tried to pass the murder off as having been an argument between two friends that had gotten badly out of hand, but Detective Bob Talbot wasn't buying any of it.

Brady was charged with the murder of Edward Evans, and a few days later, Hindley was charged as an accessory. Blood of the same type as Edward's was found on the clothing of both of them, but while they were convinced that the pair had murdered him, the police had no idea that they had actually captured a pair of serial killers—until a search of the house turned up an exercise book containing the name of a missing boy—John Kilbride.

A claim ticket found in Hindley's prayer book led police to a locker at the railway station. Inside the locker were suitcases containing personal items belonging to some of the victims. Most damning of all were photographs of a naked young girl, bound and gagged, along with a tape recording of her screaming and begging for help. That girl was, of course, Lesley Ann Downey.

Living a few doors down from Brady and Hindley was a young girl named Patricia Hodges. She had gone with both of them to Saddleworth Moor several times and had most likely escaped becoming a victim of the Moors Murderers herself only because her home was so close to theirs—if she had turned up missing, the police investigation would have come uncomfortably close to their house, putting Brady and Hindley under unwelcome scrutiny. Now, police officers questioning Hindley's neighbors learned all about their regular trips to the moor from Patricia. Detectives examining the other photographs were struck by how many of them appeared to have been taken on the moors, and they now put two and two together.

Recognizing some of the landmarks, the police began to focus their attention on Saddleworth Moor. Officers worked round the clock to locate and search the places that appeared in the pictures and the spots that Patricia remembered having been taken to. At the end of a long, grueling day of searching, one police officer saw something poking out of the ground—an arm bone. Excavating around it carefully, they found the shallow grave containing the remains of Lesley Ann Downey.

A few days later, they discovered the remains of John Kilbride buried on the opposite side of the road that wound its way across the moor. What was left of the body had to be identified by its clothing because of the advanced state of decomposition.

> In November 1965, the United Kingdom stopped using the death penalty. Had Brady and Hindley been convicted before that, they would almost certainly have been executed.

Although they strongly suspected that Ian Brady and Myra Hindley were responsible for murdering more of Manchester's missing children, the detectives could only prove their culpability in the deaths of John Kilbride, Lesley Ann Downey, and Edward Evans. In November 1965, the United Kingdom stopped using the death penalty. Had Brady and Hindley been convicted before that, they would almost certainly have been executed. Despite them both pleading not guilty, they were each sentenced to multiple counts of life imprisonment in May 1966.

Brady and Hindley moved from institution to institution, drifting in and out of the news headlines until 1985, when, in an interview Brady granted to a journalist, he dropped a bombshell: he had also killed Pauline Reade and Keith Bennett, whose bodies were still out there, waiting to be found.

Once again, tracts of Saddleworth Moor were covered with police officers searching for the graves of two missing children. While a cordon of heavily armed officers closed off the moor and helicopters kept watch overhead, Myra Hindley was brought back to revisit the scene of her crimes, ostensibly to help locate the bodies of Pauline and Keith, though it is just as likely she was simply trying to garner sympathy. If so, she failed—both to find the graves and to be seen as anything other than the most hated and despised woman in the United Kingdom. A lengthy and detailed confession to the murders of Reade, Kilbride, Bennett, Downey, and Evans did nothing more than confirm the public's suspicions that she and her lover had been blatantly lying all along.

Hindley's two visits to the moor hadn't been entirely without value, however, as her vague recollections had at least allowed the police to narrow down their search grid to something manageable. Unwilling to give up, they kept digging and digging, until three months after Hindley had left, they finally found the burial site of Pauline Read. It was located just a stone's throw away from the place where Lesley Ann Downey's remains had been discovered some twenty-two years before.

The Moors Murderers were both master manipulators, and each continued to court the British press and seek to influence public opinion until the end of their lives. Myra Hindley tried unsuccessfully to obtain parole, but each successive home secretary agreed that she should never be released from prison. Nor would she be. Hindley died at the age of 60 on November 15, 2002, succumbing to complications of pneumonia. To say that she was still universally reviled would be an understatement: the only funeral director willing to cremate her body had to be brought in from 200 miles away. Every local undertaker had flatly refused to have Hindley's corpse or ashes placed in the back of their hearse or chapel of rest. Few could blame them.

The brief funeral ceremony took place in the middle of the night, in an effort (largely unsuccessful) to avoid media attention. Paparazzi lined the street

A few miles outside of Liverpool, England, Ashworth Hospital is where Brady spent his last years of incarceration.

outside the crematorium. After searching the building for the presence of intruders or explosives, a squad of police officers stood guard outside to prevent trouble. Their presence didn't stop angry drivers on the road outside from honking their horns and screaming their contempt as they drove by. Rarely do hearses conveying dead bodies require a police escort for the protection of their deceased occupant, but Myra Hindley was a rare exception. Of the twelve people who attended the cremation, none were Hindley's family members. Her ashes were scattered in a park less than ten miles from Saddleworth Moor.

Diagnosed as criminally insane, Ian Brady spent time in several prisons and finally ended his days at Ashworth High Secure Hospital. Before his death, Brady had written a book, *The Gates of Janus,* in which he critiqued the work of other serial killers and offered his own perspective on their crimes. The public was understandably outraged, but an American publishing house released the book anyway. At the time of writing, it is still in print. Brady had made attempts to starve himself to death, stating a desire to end his life "and be done with it all," but was stymied when a nasogastric tube was inserted in order to feed him against his will.

One of Brady's greatest cruelties was the cat-and-mouse game he played with the family of Keith Bennett, torturing them repeatedly with hints that he might one day reveal the location of Keith's body. He never did. When word got out that Brady's health was declining, the Bennett family lawyer, John Ainley, wrote to Brady and challenged him to finally give them some closure.

> Now that half a century is nigh, it's time for you to end the hurt, misery, and speculation, and do the honourable thing by revealing Keith's final resting place.

> Please god, you won't take the secret to your own grave. You have spent 50 years in jails and psychiatric hospitals so what have you got to lose by being upfront with us?

Brady ignored the heartfelt plea. He died at the age of 79 on May 15, 2017. In one of life's awful coincidences, this happens to be the birthday of John Kilbride. Chronic pulmonary disease had finally induced heart failure, causing a slow, lingering decline that led to his death.

"Monster Brady Joins Myra in Hell," proclaimed *The Sun,* one of Britain's most popular tabloid newspapers. Rumors emerged that after his cremation, Brady's ashes would be scattered on Saddleworth Moor. This caused such an outcry that the coroner refused to release his body from custody until he received assurances that this would not be the case.

Mindful of the furor surrounding Myra Hindley's cremation, no flowers or music were permitted at Brady's. Although he had expressed wishes that his ashes be scattered in Glasgow, where he had spent some of his happiest days as a boy, the city council flatly refused to allow it. Instead, what remained of Ian

Brady was dumped into the sea in the middle of the night. The urn containing his ashes was made of salt, designed specifically to disintegrate in less than fifteen minutes.

Brady and Hindley may have been gone, but for the families of their victims, the pain was not yet over. More than fifty years after her death, an internal audit conducted by the Greater Manchester Police revealed that parts of Pauline Reade's remains were still in their possession. Unbeknownst to her next of kin, her jawbone and samples of her hair had been kept in storage for all that time. They were certainly not needed as evidence, as her murderers had already been caught and convicted. Nobody had ever told her family that they had been retained by the police.

In Gorton's cemetery, Pauline Reade's remains were exhumed from her grave in order for the newly discovered samples to be reburied alongside them. Other possessions of hers that the police had kept, including her shoes and some jewelry that she had been wearing, were returned to her surviving relatives.

John Kilbride's body is buried in the Hurst Cemetery in Ashton-under-Lyne, not far from the marketplace where he helped pack up stalls in order to earn a little extra pocket money.

Keith Bennett's body has never been recovered, even though Brady and Hindley accompanied detectives onto Saddleworth Moor in an attempt to

Although his body was never found, police believe Keith Bennett was hidden somewhere in Hoe Grain near Shiny Brook in the moors.

locate his grave. Keith's brother, Alan, spent over ten years looking for his brother's grave on the moor. Their heartbroken mother, Winnie, never gave up hope that her son would one day be found and his remains brought home for a proper burial. She was sometimes seen digging all alone on Saddleworth Moor, but her needle-in-a-haystack search turned up nothing. Tragically, Winnie died without seeing her only wish fulfilled.

Up on the moor can be found a marker, small and unobtrusive, but at the same time poignant beyond words. It is nothing more than a teddy bear, a few flowers, and a stone that simply reads:

To Winnie and Keith
May You Both RIP
Keith Will Come Home
We can only hope that one day, he finally does.

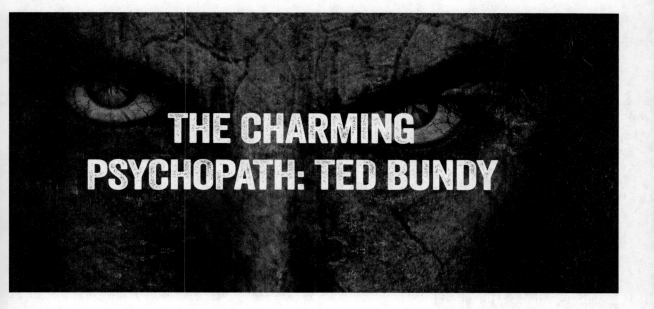

THE CHARMING PSYCHOPATH: TED BUNDY

All serial killers are, by their very nature, predatory. All of them hunt their fellow men and women. Some like to stalk their victims patiently, looking for a weakness or a vulnerability and the perfect opportunity to exploit it.

The manner in which they achieve this goal varies from murderer to murderer. At one end of the spectrum are those who use brute force to achieve their ends, such as Carl Panzram, who will be covered later in this book, and are completely devoid of subtlety and patience. This type of serial killer employs raw aggression in order to get what they want, like a sledgehammer being used to smash away any resistance.

At the other end of the scale, we find the charmers. Almost exclusively male, these men tend to be handsome, suave, and well-groomed. Their victims may either be male or female, depending on the sexual orientation of the murderer. This type of killer enjoys the thrill of the hunt every bit as much as they enjoy the adrenaline rush of the kill, sometimes even more so.

Such a man was Theodore "Ted" Bundy. According to those who knew him, Bundy's charisma was astronomical, particularly when he wanted something from a woman whom he had set out to charm. Small wonder that actors Mark Harmon, Cary Elwes, and Zac Efron were cast to play him in just three of the many different movies made about his life.

Born Theodore Robert Cowell on November 24, 1946, Bundy did not have a typical childhood. For one thing, the identity of his father is still in dispute. Certainly, he provided no support and exerted no influence, either positive or negative, on his son's life when he was growing up.

No matter what it said on his birth certificate, baby Ted was born without a father. While this wouldn't be considered a big deal in most parts of the

Western world today, things were very different in the 1940s. Unmarried mothers were seen to be a source of great shame not only to themselves and their children but also to the rest of their families—so much so, in fact, that special institutions existed in order to cater to them. It wasn't unusual for a young woman to go away for a while, ostensibly on vacation or a sabbatical but in reality to give birth in a home for unwed mothers.

That is exactly what happened to Eleanor Louise Cowell when it came time for her to have her own son. Louise, as she preferred to be known, discreetly left her home in Philadelphia and went to Vermont, where she checked into the Elizabeth Lund Home for Unwed Mothers. Rather than return to Philly as a single mother with a new son whose existence would be almost impossible to explain, she brought young Ted to live with her own mother and father, who posed as his parents for the first few years of the child's life. Louise pretended to be his grown-up sister.

> Although the Cowells seemed like a normal American family from the outside, that wasn't actually the case behind closed doors.

Although the Cowells seemed like a normal American family from the outside, that wasn't actually the case behind closed doors. Ted's grandfather, Sam Cowell, reportedly was prone to explosive anger and fits of rage that terrified those he turned it upon. He was known to abuse animals, kicking cats and dogs, and he beat his wife. Some have speculated that he may also have physically abused his grandson, though Bundy himself denied that was the case. Perhaps because of her husband's violent behavior, Bundy's grandmother suffered from severe depression and rarely liked to leave the house. Electroconvulsive therapy, a common treatment of the time, did not seem to help her at all.

It is difficult to know whether this formative environment contributed to Ted's behavior, but it is certainly a possibility. One clue can be found in a 1989 *Vanity Fair* article ("The Roots of Evil") in which author Myra MacPherson spoke with Marilyn Feldman, who administered the battery of tests for Dr. Dorothy Lewis, a psychiatrist who had interviewed Bundy personally in the run-up to his execution. According to Feldman:

> He lacks any core experience of care and nurturance or early emotional sustenance…. Severe rejection experiences have seriously warped his personality development and led to deep denial or repression of any basic needs for affection. Severe early deprivation has led to a poor ability to relate to or understand people.

In other words, as a young boy, Bundy appears to have received little, if any, of the nurturing that psychologically healthy children receive as a matter of course. The roots of his pathologically cold adult personality can almost certainly be traced back to this "seriously warped personality development." The inability to relate to other human beings and respond to them empathetically is an extremely common trait among serial killers; it's much easier to take a human life if you cannot relate to that person as a fellow human, one with similar wants, needs, and difficulties to your own.

Looking back with the benefit of hindsight, there were indeed early signs of the monster that Ted Bundy would one day become. His aunt recalled a time when she woke up to find that her young nephew had placed three kitchen knives next to her in the bed—something that not even the most curious child would be expected to think of doing. When challenged, Ted's response was simply to stare at her and smirk.

This early boyhood interest in knives—which first manifested when Bundy was little more than a toddler—was a huge red flag. Unfortunately, nobody in the household seemed to pick up on its significance, or if they did, it was never dealt with.

When the opportunity arose for Louise and her four-year-old son to uproot themselves and move to Tacoma, Washington, it was a welcome change of scene for them both. They were finally free from the cloud cast by Louise's father's perpetual state of anger. Louise married a man named John Bundy, unknowingly securing her son a surname that would one day become infamous. Although John Bundy was a calmer and kinder man than his grandfather, Ted and his stepfather did not bond like father and son or even grow particularly close—Ted would later admit to feeling nothing but jealousy for the man who had taken him on as part of a package deal with his mother. In fact, it is fair to say that Ted Bundy lacked a meaningful father-son relationship throughout his entire life.

His mother rarely, if ever, mentioned the identity of Ted's father to him. If the subject ever arose in the presence of his grandfather, he tended to fly into one of his violent rages. Yet somehow—and there are multiple stories that claim to tell the truth of how it happened, all of them different—Ted managed to find out that he was illegitimate. Psychiatrists who have analyzed the Bundy case believe that he never got over it, seeing it as a constant source of shame and resentment that would be carried with him throughout his entire life.

He had a liking for pornography and would later admit to being a chronic masturbator. While neither is necessarily unusual, Ted Bundy felt the urge so often that on more than one occasion, he masturbated in a storage closet at school. The risk of discovery may have been part of the thrill for him, but if so, it backfired on the day that he was caught by some fellow students. He was publicly shamed and humiliated at being found out and drenched in ice water by the jeering boys who had caught him red-handed.

As he transitioned from boyhood to young adulthood, on the outside Ted seemed like a clean-cut, all-American boy. He was active in the church and seemed to be civic-minded. Yet at night, a different Ted Bundy emerged, one

Bundy's high school photo seems to show a clean-cut, normal teenager. Nothing could have been further from the truth.

who would sneak around various neighborhoods looking for open windows through which he hoped to spot women undressing. Nobody could have imagined that the wholesome young Boy Scout was also a Peeping Tom.

The risky behavior he undertook also began to manifest in ways other than the sexual. Bundy took to shoplifting. Sometimes it was for items that he wanted but could not afford; other times, it was just for the hell of it. At one point, he even tried to steal a car, going far above and beyond petty theft. Getting away with these petty crimes only made him want to commit more of them.

While a junior in college, Ted began dating a fellow student named Diane Edwards. She was stunningly attractive and significantly wealthier than he was, coming from a much more affluent family background. Deep down, Ted knew that she was out of his league. When she suddenly dumped him out of the blue, he suffered a major, prolonged period of depression. Some have speculated that this rejection, which hit him extremely hard, might have been a catalyst for Bundy to begin murdering women.

In 1972, Bundy left the University of Washington with a bachelor's degree in psychology, which would assist him in playing cat-and-mouse games with the authorities when he was finally arrested for murder.

Understanding that more flies are caught with honey than vinegar, he became a master of charm and deception, keeping up appearances on the outside to maintain a carefully cultivated nice-guy persona. He took a job working on a suicide prevention hotline, which his friends and family all applauded him for. They would have been considerably less impressed had they known that whenever he grew sleepy and felt like a nap, Bundy closed his eyes and took the phone off the hook. When we consider that every missed call could have been one life potentially saved by the skills of a suicide prevention counselor, it is hard not to wonder just how many opportunities to prevent a death were missed because Ted Bundy wanted to catch up on his beauty sleep. Every time Bundy kicked back for a nap, he quite literally proved that he wouldn't lose a wink of sleep over the loss of another human life.

Bundy's desire to nap wasn't caused by fatigue or laziness. He wasn't so exhausted that he just couldn't stay awake; had that been the case, he could simply have called in sick and allowed other counselors to handle the life-or-death calls. No, this was an instance of somebody who, after accepting the responsibility of manning a crisis hotline, proved that he did not care one iota whether the people who needed his help lived or died. This is classic pathologic behavior, a pattern that Bundy would repeat over and over again.

After college, Ted got involved with political campaigning. This would stand him in good stead when he needed letters of recommendation for his next educational adventure: law school.

Some have made the obvious bad-taste joke regarding how Ted Bundy, utterly devoid of conscience and empathy, was a perfect candidate to be a lawyer. He certainly had the intellectual capacity to complete the program and pass the bar exam, but Bundy was a lazy man at heart, finding it difficult to apply himself to those things that did not truly interest him. With excellent personal and professional references, he was accepted into the law program at the University of Puget Sound in Tacoma. The young women on campus found him every bit as charming as the other women in his life before always had, but Bundy set his sights squarely on one in particular—Diane Edwards, the old college flame who had broken up with him and broken his heart in the process.

Diane was impressed that the formerly directionless Bundy, who had seemed to lack motivation or career prospects, appeared to have remade himself in the image of a budding professional. They began to date once again, with Ted suavely catering to her every wish in an old-fashioned courtship that carried her away. As 1973 ended, he had finally managed to win her over. She even went so far as to accept his proposal of marriage, but at the same time, he

Bundy attended law school at the bucolic University of Puget Sound. Here he also wooed and dumped his old flame, Diane Edwards, just to get back at her for when she dumped him back when they were undergrads.

was in a serious relationship with a different woman behind her back. Carrying on two long-term romances at the same time meant leading two entirely separate lives, something at which Ted Bundy was beginning to excel.

Soon, Ted began to ghost Diane, and on the few occasions when he did see her, he treated her coldly. The marriage was off, he finally admitted, when matters came to a head. He was dumping her, just as she had dumped him back in their college days. Now the shoe was on the other foot, and Diane was the one left heartbroken.

In hindsight, it's easy to see what Bundy was doing. He had never really intended to go through with a wedding or even commit to a long-term relationship. The whole thing was a long, drawn-out attempt to exact revenge for what she had done to him years before. Ted had transformed himself into a sophisticated, debonair success story (to outside appearances, at least), and now that he had finally met his college sweetheart's standards, he was giving her a taste of her own medicine.

He cut off all contact with her, and she never saw him again. Ted Bundy had other plans where women were concerned, and they were less pleasant by far.

Nobody knows for sure when Ted Bundy first developed a taste for murder. He himself gave contradictory answers when asked about it, making vague references to having murdered women in 1969, 1972, and 1973. It is likely that the full truth of the matter will never be known, but we know for sure that he committed a horrific attack on a female student in Oregon in early 1974. Can it be a coincidence that this took place at the same time Bundy dumped his fiancée? He was beginning to depersonalize women (if, that is, they had ever truly been people to begin with in his eyes) and treat them like disposable objects rather than human beings.

The attack by Bundy took place in off-campus housing near the University of Washington. Eighteen-year-old student Karen Sparks was fast asleep in her bed when Bundy entered the house via an open basement door and crept into her room.

In a sickening assault, he removed a thin, cylindrical section of the metal bed frame and bludgeoned the defenseless young woman repeatedly over her head with it. When she stopped moving, he inserted the metal cylinder into her vagina and thrust it in and out. The vaginal trauma and subsequent internal hemorrhage the attack inflicted were brutal and life-threatening, yet incredibly (and in no small part due to the skills of the surgeons who tended to her) she survived—albeit with significant brain damage.

Testing revealed that although Karen's assailant had penetrated her with a foreign object, he had not done so with his penis. The implication is clear: Bundy's motivation for the attack was not primarily sexual but rather one of hate-fueled aggression against a woman he had never met. This wasn't an ex-girlfriend who he felt had wronged him in some way; it was a total stranger, one whom he had intruded upon in her own home and savagely attacked while she was at her most vulnerable. There was undeniably a sexual component to the assault itself, but this was brought about by rage, not the gratification of lust.

> There was undeniably a sexual component to the assault itself, but this was brought about by rage, not the gratification of lust.

If this was his first attack, Bundy may have mistakenly believed that Karen was dead when he fled the scene of the crime. He may also have thought that the grievous injuries he had inflicted—the victim's pillow was totally saturated with blood when she was discovered by her housemates the following day—would cause her to bleed to death. He may also not have cared either way; perhaps when whatever twisted compulsion he felt had been satisfied, he simply gave no further thought to what would become of his victim.

A month later, on February 1, Bundy struck again. The similarities to the first attack were striking. Once again, he selected a victim who slept in a basement-level room in an all-female, shared house close to the university campus. He had prowled the neighborhood looking for just such an opportunity, in the same way that as a teenager he had gone looking for windows in which women could be seen undressing.

Lynda Ann Healy was a 21-year-old psychology student. When she turned up missing, her housemates became concerned and called the police. There were no signs of a struggle in Lynda's room, but when detectives looked closely at her bed, they found a sizable blood stain on the mattress. Bloodstains were also found on her nightgown. Lynda's roommates knew her habits well and insisted that although her bed had been carefully made, it had been done in a very different style to the one she usually used. Quite rightly, the police officers suspected foul play, reasoning that Lynda had been attacked and that the perpetrator had tried to clean up the scene before abducting her to try to allay suspicion. Her backpack and a pillowcase were also missing, as were the clothes she had been wearing the night before her disappearance.

It is likely that Bundy bludgeoned Lynda Ann Healy about the head while she slept to subdue her, just as he had done with Karen Sparks. That would explain the bloodstains on her mattress and nightgown. Her remains would not be found until the following year, abandoned on Taylor Mountain alongside the bones of other victims of Ted Bundy.

Two female abductions within an 11-block radius made it clear that there was a predator on the loose. One would think that Bundy would lie low for a while until the heat died down. Instead, he simply cast a wider net, going a little further afield to find his victims. Now he was beginning to abduct and murder a victim every month. In March, the next victim was 19-year-old Donna Gail Manson, who was a student at Evergreen College near Seattle. She disappeared while on her way to a concert and was never seen again. Although Bundy later admitted to killing her, the whereabouts of her body are unknown to this day.

> Claiming that he had broken his arm and was trying to load a stack of textbooks into his Volkswagen, Bundy would play the helpless nice guy and ask his chosen victim to help him out.

College campuses were Bundy's hunting ground of choice. For his April 17 abduction of 18-year-old Susan Elaine Rancourt, he chose Central Washington State. The freshman biology student was on her way to see a movie when she met Bundy. She, too, was never seen alive afterward; parts of her body were found at his Taylor Mountain dumping site long after her murder had taken place.

No longer attending law school, Bundy's focus and MO were changing. He had started out by making covert entry into the basement bedrooms of female-occupied student homes; although this gave him greater privacy, he ran the risk of alerting the housemates of his victim and also of leaving DNA evidence behind at the scene. Switching to a new method of abducting his victims in public meant that there was greater risk of his being seen (a risk he mitigated by only prowling after dark), but once he was able to charm the women into his car, he was less likely to be caught after the fact—or so he believed.

As detectives investigated the spate of missing young women from college campuses across the state, other students shared a crucial piece of eyewitness evidence: they had seen a man lurking around the areas of the disappearances with one arm holding books and the other arm in a sling, as though broken. All the witnesses were female, and all of their stories matched.

The man they saw was Ted Bundy, and the sling was a key part of his abduction routine. Claiming that he had broken his arm and was trying to load a stack of textbooks into his Volkswagen, Bundy would play the helpless nice guy and ask his chosen victim to help him out. The women who came forward to share their experience with the police were the lucky ones—they evaded kidnap, rape, and murder. Others were not so fortunate. Once they agreed and were distracted by trying to load the books, he would strike, shoving them into the car and driving away.

Less than a month later, on May 6, Bundy abducted and murdered Kathy Parks, 21, a student at Oregon State, as she was on her way to the student union. Far from keeping a low profile, the serial killer was actually ramping things up. In June, he killed two more women, Brenda Carol Ball, 22, and Georgann Hawkins, 18; on July 14, Bundy murdered Janice Ott, 23, and Denise Naslund, 19, both in Lake Sammamish State Park. Bundy's new trick was to approach young women and claim to need help lifting a sailboat up onto his VW Bug. What could be more harmless than a charming young man (with an injury, no less!) asking for a little help on a nice day? As the day ended, both women had disappeared. Denise Naslund's dog was found wandering around the park, with no sign of its owner anywhere.

Ted Bundy's confidence had reached new heights. Gone were the days of using the hours of darkness for cover. The last two kidnappings had taken place in a very public place in broad daylight. It wasn't that the police had nothing to go on. Multiple eyewitnesses had given them a description of Bundy and his brown Volkswagen, including the fact that he appeared to be injured; Ann Rule, who would later write one of the definitive books about Ted Bundy, *The Stranger Beside Me*, and worked with him on the suicide prevention hotline, thought that the description matched her colleague a little too closely and reported her own suspicion to the police department. As with so many high-profile murder cases and disappearances, however, detectives had been deluged with tips and leads from well-meaning members of the public. It took time and manpower to run them down, and not all of them were followed through to completion.

One of those loose ends was Ted Bundy. On paper, Bundy appeared squeaky clean and devoted to getting his law degree and serving his community. He wasn't given any further scrutiny, and he got lost in the background noise of the criminal investigation.

Then, just like that, the disappearances of young women stopped—not because the killer had been caught, but because after brutally assaulting one woman and murdering eight others, Ted Bundy had moved on to new pastures. Thanks to his acceptance by a different law school, Salt Lake City was to be his new home for the last few months of 1974. Although he had performed poorly on his first attempt at law school, the political connections he had made now stood him in good stead.

Ted would be starting over, beginning at the University of Utah Law School. His confidence soon evaporated, however, and he began to realize that he was in over his head.

From fall 1974 to 1975, Bundy stayed at this rooming house in Salt Lake City, Utah. This, according to investigators, is likely where victims Melissa Smith, Laura Aime, and Debra Jean Kent met their ends.

He was not as smart as his classmates were, and he was less capable of coping with the academic workload. Bundy had overestimated his abilities, and as his frustration grew, he took it out on a new group of unsuspecting victims.

There were no murders in August and September, doubtless because Bundy was still finding his feet in a new area. On October 2, 1974, however, he raped and murdered a 16-year-old cheerleader named Nancy Wilcox. After seeing her walking along the roadside near the town of Holladay, Bundy pulled a knife on the girl and forced her into a nearby orchard. After fatally strangling Nancy, Bundy loaded her body into his car and drove it 200 miles away to south-central Utah for burial in Capitol Reef National Park—or so he claimed. The body of Nancy Wilcox has never been found, and we only have her murderer's word for what happened. Despite the best efforts of law enforcement, the location of her grave has never been discovered.

Decades later, Rhonda Stapley came forward and told of her own harrowing encounter with Ted Bundy more than forty years before. Stapley claimed that on October 11, 1974, she accepted a ride in the serial killer's VW Bug rather than continue to wait for a bus.

According to her interview with TV personality Dr. Phil, Bundy took Stapley to an isolated canyon and said, "You know what? I'm going to kill you," before putting his hands around her throat and beginning to strangle

The now-defunct National Museum of Crime and Punishment in Washington, D.C., once had this display of Bundy's 1968 VW Bug. You can now see it at the Alcatraz East Crime Museum in Pigeon Forge, Tennessee.

her. What followed was an ordeal of rape and battery, which ended only when Stapley bolted and, she says, fell into a fast-flowing river, which swept her away from her tormentor before he had a chance to murder her. She would later publish a book, *I Survived Ted Bundy: The Attack, Escape, and PTSD That Changed My Life*.

On the night of October 18, Bundy killed 17-year-old Melissa Anne Smith, from the town of Midvale. She was the daughter of the local chief of police, and like the rest of Bundy's victims, she was dark-haired and attractive. Melissa had also been struck repeatedly about the head with a blunt object. Her naked body was abandoned on a mountainside many miles away from Midvale and discovered nine days later.

This was every parent's worst nightmare, but one can only imagine how her father must have felt. As a law enforcement professional charged with protecting not just his own family but also an entire town, he was aware of what the coroner's findings would have portended. Injuries inflicted upon his daughter's body had occurred prior to her death (this was apparent from the nature of the bruises) and indicated that she had been viciously battered, in addition to being anally and vaginally raped by her unknown assailant. She had finally died of strangulation.

Ted Bundy struck again on Halloween night. Laura Aime, 17, disappeared without a trace. Her body would not be found until Thanksgiving, nude and beaten beyond all recognition other than some distinctive scars from a childhood riding accident. The patterns of sexual molestation and physical injury were extremely similar to those of Melissa Anne Smith.

Eight days later came the botched kidnapping of Carol DaRonch, 18, whom Bundy approached while she was browsing in a book store in Murray. Changing up his act a little, he professed to be a police officer who had witnessed her car being broken into outside in the mall parking lot.

> A married couple driving by stopped to pick up the now-hysterical girl. Her story was completely believable, particularly as she still had a set of handcuffs attached to one wrist.

"Come to the police station so we can file a report," the so-called detective told her. DaRonch got into Bundy's car, mentally questioning the idea of an on-duty cop driving a VW Bug, but her suspicions were really aroused when she realized that the road he was taking did not go anywhere near a police station. The man's initially pleasant affect had changed to something coldly dissociated, and it frightened her—so much so that she attempted to jump out of the car at the first opportunity when the driver pulled over. Bundy attempted to handcuff her, but he wasn't agile enough.

Carol DaRonch then did what anybody in her situation should do: she fought back. In addition to hollering at the top of her lungs, she lunged for her abductor's eyes with her fingernails. Bundy pulled a gun and threatened to shoot her, but when she either fell or threw herself backward out of the car, he came around to the passenger side of the car brandishing a metal bar. To her credit, Carol refused to be intimidated. She knew the stakes were now life and death, and she kept fighting. Bundy—heavier, more muscular, and utterly deranged—had the advantage, but she managed to plant a foot in his crotch before turning and fleeing into the night.

A married couple driving by stopped to pick up the now-hysterical girl. Her story was completely believable, particularly as she still had a set of handcuffs attached to one wrist. Officers were immediately dispatched to the scene, but the man was long gone. What they *did* have was a detailed description of their suspect and his vehicle. Ted Bundy was starting to slip up.

Unfortunately, he did not take the near-miss as a warning, and he continued to cruise the streets looking for another victim that night. He found one in the form of Debra Jean Kent, who was snatched from the nearby town of Bountiful after visiting the theater. After the fact, a number of those present in the audience that night would recall seeing a strange man lurking at the back of the auditorium. Following Debra Jean's disappearance, two of them told police that he had attempted to lure them out into the parking lot, but both had refused. That refusal almost certainly saved their lives. When officers checked, they found a key that they recognized as the type that opened handcuffs. It popped open the cuffs attached to Carol DaRonch's arm on the first attempt.

Bundy's long-term girlfriend, Elizabeth Kloepfer, whom he had first met at the University of Washington back in 1969, thought that the descriptions of the man police were looking for sounded too close to that of her boyfriend for comfort. She reported her suspicions to the police on multiple occasions, with the promise that detectives would look into the matter when time allowed.

No other victims died in 1974, but in January 1975, Ted Bundy was up to his old tricks again—this time in the Colorado ski resort of Snowmass. His target was a 23-year-old nurse named Caryn Campbell. Bundy abducted her from inside the hotel where she was staying, the Wildwood Inn. She had gone to fetch a magazine from her hotel room, leaving her husband and friends downstairs in the lobby, and was never seen alive again.

Her naked body, partially buried beneath the snow, was discovered five weeks later. Although animal predators had eaten away parts of it, the coroner was able to determine that she had sustained significant blunt force trauma to the head prior to her death. Both hands were bound behind her back. Police believed that Caryn's body had been pushed from a moving vehicle on Owl Creek Road.

One month later, on March 15, Bundy abducted Julie Cunningham, 26, in the ski resort town of Vail. He drove her 90 miles away, raped and strangled her, then buried her remains in a grave that has never been found. Three weeks after that came the murder of 25-year-old Denise Lynn Oliverson, who was taken during a bicycle ride in the city of Grand Junction. Her body remains undiscovered to this day.

Back in Utah on June 27, Bundy killed 15-year-old Susan Curtis. He would later claim that her body was buried along the side of the highway near Provo. If so, it lies there still.

After having gotten away with raping and killing so many innocent victims, it ultimately took something as mundane as a routine traffic stop to finally turn the tables on Ted Bundy. In the early morning hours of August 16, 1975, a Utah Highway Patrol sergeant spotted a tan Volkswagen Bug driving through his own neighborhood and thought it strange. It was the kind of area where everybody knew everybody else, and the VW didn't belong to any of the police officer's neighbors.

When the driver of the Bug saw that he was being watched, he took off with a screech of rubber—hardly the actions of an innocent man. A chase ensued, and when the car pulled over and its occupant claimed to be lost, the sergeant smelled a rat. Looking inside the Volkswagen, he noticed some items that were somewhat unusual. A ski mask and crowbar practically screamed "home invasion," but more worrisome was the fact that the passenger seat had been unbolted and placed in the back (this was how Bundy managed to stuff struggling victims inside the vehicle). Was this a burglar casing his neighborhood? the cop wondered. He could have no idea that he had inadvertently stumbled upon one of the most sadistic serial killers in American history.

Although possessing such tools wasn't a crime, fleeing from a cop was. Bundy found himself behind bars before daybreak. A good police officer has a mind for connecting dots, and the description of a tan or brown VW Bug given during the 1974 spate of abductions rang a few bells around the department. Ted Bundy had to be released, but he was now a suspect for something far bigger than evading police, and he was placed under round-the-clock surveillance. His girlfriend was interviewed, and she conveyed her suspicions that Ted was involved in some of the disappearances she had seen on the news. Furthermore, she reiterated her concern that her boyfriend fit the description of the suspected perpetrator almost exactly.

Ted Bundy had no alibi for any of the nights on which the young women had been taken. When forensic officers went over the VW with a fine-tooth comb, they found DNA evidence belonging to multiple victims. Then came the biggest nail in the coffin yet. Bundy was placed into a police lineup with several other men. In came Carol DaRonch, who made a positive identification of the phony police officer who had handcuffed her and then pulled a gun on her.

Detectives from all the states in which Bundy had abducted victims were now collaborating, pooling their evidence and sharing their expertise. A case was slowly but surely being built against him. Nobody was in any doubt that Ted Bundy was the guilty man. The only question was—just how guilty was he?

His first trial took place in Salt Lake City in February 1976. The presiding judge found him guilty not of murder, but rather of kidnapping Carol DaRonch. He would still do jail time, but the bulk of his crimes remained undiscovered. But that October, detectives from Colorado formally charged Bundy with the abduction and murder of Caryn Campbell.

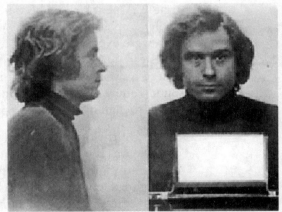

Bundy's mugshot in 1975 after he was arrested for burglary in Utah, a charge that later led to kidnapping, but not murder, charges.

January 1977 saw him extradited to Aspen for his first murder trial. The wheels of justice moved slowly, and by the time June came around, Ted Bundy decided that he was tired of waiting for a jury to decide his fate. Biding his time, Bundy saw an opportunity to escape when he was left alone in one of the second-story rooms for a brief period. In a scene reminiscent of a Hollywood crime thriller, he jumped out of the window and hit the ground hard, twisting his ankle in the process. It was a fall of some 25 feet, and he was lucky not to have broken his legs—or his neck.

While the local police frantically threw up roadblocks and assembled K9 search teams, trying to throw a cordon around the town, Bundy avoided the roads leading out of Aspen and instead headed for the mountains. The entire town went on lockdown.

They needn't have bothered. After six days on the run in the wilderness, cold and sleep-deprived, Ted Bundy was arrested on the streets of Aspen while driving a stolen car. By all accounts, he was relieved to see the inside of a warm jail cell again and to be given three square meals a day. For a narcissist such as Bundy, any romantically held notions of being a desperado on the run must have quickly evaporated in the face of cold, hard reality.

The smart thing to do would have been to sit quietly, finish serving his sentence for kidnapping (less than two years remained on it by the time of his 1977 escape), and hope that he would not be convicted of Caryn Campbell's murder. If Bundy's track record tells us anything, however, it is that he was not a man capable of doing the smart thing. Another audacious escape attempt was soon in the cards.

It was impossible for Bundy to get anything even approaching a fair trial in Aspen. He had become the talk of the town, the subject of daily water cooler conversation. In the bars and restaurants, gossip and rumor concerning him were everywhere. The court system recognized this fact, so Bundy was transferred to the city of Colorado Springs in the southern part of the state, where he was likely to get an even less welcome reception than in Aspen. Bundy knew that he had to make a break from his current place of imprisonment, the jail in Glenwood Springs, before then.

On the night of December 30, he made his move. Thanks to the holidays, he was the only prisoner, and staffing was light. It was now or never. He had been planning the escape for months, surreptitiously sawing his way through the ceiling above his bunk. Now his patience paid off. Ted Bundy punched his way up through the ceiling into a floorspace that led to the living quarters of the jailer, who was eating dinner with his wife at the time. He lay there in the darkness, listening to them finish their meal and then head out for the evening to see a movie.

Seizing the moment, Bundy dropped down into the now-empty apartment. Conveniently, the jailer was of a similar size and build. His civilian clothes fit Ted almost perfectly. After lacing up his shoes, Bundy was able to make his way outside to freedom. By a combination of car theft and hitchhiking, he reached Denver's Stapleton Airport and caught a flight to Chicago before anybody noticed he was missing.

For the corrections and law enforcement officers of Glenwood Springs, it was to be anything but a happy New Year.

On the run and in disguise, Bundy spent the first week of 1978 making his way across the country. His goal was to get as far away from Colorado and Utah as he possibly could. So far, he had been extraordinarily lucky when it came to his escapes from the law. How long that luck would hold out was anybody's guess.

When he reached Florida, Bundy finally felt safe. Living under an alias, he took to petty crime to feed himself and pay hotel bills. Getting a regular job was out of the question; every piece of identification he owned listed him as one Theodore Bundy, a wanted man who was on the run from police.

Any hopes that his murderous impulses had been left behind with his old life proved to be mistaken only a week after he had arrived in the Sunshine State. The female students of Florida State University in Tallahassee were no longer safe. Bundy was going back to his original MO—that of breaking into properties under cover of darkness—but this time, the number of victims he attacked was unprecedented.

Bundy's first murder in two and a half years took place when he entered the Chi Omega sorority house. It was a little before three o'clock in the morning on January 15. He used a makeshift wooden club to beat his first victim, 21-year-old Margaret Bowman, into submission, then used one of her own stockings to strangle her—something he had done on a number of previous murders.

His next target was Lisa Levy, 20, who was assaulted in the same vicious manner. Bundy's pent-up hatred of women was given

Bundy shown here in 1978. He had escaped that year only to kill again and find himself in prison ... again.

free rein, as he battered her about the head, tore off most of one nipple with his teeth, and in an awful echo of the Karen Sparks assault, brutalized her internally by forcing a bottle of hairspray into her vagina. He had also bitten her buttock, leaving a deep bite mark that would one day come back to haunt him in the courtroom.

Neither Bowman nor Levy survived the attack. Kathy Kleiner and Karen Chandler, however, were somewhat more fortunate; they shared a room, but that didn't stop Bundy from slamming the piece of firewood he was using as a weapon into both of their skulls, one after the other. Each of them sustained serious injuries, including broken jaws and knocked-out teeth, but Bundy was interrupted before he could murder them both. It is believed that the arrival of another sorority sister may have spooked him. Having murdered two women and badly beaten two others, the killer ran off into the night.

Shortly afterward, police officers and paramedics would descend upon Chi Omega in a storm of flashing lights and wailing sirens. Bundy had gotten off scot-free yet again, but his murder spree wasn't over. Rather than lie low, he went in search of another victim, perhaps figuring that every spare police unit in the county would be tied up at the sorority house. He crawled through a kitchen window into an apartment just a few blocks away, where another student, Cheryl Thomas, 21, was fast asleep. Bundy struck her over the head with the improvised club several times, making so much noise that he woke up the next-door neighbors, who immediately called the police.

> Bundy had gotten off scot-free yet again, but his murder spree wasn't over. Rather than lie low, he went in search of another victim....

That prompt phone call saved Cheryl's life. The police, already on high alert after the events at Chi Omega, were there in just minutes. They found her lying in a pool of her own blood, badly injured but still alive. There was no sign of her assailant. She would never regain the hearing in one ear.

It had been a horrific night on the Florida State University campus. Two students were dead and three more were seriously injured in a series of brutal assaults by an as-yet unknown perpetrator.

Bundy killed his last victim on February 9 in Lake City, Florida. It was arguably his most sickening act yet. Twelve-year-old Kimberly Leach was just a schoolgirl, not yet old enough to be called a woman. Bundy didn't care. After abducting and raping her, he left her body in a shed some miles away. He didn't know it, but time was running out.

In order to get around, Bundy had stolen an orange Volkswagen Bug, one that reminded him of the tan model he had formerly owned. He was out of money, unable to pay his rent, and getting by on stolen credit cards. On the verge of being evicted, he decided to get out of Tallahassee and start over somewhere else.

For the second time, a traffic stop proved to be his undoing. A sharp-eyed patrol officer spotted the Bug and ran a records check. The vehicle, as it turned out, was stolen. When he hit the overhead lights and sirens, the Volkswagen took off. The officer chased Bundy for about a mile before he pulled over. Most likely, this was a panicky reaction followed by a short period of frantically cooking up a convincing story, which would then be delivered in a suitably contrite way and backed up by the usual Ted Bundy charm.

This time, he tried a different tactic: he fought. Taking the police officer by surprise, Bundy knocked him down and ran away as fast as he could. The officer gave chase, firing a warning shot that caused Bundy to drop down onto the ground, no doubt afraid that the next shot would kill him. When the officer attempted to cuff him, Bundy went for his gun. The cop was better at handling himself than Ted was, and after a desperate struggle, he finally managed to wrestle the perpetrator under control and get the cuffs on him. Although he gave a false name to the booking sergeant, Ted Bundy was back behind bars.

The seasoned officers of the Pensacola Police Department knew that something was wrong from the outset. For one thing, the man they had just taken into custody was carrying a number of identification and credit cards that didn't belong to him—all of them belonging to females. He admitted to having stolen them all, but he still would not give up his real name until the following day, after he had spoken with a lawyer. It was only then that it became clear that one of the FBI's 10 Most Wanted fugitives was sitting in one of their jail cells.

Over the next few weeks, simply being incarcerated and questioned repeatedly by detective after detective finally seemed to wear Bundy down. He began letting slip cryptic hints about what he had done, never directly admitting to murder but placing himself ever more squarely in the frame for the Chi Omega sorority house attack and those on Cheryl Thomas and Kimberly Leach.

It has already been said that narcissism was a key part of Bundy's personality. There's an old saying that any man who represents himself in court has a fool for a lawyer, and this was never truer than in the case of Ted Bundy. Attorneys had been appointed to him at the public's expense, but he was simply too egotistical to sit back, shut up, and let them do their job. He insisted upon forcing his way into proceedings, talking over his appointed

Captured again, Bundy is shown here in a court in 1979. He finally pled guilty and was sentenced to life in prison.

defenders, generally grandstanding and trying to manipulate the course of events in his own Machiavellian way. Unfortunately for him, Bundy was not nearly as intelligent as he liked to imagine.

Prosecutors had hashed out a possible plea deal with his attorneys, one that would see him plead guilty to the Chi Omega attacks and send him to jail for life, but would at least keep him out of the electric chair. Although it would have spared him from being executed, it would also have required Ted Bundy—one of the most narcissistic, ego-driven men alive—to take responsi-bility for the horrific things he had done to some of his vic-tims. He backed away from the deal, and the case went to trial, putting Bundy front and center in the spotlight of public scrutiny. In the courtroom, a smirking Bundy often disrupted the proceedings with snide remarks.

> **D**ental experts proved to the jury that the bite mark on Lisa Levy's buttock was an exact match with the teeth of Ted Bundy.

Dental experts proved to the jury that the bite mark on Lisa Levy's buttock was an exact match with the teeth of Ted Bundy. This act of spur-of-the-moment savagery went a long way toward incriminating him, placing him squarely in the Chi Omega sorority house on the night of the assault. There was no way he or his defense team could argue their way around it. Bundy was duly found guilty and given two death sentences by the judge, one apiece for killing Lisa Levy and Margaret Bowman.

Bundy would never murder again, but the after-echoes of his crimes would go on for years. He received another conviction for the murder of school-girl Kimberly Leach. Bundy had insisted upon representing himself completely this time, which spectacularly backfired. Perhaps frazzled at the double date with the electric chair to which he had already been sentenced, Bundy lost his cool in the courtroom. Gone was the charming, sophisticated Ted Bundy, replaced by an angry, childlike man who seemed incapable of keeping his temper.

At last, the real Ted Bundy had shown his face to the public. The suave facade was gone, perhaps forever. The trial became something akin to a circus sideshow when a former colleague of Ted's named Carole Ann Boone, a woman with whom he had grown increasingly close, stood up unexpectedly and announced to the entire courtroom that she intended to marry "the love of my life"—Ted Bundy. She had already applied for a marriage license in advance, and the state of Florida had an arcane law on the books that held that if such a declaration was made in open court, with a valid marriage license in hand, then she and Ted could lawfully become husband and wife—which is exactly what happened.

Jaws dropped across the courtroom as the couple became Mr. and Mrs. Theodore Bundy right then and there, in the middle of a murder trial. Carole Ann Boone evidently wanted to become the wife of a man accused of raping and murdering a 12-year-old child, a man already on his way to the electric chair for having killed two young women and brutally assaulted two more. It was practically beyond belief.

If the marriage was nothing more than a calculated ploy, one contrived to portray Ted in a sympathetic light in the eyes of the jury, then it was a waste of time. It took them less than an hour to find him guilty of murder. Once again, the judge sentenced him to death by electrocution.

Bundy was sent to death row. Remarkably, he was somehow able to get his wife pregnant while still incarcerated there—most likely by bribing the guards. Carole Ann gave birth to a daughter nine months later.

Years passed. Bundy tried a variety of shenanigans to try to evade the electric chair, including offering in-depth confessions to a number of murders in the hope that he would gain a stay of execution in return. The state of Florida was having none of it. As with so many of Ted Bundy's flawed strategies, his confessions had unforeseen consequences: this time, his wife, who had insisted throughout his trial that her husband had been innocent, took it as a personal betrayal when he finally admitted his guilt. She cut off all contact with him, an ironic—some would say karmic—mirroring of the way that he had treated his first fiancée, Diane Edwards.

After spending the better part of a decade on death row, it all came to an end for Ted Bundy on January 24, 1989. Now 42 years old, his boyish good looks had been replaced by the sallow and haunted air of a man who had been living under a death sentence for years upon end. His date with the electric chair was set for first thing in the morning in the execution chamber of Raiford Prison. Across the state of Florida—not to mention Utah, Colorado, and every other state of the union, one presumes—people celebrated the impending death of a monster.

An executioner threw the switch that sent high-voltage electricity coursing through a heavily sedated Ted Bundy's freshly shaved head. Once a physician had examined him and pronounced him dead, his body was taken by hearse for cremation. He had chosen to leave his few belonging (and control over what happened to his cremains after his death) to his attorney, with the stipulation that his ashes be scattered somewhere in the Cascade Mountains of Washington State. This seems particularly callous in light of the fact that he had dumped the bodies of several victims in those same mountains, but the request was carried out nevertheless.

Ted Bundy's story does not end with his death in 1989. In many ways, it is still unfolding. In addition to denying involvement in murders that police

FBI agent Bill Hagmaier (left) interviews Bundy one
last time before his execution in 1989.

suspected he had committed, Bundy would sometimes accept responsibility for others in which his involvement was possible but highly questionable. One such instance was the killing of 12-year-old Lynette Dawn Culver in the summer of 1975. According to Bundy, he snatched the Idaho schoolgirl and took her to a Holiday Inn, where he claimed to have raped and then drowned her (a method that was not consistent with his usual MO) before throwing her body into a river. Detectives found his claim to be dubious, and at the time of writing, her murder is still an open case.

In interviews that he gave in the days leading up to his execution, Ted Bundy confessed to having committed a grand total of 30 murders. While it is reasonable to assume that he was responsible for more murders than he was ultimately convicted for, the true number of his victims will never be known; tragically, their remains may never be found and laid to rest.

Ted Bundy was nothing less than a superb actor. He managed to fool practically everybody in his life, successfully concealing his sadistic and predatory nature even from those who knew him best. When the police announced that he was the prime suspect in a series of brutal sexual murders, none of his friends, family members, or associates could believe it. While one expects denial from a mother or a spouse, past girlfriends, teachers, and those he had worked with all thought it was a ghastly mistake. Surely it couldn't be true— not *Ted Bundy*, of all people? After all, he was *such a nice guy!*

This off-the-charts level of charisma is arguably the main reason that Ted Bundy was such a successful predator. People instinctively *liked* him. For the most part, women found him attractive and believed him to be trustworthy, especially when he turned on the charm or—equally effectively—portrayed himself as the vulnerable nice guy in need of help. The crutches, sling, and stack of books served as props in the arsenal of a highly skilled actor.

Many serial killers attract a following, a fan base of sorts, and one that is predominantly female. Ted Bundy received countless marriage proposals during his trials and incarceration on death row, even after his impromptu wedding. True crime author Ann Rule, arguably the single greatest expert on Bundy (she worked next to the serial killer on the suicide prevention hotline and maintained a long-term correspondence with him after his capture), observed that she had never seen so many beautiful women sitting in the public gallery at any other trial she attended in her career.

Part of Bundy's attraction was his charm, and another part was his undeniable physical handsomeness, so a certain "cult of Bundy" grew up in the media, one that still persists to this day. As mentioned earlier, there have been multiple Bundy biopics. The most recent, *Extremely Wicked, Shockingly Evil and Vile* (2019), starring Zac Efron as Bundy, has drawn the ire of critics, who point out that it portrays its subject in far too flattering a light, making him a borderline sympathetic character and glossing over the horrific nature of his crimes.

Sometimes, reality mirrors art. Watch an interview with Bundy on YouTube, and you will see a literate, thoughtful, apparently reasonable man giving thoughtful answers to the questions that are put to him. It is sometimes all too easy to forget just how depraved the man was, and just as easy to see how so many were taken in by his apparently affable demeanor.

THE LONELY MURDERER: DENNIS NILSEN

It is only to be expected that for many people, the details of many serial killings are the subject of equal parts fascination and revulsion. Much of this has to do with the taboo nature of not just the act of murder but also the disposition of the victim's body afterward.

Taboos—subjects that must never be spoken about or engaged in, by collective agreement of the members of a society—are, for some people, made to be broken. For the serial murderer, the things that bring revulsion to most people are something to be indulged in, experimented with, even celebrated.

One such taboo is necrophilia, the act of sexual intercourse with the dead. Several of the serial killers who appear within these pages were necrophiles, taking great pleasure in having sex with their victims once their hearts had finally stopped beating. For some, such illicit congress was the main reason they had committed the murder in the first place.

The Milwaukee cannibal Jeffrey Dahmer is the serial killer most Americans think of when they hear the term "necrophiliac." For Britons, on the other hand, that man is Dennis Nilsen.

Nilsen was of Norwegian Scottish descent and was born in Scotland on November 23, 1945. While his childhood was not a particularly stable or happy one (his parents' marriage lasted six years before ending in divorce), neither was it a deprived or abusive one. After his father left home, Nilsen's only male role model was his maternal grandfather, a fisherman for whom he felt something very much like hero worship.

On Halloween of 1951, Nilsen's grandfather died at sea, suffering a massive heart attack. Young Dennis was five years old at the time and would later claim that the aftermath of the old man's death would be one of the causal factors that led him to a life of murder. The body of his deceased grandfather was returned to the Nilsen household by his fellow fishermen, who laid it out respectfully and left their friend's family to grieve over him.

The young boy lacked a true understanding of the nature of death. When he asked his mother what was happening to his grandfather, who lay still and silent in an open-topped coffin with his eyes closed, she lied to him, dodging the straightforward explanation that the man was dead and gone forever. It would be fair to assume that she did this out of a desire to spare her son's feelings, but if the claims he made in later years were to be believed, it was a lie from which he would never recover.

Young Dennis was five years old at the time and would later claim that the aftermath of the old man's death would be one of the causal factors that led him to a life of murder.

Nilsen's schoolteachers noted that the boy was a loner and was "full of anger," lacking the friendships that the other children seemed to form with relative ease.

Author Russ Coffey interviewed Nilsen extensively for his biographical book about the serial killer and engaged in a lengthy correspondence with him, writing to Nilsen while he was serving his jail sentence. Coffey picked up on one of the early indicators that a child may be destined to grow up to become a killer: he once strangled a cat to death, watching it struggle helplessly until it finally expired. While this fits well with the traditional "childhood molding of a serial killer" narrative that we see in so many other cases, Nilsen does not quite fit the stereotype. Rather than become euphoric or sexually aroused by the poor creature's death, he instead claimed to have felt a sense of self-loathing and disgust at having caused the cat's suffering. This atypical reaction forms part of the fascination so many people have with Dennis Nilsen. The man was a true paradox, growing up to respect and appreciate animal life while simultaneously being capable of murdering other human beings without showing any sign of apparent remorse.

Nilsen followed in his father's footsteps by enlisting in the army at the age of 14, serving as a member of the Catering Corps for over ten years. During his term of service, he was deployed to a number of overseas posts around the world. The infamous British Army social culture also taught him how to drink to excess.

He had experienced homosexual desires and fantasies for several years before enlisting and wisely made of point of keeping them well hidden during his military term of service. The British Army was an extremely homophobic institution during the 1960s, and even the mere suggestion that a soldier might be gay could be enough to earn them a ferocious beating and, almost certainly, a discharge on the grounds of being "unsuited or unfit for military life." While a competent cook, he was not a particularly professional soldier. Nilsen had a habit of getting into fights when drunk and was not permitted to extend his enlistment when the time came to do so. He found himself out of the army, adrift on "Civvy Street," as soldiers like to call it, and desperately in need of a job. Despite the briefness of his military stint, the army did teach him at least one skill that he would use in later life: the art of butchery.

A wayward son is often drawn to his childhood home. Nilsen moved back in with his mother and siblings in Scotland, but after a listless and unhappy year, he decided to move to London and apply for a job as a police officer. With his military background and clean service record no doubt helpful, he was accepted, graduating from basic training in the spring of 1973. Yet Dennis's law enforcement career was to be short-lived. Not only was his drinking problem getting out of hand, but Nilsen was also a lonely gay man living and working in the nation's capital. The Metropolitan Police were a little more tolerant of the homosexual lifestyle than the army had been. As he sought out more sexual encounters with other men, Nilsen realized that he had a choice to make—keep his job or fulfill his personal desires.

His personal desires finally won out. By Christmas of 1973, he had quit the police force and was looking for work in the private security sector. After a brief spell there, he entered the beginnings of an administrative career by taking a position at a job center, helping the unemployed find work.

> The honeymoon period lasted for just a few short months. Nilsen and Gallichan, infrequent lovers at the best of times, began to gradually grow apart.

All that was missing was a steady relationship, and Nilsen believed he had finally found one in November 1975 when he met an 18-year-old gay man named David Gallichan in a pub. Gallichan became very enamored of Nilsen despite Nilsen being eleven years older. Before long, the two men had moved into a flat together on Melrose Avenue in Cricklewood.

The honeymoon period lasted for just a few short months. Nilsen and Gallichan, infrequent lovers at the best of times, began to gradually grow apart, until finally each of them was openly seeing other men—sometimes even bringing them back to the flat while the other was still there. Less than two years after they had first begun living together, they broke up. Gallichan moved out of the flat, leaving the lonely civil servant with only the bottle for company.

Home movie footage of the two men, with each taking turns filming the other, suggests an obviously unhappy relationship that was fraught with tension. Nilsen comes across as by turns petulant, angry, and judgmental, deriding his lover for the way he operates the camera ("It's like training fucking chimpanzees," he snorts at one point). Gallichan, for his part, comes across as embarrassed and uncomfortable while lounging shirtless in bed.

The classic contemporary account of the Dennis Nilsen murders was the appropriately titled *Killing for Company* by Brian Masters. It was published in 1985, just two years after Nilsen was apprehended, and it set forth the idea that he picked up other gay men and murdered them primarily because he was lonely.

While many have likened Nilsen to Jeffrey Dahmer, there are also striking parallels with Herbert Baumeister, the I-70 Strangler. Both Baumeister and Nilsen were intelligent and socially awkward individuals who deliberately picked up other homosexual men that (they hoped) would not be missed, bringing them home and plying them with alcohol before murdering them. All three men preferred strangulation as their primary method of killing. Nilsen was not above targeting the homeless, correctly reasoning that fewer questions would be asked when they disappeared without a trace. Both Nilsen and Dahmer were extremely heavy drinkers, having developed a problem with alcohol as young men that only grew worse as their mental and emotional states began to deteriorate.

In all three cases—Baumeister, Dahmer, and Nilsen—there was a significant degree of loneliness. All were outsiders, in one way or another. Baumeister was a gay man who never officially came out, one who felt forced to hide his homosexuality behind the facade of a "normal" heterosexual family man. Dahmer was a social recluse, venturing out to bars mostly when he wanted to hunt for new victims. Nilsen was a quiet man with few friends, who spent much of his time working his day job as a civil servant before coming home and drinking himself to sleep.

Nilsen didn't want the young Holmes to ever leave him, and the only way to assure that was to kill him, so Nilsen filled a bucket with water and drowned the 14-year-old boy.

Dennis Nilsen had long harbored dark sexual fantasies, but they did not turn into murder until the night of December 30, 1978. For him, as for so many people, the Christmas to New Year holiday season had been a bleak and lonely one. His closest family were far away in Scotland, and even had they not been, they were no longer emotionally close with one another. Although he was not averse to one-night stands, these passing sexual encounters never amounted to anything more substantial, and the only source of constant company that he had was his dog. He loathed the emptiness of these hollow encounters, and he turned that sense of disgust inward on himself. The more self-loathing Nilsen felt, the more he anesthetized himself with alcohol, entering a downward spiral that cost him much of his self-control.

One day, he met a 14-year-old Irish boy, Stephen Holmes, in a pub. They drank together, and Nilsen invited him back to his home. Stephen went with Nilsen willingly (doubtless influenced by all the alcohol he had consumed), and when the two got back to 195 Melrose Avenue, they stayed up late drinking until they both passed out.

When a groggy Nilsen finally awoke, Holmes was still sleeping. He ran his hands over the boy's body and, he claimed, felt a sudden compulsion that Holmes absolutely *must* be his companion over the coming holidays. Anything would be better than spending another New Year alone. To that end, Nilsen made sure that Stephen Holmes would be incapable of leaving—ever. He slipped a tie around the sleeping boy's neck and strangled him. This rendered him unconscious but was not immediately fatal, so Nilsen filled a bucket with cold tap water, then immersed Stephen's head in it until he had drowned.

Dennis Nilsen now had company for New Year's Eve and New Year's Day—the company of a dead teenager lying motionless on his bed. Nilsen used the body as a masturbatory aid. He had to wait for the condition of rigor mortis to dissipate before pulling up floorboards and placing Stephen Holmes's body underneath them. The week that followed was a nervous one for Nilsen. He lived under the continual threat of discovery, convinced that there would be a knock on the door, and when he opened it, the police would be standing there, ready to arrest him.

It never happened. Finally, curious as to what Stephen Holmes's remains might look like after a week in the ground, Nilsen uncovered the body to gauge its condition. The body was grimy and dirt-stained but had not significantly decomposed—possibly due to the cold weather and temperature of the ground. Nilsen felt the urge to drag the body back up into the apartment and wash it clean, then return it to its makeshift grave, where it would spend the next seven months.

Nobody came looking for Stephen Holmes, and after the first weeks of 1979 turned into months, it slowly began to dawn on Dennis Nilsen that he had gotten away with murder. In August, he burned the dead boy's remains, doing his best to get rid of the evidence of his crime. Had he stopped there, it is likely that the murder would have gone undetected. Stephen would have become one of the thousands of unexplained disappearances that happen each year, and nobody would ever have heard the name Dennis Nilsen.

Instead, on October 11, he tried to kill another young man that he met in a pub. This time, his intended victim was a student named Andrew Ho. After a few drinks, Ho accompanied Nilsen back to his flat, but when Dennis attempted to

> Nobody came looking for Stephen Holmes, and after the first weeks of 1979 turned into months, it slowly began to dawn on Dennis Nilsen that he had gotten away with murder.

strangle him with a tie, Ho fought back and managed to escape. He went straight to the police and reported the attempted murder. Nilsen was later questioned by officers, but he managed to talk his way out of it, and unfortunately no legal case was pursued against him. If it had been, many other lives might have been saved.

Two months later, Nilsen killed again. Kenneth Ockenden, 23, was also a student and made the same mistake of accompanying the serial killer back to his home. The young Canadian was taking in the sights of London, and after a few hours drinking with Nilsen in a pub, he accepted his offer to be a tour guide. According to Coffey, Nilsen used the young man's love of music against him. Back at 195 Melrose, Ockenden was listening to an album, with a pair of headphones over his ears. He was caught totally off-guard when his seemingly gracious host began to strangle him with the headphone cord, tightening it around his neck and pulling it taut until he was dead.

Dennis Nilsen's sex fantasies had sometimes centered upon death and dead bodies. He took photographs of Kenneth Ockenden's corpse with a Polaroid camera, keeping the pictures hidden for future enjoyment. Nilsen took the headphones from the dead man's head and put them on himself, listening to the music while he enjoyed a drink. The life he had just taken didn't seem to bother him in the slightest.

Recounting the murder afterward, Nilsen claimed to have watched some television in bed—with his victim's naked corpse resting on top of him. The presence of Ockenden's body helped Nilsen stave off the ever-encroaching feeling of loneliness that haunted him. He would sometimes place the body in an armchair, sitting up and seemingly watching the television alongside him. He got used to talking to it, as one might speak to an unusually quiet room mate. When he tired of this, Nilsen put the body underneath the floorboards, just as he had done with that of Stephen Holmes.

Kenneth Ockenden had family, however, and he was reported missing. Nevertheless, there were few solid leads, and it would take a confession from Nilsen himself several years later before the truth came out. Most of his future victims would prove to be even harder to trace.

Six months passed without there being another murder. Nilsen's twin traits of alcoholism and workaholism combined to keep him busy and out of trouble. On May 17, he saw an opportunity to kill again in the form of Martyn Duffey, 16. The young man was homeless, sleeping on the streets and scavenging food wherever he could. The offer of a soft bed in a warm flat, along with a free meal thrown in, were all the inducement he needed to go back to Melrose Avenue with Dennis Nilsen.

Nilsen inflicted what was now becoming his traditional method of murder upon the boy as he lay in bed: strangulation, followed by drowning, and cleaning his body in the bathtub while he also sat in there with it. After masturbating on it, Nilsen buried the corpse beneath the floor.

With no apparent notice being taken by the police, Dennis Nilsen's confidence was growing. Whenever he wasn't at work, he kept a watchful eye out for other potential victims. Through the remainder of 1980 and on into the spring of 1981, he killed on average of once every month. To this day, police still do not know the identities of many of these unfortunate individuals. During his interrogation, Nilsen would describe his recollections of each one, such as a tattoo around one man's neck that bore the words *cut here*. Attempts to match them against lists of missing persons were largely unsuccessful.

After Nilsen kept company with a corpse for a while, he would bury each body underneath the floor of 195 Melrose Avenue. Small wonder that as the weather turned warmer, the place began to stink. Nilsen used air fresheners and other chemicals in an attempt to mask the stench, but he was fighting a losing battle. Whenever the mood took him, he would pull up the floorboards and extract a body at random, which he would then cut open and dismember. He would dispose of some of the remains by burning them on a makeshift bonfire behind the property, in an attempt to rid his flat of not just the evidence but also some of the smell.

After a string of unidentified victims met their untimely end there, the last person to die at 195 Melrose Avenue was 23-year-old Malcolm Barlow, whom Nilsen also strangled while he was sleeping. Not long afterward, Nilsen's landlord dropped a bombshell: he wanted to fix up the flat to a higher standard, which meant that Dennis would be forced to move out. Nilsen lit one last bonfire, disposing of Barlow's body, before he moved out to his next address—an attic flat located at 23 Cranley Gardens in Muswell Hill.

When it came to the matter of killing, Dennis Nilsen now found himself in something of a quandary. Although he still felt the urge to murder, his new residence was no longer on the ground floor—which meant that he would be unable to simply conceal the bodies beneath the floorboards. He would have to find a different solution. He mulled it over for a few months, and by the time he killed his first victim at Cranley Gardens (John Howlett, also 23) in March 1982, he had hit upon a new idea.

Nilsen moved into the Muswell Hill neighborhood in North London, but his new residence was not on the ground floor, and there was no way to hide bodies under the floorboards.

Nilsen's latest method for disposing of his victims' bodies was not well thought out: he would cut up the bodies and then flush the constituent parts down the toilet, one piece after another. The heads were an exception: these he boiled on the kitchen stove. This was more than the sewage system at Cranley Gardens could handle, and it wasn't long before the odor of rotting flesh and tissue began to draw complaints from Nilsen's neighbors. This would ultimately prove to be his undoing.

Six months went by without another murder, but in September, Nilsen could no longer help himself. He strangled 27-year-old Graham Allen as he ate. In early February of the following year, Nilsen murdered 20-year-old Australian Stephen Sinclair. While the bones had been dumped in the trash, the softer remnants of both men were cut up and flushed down the toilet, albeit several months apart. Large portions of Sinclair's dissected body were retained by Nilsen and kept in various places inside his flat.

On February 8, 1983, a plumber was brought in to scope out the drains in an attempt to identify the source of a rancid odor that permeated the building and surrounding area. When interviewed later, the plumber described it as a stench that smelled like that of a slaughterhouse. He found flesh and bone fragments clogging the sewage pipes. The bones had knuckles and had quite clearly come from a human hand.

The police were immediately called. A quick search of 23 Cranley Gardens turned up the remains of three victims, cut up and contained in black trash bags that Nilsen had stored in the wardrobe. A pathologist soon confirmed what officers already suspected: the pipes at Cranley Gardens had been blocked by human remains.

The lead detective confronted the resident of flat 23 with a dry, "I have come about your drains." The serial killer initially tried to be brazen, but when pressed, Nilsen confessed openly to having murdered at least 15 men and boys. Police found the bagged remains of two victims stuffed inside the wardrobe, along with a skull that Nilsen had boiled in a cooking pot that had been placed on the stove. A decapitated head found nearby was in equally bad shape. Despite this, Nilsen always insisted that he had no interest in cannibalism and had never eaten the flesh of any of his victims. As he openly admitted to masturbating both on and over their bodies, it seems unlikely that he would have lied about this single detail, although it is impossible to be absolutely certain of it.

A more extensive search of the property revealed still more body parts. Detectives soon reasoned that if Dennis Nilsen had killed men at 23 Cranley Gardens, he had almost certainly done so at his former address as well. Officers went to Melrose Avenue, where a blackened section of the garden yielded hundreds of charred bone shards scattered among the remnants of a tire that Nilsen had burned to hide the smell of melting flesh.

It took just one day for the jury to find Dennis Nilsen not only guilty of several counts of murder but also fully capable of understanding his actions—and therefore of taking responsibility for them. He was sentenced to life sentences in prison, not in a secure hospital facility.

While he was incarcerated, Nilsen wrote an autobiography that he titled *History of a Drowning Boy*. Author Russ Coffey was one of the few people who had access to the written work, which was blocked from publication by the British Home Office, and he used it as part of his own book about Nilsen. He provided great insight into the mind of his subject. Brian Masters also produced a very competent biography of Nilsen. Both books are essential reading for those who wish to understand Nilsen on some level. Nilsen's own work, which may never see the light of day, is by the accounts of some who have read it

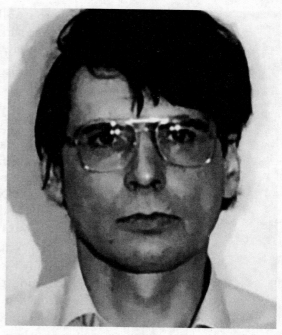

Dennis Nilsen's mugshot. He died in prison in 2018.

rather pretentious and deceptive, full of self-justification and skewed self-perceptions. To get a look at Nilsen in person, the author recommends watching a BBC TV documentary titled *Bookmark: Killing for Company*, which presents not only extracts from Nilsen's prison journals but also home movie footage taken of Nilsen by his live-in boyfriend.

While the idea of a lonely, isolated man who was "killing for company" is still a valid one, Brian Masters describes Nilsen having made a confession to him: "I've got to come clean with you, Brian. *I killed them because I enjoyed it.*" One is forced to wonder whether, had Dennis Nilsen been living in a relatively normal, well-adjusted relationship during the late 1970s and early 1980s, he would still have felt the compulsion to commit murder.

During the sentencing process, Nilsen received the Whole Life Tariff, a stipulation made by the presiding judge that he would never be released from prison during his lifetime—or, "life means life."

A ruptured abdominal aortic aneurysm is not a pleasant way to die. The aorta is the body's major artery, curving up from the heart into an arch before descending downward, passing through the chest into the abdomen. Some people, usually after years of poorly managed high blood pressure, develop a weakened pocket in the wall of the blood vessel. The aneurysm throbs, bulging in and out in time with every heartbeat, a silent time bomb waiting to go off … until finally, one day, it tears.

This was how Dennis Nilsen died on May 12, 2018. He had been imprisoned since 1983. Two hours after his first complaints of abdominal pain were ignored by prison medical staff, the serial killer was found on the toilet, his body splashed with his own feces.

Hours passed. Nilsen's condition worsened. Finally, an ambulance arrived and rushed the dying prisoner to the hospital. It was too late. When an aortic aneurysm finally gives out, the chances of survival—even with surgical intervention—are not good. Nilsen died following an emergency surgery that had attempted to stabilize and repair the rupture. The surgery was successful, but a blood clot made its way to his lungs, finally finishing him off.

Whenever a prisoner dies in a British prison, an independent investigation is conducted, usually by an ombudsman. In Nilsen's case, the ombudsman's official report found that his reports of a medical emergency were overlooked by the prison guards and not taken seriously until it was too late to save him.

Predictably, the British public couldn't have cared less. Not only had Dennis Nilsen wasted large amounts of taxpayer money on fatuous legal complaints and appeals during the course of his prison stay (he once famously claimed that his rights were being infringed because the pornographic material he received was being censored), but he was also one of the most reviled men in the country.

"Fiend's Boiling in Hell," exclaimed *The Sun* newspaper, a play on the fact that Nilsen had boiled the bones of his victims. These four words completely encapsulated the mood at large. Few, if any, were saddened by the death of Dennis Nilsen. His body was cremated in secret, well out of the public eye, and his ashes were given to his surviving family members.

One final postscript concerns Nilsen's apartment in Cricklewood, London. If one didn't know the history of the anonymous-looking flat on Melrose Avenue, there was nothing particularly out of the ordinary to give away the horrific things that had happened there. Now, forty years after Nilsen's atrocities were uncovered, the flat is at last a happy home, lived in by a professional couple who are not remotely bothered by its macabre past.

How fitting it is that at least one small piece of Dennis Nilsen's evil legacy has been transformed into something good.

THE NIGHT STALKER: RICHARD RAMIREZ

"**D**o you admit to being evil, Richard?" Reporter Mike Watkiss asks a simple question. His interviewee, a straggly haired man with dark, piercing eyes and wearing a prison inmate's boiler suit, smiles wolfishly for the camera.

"We are *all* evil, in one way or another, are we not?" The man has a point. He should know, after all, for he is none other than Richard Ramirez—serial murderer, rapist, and self-professed son of Satan. He is more commonly known as the Night Stalker. "Yes, I *am* evil. Not a hundred percent, but I am evil."

The interview is taking place in the confines of a cell on California's death row. Ramirez insists that much of what has been said about him in the media is not true, yet when the veteran journalist gives him the opportunity to clarify things, he blows it off.

"*Who are you?*" Watkiss asks bluntly.

Ramirez is silent for a while, either pondering the question or at least pretending to, before finally exhaling in a way that suggests it is much too complex for a simple answer.

"Just a guy."

Yet for somebody who was such a loose cannon in the courtroom (Ramirez was famous for displays of contempt, disrupting the flow of events however he could contrive to), he suddenly becomes coy, bordering on the clinically detached, when asked whether he truly is guilty of 13 murders.

"It would be improper for me to comment on my LA convictions and my pending case here in San Francisco," he replies with great care and deliberation, "because of my appeal."

However, Ramirez being Ramirez, he cannot help rising to the bait when Watkiss compares him to Charles Manson.

"Serial killers do on a small scale what governments do on a large one," Ramirez points out. "They are a product of the times, and these are blood-thirsty times. Even psychopaths have emotions if you dig deep enough, but then again, maybe they don't."

Watkiss sees an opportunity and takes it. "Do *you* have emotions, Richard?"

A smirk. *I know something you don't know,* it seems to say. "No comment."

There's the definite sense that a game is being played and that Ramirez is enjoying it a great deal more than his opponent, who seems to be having a hard time concealing his disgust at being in Ramirez's company.

"Killing is killing, whether done for duty, profit, or fun," Ramirez adds. "Men murder themselves into this democracy."

> This idea that a criminal such as himself is no different from a national government furthering its ends with violent means is a staple argument for Ramirez....

This idea that a criminal such as himself is no different from a national government furthering its ends with violent means is a staple argument for Ramirez, something to be conveniently trotted out during an interview in the hope that it won't be considered too carefully. *I'm no different from the good old U.S. of A.,* the serial killer is basically saying, and while even the most casual study of history demonstrates that governments have indeed been responsible for murder and torture, they do not delight in carrying out such horrific acts in the way that Richard Ramirez plainly did.

Much was made of Ramirez's supposed connection to Satanism, both during his murder spree itself, when occult symbols were found daubed on the walls at some of his crime scenes, and also during his trial when Ramirez flashed a palm with a pentagram symbol on it toward the TV cameras. Trying out a new avenue of questioning, Mike Watkiss asks him whether he is a Satanist. Ramirez admits to having studied Satanism but refuses to comment on whether he is a "worshipper of the Devil."

Satanism, in Ramirez's words, is "undefiled wisdom instead of hypocritical self-deceit" and "power without charity." He notes that there has always been evil, which would never come to pass in a perfect world, and he predicts that "it is going to get worse." Few of us who keep up with current events in the 21st century, some 30 years after the serial killer first made this observation, would disagree with him on that score.

Ramirez's crimes were utterly heinous, yet he developed quite the following of admirers (most of them female) during his incarceration. In a particularly surreal twist, the phalanx of Ramirez groupies included a woman who had been part of the jury that sent him to death row for the crime of murder.

He would ultimately go on to get married while awaiting execution, and he never lacked for letters from his female fans, many of which contained heavy sexual overtones. With long dark hair framing a Saturnine face, it is not difficult to see why so many women found Richard Ramirez attractive ... until, that is, one looks into his eyes.

Ramirez considered himself a Satanist and would mark the walls of murder scenes with Satanic symbols.

Of Mexican descent, Richard Ramirez was born on February 29, 1960, in El Paso, Texas. His parents were both immigrants and had four other children prior to him. As a boy, he was diagnosed with epilepsy, and although his seizures gradually diminished in frequency and intensity before finally stopping, author Philip Carlo observes that such a condition can be linked to hyperaggressiveness in later life.

Carlo also relates an account of Ramirez's cousin, Miguel (known as Mike), who had served in Vietnam as a member of the U.S. Special Forces. The 12-year-old Richard had listened spellbound to the older man's tales of intense firefights against the Viet Cong and his forcible "conquests" of Vietnamese women afterward. Cousin Mike had saved the best for last, however: he kept a box full of photographs, some of which showed those women performing oral sex on him. The gun Mike held to their heads kept the women both motivated and scared, a lesson in power that the young Richard Ramirez never forgot. Nor did he forget the image of his cousin holding one of those same women's decapitated heads in his hand while posing for the camera.

Special Forces soldiers are particularly adept at moving stealthily, using the shadows and darkness as a natural form of cover. These are skills that Richard's cousin was able to teach him. He found the boy to be a surprisingly quick and enthusiastic learner.

Their relationship came to an abrupt and unexpected end in 1973 when Mike had a domestic argument with his wife. Right in front of Richard and his own younger children, Mike shot her in the head, killing her instantly. He made his cousin flee and promise never to breathe a word about what had happened that day, primarily so that the boy would not somehow implicate himself or be tainted by association. Richard did as he was told and kept the secret to himself just as he had promised, but the impressionable youth never forgot what he had witnessed and the way it made him feel. Cousin Mike soon found himself in jail awaiting trial for murder. It would take Richard Ramirez a few years longer to reach the same place for the same reason, but he would get there in the end.

A stint spent living with his older brother, Ruben, in Los Angeles was equally formative, further helping mold Richard Ramirez into the monster he would one day become. Ruben was a drug addict and a petty thief. Richard had learned how to move covertly from his cousin Mike; now he became adept at breaking into buildings, thanks to a crash course from his brother.

Ruth Ramirez, Richard's older sister, had married a man with somewhat unusual sexual tastes. Despite having sex with his wife as often as she would allow, Roberto Avala wanted more than she was prepared to give him. He made a habit of prowling the back alleys and yards late at night, a Peeping Tom out for a glimpse of nudity from any available female. Already developing his own warped form of sexuality, in no small part thanks to the influence of his cousin Mike, Richard was more than happy to go along with him. Peering into backlit windows, the two often caught women in various stages of undress. It didn't take long for the youth to begin fantasizing about breaking into their homes, tying them up, and forcing them to have intercourse with him. Sometimes he would even go inside, although he wasn't engaging in any sort of physical interaction with the unsuspecting occupants—yet.

If Richard Ramirez had a love affair, it was with Satanism. He was fiercely attracted to the sense of freedom and power it offered him. The intensity of emotion was heightened through his abuse of recreational drugs, which further skewed his perception of reality and contributed to his increasingly delusional view of the world. He believed that no matter what he did, no matter what risks he took, Satan would protect him.

With little in the way of formal schooling under his belt, life held few options for Richard Ramirez. Others in his position might have enlisted in the military (as Jeffrey Dahmer did), but unlike his cousin Mike, who came back on the scene when he was released from the secure medical facility where he had been kept for treatment, he lacked the self-discipline and willingness to conform to authori-

The Church of Satan is currently led by its high priest Peter H. Gilmore. Members say their church is not about worshipping Satan but, rather, about being skeptical atheists. Ramirez, though, was attracted to the Hollywoodized, evil depiction of murderous Satanists.

ty that such a career choice would have required. Instead, at 22 years of age, Ramirez left Texas behind forever; on a shoestring budget, he relocated to the West Coast and supported himself with a life of petty crime and, eventually, murder.

It would take 25 years for the identity of Richard Ramirez's first victim to come to light.

The date was April 10, 1984. Nine-year-old Mei Leung lived in an apartment at 765 O'Farrell Street in the Tenderloin district of San Francisco. She had been playing with her brother when she realized that she had dropped a dollar bill somewhere in the apartment building. Mei went off to find it, leaving her brother alone. When she didn't come back, he went looking for her.

Richard Ramirez had beaten the little girl to within an inch of her life, then raped and killed her, before hanging her dead body from a water pipe down in the basement. She had been repeatedly stabbed and strangled. In an even more disturbing turn of events, her killer had deliberately left her dangling with the tips of her toes just a few centimeters above the floor.

"Had she been a little taller, she could have transferred her weight to her feet on the ground and screamed and somebody could have come and helped her," San Francisco Police Department inspector Michael Mullane recalled in an interview with the *Daily Mail*. "This was one of the tougher ones. One of the ones you'd like to solve. I had little children at the time."

Back in 1984, the police had no real suspect in the slaying, but they were able to collect DNA evidence, which they kept in storage for over a quarter century before finally getting a hit. The cold case suddenly became hot.

The result of the DNA match made complete sense to detectives in 2009 when it was finally flagged. They knew that in the spring of 1984, Richard Ramirez had lived just a short distance away from Mei Leung, also renting a place in the Tenderloin. He certainly had the means, the motive, and the opportunity to commit the crime.

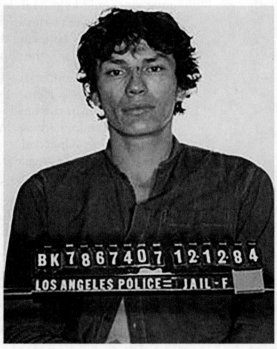

Ramirez was arrested just before Christmas 1984 for auto theft.

Until the discovery of this missing link, the first "official" Richard Ramirez murder was believed to have taken place on the night of June 28, 1984, when he broke into the home of 79-year-old Los Angeles resident Jennie Vincow. After pulling away a protective screen, Ramirez had climbed in through an open window and found his victim fast asleep in her bed. The intruder stabbed her over and over again, and then he slit her throat. By the time she finally stopped moving, the bed was drenched in blood. Despite the fact that Vincow had screamed during the early stages of the attack, nobody called the police or came to check on her. Rather than immediately flee the scene of the crime, Vincow's killer stuck around long enough to wash off some of the blood splatter and to see what there was in the apartment worth stealing.

The body of Jennie Vincow would not be discovered until much later that day, when her son came to visit. By then, Richard Ramirez was long gone.

He would not kill again for nine more months. That's not to say that Ramirez wasn't committing crimes; he was breaking and entering into homes on a daily basis, taking what valuables he could find and fencing them to feed himself and support his cocaine habit.

For his first two murders, Ramirez had favored a knife. During his following crimes, he made use of a .22 caliber pistol, a gun that was relatively quiet and could be used indoors, at close quarters, without fear of the round going through the victim and into an adjacent room or apartment. He was all about power, fully believing that Satan had bestowed both power and purpose upon him, and he saw the gun as a tangible extension of that power.

Richard Ramirez struck again late on the night of March 17, 1985. He lay in wait for Maria Hernandez, 22, outside her Rosemead home and attempted to shoot her in the head when she parked her car in the garage. It was a completely random attack. Maria had not been targeted for any specific reason. She simply happened to be in the wrong place at the wrong time, which somehow managed to make the ambush seem even more terrible.

> I turned around and I saw a man pointing a gun at me. He started walking toward me … and he pointed it right up at my face and shot me from a range of about one foot. I put my hand up for protection. I heard a shot. I felt a cross between pain and heat on my right hand. I fell to the ground.

In an incredible twist of fate, a million-to-one chance, the relatively small .22 caliber round had bounced off Maria's car keys. Ramirez apparently hadn't been paying close attention, because when Maria wisely chose to play dead, he fell for it. Her roommate wasn't as fortunate. Ramirez went into the condominium, found 34-year-old Dayle Okazaki, and shot her in the head from extremely close range. On conducting her autopsy, the coroner noted that powder burns from the muzzle of her killer's pistol were ingrained on Okazaki's face.

Ramirez made a fast getaway, but an extremely shaken Maria Hernandez was able to give police a general description of the killer: a tall, thin male dressed in black from head to toe. While the police department was securing the crime scene and starting their investigation, Richard Ramirez was getting ready to murder again for the second time that night.

He drove from Rosemead to Monterey Park—about five miles—and attempted to drag student Tsai-Lian Yu, 30, out of her car, which was stopped at a red light. Tsai-Lian fought back, but Ramirez overpowered her. Pulling her into the street, he shot her multiple times at close range. She did not survive.

Ten days later, Ramirez set out to kill again, this time in Whittier. His latest target was a married couple, Vincent Zazzara, 64, and his wife, Maxine, 44. He shot Vincent in the head with the .22 and then turned his attention to Maxine, whom he battered, shot in the head and the neck, and then stabbed repeatedly after she was dead. Some of Maxine's stab wounds were to her pelvis, hinting at the pathologic loathing for women that Ramirez had been nursing. Most disturbing of all, he cut out the dead woman's eyes with a knife and took them with him as a trophy or souvenir.

> **R**amirez made a fast getaway, but an extremely shaken Maria Hernandez was able to give police a general description of the killer.

Ramirez's MO was starting to form. Reasoning that the male was usually the more physically powerful member of a couple, and therefore the greater threat, he began to develop a habit of shooting the male dead first, which would then give him greater time and opportunity to brutalize the female.

He employed exactly this method on May 14, in the murder of Bill and Lillian Doi. Ramirez had been prowling in Monterey Park, the same place in which he had murdered Tsai-Lian Yu two months before. After forcing entry into their home, the intruder shot Bill Doi, 66, who would nonetheless manage to make a desperate call to 911 in spite of the fact that he was bleeding to death from a bullet hole in his face.

Lillian Doi, ten years younger than her husband, was physically disabled and unable to put up a fight, especially as they had both been taken by surprise. Her husband had attempted to get a gun to defend them both and would pay the ultimate price for it. Now, Richard Ramirez showed her no mercy whatsoever. He cuffed the poor woman, then sexually assaulted her. She was left alive (and emotionally scarred forever) when their attacker fled the scene with a host of stolen valuables. Her husband would die shortly afterward.

The police were now on high alert, aware that a serial offender was at work in what was beginning to look like a series of interconnected home invasion crimes. On May 29, Ramirez raped two elderly ladies, Mabel Bell, 83, and Florence Lang, 81, in their Monrovia home. Both women were physically frail

Ramirez would often handcuff, torture, and rape his victims before killing them. Weak, elderly, or disabled women were common prey.

and could not have defended themselves from a man of Ramirez's age. Nevertheless, he tied them up and tortured them both. In what would become known as a characteristic signature of his crimes, Ramirez introduced a Satanic element by drawing a pentagram on the bare thigh of one of his victims. Mabel would ultimately succumb to the injuries Ramirez had inflicted upon her.

One night later, Ramirez viciously raped Carol Kyle, 42, at her home in Burbank. Carol, a nurse, showed almost superhuman discipline and restraint, enduring violent acts of sexual humiliation that were both intensely painful and extremely degrading. She was motivated to endure her ordeal by just one thing: having her attacker spare the life of her 11-year-old son, whom the intruder had restrained in the closet while he assaulted his mother. Kyle's actions were nothing less than utterly heroic. As repugnant as her brutal mistreatment at the hands of Richard Ramirez had been, this expression of motherly love paid off in the end: Ramirez let them both live, cuffing them to one another before leaving the house.

Californians were now living in fear, a fear that fed the confidence and narcissism of Richard Ramirez. The local press came to dub him "the Valley Intruder." The more that he got away with, the more compelled he felt to strike again. Even in something as grotesque as serial murder and rape, it was possible to develop a "success begets more success" mindset. He believed wholeheartedly that Satan had his back. When it came to the law, Ramirez believed that he was effectively bulletproof.

On July 2, he murdered Mary Louise Cannon. There was no husband for him to kill first; the 75-year-old was a widow and lived alone. This time, Ramirez did not rape his victim, either before or after stabbing her and cutting her throat. The reason for this is unknown. He had shown no reluctance to sexually molest women in their eighties before, so it could not have been her age. It may be that something spooked him, causing him to cut his attack short. Nonetheless, after killing his victim, he ransacked her home for valuables and disappeared into the night.

He severely battered another victim three nights later but left her alive. Two nights after that, he beat Joyce Lucille Nelson, aged 61, to death in her own home, killing her without using either a knife or a gun. This was another break from routine.

Throughout the summer of 1985, Richard Ramirez robbed, raped, and murdered his way across several different cities, leaving a trail of terror and death in his wake. Some victims he chopped up with a machete; others were shot with the .22, usually in the head. Most female victims were raped, with sodomy being Ramirez's preferred method of abuse. The police were gradually putting the pieces together, but as an August 10, 1985, article in the *Los Angeles Times* shows, they were not yet aware of the true scale of Ramirez's crimes:

> The March 17 shooting death of a 35-year-old woman in her Rosemead condominium may have been the first in a countywide series of at least 6 slayings linked to a killer who enters unlocked homes at night to attack his victims as they sleep, authorities said Friday.

Reporters David Freed and Mark Arax were largely right, of course; the article listed the attack on Maria Hernandez and concomitant murder of Dayle Okazaki as the first crimes in the spree. There was no mention of the murder of Jennie Vincow, which is unsurprising, as it took place in 1984 and was not immediately linked to what would soon become known as the Night Stalker murders. Detectives gradually began casting a wider net, scrutinizing unsolved murders, assaults, kidnappings, and sex crimes to see whether they fit the Night Stalker's pattern.

The same article continues:

> Another high-ranking police officer said that although there are many similarities between the assaults and slayings, it is the dissimilarities that confound investigators. "The strange part is that he doesn't meet any profile we've ever seen," said the officer, who spoke on the condition that he not be named. "Guys that have worked 15 to 20 years investigating homicides are pulling their hair out over this. They say this is the most perplexing case they've ever worked on."

This was a direct result of Ramirez varying his MO whenever it suited him to do so. He would stick with the "shoot the male, rape the female" approach for a while, then switch to stabbing his victims or punching and kicking them to death. Every once in a while, he would leave one alive, sometimes intentionally, sometimes by accident. Sometimes he would scrawl dark messages upon the walls or leave a pentagram as part of his signature "calling card," but during other home invasions, he left nothing at all.

It is easy to see why the homicide detectives found the hunt for the Night Stalker so infuriating. There was physical evidence—Ramirez had inadvertently left his fingerprints and shoe prints at some of the crime scenes—but

> He would stick with the "shoot the male, rape the female" approach for a while, then switch to stabbing his victims or punching and kicking them to death.

Road checkpoints were deployed by the police to stop any suspicious-looking automobiles in an effort to trap the Night Stalker.

as the summer of 1985 slowly passed, the police seemed no nearer to establishing his identity.

Adding to the problem was a frightened public who desperately wanted to see the Valley Intruder/Night Stalker caught. To that end, they deluged police tip lines with a torrent of leads, the vast majority of which were nothing more than sources of well-meaning distraction for the detectives who were charged with sifting through them all and chasing down the more promising ones. Although the police departments involved had established a task force and invested significant amounts of time, effort, and money into the manhunt, their resources were not infinite.

Meanwhile, the attacks continued with impunity. Nocturnal police patrols were stepped up throughout the Los Angeles region. In a desperate attempt to catch the Night Stalker, random vehicle checks were implemented at the end of August. Police officers were empowered to stop any car whose driver "looked suspicious," which basically meant any male who was seen driving alone after nightfall. Surely, police chiefs reasoned, they would have to catch their man sooner or later.

After yet another brutal assault and rape, Ramirez had blithely instructed his female victim to tell authorities that "the Night Stalker was here." He felt invincible. Invulnerable. Untouchable. Satan was protecting him, after all.

In the end, Richard Ramirez's overconfidence turned out to be his undoing. On that same night, a teenager in the victim's neighborhood watched him slowly drive by. Ramirez looked sufficiently creepy to 13-year-old James Romero III that he immediately became suspicious and was savvy enough to commit the color and make of the car to memory. He also remembered a section of the vehicle's license plate number, which was enough to allow police to trace the car. It had been stolen and, based on Romero's description of the man in black who had been driving it, they had reason to suspect that its driver was none other than the Night Stalker himself.

Finally, the police had caught a lucky break. Forensic technicians were able to lift a fingerprint from the car's rearview mirror. The print belonged to one Richard Ramirez. A background check revealed that the 25-year-old petty theft criminal had a lengthy rap sheet and was obviously a very shady character indeed. His mug shot was also on file, and detectives wasted no time in putting his photograph and identity out to the general public, letting them know that this was the number-one suspect in the Night Stalker slayings.

Now it was just a matter of time.

Every network TV news broadcast and the front pages of every newspaper were carrying his face. Millions of people were on the lookout for Richard Ramirez—people who had been living in a state of perpetual fear for months. Now, that fear had turned into something different: anger.

The Night Stalker's luck finally ran out on Saturday, August 31. Ramirez, still oblivious to the fact that his secret was well and truly out, blithely walked into a liquor store and stopped dead in his tracks. There, looking right back at him from the front page of a newspaper, was his own face. He looked at the newspaper next to it. There he was again. Richard Ramirez was the lead headline on each and every one of them.

He walked out of the store, his head on a swivel. People were coming toward him. They knew who he was, Ramirez realized, and he broke into a run. But you can't outrun an entire neighborhood. Desperately, he tried to hijack a car, but it was too late. A small mob was on him. They laid into him with fists, feet, and even a metal bar, meting out just a small fraction of the pain and trauma that he had inflicted on so many others over the course of the summer—vigilante justice.

> **P**eople were coming toward him. They knew who he was, Ramirez realized, and he broke into a run. But you can't outrun an entire neighborhood.

It was a bruised and bloody Richard Ramirez that police officers rescued a few minutes later. "Thank God you came," was all he could say when the cops forced their way through the attackers and pulled him out. If they had arrived just a few minutes later, the odds were good that he would not have survived the assault. Most California residents would have been perfectly okay with that.

Ramirez was taken to the police station and booked into protective custody, and additional measures were taken to ensure that he would survive to stand trial. One man, armed with a knife, was apprehended trying to get close to Ramirez; he said he was the husband of one of the victims. There would be no shortage of individuals who wanted to see the Night Stalker dead before he was even tried.

After languishing in jail for three years, Richard Ramirez finally went to trial in July 1988. If he hoped to have any chance of escaping the death penalty, the serial killer did not help his case any by making statements such as "I love to kill people. I love all that blood. One time, I told this lady to give me all her money. She said no. So, I cut her and pulled her eyes out."

Undercutting the odds of successfully employing the insanity defense, Ramirez declared himself to be absolutely sane. At this point, he still believed that Satan was protecting him. Far from being a model prisoner, he disrupted

A mugshot of Ramirez in 2007; he would die of cancer six years later.

the courtroom by flashing a palm on which an occult symbol was displayed. He wore sunglasses for much of the time, cultivating a look that was as much wannabe rock star as it was serial killer. Finally, there was a lengthy trial in which there was almost as much drama associated with the pool of jurors as there was with the defendant. It took six months just to select the jury from a pool of more than 1,500 potential jurors. Ramirez laughed out loud when the details of his crimes were read out. He expressed an intention to smuggle a pistol into the courtroom and kill the prosecuting attorney. One of the jurors was murdered by her own boyfriend, who was not connected with Ramirez; nevertheless, the tragedy cast a pall over the entire proceedings. Ultimately, after six months had passed, the jury finally found Richard Ramirez guilty of multiple counts of murder. He was sentenced to death.

"I will be avenged," Ramirez declared after being informed that he had a date with the gas chamber at San Quentin. "You don't understand me. You are not expected to. You are not capable of it. I am beyond your experience. I am beyond good and evil. I will be avenged. Lucifer dwells in us all."

What followed was a deranged tirade in which Ramirez invoked the powers of darkness before he was led back to his cell by the guards.

The process of executing a prisoner in the United States is rarely a quick affair (with the possible exception of the state of Texas), and it is not at all unusual for a convicted felon to spend years, if not decades, sitting on death row while the mandatory appeals process plays itself out. So it was with the Night Stalker, who spent 23 years awaiting execution before nature beat the state of California to the punch.

In 2013, at the age of 53, Richard Ramirez died of cancer. Many would say that it was a much kinder ending than he deserved. Yet that hasn't stopped him from making an appearance in the fictional TV anthology series *American Horror Story* as a recurring character, sparking a new wave of interest in the serial killer and his crimes. Despite the fact that *AHS: 1984* portrays him as a relatively cool and hip character, it's important that we should remember Richard Ramirez—if, that is, we remember him at all—for what he really was: one of the vilest monsters to ever walk the face of the earth.

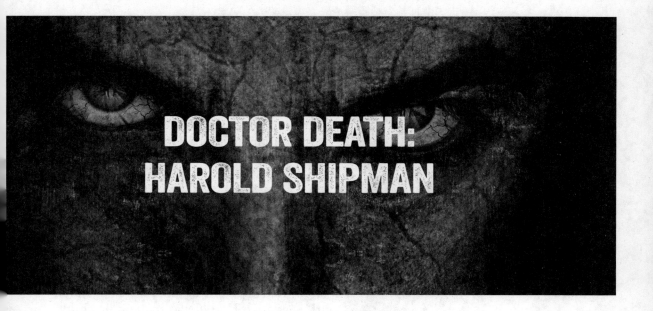

DOCTOR DEATH: HAROLD SHIPMAN

We live in a culture that is obsessed with lists, rankings, and ratings. It should, therefore, come as no surprise that so many people want an answer to the question of just who, exactly, is the most prolific serial killer in history.

At first glance, one might think that the so-called Devil in the White City, H. H. Holmes, would be a good candidate, but as we shall discover elsewhere in this book, the claim that Holmes killed somewhere between 100 and 200 victims is vastly overblown.

At the time of writing, most experts on serial murder agree that the British doctor Harold Shipman probably holds that title. At the very least, he has an extremely strong claim. Between 1975 and his capture in 1998, this affable and seemingly mild-mannered family practice doctor was responsible for killing at least 215 victims, the majority of them older women. After close scrutiny of his patient care records, investigators considered it entirely possible that the total number of deaths could have exceeded 250. Small wonder that he would earn the nickname "Doctor Death."

The idea of one individual being responsible for so many deaths is hard to comprehend, let alone stomach. Like almost all serial killers, Shipman was adept at hiding in plain sight. As a doctor, he held a position of great trust in the community. People welcomed him into their homes and bedrooms when they were at their most vulnerable, putting their lives into his hands. Harold Shipman repaid that trust with murder.

Striking at the very heart of the sacred doctor-patient relationship, the Shipman case created shockwaves in the medical community that are still felt to this day. One of the biggest unanswered questions is, What was Shipman's

It is estimated that Harold Shipman may have murdered over 250 people during his crime spree from 1975 to 1998.

motivation for killing? Taking a look at his formative years may help to shed a little light on why he was the way he was.

Harold Shipman was one of many children born in the post-World War II baby boom, on January 14, 1946, in Nottingham, England. Growing up, he fit the serial killer stereotype of being a friendless loner, more inclined to stay indoors by himself than to spend time playing outside with the other children in the neighborhood. The Shipmans were hard-working, salt-of-the-earth people. Harold's father, Harold Sr., drove a truck for a living, while his mother, Vera, kept house and raised their three children—two boys and a girl—of which Harold was the middle child. It's fair to say that he was the apple of his mother's eye, enjoying the status of most favored child within the household.

Smoking was a common social pastime during 1940s and 1950s Britain, bringing with it a large increase in the number of lung cancer diagnoses. Vera Shipman fell ill to the disease when Harold was a teenager. The young Shipman raced home from school at the end of each day to help tend to the mother he doted upon. Mother and son were already close, but Vera's illness strengthened the bond.

Despite the best efforts of her physicians, Vera Shipman slowly began to succumb to the ravages of cancer. Unlike today, doctors regularly made house calls back then. The worst side-effects of the cruel and painful disease were only ameliorated by regular injections of pain medications, which would be delivered by a friendly physician who came and knelt at Vera's bedside. The drug of choice was morphine, an opioid analgesic with long-lasting effects. For somebody suffering from cancer, morphine could be the best friend in the world, making the agony at least somewhat bearable. It is easy for us to picture the teenaged Harold Shipman sitting in the same room as his mother, watching the visiting doctor insert a needle into her vein and administering the one thing other than death that could take away her pain.

Although Harold always remained tight-lipped about his private life, it is reasonable to conclude that these regular pain-relieving sessions helped set the young man on the path to becoming a physician himself. Perhaps he started out wanting to provide the same level of care and comfort to others as his own mother was given by the general practice (GP) physician in the Shipman household. Had it not been for Vera's terminal illness, Harold Shipman might have gone on to choose any one of a hundred different professions. If that had been the case, the chances are that he would never have been given the opportunity to kill. It's a tantalizing "what if" scenario to consider: Had he been an accountant, a financier, or a teacher, for example, then the potential serial killer waiting within him may never have reared its head.

But he wasn't. Instead, no doubt influenced by the kindly family doctor who had ministered so compassionately to his mother, Harold Shipman elected to become a physician. He was admitted into the medical training program at the University of Leeds on his second application attempt.

Shipman's girlfriend, Primrose Oxtoby, became pregnant at the age of 17. In the eyes of society, there was only one decent thing for them to do: tie the knot. She and Harold, now 19, dutifully got married and began to plan for a life together that centered on raising their coming child.

The initial period of education for an aspiring doctor was five years. While not at the top of his class, Harold worked hard and put in the long hours of study required to graduate, while also dealing with the stresses and

Shipman found a job here at the Pontefract General Infirmary in West Yorkshire after finishing medical school. (The infirmary closed in 2010 to be replaced with a new, modern facility.)

challenges of a new marriage and having a young child at home. Primrose was extremely supportive, which helped him to cope more effectively, and the sports field provided a welcome outlet for him to blow off steam, just as it had during his school days. Life settled into a comfortable familial rhythm, and more children would soon follow the first.

After completing his medical schooling, the next phase was to take place in the field. Harold was assigned to the Pontefract General Infirmary in West Yorkshire, where he was responsible for delivering patient care under the supervision of more experienced doctors. It was an opportunity for them to assess his level of knowledge and practical skills in a clinical setting—a probationary period prior to him being awarded the status of physician. Shipman passed his final evaluation with flying colors. Now a "proper doctor," he remained at Pontefract General, gaining experience and putting his training to good use.

Once he had gained experience in a hospital setting, Shipman decided to transfer into general practice. In 1974, an opportunity arose for him to transfer to the Abraham Ormerod Medical Centre in the Yorkshire town of Todmorden. This was essentially a local healthcare clinic, exactly the sort of place to suit Shipman's ambitions of becoming a GP.

The new doctor was well liked by his fellow physicians, and it wasn't long before he was offered the chance to become a junior partner in the practice. Yet the truth was that Shipman was just putting on a show for his peers. The superiority complex that he had begun to develop as a young man was getting stronger all the time, particularly as he gained confidence as a doctor, and those he considered to be his inferiors, such as staff members, patients, and members of the public, were often treated to glimpses of Shipman's true self. He was irritable and quick to anger. Never one to suffer fools gladly (or simply those who took a different point of view from his own), the young doctor would verbally lash out whenever one of them contradicted him.

It didn't take long for him to begin taking advantage of his newly acquired position of authority. Even during the 1970s, prior to the opioid crisis that is so often splashed across the news headlines today, the distribution of narcotic drugs was tightly controlled. The primary point of contact for the ordering and dispersal of drugs at Abraham Ormerod was Dr. Shipman, who filled out all the required paperwork and stored the medications personally. Although it isn't clear exactly why he first began to abuse meperidine, an extremely potent opioid that behaves in the same way as morphine does within the body, the fact is that Shipman began to inject the drug intravenously and was then forced to falsify the records to conceal his behavior. It may well be that he began to inject narcotics long before coming to Todmorden; even as a very junior doctor, he would have had access to them at Pontefract General.

In 1975, Harold Shipman murdered his first confirmed victim. Eva Lyons, 70, was suffering from terminal cancer. The physician administered a fatal dose of narcotics to her while kneeling at her side. Although it is possible to conclude that this was physician-assisted suicide, a kind act meant to relieve a dying woman of her pain and suffering, the same cannot be said of the vast majority of the deaths Shipman caused. Most of his future patients would have little or even nothing wrong with them at the time of their demise.

The amount of meperidine that Shipman was ordering eventually raised a red flag with the supplier. There was no way that such a relatively small medical clinic should need such large amounts of a pain medication; this wasn't a major trauma center or a big city hospital. Alarmed by the official scrutiny they were suddenly attracting, the other partners in the practice demanded answers from Shipman. Displaying character traits more befitting a narcissist than a respectable physician, he didn't even bother to deny it. Yes, Shipman admitted, he was taking the meperidine for his own use. What, exactly, were they going to do about it?

> **A**lthough it isn't clear exactly why he first began to abuse meperidine, ... Shipman began to inject the drug intravenously and was then forced to falsify the records.

One can only imagine the shock felt by the other partners as their junior member calmly recommended that, rather than report him to the authorities, they would be better off helping Shipman cover up his "harmless addiction"—all for the good of the practice, of course. If they declined to help, Shipman declared casually, then he would dig in his heels and fight. There would be an ugly scene, at the very least, and the only way they were going to get rid of him was to fire him, giving the Abraham Ormerod Medical Centre a black eye in the process.

To their credit, they *did* fire him. Shipman went berserk, throwing a huge temper tantrum, all to no avail. The police were informed of his criminal behavior, and despite denials and protestations on Shipman's part, he was found guilty of forging prescriptions and diverting narcotics for his own private use.

Shipman spun the police a sob story about his supposedly getting hooked on drugs to help deal with the difficulties of life as a doctor. Whether this was true is debatable, because Shipman was a convincing liar when he chose to be. He went to rehab, trying to put a positive spin on the situation by making it appear that he was trying to get clean and beat his addiction. While it is conceivable that this was a genuine attempt on his part, it is more likely that this was just another cynical move on the part of a calculating and manipulative man who suddenly found himself with his back to the wall.

Despite his having spent over a month in rehab, criminal charges were still levied upon Shipman. Pleading guilty, he managed to avoid going to prison, escaping with nothing more than a moderate fine. For most people, this would have marked the end of their medical career, but Shipman wasn't going to let something he considered to be relatively trivial stop him from practicing as a doctor. He simply moved on, leaving Todmorden behind him.

Surprisingly, Shipman was permitted to continue working as a physician. After a couple of short-term interim jobs, he relocated to the town of Hyde, near Manchester. He was selectively honest about his reasons for having left Abraham Ormerod, but he then painted himself as a recovering addict who was looking for a second chance and the opportunity to serve future patients. His authorization to function as a doctor and to have access to controlled substances such as meperidine could have been revoked. It wasn't. As a direct consequence, hundreds of people would die.

Built in 1968, the Donneybrook Medical Centre is still a functioning clinic today. Harold Shipman began working there in 1977, a doctor with a troubled past who seemed to be earnestly seeking a fresh start. In a repeat of the situation at Todmorden, he was friendly with his fellow doctors, but he treated his coworkers with disdain whenever they crossed him. In other words, it was business as usual—but with a distinctly darker aspect that would only emerge years later.

> In a repeat of the situation at Todmorden, he was friendly with his fellow doctors, but he treated his coworkers with disdain whenever they crossed him.

By and large, Shipman's patients loved him. Being a G.P. is a busy and time-consuming profession. Along with an ever-increasing patient base come a host of other demands on the physician's time. Nevertheless, Harold Shipman took the time to sit and talk to his patients, patiently listening to their concerns, complaints, and even the general ups and downs of their lives. The honeymoon period he enjoyed with his colleagues eventually soured, due largely to his "my way or the highway" approach to doing things, and by New Year's Day of 1992, Shipman had moved on to set up his own private practice in the same area. The patients who were so fond of him flocked to join him.

As something of a minor celebrity in Hyde, Dr. Shipman saw his popularity reach new heights. His availability to make house calls was a significant factor in this, demonstrating his willingness to put the comfort and convenience of his patients first—or so it appeared. The reality was quite different. Shipman was killing his patients off one by one, injecting them with fatal doses of narcotic drugs such as morphine and diamorphine.

His MO remained consistent throughout his entire 23-year killing spree. He targeted the elderly, though not necessarily the sick and infirm; in fact, many of his victims were very healthy, complaining only of a relatively minor ailment, until after Dr. Shipman made his house call. The massive overdose of medication knocked out the patient's respiratory drive, suppressing or completely eliminating the signals sent by the central nervous system that kept them breathing. The patient would then go into respiratory arrest, followed by cardiac arrest—the lack of oxygen caused their heart to either stop beating or to go into a fatal arrhythmia from which it would never recover. Each of Shipman's patients essentially died in their sleep. It may have been a relatively peaceful passing, but it was still nothing less than cold-blooded murder.

In order to cover his tracks, Shipman would then falsify the patient's death certificate, inventing fictional strokes, heart problems, diabetes, and other diseases as a probable cause for their demise. One of his favorites was the global catch-all diagnosis of "old age." Medical professionals have an informal saying: "We can't fix old." This may sound callous, but it essentially means that there comes a point in every human life when the various bodily systems have deteriorated so much, the entire organism begins to break down. The natural end point of that is death. Old age was the documented reason for many of the Shipman murders, and one that usually wouldn't raise an eyebrow—unless there were a lot of them. And in Harold Shipman's district, there were *a lot*.

For something as important as certifying the natural, lawful end of a human life, it is wise for there to be no single point of failure—in other words, no one individual should have that much power and responsibility vested in them. Nor did they. The law required a second physician to scrutinize and sign off on the findings of the first doctor, the one to pronounce the patient dead.

Shipman would kill his patients with drug overdoses and then forge their death certificates to cover his tracks, declaring they had died of strokes, heart attacks, or a disease. His victims were often elderly but not necessarily in bad health.

There was no way around this safety precaution. Harold Shipman used the services of a nearby medical practice, and in early 1998, Linda Reynolds, one of the doctors from that practice, began to feel deeply uneasy about the number of deaths that were occurring around Dr. Shipman. She noticed a pattern: almost all the decedents were female, of late middle or old age, tended to live alone, and were in reasonably good health. Perhaps most damning, Shipman was either in the room at the time they died, or they were conveniently found dead by him during a visit to their home. She sensed something wasn't right and expressed her concerns to the coroner.

Nor was she the only one becoming suspicious. Staff at the funeral home that dealt with the remains of Shipman's dead patients were growing alarmed at the number of cremations that the doctor was requesting. With hindsight, it would become obvious that Shipman always recommended his patients' bodies be cremated rather than buried because it was the perfect way to ensure that all chemical evidence of his crimes was destroyed. With no autopsy performed on any of the victims' bodies, the possibility of the coroner realizing that they had died with massive amounts of morphine and diamorphine in their bloodstream and tissues was effectively zero.

It was almost the perfect murder, repeated hundreds of times over without anybody noticing, until the scale of Shipman's crimes finally became so great that it began to attract attention. The pattern of eerily similar deaths was finally brought to the attention of the police, who started a formal investigation.

One red flag that raised suspicions was the number of cremations that Shipman was requesting be done. He also neglected to request autopsies.

The fact that Shipman had flown low enough under the radar to get away with murdering around 250 patients is both remarkable and abhorrent, but as with almost all serial killers, his behavior ultimately became erratic enough that he gave himself away. He finally went too far with the murder, in June 1998, of 81-year-old Kathleen Grundy, a former mayoress of the town, who had received a visit from Dr. Shipman in order to treat her for chest pain—according to him, at least. Grundy's daughter found it hard to believe that her mother, who had been spry and in good health for her age, had died of Shipman's favorite stated cause, old age, particularly as the doctor had not requested an autopsy be performed on her prior to her funeral.

The biggest red flag, however, was that Grundy had left Dr. Shipman a large sum of money in her last will and testament. That alone was reason for suspicion, particularly as none of Grundy's family members were bequeathed any money at all in the same document. An attorney by profession, Kathleen's daughter traditionally dealt with any legal matters that her mother needed help with and found the new will to be highly dubious. She reported her concerns to the police, who, learning that the beneficiary of the will was Harold Shipman, a doctor who was already on their radar, decided to exhume Grundy's body and check for foul play. She was one of the few patients of Dr. Shipman who had been buried rather than cremated. In the end, this would prove to be his undoing.

The toxicology screen revealed that large levels of opioid drugs were present in Kathleen Grundy's body. The dosages that had been administered were too high to be therapeutic, and at a bare minimum had almost certainly contributed to her death. There was also the fact that she had not been prescribed morphine for any preexisting medical conditions, which meant that the person who most likely gave it to her was Dr. Shipman. As detectives dug deeper into the case, exhuming the bodies of other deceased patients, they found the same pattern repeating itself: no prescription for morphine or diamorphine, but amounts of the drug were present in their bodies nonetheless.

Close scrutiny of those patients' medical records revealed that Shipman had gone back and retroactively altered them, adding in false complaints and illnesses in order to support whichever cause of death he had entered on the death certificate. It soon became obvious that they were dealing with a killer who was trying to cover his tracks, but the sheer scope of the murders had yet to be uncovered.

Harold Shipman was duly arrested and tried for multiple counts of murder and one count of fraud. The jury saw right through his protestations of innocence, sentencing him to fifteen life sentences without the possibility of parole. Both he and his wife, Primrose, continued to deny any wrongdoing on his part, despite the overwhelming evidence against him.

After spending four years in prison, Harold Shipman finally met his end in the early morning hours of January 13, 2004. Using the sheets from his bed, he fashioned a noose in one end and tied the other end to the bars of his cell window. Although it is commonly stated that he hanged himself, in such cases death is usually caused by strangulation and asphyxiation. The fact that Shipman's death would have been neither quick nor easy came as a comfort to some of the families of his victims, but others felt that he had taken the easy way out and had gotten off far too lightly.

An official inquiry considered hundreds of patient deaths that may have had a connection to Harold Shipman. Once the dust finally settled, it was concluded that he had murdered 215 people, primarily women. There is reasonable doubt in a number of other cases too, so a completely accurate final tally is impossible to provide, but 250 is a commonly accepted figure.

He began by killing a handful of patients each year—typically three or four—but by the time he was finally stopped, that number had increased by an order of magnitude. The fact that he was not found out and stopped earlier is horrifying.

The study of serial killers generally turns up some common motivations among them. For the vast majority, it is a matter of enjoyment. They simply *like* killing, the unsurpassed sense of power that ending another human life can bring them. Others simply feel compelled to kill; they initially fight to suppress the urge but ultimately succumb to it. After getting away with their first murder, they develop a taste for it. Many have dysfunctional childhoods, displaying early tell-tale signs such as bed-wetting and torturing or killing animals. Yet Harold Shipman is a more complicated case.

> Although he was a relatively antisocial child and something of a loner throughout his life, Harold Shipman did not fit the classic serial killer profile.

Although he was a relatively antisocial child and something of a loner throughout his life, Harold Shipman did not fit the classic serial killer profile. His motivations remain somewhat opaque. It is difficult to understand what drove him to kill. It is likely that he was strongly influenced by the home visits to his mother that doctors made, and it is no coincidence that his chosen murder weapon was the same thing that brought her relief from her suffering: a syringe full of pain medication. How is it that once he became a doctor, Shipman managed to pervert something fundamentally decent and good into an instrument of pure evil?

Harold Shipman liked to keep himself to himself. He had few close friends, if any, and except for his wife, it is safe to say that nobody really knew him well enough to offer much insight into his murderous behavior. It may be that Shipman's ego had simply gotten so inflated that he reveled in having the power of life and death over his patients and that this was something he was able to conceal from everybody else. Primrose stood by him to the end, accepting his denials at face value. Shipman's nice-guy facade often slipped, giving way to flashes of anger and irritation that were symptoms of an underlying god complex. Harold Shipman went to his grave refusing to confess his guilt, unwilling to acknowledge a single crime—not even that of defrauding Kathleen Grundy and her family. The man lived in complete denial until his dying day, and even then, he chose to take his own life rather than face the life behind bars imposed upon him by the justice system.

The medical field is one of the most respected professions in existence. Over the space of 23 years, a monster exploited loopholes in the system to run rampant, taking lives whenever he felt the desire to do so. We can only hope that there are no more Dr. Harold Shipmans out there, practicing medicine today.

THE UNREPENTANT MANIAC: CARL PANZRAM

"In my lifetime, I have murdered 21 human beings, I have committed thousands of burglaries, robberies, larcenies, arsons, and, last but not least, I have committed sodomy on more than 1,000 male human beings. For all these things I am not in the least bit sorry."

These are the words of Prisoner 31614, who lies buried in row 26, grave number 24, at the U.S. Penitentiary Cemetery in Leavenworth, Kansas. The grave is marked with a simple stone, worn and weatherbeaten. Few who pass by are aware that it contains the earthly remains of one of the world's most vicious serial killers, a predator who was completely devoid of conscience or compassion for his fellow human beings. His name was Carl Panzram.

Panzram was born on June 28, 1892, in East Grand Forks, Minnesota. Minnesotans were a tough and hardy people then as now, and from an early age, the young Carl carried out chores on his parents' small farm. The Panzram family were German immigrants and, in the words of their infamous son, were "hardworking, ignorant, and poor."

In what would amount to his final confession, Panzram wrote of them:

All of my family are as the average human beings are. They are honest and hard-working people. All except myself. I have been a human animal ever since I was born. When I was very young at five or six years of age, I was a thief and a liar, and a mean, despicable one at that. The older I got, the meaner I got.

What is most striking about this statement, in addition to its sheer bluntness, is what it says about the "nature vs. nurture" argument. For decades, it has been hotly debated whether serial killers do what they do because they are simply "wired wrong" and evil by nature, or whether they are nothing more than a product of their environment. Many serial killers experienced abusive environments when they were growing up, but this is by no means always the case. For every Fred West, there is a Harold Shipman. In the case of Carl Panzram, we have a clear-cut admission that he was the black sheep of an otherwise decent and honest family long before that family environment turned sour—a strong argument for nature being the culprit, rather than nurture, in this particular case at least.

> In the case of Carl Panzram, we have a clear-cut admission that he was the black sheep of an otherwise decent and honest family....

Things changed drastically when he reached the age of seven. Carl's parents separated, with his father disappearing to parts unknown. For several years, Panzram's mother, now the family matriarch, rode herd on her children and had them help her run the farm. As her older sons grew up and matured, however, they began to leave home themselves, until finally there was just Carl, an older brother, and their sister left to help. Their workload doubled. The only way for the children to get any kind of an education was for them to attend school during the daytime and then, once they came home in the evening, head out into the fields and start working on the farm chores late into the night.

It was a tough upbringing, and while it was not atypical of social conditions during the late nineteenth century, today we would think of it as being a physically and emotionally abusive one. Looking back, Panzram would recall of his time on the farm:

> My portion of pay consisted of plenty of work and a good sound beating every time I looked cock-eyed or done anything that displeased anyone who was older and stronger and able to catch me and kick me around whenever they felt like it, and it seemed to me then and it still does now that everything was always right for the one who was the strongest and every single thing that I done was wrong.

Now that his father was gone and life had gotten even harder, young Carl Panzram's world had become a dog-eat-dog environment, one in which the strongest and toughest came out on top. It was a lesson that every beating he endured only served to reinforce. Always the underdog (in his own mind, at least), Panzram maintained this victim mentality until around the age of 11, when he "began to suspect that there was something wrong with the treatment I was getting from the rest of the human race." It is most likely that this was the time at which he first began to see other people as targets of opportunity and potential victims, rather than as actual human beings.

His first mark was a neighbor who lived in a nicer house than the Panzrams did and was much better off, materially and financially. The first criminal act that Carl Panzram ever admitted to was breaking into the neighbor's house and helping himself to a few items that took his fancy, including a cake (such luxuries were a rarity at his own home) and a revolver, which he intended to use to "shoot Indians."

His plans to hop on a train and head west were stymied when the burglary was discovered and the culprit quickly arrested. Carl received a ferocious beating for his efforts, was jailed briefly, and then was sentenced to serve time at the Minnesota State Training School at Red Wing, a correctional facility for wayward young men.

An imposing building complex since renamed the Minnesota Correctional Facility, the "school" (if it can truly be called that) introduced 11-year-old Carl to a whole new world of brutality. The school was heavily grounded in religion. The juvenile offenders were beaten regularly by staff members, ostensibly to get them to adopt Christianity and its principles as their personal form of faith. In any case, the regime had precisely the opposite effect. For Panzram, each beating only intensified his hatred for the institution. He also hated the abusers, and as the long weeks passed into years, his mind began to formulate revenge fantasies, thinking about the many ways in which he could repay them for the pain they kept inflicting on him.

The inmate population at Red Wing was close to 250, all boys and young men who had committed crimes ranging from minor to extremely serious. Some boys were as young as seven, and they were easy prey for the older boys. Violence and sexual abuse were rampant, especially in what was referred to as "the paint shop," so called because victims would leave there covered in multicolored bruises. Boys were made to bend over a large block of wood and take a whipping, after which salt water was applied to their wounds. The pain it caused would have been excruciating.

So great was Panzram's hatred of the dreaded paint shop that one day, he decided to burn it to the ground. All it took was a long wooden stick around which was coiled a length of string. He lit one end and secreted it in a heap of rags that had been dipped in oil. The rag pile smoldered, finally caught light, and then set the entire room ablaze.

Considered to be too unintelligent to take lessons in the classroom, Panzram was instead assigned duties in the kitchen of the corrections officers' dining hall. He was able to exert a small measure of revenge on those men

The young Panzram's first experience with incarceration was at the Minnesota State Training School. He was only 11 at the time.

he considered to be his tormentors by surreptitiously urinating and masturbating into their food, then standing silently by and watching as they ate every last bite. Panzram once attempted to murder one of his overseers by putting rat poison in his meal, but it was discovered and he was given a severe beating for it.

Some fellow inmates pointed out that if Panzram ever wanted to get out of the State Training School, he needed to reform or at the very least *appear* to have been reformed. After mulling the idea over, he soon concluded that they were right. From that moment on, Carl Panzram made a conscious effort to always appear diligent, humble, and contrite. Inside, he was a seething mass of hatred and resentment, but to all outside appearances, he seemed to have become a model inmate. While far from perfect, Panzram's act was at least convincing enough to fool the parole board.

> By the time he had served two years and was eligible for release, Panzram was the furthest thing imaginable from being reformed.

By the time he had served two years and was eligible for release, Panzram was the furthest thing imaginable from being reformed—in fact, he now wanted to hurt people more than ever before. Not just the abusers; *anybody* would do, as long as he could get away with it. He was angry at the world, and after years of physical punishment, the 13-year-old boy wanted nothing more than to hurt it right back.

I had learned more about stealing, lying, hating, burning, and killing. I had learned that a boy's penus [sic] could be used for something besides to urinate with and that a rectum would be used for purposes other than crepitating.

… I had fully decided when I left there just how I would live my life. I made up my mind that I would rob, burn, destroy and kill everywhere I went and everybody I could as long as I lived.

The boy had undergone a massive fundamental change in the two years he had spent within the walls of the correctional facility. While the conditions there were undeniably brutal, it takes more than one harsh spell in prison to create a serial murderer. After all, what of the other 250 boys who were Panzram's fellow inmates? There is no evidence to suggest that any of them went on to commit the kinds of atrocities that Carl Panzram did. It is far more reasonable to conclude that all the building blocks of a severely deranged personality were in place when the 11-year-old was sentenced. What the correctional institute really did was bring it out of hiding and put that personality squarely in the driver's seat.

As the Training School gates closed behind him, 13-year-old Carl Panzram wore a brand-new suit and had five dollars in cash and a copy of the

Bible to his name. The State of Minnesota had also provided him with a free train ticket that would take him back home. Panzram spent the money on sweets to help him while away the journey, his first real taste of luxury in two years.

Rather than arrive home to a warm welcome, the boy was immediately sent back to working in the fields. Incarceration had taught him to lie convincingly, however, so he began to tell stories about wanting to become a preacher to save the souls of his fellow men and women from the eternal hellfire of damnation. This cunning ruse earned him enrollment in a German Lutheran school, which seemed like an easy ticket away from the drudgery of farm work at first, but Panzram's reputation as a reform schoolboy soon caught up with him. The other children laughed and made fun of him; he, in turn, reacted with explosive fits of violence. Carl Panzram had had his fill of being tormented, and he lashed out at the slightest provocation. When the preacher tried to discipline him, the teenager fought back. Although quite handy with his fists, Panzram was no match for a fully grown man, and he ended up on his back.

The preacher beat his troublesome young charge on a regular basis. Carl knew that if he was going to protect himself, he needed an equalizer. It came in the form of a revolver that he took from another kid and brought with him to school.

"Lay off me," Panzram snarled at the preacher, "or I'm gonna *fix* you."

Unaware of the very real threat that Panzram posed, the preacher took out his whip, ready to instill a little discipline yet again, but suddenly found himself looking straight down the barrel of a gun.

Panzram pulled the trigger. *Click.* The hammer fell on an empty chamber. *Click. Click.* Pandemonium erupted in the classroom. Carl used the commotion to escape, concealing the pistol as he went. Word of what he had done somehow managed to reach his home before he did. His older brother choked the gun's hiding place out of him. While his brother went to search for the weapon, Panzram fled. Heading to the nearest railway track, he jumped the first train that came along and rode the rails west.

He did this for the next few months, living the hobo life and seeing a good portion of the United States along the way. Sleeping rough in the countryside and hiding out in

Fleeing his family home, Panzram took to the rails to live the life of a hobo. He panhandled for food and was molested and raped by strangers, hardening him even more.

deserted railroad cars, he panhandled for food and money to feed himself, concocting hard-luck stories that were carefully calculated to tug at the heartstrings of even the most hardened cynic.

The railroad boxcars could be a dangerous place sometimes. One night, the teenager was brutally gang-raped by four men who were riding the rails just as he was. The experience was repeated with a second group of men he chanced upon in a small-town stable. They plied him with drink and then, when Panzram was unconscious, took their turns molesting him.

His hatred and distrust of his fellow man grew exponentially with each assault. In his memoirs, Panzram would observe that the two rapes he suffered taught him one crucial lesson about the way in which the world really worked: *Force and might make right.*

Carl Panzram thought nothing of using petty crime to advance his way in the world. A robbery here, a spot of grifting there—none of it was a big deal in his eyes. The court saw it differently when he was arrested for burglary again, this time in Butte, Montana. It cost him a year, incarcerated in yet another reform school. Working in the fields again as he served time, just as he had back home on the farm, Panzram was a hostile and unruly prisoner. As such, he soon drew the ire of one of the guards, a man named Bushart. Bushart was tough, having been a fighter before taking a job in corrections, and he wasn't willing to give a troublemaker like Panzram an inch. Believing that he was being singled out by another tormentor, the teenage prisoner decided there was only one way to solve the problem: Bushart had to be killed.

One evening, as the guard was sitting at the front of the classroom letting one of the inmates polish his boots, Panzram snuck up behind him and slammed a heavy wooden board across the back of his head. Bushart went down as though poleaxed. At first, Panzram thought he had succeeded in killing the man, but it soon became apparent that although Bushart had a serious closed head injury, he was still alive.

The other guards made Panzram pay dearly for the attack, repeatedly beating him mercilessly. Whether or not he had been singled out before, he most definitely was now. Bushart's colleagues made a point of targeting him for their special attention morning, noon, and night.

Masturbation was frowned upon in such institutions, particularly those with a religious bias (which was most of them), because it was believed to be inherently sinful. While serving time in the Montana reformatory, Panzram claimed to have been forced to undergo involuntary circumcision to prevent him from masturbating. This painful and unnecessary surgical procedure gave him yet another cause to resent "The Man."

Panzram and another inmate escaped from the reformatory and went on a two-man crime spree, burgling buildings and setting fire to them, then jumping on trains once more to escape the area. When they reached the next stop, they'd do it all over again. Finally, the wanderlust seemed to ebb, and the two of them went their separate ways.

For someone with a deeply ingrained hatred of authority, Panzram's next move was somewhat unusual. He may have wanted a little more stability in his life, or perhaps it was simply a spur-of-the-moment impulse, but whatever the reason, Carl Panzram walked into a military recruiting office, took the oath of enlistment, and signed up for service as an infantryman in the U.S. Army.

Any possibility that the army life might have made him straighten up and fly right was dashed after just the first few weeks. Panzram's thieving ways soon came to the fore once more, and he soon found himself sentenced to three years at Fort Leavenworth, the much-feared military prison. Many of his fellow inmates were hard-as-nails types, more than capable of killing a man with their bare hands. Some had been specifically trained to do just that.

> While serving time in the Montana reformatory, Panzram claimed to have been forced to undergo involuntary circumcision to prevent him from masturbating.

On his release in 1910, the six-foot, 190-pound Panzram was immensely strong after spending months breaking rocks for hours upon end. Having an iron ball weighing 50 pounds chained to him while he swung a heavy hammer over and over again had given him a frame of pure muscle. Without anybody knowing it, Fort Leavenworth had served as the training ground to prepare him for life as a serial killer.

Looking back at this period of his life, Panzram reflected:

I was the spirit of meanness personified. I had not at this time got so that i hated myself, I only hated everybody else.

Everybody else would soon be made to pay.

After his release from Leavenworth, Carl Panzram went to Denver, Colorado, where he took a job skinning mules. His combative personality got him thrown out of the mule skinner's camp. "I licked every one in it and was getting all set to work on the boss-man when he fired me, pulled a gun on me and drove me out of camp."

Heading straight for the city's red-light district, Panzram proceeded to go on a drinking and whoring spree of epic proportions—one that ended with him waking up naked, penniless, and sporting a newly acquired case of gonorrhea that helped put him off sex with women for the rest of his life. Finally admitting defeat, he returned to the only thing he knew how to do: living the

Panzram spent three years at Leavenworth Penitentiary, a prison for those in the military. His time there only served to make him harder physically and emotionally.

life of the hobo, riding the railroad tracks for free, and fighting and stealing his way across America.

For the next few years, Carl Panzram, using a number of aliases, drifted in and out of prison, always for the same old causes—theft and robbery. But now there was a new element. Panzram's behavior was growing increasingly violent, and he began to forcibly sodomize some of the men he fought and robbed.

On one of his train journeys, Panzram was relaxing in a railroad car with two other men when they were suddenly discovered by a railroad brakeman, who threatened to have them all thrown off the train. Without batting an eye, Panzram pulled out his gun, forced the brakeman to drop his pants and underwear, and then raped him in front of the two other doubtlessly horrified hoboes. When he had finished, Panzram politely offered them both the opportunity to do the same thing to the brutalized brakeman. Both men declined, but Panzram wasn't taking no for an answer, later writing:

But by my using a little moral persuasion and much waving around of my pistol, they also rode Mr. Brakesman around.

The triple rape now over, Panzram made all three men jump off the railroad car—while it was still rolling forward at 20 miles per hour. Fortunately, none were injured further.

As time passed, Panzram's spells behind bars became more frequent. He took an active delight in causing as much trouble and damage as he possibly could while he was incarcerated. When he got out, Panzram found unskilled work on merchant ships, sailing to places as far away as London, Hamburg, and Le Havre.

Still bearing a grudge against the man who had approved his incarceration at Leavenworth all those years before, on a whim, Panzram broke into and robbed the New Haven, Connecticut, house of William Howard Taft, former secretary of war and president of the United States, who was now a law professor at Yale University. One of the things Panzram stole was Taft's personal Colt .45 pistol, which would soon be put to murderous use. The burglary made him enough money to buy a yacht, which he named the *Akista*. His plans for the yacht were both simple and chilling.

> I figured it would be a good plan to hire a few sailors to work for me, get them out to my yacht, get them drunk, commit sodomy on them, rob them, and then kill them.
>
> This I done.

Panzram's MO for achieving this was simple and effective. He hung out at bars and in areas that he knew sailors regularly frequented, such as the vicinity of South Street. Once one or two of them took his fancy, he would sidle up to them and genially make their acquaintance. Panzram would casually mention that he was hiring sailors for his yacht. The work wasn't particularly demanding, he promised, and the pay was excellent.

Once the sailors turned up at Panzram's yacht, the liquor soon began to flow. He fed them well, got them roaring drunk, and then sent them off to bed. Once the sailors were fast asleep, he shot each one in the head with the .45 he had stolen from Taft. (It is likely that Panzram raped them first, though he never admitted to doing so in his written confession.) The dead bodies were then taken out onto the deepest parts of Long Island Sound and dumped overboard, weighted down with heavy rocks to ensure that they would sink all the way to the bottom of the river and stay there.

Carl Panzram had taken to murder without a single qualm or pang of conscience. He kept the dead men's possessions, filling up the spare storage space on the *Akista* with their belongings. Ten men died in this way. Their remains were never recovered from the watery graves to which he consigned them.

It is likely that Panzram would have kept on murdering sailors in this way had it not been for a boating accident that sank the *Akista* in the river near Atlantic City. Swim-

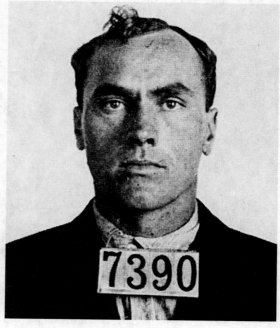

A 1915 mugshot of Panzram.

ming ashore with what little he could carry, a physically sick Panzram was cared for by a local physician, who took him into his own home. Showing a rather twisted form of gratitude for the doctor's kindness, Panzram gifted him with the stolen Colt .45, never telling him that it had been used to murder ten men in cold blood.

After serving still more jail time for the usual reasons, Panzram decamped for Africa to continue his crime spree. His behavior became, if anything, even more heinous. While in Angola working for an oil company, he bought a 12-year-old African girl, paying a considerable sum of money because of the girl's father's claim that she was a virgin. After spending one night with the girl, Panzram insisted that she was not, and demanded a replacement—this time, the child was only eight. After forcibly molesting her, he "decided to quit looking for any more virgins," and turned his attentions to young boys instead.

One day, Panzram wrote, as he was sitting in a park deep in thought,

A little nigger boy about 11 or 12 years old came bumming around. He was looking for something. He found it too. I took him out to a gravel pit about 1/4 mile from the main camp of the Sinclair Oil Company at Loanda. I left him there, but first I

One of Panzram's many murderous sprees while in Africa involved killing people on a hunting expedition and feeding them to the crocodiles.

committed sodomy on him, and then killed him. His brains were coming out of his ears when I left him and he will never be any deader. He is still there.

Panzram had "graduated" from raping and murdering adults to doing the same thing to innocent children. His self-professed hatred of all humanity meant that there was no crime too heinous for him to commit, and no potential victim was off limits.

Putting some distance between himself and his latest atrocity, Panzram boarded a ship that took him further down the coast. When he disembarked, he developed a sudden hankering to try his hand at crocodile hunting. Hiring six native men to act as rowers and guides, he and his small group headed upriver, deep into the jungle. There was no shortage of crocodiles to be found, but the unfortunate natives got far more than they bargained for when they signed on to row a serial killer on his hunting expedition. He shot them all, one by one, and then pushed their dead bodies into the river for the crocodiles to feed on.

Word about Carl Panzram was spreading fast among the various U.S. consulates and managers of the Sinclair Oil Company, so much so that he was forced to stow away on several ships in order to make his way back to New York. Panzram's time at sea did nothing to curb his perverted tendencies. Not long after stepping foot on American soil again, he raped and murdered a 12-year-old boy, battering his skull in with a rock. It was now 1922, and Panzram unleashed a one-man crime spree on the East Coast, heading from state to state and wreaking havoc wherever he went. By 1923, he had worked through a series of menial jobs that he used as an opportunity to seek out further criminal opportunities.

A man who pretended to be interested in buying a yacht from Panzram found the tables turned on him when he attempted to steal it out from under him. Panzram shot him dead, dumping the body into the river, and went on his merry way.

At this time of his life, Panzram was accompanied by a 14- or 15-year-old boy named George, to whom he had "attempted to teach the fine art of sodomy." After spending some time with the temperamental serial killer, George soon decided that he had had enough. Surprisingly enough for a man who had shown no compunction about murdering children much younger, Panzram allowed him to go home to his parents. The boy wasted no time in telling them all about his former companion's violent ways. The police were informed, and Panzram yet again found himself behind bars.

Instead of his usual attempt at a jailbreak, Panzram retained the services of a lawyer to get him out of jail. Incredibly, his novel plan worked. Instead of paying the attorney in cash, Panzram offered the lawyer ownership of the boat he had stolen if he could somehow manage to secure Panzram's release. The attorney was as good as his word, but he found himself conned by his own client. While Panzram got off scot-free, the less-than-savvy lawyer was lumbered with a boat that turned out to be stolen and had to be returned to its rightful owner shortly thereafter.

Anybody in their right mind would have taken this as a sign to lie low for a while. Carl Panzram, of course, was not in his right mind. His next act was to rape and murder a 12-year-old boy, strangling him to death with a belt and discarding his corpse behind some bushes, with no more afterthought than if it had been a piece of trash.

Still more murders, rapes, robberies, and prison time constituted the remainder of Carl Panzram's life, which spanned the rest of the 1920s. In 1930, he was behind bars for the final time. Remarkably, his arrest in 1928 had been for something as mundane as a robbery, yet during his interview with the arresting officers, for some reason, Panzram confessed to having committed several of the many murders he would later lay claim to. Perhaps he was sick of it all, living life on the run and always having to look over his shoulder.

> **P**anzram confessed to having committed several of the many murders he would later lay claim to. Perhaps he was sick of it all....

The judge took a hard line. Given a life sentence, Panzram had come full circle. He was sentenced to serve out his time at a very familiar place: Fort Leavenworth.

Evidently deciding that there was nothing left to lose, Panzram's behavior became even more unhinged, culminating in his savagely using a thick metal bar to beat to death Robert Warnke, a civilian employee in charge of the prison laundry. This resulted in Panzram's life sentence being upgraded to a death sentence, which may well have been his intent all along; on the other hand, it may simply have been just another homicidal act of violence in a life that was filled with them.

Panzram certainly had no fear of death and rejected out of hand any possibility of appealing the verdict of the court. Because of this, the process of execution was relatively quick, even by the standards of the time. Fifteen months after committing his final murder, Carl Panzram mounted the scaffold and allowed the hangman to tie a noose around his neck and place a hood over his head.

Defiant to the last, an impatient Panzram screamed that he could murder a dozen men in the amount of time it was taking them to hang him. Those were his final words on this earth before the executioner pulled the lever, opened the trapdoor, and sent his body plunging down into the hanging pit.

The primary source of information for Carl Panzram's life story is the testimony of the man himself, written at the end of his life during his final period of incarceration. For as much as Panzram hated humanity, both individually and as a collective, a prison guard named Henry Lesser, to whom we owe a huge debt when it comes to obtaining Panzram's story, somehow managed to strike up a strange sort of friendship with Panzram, and the latter gifted him with his final recollections in the form of a handwritten manuscript. This document, along with Panzram's criminal record and others pertaining to him, is now stored in the archives of San Diego State University, in a special collection known as the Carl Panzram Papers.

Panzram is most definitely not the typical serial killer, if indeed there is such a thing. He did not kill for sexual gratification or put much effort into covering his tracks. He did not target his victims carefully, disdaining to choose those who would not be missed. Carl Panzram was no careful hunter, using charm and social skills to seduce his targets and get them to drop their guard. On the contrary, he was a blunt instrument of destruction, more prone to bludgeoning than seduction in order to get what he wanted.

When it came to sexual gratification, the solution for him was simple: he raped. If he is to be believed, Panzram sodomized over a thousand men during his lifetime, most of them against their will. After being molested himself as a boy and young man, Panzram may well have been inflicting the same type of suffering he'd endured upon other males of all ages—by using them as proxies for the men who had caused him great pain and humiliation.

Carl Panzram was something akin to a human battering ram. Utterly remorseless and completely without mercy, he was a machine fueled by hatred and spite—a man with few redeeming virtues, if any. It is fair to say that there has never been another serial killer quite like him. As we close this chapter out, it only seems right to leave the last words to Panzram himself:

> I started out in life enjoying it and hating no one. I am winding it up now by hating the whole human race including myself and having no desire to live any longer. For all the misery and tortures that I have went through, I have made other men go through many times over, only worse.

Quotations in this chapter are drawn from the Carl Panzram Papers, Special Collections & University Archives, San Diego State University Library, Boxes 1 and 3. The collection was donated by Henry Lesser.

HOLLYWOOD MONSTER: AILEEN WUORNOS

There's a common perception that there are practically no female serial killers. While the overwhelming majority of serial killers *do* tend to be men, there are exceptions. Some, such as Moors Murderer Myra Hindley and Rose West, infamous for her role in the Cromwell Street House of Horrors, have already been profiled in this book. Others have received coverage elsewhere, perhaps most notably in Peter Vronsky's excellent study of women who kill, *Female Serial Killers: How and Why Women Become Monsters*.

Hindley and West were similar in that both killed in conjunction with a male partner. The legal defense teams for each woman argued that each of them was nothing more than an assistant to the more dominant male perpetrator, who they claimed had taken the lead in carrying out the murders and therefore should bear the lion's share of the guilt. While that may perhaps have been true in Hindley's case, a very strong argument can be made that West was the more vicious and dominant personality, one who attempted to get her decidedly less-than-intelligent husband to take the fall for her many heinous acts.

One of the handful of examples of female serial killers who acted alone, without a male accomplice, is Aileen Wuornos. In fact, it is safe to say that since the release of the biopic *Monster*, starring Charlize Theron in the titular role, Wuornos has become the poster child for the female "lone wolf" murderer. Just how much of that image is true, and how much is a misperception, is hotly debated to this day.

As we have seen already throughout this book, one common theme seems to repeat itself: many serial killers come from broken homes, dysfunctional families, and an abusive background.

Aileen Wuornos is no exception. She was born on February 29, 1956 (a leap year), in Rochester, Michigan. Aileen's mother, Diane, was married but raised her two children alone for the first four years of Aileen's life because her husband, Leo Pittman, was serving time in prison. Diane was just 14 years old when she gave birth to Aileen.

Aileen would have no contact with her father and would soon abandon his surname in favor of her mother's. By all accounts, Pittman was not a nice man. He had been jailed for raping a seven-year-old girl and would ultimately take his own life by hanging himself in his cell. One has to wonder just how much influence her mentally disturbed father's genetics had on Aileen's behavior later in life.

As we have seen already throughout this book, one common theme seems to repeat itself: many serial killers come from broken homes, dysfunctional families, and an abusive background.

When Aileen was four, her mother took off for good and abandoned her children, leaving them in the care of Aileen's maternal grandparents, Lauri and Britta Wuornos. There was certainly no love lost between mother and daughter; Aileen would later refer to her as a "motherfucking bitch whore."

The primary source for much of Aileen Wuornos's story is Aileen herself, which should lead us to tread carefully. In addition to giving interviews, she also wrote about her background and life experiences in her own unique way. Other serial killers have done the same thing, and in almost every case there is some attempt by the subject to twist reality, to skew things to paint themselves in a better light. In addition to this, we must also consider that the writings of serial killers such as Carl Panzram and Aileen Wuornos are the products of pathologically sick, diseased minds. Thus, it behooves us to be skeptical of everything that cannot be independently verified.

According to Aileen, her grandfather was an abusive alcoholic with a sadistic streak—which we also see in several other serial killer backgrounds. Allegedly, he would strip young Aileen naked and force her to lie face down on the bed with her arms and legs spread wide apart, before beating her mercilessly with a leather belt—all in the name of "discipline." To add insult to injury, he would force her to clean and oil the belt afterward, intentionally putting Aileen in close proximity to the object that had just been used to inflict excruciating pain upon her. Aileen later recalled that while she was being lashed by her drunken, abusive grandfather, he liked to berate and belittle her, screaming his opinion of the little girl's inadequacies in between strokes of the belt. (In the interest of fairness, it should be pointed out that Aileen's older brother, Keith, vehemently denied her claims about there being an abusive family environment during their shared upbringing).

If this truly happened, one can see where the seeds of Aileen's pathologic hatred of men were sown. With both her biological mother and father now permanently out of the picture, Aileen's grandparents adopted her. Unfortunately, they did not tell her that she was their granddaughter, choosing instead to pass themselves off as her parents. When 11-year-old Aileen finally found out the truth, she quite understandably went berserk. She already had severe trust issues where her "father" was concerned. Now that she knew that he wasn't who he claimed to be, she began to detest him even more.

Growing up, Aileen Wuornos did not have a normal, healthy attitude toward sex. She developed a reputation among the other neighborhood children for having sex with her older brother, Keith. Unpopular with others her own age (both boys and girls), Aileen was known as a girl who would "put out" sexually for the price of a few cigarettes. In addition to the physical and emotional abuse inflicted by her grandfather, this could only have destroyed whatever shred of self-esteem Aileen had left.

As Aileen grew older, the level of abuse that she suffered only worsened. As far as her grandfather was concerned, he was trying to raise his increasingly rebellious "daughter" right. In reality, he was torturing the poor girl. For example, he locked her out of the house multiple times and forced her to fend for herself—usually in subzero winter conditions. It was nothing short of a miracle that the teenage girl didn't freeze to death in the woods.

Even before she reached early adulthood, young Aileen had developed the habit of binge drinking. Considering the quality of life she had at that time, it's completely understandable; she was a deeply troubled young lady, emotionally volatile with the behavior to match. Sleeping around, starting small fires, and getting into fights whenever she felt threatened were all potential warning signs that an observant parent could have picked up on, but Aileen lacked caring parents who could provide any kind of emotional support system.

When she was 14—the same age at which her own mother had given birth to her—Aileen became pregnant herself, the product of a sexual assault. Her grandfather predictably blew a fuse. This was 1970, and being an unmarried mother was still seen as shameful and a great stigma across most of the United States. Babies born out of wedlock were often not talked about and their mothers sent off to homes for unwed mothers to give birth away from the glare of public scrutiny. Enraged that his "daughter" was pregnant, Lauri Wuornos threw her out of the house

According to Aileen Wuornos, she suffered from abuse at the hand of family members when she was a girl.

again, and this time he told her that if she ever came back, he would kill her. It's possible that Aileen's grandmother would have defended her had she not recently died as a consequence of a failing liver.

As things turned out, Lauri Wuornos would die before his "daughter." Supposedly deranged by the death of his wife and the disintegration of his family, he attempted suicide on multiple occasions, until he was finally successful.

Now a homeless and destitute teenager, Aileen quickly learned the hard way that the only person she could truly depend on was herself. Furthermore, never a strong student and lacking in any sort of career prospects, Aileen turned to prostitution to make money and support herself. She saw few other choices, and it wasn't a big leap to go from trading sexual favors in exchange for cigarettes to trading them for cash. Her infant son was put up for adoption. To this day, his whereabouts are unknown; he almost certainly does not know the identity of his infamous mother, which is probably for the best.

> Now a homeless and destitute teenager, Aileen quickly learned the hard way that the only person she could truly depend on was herself.

Now free of any social or familial obligations, Aileen dropped out of school and became a drifter, living in motels, cars, or outdoors when there was no other alternative. As she wandered from town to town and from state to state, Aileen continued to engage in prostitution, and she also took up other petty crimes. She was quick to anger and refused to back down when riled, which did her no favor whenever she was confronted at a bar. She also frequently drove under the influence of alcohol, a crime for which she was arrested in Colorado in 1974—along with disorderly conduct and firing a handgun while driving on a public highway. Although a court date was set, Aileen simply skipped town and never looked back, the start of a long criminal record she would accrue throughout the 1970s and 1980s.

Largely because of the warm weather, Florida attracts a significant number of homeless people. Aileen Wuornos arrived there in the spring of 1976. Ever the opportunist with the eye of a grifter, she soon latched onto a wealthy single man named Lewis Gratz Fell. The great disparity between their ages (Aileen was 20; Lewis was 69) must have been offset in her mind by the fact that he was a millionaire and the president of a yacht club. If ever there was a case of two people being absolute polar opposites, this was it: Whereas Fell was refined and cultured, used to moving comfortably in the upper echelons of Florida society, Aileen Wuornos was crude and unsophisticated, better suited to bar fights and bouts of heavy drinking than haute cuisine and conversation.

Nevertheless, after a whirlwind "courtship," the two ended up getting married. It would be ludicrous to suggest that Aileen actually loved her husband (and, most likely, vice versa). It is more likely that she saw her marriage to Fell as nothing more than a higher form of the prostitution she was so used to using to keep herself afloat.

Predictably, the marriage was short-lived, ending in a legal annulment after just a few weeks. While it's difficult to say at which point the aging multi-millionaire first realized he had made a horrible mistake in his choice of a trophy bride, it may well have been the occasion on which she punched him in the face during what started out as a mild disagreement. It was Aileen's philosophy that most, if not all, problems could be solved with violence, an attitude that would only grow stronger over time.

When Aileen snatched his walking stick away from him and beat him with it, Fell decided that enough was enough. His wife was no longer bothering with even the pretense that she was a nice person. The increasingly frail Lewis realized that he had married a predator, and unless he broke the cycle of domestic violence that he now found himself caught up in, it was almost guaranteed to end badly. Fortunately, thanks in no small part to the restraining order he managed to obtain, Lewis Gratz Fell escaped from Aileen Wuornos with his life. Not all the men who fell into her sphere of influence would be as fortunate.

Aileen returned to the itinerant lifestyle. Being married to a wealthy man for such a short period of time (and then getting an annulment) meant that she walked away from Florida with little more than an expensive engagement ring, which she immediately pawned for cash, and an addition to her criminal record for assault and battery. Her brother, Keith, died at the age of 21 from esophageal cancer. His life insurance paid out $10,000 with Aileen as the main beneficiary. Rather than use the money to start turning her life around, however-er, Aileen did what a lot of people with really terrible impulse control might do: she bought herself a muscle car.

In addition to the shiny new car, Aileen went on a shopping spree for gadgets and other luxury items. She kept buying and buying until all her money was gone. Broke and homeless again, she had little choice but to return to prostitution.

Despondent almost to the point of becoming suicidal, Aileen continued to drift aimlessly from place to place. Her downward spiral progressed from petty crime to armed robbery, for which she spent over a year in jail. Far from being a model inmate, she got into multiple altercations during her first term behind bars. On her release, she immediately

When her brother, Keith, died and left her with $10,000, Wuornos blew all the money by buying a muscle car and going on a shopping spree.

went back to her old ways, using a series of aliases in an attempt to stay one step ahead of the law.

It is uncertain when Aileen Wuornos first began to have sexual relationships with women. As she became increasingly disillusioned with the men in her life, starting with her father and her grandfather, then moving on through her husband, casual boyfriends, and the many johns who had paid her for sex, it makes sense that she might have felt more comfortable in the company of other females. Arriving back in Florida once more, Aileen met a woman in a Daytona Beach gay bar with whom she would enter into a long-term relationship and fall head over heels in love—at least, as much as Aileen Wuornos was capable of falling in love. Her name was Tyria Moore.

The two women were soon living together. Aileen was sufficiently smitten that she worked extra hours as a prostitute to keep them both financially afloat. Behind the scenes, all was not sweetness and light, however, with much of the stress and tension between them being directly attributable to Aileen's increasingly volatile personality. She seemed to walk around on a perpetual hair trigger, ready to be set off at even the slightest provocation, and she soon developed a reputation for being a troublemaker, somebody to be avoided if at all possible. As her binge drinking reached new heights, so too did her violent behavior. Eventually, none of the motel owners in the area would rent the pair a room for fear of having it trashed.

Aileen's acts of violence thus far were relatively moderate—for example, a punch in the mouth, a thrown billiard ball, or pulling a gun on somebody who had angered her. Nobody was seriously injured or killed. That would change on November 30, 1989, when a client named Richard Charles Mallory picked her up.

Based upon his reputation, it seems fair to say that Mallory was no saint. A small-business owner by day, the 59-year-old liked going to strip clubs in his spare time. He drank heavily, indulged in drugs, and regularly engaged the services of prostitutes—which is how he came to encounter Aileen Wuornos. He did not treat the women he paid for sex particularly well and was said to get off on humiliating them and inflicting pain. In the end, that would cost him his life.

When she was working as a prostitute, Aileen generally preferred one of three location types in which to turn her tricks: the customer's car, a motel room procured specifically for that purpose, or the woods. On this particular night, she was hitchhiking, catching rides from kindly drivers after a long drinking session. It may well be that Mallory guessed the manner in which she made her living, either from the way she was dressed or simply because he was familiar with the hooker stereotype, and noticed that the lonely-looking woman walking along the side of the road fit the mold perfectly. His instincts were proven correct when his passenger made a sly reference to trading money for "a little fun." Aileen Wuornos was exactly what he had been looking for—or so he thought.

In the early hours of the morning, on a lonely road that was far enough away from passing traffic that they likely wouldn't be disturbed, Mallory offered to pay Aileen for oral sex. This was nothing she hadn't done many times before, and, as her legal defense would remind the jury at her trial, she usually performed the sex act without complaint and simply took the money. She had never turned violent and attacked the customer she was pleasuring before then.

We only have Aileen's word for what happened next, as the only other person present did not survive the encounter. According to Aileen, she began to undress in preparation for fellating her customer. The half-drunk Mallory then attacked her and, depending upon which version of her testimony one chooses to believe, he either raped Aileen or threatened to rape her *or* paid for sex and then demanded his money back. Whichever may be the case, we do know that she took out a .22 pistol and shot him repeatedly in the chest, then dragged his body into the woods and left it there. Ballistic evidence suggested that he may also have been shot in the back while attempting to flee.

> The half-drunk Mallory then attacked her and, depending upon which version of her testimony one chooses to believe, he either raped Aileen or threatened to rape her.

Although Richard Mallory's car would be found by police the following day, the whereabouts of its owner were unknown. His body would turn up two weeks later, discovered by two men who were out for a walk. Two weeks' worth of exposure to the elements had not been kind to his remains. The former businessman was in a state of advanced decomposition. Identifying him would be a challenge. When the remains were finally identified as being Mallory, the police department launched a murder investigation—which went nowhere. Few of the people questioned had anything positive to say about the victim, and it didn't take long for detectives to uncover some of the more unsavory details about his sexual behavior. He was reputed to have abused a number of prostitutes, any one of whom might have had cause to murder him. The problem was, none of them ultimately panned out as viable suspects, and the trail went cold. Had it ended there—had there been no more killings—it is possible that Aileen Wuornos would have gotten off scot-free.

But six months later, on February 19, Aileen killed 47-year-old construction worker David Spears. As had been the case with Richard Mallory, Spears picked Aileen up as she was walking along the side of the highway trying to thumb a ride. Her account of the moments leading up to his death was rambling and incoherent. She claimed that while she and Spears were drinking and stripping off their clothes (presumably a prelude to having sex), he attacked her. Her

Wuornos started murdering the men who picked her up when she was hitchhiking and then asked for sex.

statement, however, was questionable, because everybody who knew Spears—including his ex-wife—swore that he was a kind, gentle, and amiable man. David Spears was about as different from Richard Mallory as it was possible to be. Either he disguised his true nature, or Aileen Wuornos killed him in a fit of drunken rage. It is likely that due to her heavy drinking and propensity to black out, even she—the sole witness to survive their encounter—couldn't remember exactly what had happened between the two of them.

One thing is clear: Aileen shot David Spears six times and dumped his naked body amidst some trees at the side of the road. She stole his truck, a few of his personal possessions, and all his cash.

There had been a gap of six months between Aileen's first and second killings. Only a few days separated the second and the third. It is believed that 40-year-old Charles Carskaddon also offered her a ride, a fatal mistake that resulted in him being shot nine times and his body dumped at the side of the road, covered up with leaves and a blanket. When asked about her motivation for killing Carskaddon, Aileen claimed that she had acted to protect herself from attack, yet closer examination of her story by detectives strongly suggested that she murdered him in a fit of unprovoked, homicidal rage.

In each case up to this point, once her victim was dead and had been robbed of whatever money they possessed, Aileen took their car and drove it away from the scene, abandoning it when she got to her destination. This time was no different. She made a half-hearted attempt to throw police off by removing the registration tags, but this was nothing more than a mild inconvenience to the detectives. Once the vehicle was traced back to Charles Carskaddon and connected with the discovery of his body, detectives questioned his friends and family members and found that just like David Spears, the latest victim of an as-yet unidentified murderer appeared to be a friendly, wholesome man with no history of violence or shady past. The same would hold true with her fourth victim, a 65-year-old retiree named Peter Siems.

Siems was a quiet and deeply religious man. A missionary, he carried his Bible with him when he set out on a long road trip to visit his mother in

New Jersey on June 7, 1990. He made it as far as Georgia. According to Wuornos, after he picked her up, the pair went into the woods, where Siems supposedly got undressed; she then killed him in order to "prevent him from raping her." His remains were never recovered.

After the murder, an extremely drunk Aileen Wuornos stole Peter Siems's car and drove it so recklessly that she ran it off the road, wrecking it in the process. Accompanying her was her girlfriend, Tyria Moore, whom Aileen was still supporting financially with the proceeds of her prostitution and murders/robberies. The two women suffered only minor injuries, but more importantly, several eyewitnesses saw them.

Victim number five was Florida salesman Troy Burress. On July 30, 1990, he was on the road, visiting a number of customers, when he apparently disappeared. The sausage company delivery van that he had been driving was soon located; five days later, his body was found. Despite the body's state of decomposition, the coroner was able to determine that the cause of death was two rounds to the torso from a .22 caliber handgun, the type favored by Aileen Wuornos.

> It had been yet another rape attempt, she claimed after her capture, which was why she had shot Troy Burress dead.

It had been yet another rape attempt, she claimed after her capture, which was why she had shot Troy Burress dead and taken not only his own personal money but also his company's money.

Aileen was now killing an average of one man per month. Afterward, she would exhibit little remorse for any of the murders, justifying them as self-defense acts. She claimed that all her victims were potential rapists who deserved everything they got.

Charles Humphreys, 56, also fit the mold for what was fast becoming Aileen's general victim type: a middle-aged male, often respectable in his private life, and most importantly, traveling alone. Humphreys was a veteran of both the military and law enforcement. He went missing on September 11 and was found shot dead the following day. Most of his wounds were to his torso, but Aileen had also shot him in the head. In a departure from her usual MO, Humphreys's body was fully clothed when it was discovered.

Aileen's killing spree finally came to an end with the murder of her final victim on November 17. Walter Jeno Antonio, 62, also had a law enforcement background. She shot him four times, for reasons that she found difficult to articulate beyond the now-standard fear that he was going to rape her. The fact that he had bullet entrance wounds in his back made that claim somewhat questionable. When his body was found, Walter was wearing only his socks.

At this late stage, nobody in law enforcement could miss the fact that middle-aged men were turning up dead along Florida highways, all of them murdered with .22 caliber bullets. It was no great stretch to conclude that all the murders were perpetrated by the same individual. When witnesses were questioned, several described having seen a woman fleeing the scene after abandoning a vehicle or paying for supplies at a store. That woman, of course, was Aileen Wuornos.

The presence of condoms at several of the crime scenes made detectives suspect that the perpetrator was a female prostitute, as did the small caliber of the murder weapon. The state of undress many of the victims were found in also strongly suggested a sexual element to the string of crimes.

Despite Aileen's best efforts to persuade her otherwise, Tyria finally left her in December. Aileen began to pawn off some of the valuables she had stolen from the bodies of her victims. Unbeknownst to her, this would make it easier for the police to track her down.

Aileen Wuornos spent a lonely and miserable Christmas holiday season living at a motel, drinking away what little money she had and blissfully unaware that a police dragnet was slowly closing in on her. Soon, undercover detectives tracked her to her favorite bar, The Last Resort in Port Orange, Florida. Officers moved in on January 9, 1991, taking Aileen into custody on a

Officers finally caught up to Wuornos at The Last Resort in Port Orange, Florida, in 1991.

relatively minor charge. For the woman who had recently been evicted from her motel when her money ran out, a warm cell with guaranteed hot meals might have been a step up.

Much speculation has taken place about exactly how much Tyria Moore knew about the murders her lover was committing. Moore had ridden in several of the victims' cars and had been spotted in Aileen's company after some of the killings had taken place. When detectives contacted her, Tyria jumped at the opportunity to speak out against Aileen.

"I would die for you," Wournos told her erstwhile lover during a phone conversation that was monitored by law enforcement. As things turned out, that was exactly how things would play out.

To make good on her promise to get Moore off the hook, Wuornos confessed to the murders in an attempt to exonerate Moore. Hedging her bets, she maintained that each killing had been an act of self-defense against an aggressive male who wanted to sexually assault her. This was essentially the only card she had left to play. There was no denying her culpability: it could be proved she had pulled the trigger in each case, sometimes shooting her victims in the back, which rendered the self-defense argument highly questionable.

A deeper background investigation would reveal that Richard Mallory had spent time in prison for attempted rape, a fact that lent a great deal of credence to Wuornos's insistence that he had tried to rape her and that she had shot him in self-defense. Unfortunately for her, however, none of this information was brought up at her trial, so the jury was unable to take it into account when determining her guilt. It is difficult to determine whether this knowledge would have truly made a difference in the eventual outcome, however, because even if the jury had bought her argument and cleared her, there were still five other murders for which she would be charged (the murder of Peter Siems stayed off the docket because without the presence of a body, there was no way to prove that he *had* been murdered).

On January 27, 1992, she was found guilty of murdering Richard Mallory. She did not take the guilty verdict well, screaming, "I'm innocent! I was raped! I hope *you* get raped! Scumbags of America!"

Despite the best efforts of her attorney to mitigate the sentence to one of life imprisonment, the image of a deranged Aileen Wuornos spitting hatred in their faces was still fresh in the minds of the judge and jury when they handed down a sentencing recommendation of death, to be carried out by electrocution.

More murder charges followed, but those who anticipated another courtroom outburst were to be disappointed. Aileen pled no contest to the charges, refusing to accept direct responsibility but making no argument against the accusations either. While incarcerated on death row, she waived the right to an appeal and dismissed her defense counsel. Aileen Wuornos was resigned to her own death, it seemed, and on the morning of October 9, 2002, she prepared for death via lethal injection and had her last breakfast—a cup of coffee.

An IV was started in her arm, and the cocktail of lethal drugs was administered under the close supervision of a doctor. Her last words were confusing and nonsensical, making them an appropriate capstone to an equally confusing life: "I'd just like to say I'm sailing with the Rock and I'll be back like Independence Day with Jesus, June 6, like the movie, big mothership and all. I'll be back."

> She did not take the guilty verdict well, screaming, "I'm innocent! I was raped! I hope *you* get raped! Scumbags of America!"

Moments later, the medications did their work. Aileen Wuornos went into cardiac arrest. A hearse took her body away for cremation, after which the closest thing she had to a best friend, a woman from their high school years named Dawn Botkins, was given the ashes to dispose of. She chose to scatter them in Aileen's home state of Michigan.

Contrary to her prediction, she would never be back—but after her death, Aileen's media presence exploded, due in no small part to two documentary movies. *Aileen Wuornos: The Selling of a Serial Killer* and *Aileen: Life and Death of a Serial Killer* were both directed by filmmaker Nick Broomfield. The second documentary contains an on-camera interview that she had granted just before her execution. This puts a human face on the film's subject, and while it does not necessarily engender much sympathy for Aileen Wuornos, the interview does raise several questions relating to how she was treated during the criminal investigation and her subsequent trial.

After her death, the motion picture *Monster* (2003) cast Charlize Theron as Aileen. Critics loved the movie, which secured Aileen's place in the pantheon of notoriety alongside other infamous serial killers. Theron's performance garnered her much acclaim, but not everybody was happy with the movie's portrayal of Aileen Wuornos or her victims.

In a 2004 *Washington Post* op-ed piece, Wuornos biographer Sue Russell criticized *Monster* for twisting Aileen's story into something a little more palatable for the audience to stomach. Russell, who researched Wuornos extensively for her book *Lethal Intent* and is therefore familiar with the facts of the case, sees her as a cold-blooded killer rather than a victim. The movie ignores Aileen's difficult upbringing and pathologic mental/emotional state as causative factors, spinning a tale of a rape victim who goes looking for revenge after being brutally assaulted. Despite the title, it does not depict Aileen Wuornos as the homicidal monster that she almost certainly was. Russell also makes the valid point that the movie demonizes Aileen's victims, portraying them as being seedy johns looking to use Aileen for sex.

Speaking to Nick Broomfield, Aileen Wuornos famously stated: "You sabotaged my ass! Society, and the cops, and the system. A raped woman got executed and was used for books and movies and shit." Yet contrary to these words, Sue Russell also makes a convincing case for Aileen wanting to be a "star" in some form or other and believes that the notoriety she received because of the murders achieved exactly that:

> Aileen craved fame. She had told friends that she wanted to do something that no woman had ever done before. She had repeatedly expressed fantasies of leading a Bonnie-and-Clyde-style outlaw existence (though she ultimately acted alone) and going down in history. She wanted a book to be written about her life. She wanted society to view her as a heroine.

If that was indeed true, then Aileen Wuornos got what she wanted in the end—albeit at the cost of her own life. It is difficult to avoid concluding that she was little more than a cold-blooded killer, rather than the sympathetic antiheroine that some have made her out to be.

Actress Charlize Theron portrayed Wuornos in the 2003 film *Monster*.

Aileen's victims were all middle-aged men who picked her up and offered her a ride, in some cases probably just trying to help out a stranger in distress (she was known to falsely claim that her car had just broken down). While some may have taken her up on her offer of sex for pay, what are the odds that all of them did—and in the unlikely event that this was the case, are we expected to believe that *all* of them attacked her?

During her time in prison, Aileen initially justified the killings by claiming that she was doing society a favor. If she had not killed the men, all of whom wanted to rape her, then they would not only have abused her but also gone on to do the same to other women. Besides, she added, she was having sex for money with literally *thousands* of men (the number Aileen laid claim to was 250,000), the vast majority of whom she *didn't* kill. But she ultimately changed her tune, finally admitting that none of her victims—with the exception of Richard Mallory—had actually raped her. She stuck to her guns where Mallory was concerned, which seems to be a credible claim. They "began to start to rape her," she said, although what that actually meant is impossible to determine.

Her version of the story changed over time, meandering from "I killed them all in self-defense," to "I killed *one* in self-defense," and then to "I wanted to rob them and leave no witnesses." The truth most likely lies somewhere in the middle. The explosive outbursts of rage Aileen was prone to became increasingly more violent. Her heavy drinking removed any inhibitions she might have had. If she truly believed that some of the men intended to rape her, as she contended several times, then it is possible that in her drunken state, she misinterpreted an innocent phrase or action and was triggered to commit murder.

Aileen Wuornos maintained a victim mentality until the very end, vehemently insisting that society had railroaded her and chastising it for executing a woman who had been raped. Despite her violent mood swings and increasingly paranoid, irrational behavior behind bars, the clinicians who assessed her agreed that she was sane and competent to stand trial. Thanks to the movie *Monster*, her public image has often been that of the wronged woman seeking revenge on her abusers, but the truth is colder than that.

"I robbed them," she said while incarcerated on death row, "and I killed them as cold as ice, and I would do it again, and I know I would kill another person because I've hated humans for a long time."

The final word on Aileen goes to an unnamed source associated with the criminal investigation, who put it best when they stated that Aileen Wuornos was "a killer who robs, not a robber who kills."

MINDHUNTED: EDMUND KEMPER

In October 2017, Netflix, arguably the world's most popular video streaming service, premiered an eagerly anticipated TV show from producer/director David Fincher (*Fight Club*, *The Girl with the Dragon Tattoo*). Fincher had delivered Netflix one of its most successful TV series ever, the smash hit drama *House of Cards*, starring Kevin Spacey, and was looking for another drama project on which to work with the network.

It came in the form of *Mindhunter*. Based upon the book of the same name, an autobiographical account of the career of FBI profiler John Douglas and the serial killers he had pursued and whose habits he had analyzed, *Mindhunter* had all the earmarks of success. Fincher was no stranger to serial killer material, having already directed the fictional *SE7EN* and the based-on-a-true-story movie *Zodiac*. Such dark subject matter was his forte.

Audiences took to *Mindhunter* in droves. One of the standout performances in the show's first season was delivered by actor Cameron Britton, playing the relatively unknown serial murderer Edmund Kemper. Up to that point, practically nobody outside the circles of serial killer aficionados had heard of Kemper; after *Mindhunter* began streaming, he was mentioned in the same breath as Gacy, Dahmer, and Bundy. Kemper looms like a shadow over the first ten episodes of the show, and viewers took to the internet in droves in an attempt to learn more about him.

Edmund Kemper is a big man, standing some six feet, nine inches tall and weighing in at a hefty 300 pounds. Despite being physically imposing, he is soft spoken and usually presents with a calm, almost placid affect. This can be misleading, because it masks the ever-present capacity for rage and extreme violence that lurks just beneath the surface.

Actor Cameron Britton portrayed Edmund Kemper in the TV series *Mindhunter.*

Equally misleading would be the stereotype of the big man being dumb. Kemper is an intelligent and literate man with a high IQ. He is thoughtful and patient, not to mention extremely cunning when the need arises. This is not a man to be underestimated.

At the same time, Edmund Kemper is deeply disturbed. A clinically diagnosed schizophrenic, his practically nonexistent impulse control and violent, paranoid tendencies led him to commit a string of brutal murders that meant he will never see the outside of a prison cell ever again. They also earned him the sobriquet of the "Co-ed Killer."

Edmund Kemper III was born in Burbank, California, in 1948. Many of the major Hollywood movie studios are headquartered in Burbank, including Warner Bros. and Walt Disney. He was the middle child of three, having both an older and a younger sister.

The Kemper household was not a happy one, and young Edmund's parents separated when he was nine years old. Of the two parents, Kemper much preferred his father, also named Edmund, but his mother, Clarnell, kept custody of the children, moving out of state and taking them away from their father. It was a betrayal that young Edmund neither forgave nor forgot.

Having involuntarily traded the delights of California for a rather more mundane life in Montana, Kemper was not a happy kid, and it is therefore not surprising that he began to act up. His volatile temperament was already beginning to rear its head, and it wasn't helped any by his mother's habit of locking him in the basement whenever she felt like having a little peace and quiet. His hatred and resentment of her grew with every hour he spent alone down there with nothing but time on his hands—time to dream up a multitude of ways to kill his domineering mother.

An early red flag was young Kemper's desire to harm animals. Somewhere around the age of ten, he killed the family cat, buried it, then dug it up again and cut off its head. As he grew up, other pets would die, feeding his twisted desire to inflict pain and injury on living creatures.

The macabre fascination Kemper had for decapitation also manifested itself when he tore the heads off his sisters' toy dolls. He also cut off their hands. Looking back and reflecting upon his childhood, Kemper rejected the notion that this obsession stemmed from his father cutting the heads off a pair of chickens and his mother forcing him to eat them, saying that the reason was "nothing that simple."

If only Kemper's mother had been paying closer attention, she may have realized that her son was developing some truly alarming habits. One day, she would pay for that lack of attention with her life.

By the age of 15, Edmund Kemper had had enough. He could not stand another day of living under the same roof as a mother who detested him, a woman he wanted nothing more than to murder with his own hands. He ran away from home, heading off in search of his father, taking with him little more than the clothes he wore.

Most of the boyhood fantasies Kemper dreamed up were twisted and macabre, but this was one of the few exceptions: it is easy to imagine the images of a happy family reunion that sustained him during the long journey west. The teenager's hopes were to be completely dashed; when he finally arrived at his father's home, he was devastated to find that he had remarried and started another family, one that had no room in it for a son from a past life.

It is fascinating to wonder what might have happened had the young Edmund Kemper III been fortunate enough to grow up in a loving, nurturing family, rather than be bounced between a mother and a father who either had no time for him or actively disliked him. Would he ever have made the transition into becoming a serial killer, or would he have grown up to be relatively normal?

Unfortunately, we shall never know. Under pressure from his new wife to get rid of this unwelcome reminder of his first marriage, Ed Kemper Jr. sent his son back home to a mother who wanted no part of him either. She, in turned, packed Edmund off to live with his grandparents in California. Rejection was piled on top of rejection.

Edmund already hated his mother. Whether that colored his attitude toward his grandmother, Maude, is not known, but the teenager soon grew to loathe her every bit as much. His grandmother "thought she had more balls than any man and was constantly emasculating me and my grandfather to prove it," Kemper told reporter Marj von Beroldingen during an interview he granted after his capture.

Edmund and Maude began to clash more and more often. His grandfather, who was also named Edmund, generally kept out of it (Kemper believed that he was senile). In Maude's eyes, young Edmund could do nothing right. Finally,

> By the age of 15, Edmund Kemper had had enough. He could not stand another day of living under the same roof as a mother who detested him.

he stopped even trying. As is the case with many serial killers, the youth had developed a pathological hatred for the opposite sex.

In August 1964, the 15-year-old Edmund Kemper finally reached his breaking point. He had had enough of his grandmother's acerbic ways. While she was sitting at the kitchen table, he walked calmly out of the room. When he returned, he was holding a rifle. As casually as one might fire at a target on a firing range, Kemper placed Maude's head squarely in the center of the sights and pulled the trigger. Although the weapon was a .22 caliber, relatively small-bore, the bullet had a devastating effect on Maude's skull at such close range. For good measure, Edmund then put a couple of rounds into Maude's back before stabbing her several times with a knife.

His grandfather was at the store getting supplies. Kemper reloaded the rifle and waited patiently in the kitchen until he heard the car pull up outside the house. The teenager was a competent marksman. As the old man began to unload grocery bags, his grandson shot him in the head, dropping him instantly.

Rather than go on the run as a fugitive, Edmund Kemper set down the weapon and called his mother, telling her that he had just killed both his grandparents in cold blood. Once the news had sunk in, she told him to hang up the phone and call the police. For once in his life, he obeyed her instructions. When officers arrived at the ranch to arrest him, Kemper went without a struggle.

While there was no argument about the fact that he had committed murder, the psychiatrists who assessed him determined that he was a paranoid schizophrenic who belonged in a secure mental health facility instead of a prison; his actions, after all, had hardly been those of a sane and well-adjusted teenager. When questioned, he was unable to articulate a specific reason for murdering his grandmother, other than wanting to know what it would feel like to kill her.

Located roughly halfway been San Francisco and Los Angeles, the Atascadero State Hospital for the Criminally Insane was where the state of California sent its most dangerous mentally ill patients and convicts. The sprawling secure medical complex has always been huge; today it occupies a campus some 700 acres in size and employs over 2,000 people to care for the needs of its inmates. In 1964, it became Edmund Kemper's new home.

The psychiatrists at Atascadero disagreed with the clinical assessment of their peers who had sent Kemper to their facility. Yes, the boy was disturbed, but in their view, he did not meet the criteria for paranoid schizophrenia. Then there was the matter of his behavior while incarcerated: he was a model patient. The smart, bookish Edmund did not cause trouble, as some of the other patients did, and kept to himself.

His prodigious intellect was matched with an innate sense of cunning. Seen as no great threat by the staff, Kemper was even allowed access to the tools and techniques that were used to gauge the mental and emotional state of other patients. These directly impacted their eligibility to be released into the real world. Through diligent study and making use of his natural gifts, he was able to memorize the correct outcomes to all of the tests—practically guaranteeing that when the time came for him to be assessed some six years later, he was sure to pass. And pass he did, with flying colors. Kemper put on such an impressive show that he convinced the clinicians charged with determining whether he was a danger to society that he was pretty much harmless. After turning 21 and legally becoming an adult, he was discharged from Atascadero and given back his freedom. This would prove to be a terrible mistake.

The wise thing for Edmund to have done would have been to find a place of his own and begin to make his own way in the world, getting a job and learning to become self-sufficient, perhaps furthering his education in the process. Instead, he did the worst thing imaginable: he moved back in with his mother, the woman he reviled most in the entire world. The psychiatrists who had cleared him for release had expressly warned against it. Clarnell Kemper, for her part, had not grown any fonder of her son during his absence; if anything, she was even more resentful of his presence in her life than she had been before his incarceration, and she treated him accordingly. One would have thought that after what he had done to his grandparents, she would perhaps have treated the volatile Edmund with kid gloves.

> The smart, bookish Edmund did not cause trouble, as some of the other patients did, and kept to himself.

To his credit, Kemper did at least *try* to build a normal life for himself. He attempted to date girls, but try as he might, he just couldn't find a way to relate to the opposite sex. Enrolling in a few college classes ultimately led nowhere, as his huge frame meant that he was too big to work in law enforcement (we can only imagine what Edmund Kemper could have gotten away with if he had possessed the benefit of a police officer's shield).

Taking a highway construction job with the state of California allowed him to save some money, which led to him finally move out of his mother's home and rent a place of his own. Their home life had been every bit as confrontational as it was before he went away. Mother and son fought like cat and dog, often over the most inconsequential of issues. It had to have been one of the happiest days of Edmund Kemper's life when he walked out from beneath his mother's roof for the last time, moving in with a friend instead.

One of the few nice things Clarnell did for her son was to get him a staff access sticker for the university campus where she worked. There was no way she could have known that he would use it as a means of committing murder.

This was the 1970s, and hitchhiking was in vogue. Driving around the university campus, Kemper soon realized that female hitchhikers were *everywhere*. At that time, nobody thought too much about the safety concerns of getting into a car with a complete stranger.

In a video interview recorded shortly after his capture and imprisonment, Kemper expounded on this:

Interviewer: "You were involved with the [UC Santa Cruz] campus because your mother worked there." (His mother was an administrative assistant there at the time of the so-called co-ed murders).

Kemper: "Yes. I was also involved in killing co-eds because my mother was associated with college work, college co-eds, women, and had had a very strong and violently outspoken position on men for much of my upbringing. They [his female victims] represented not what my mother was, but what she *liked*, what she coveted, what was important to her—and I was destroying it."

Kemper began not with murder but rather with simply picking up female hitchhikers and giving them rides to wherever they wanted to go. Unbeknownst to the first string of young women who got into his yellow Ford Galaxy, he had stashed a rape-and-murder kit in the car, but he initially lacked the nerve to use it. That would change as his confidence grew.

At that time, nobody thought too much about the safety concerns of getting into a car with a complete stranger.

"I'm picking up young women, and I'm going a little bit farther each time," he recalled. Kemper got incrementally closer to murder one stage at a time. At first, he picked up women, took them to an isolated place where he could easily have killed them, but didn't go through with the act. Then he took a gun along with him. Slowly but surely, he was working up the courage to act out his deepest, darkest fantasies, fueled by what he called "this craving, this awful raging eating feeling inside."

Each time, he would pull back from the brink—until one day, he could no longer control it. It was then that he started to kill. Once he found that he had a taste for it, he could no longer restrain himself from doing it.

Mary Anne Pesce and Anita Mary Luchessa were the first to fall victim to Kemper's murderous urges on May 7, 1972. The two 18-year-old students were hitchhiking when they accepted a ride from Kemper. An hour later, rather than arriving at the promised destination, the confused young women found themselves stuck in the middle of nowhere with a man who turned out to be a killer. Despite there being two of them and only one of him, Edmund Kemper was a physical powerhouse. There was no way they would have been able to overpower him, certainly not within the close confines of a car interior. But by the same token, Kemper couldn't handle both of them at the same time.

His solution was to truss up Anita and lock her in the trunk, threatening both women with a pistol and keeping them too scared to resist.

With Anita out of sight and out of mind for the moment, he switched his attention to Mary Anne. Kemper's attempt to sexually assault her in the back seat failed because he was physically unable to go through with it; this lack of capacity was not due to squeamishness or a fit of conscience, however—Edmund Kemper would demonstrate a distinct lack of both traits on more than one occasion. His psychological hangups regarding females prevented him from carrying out the rape, one small mercy that preceded a horrific knife attack on his victim.

Kemper explained his hatred for women and primary reason for killing them thusly: "My frustration. My inability to communicate socially, sexually. I wasn't impotent, but I was emotionally impotent. I was scared to death of failing in male/female relationships. I knew nothing about that whole area." Women

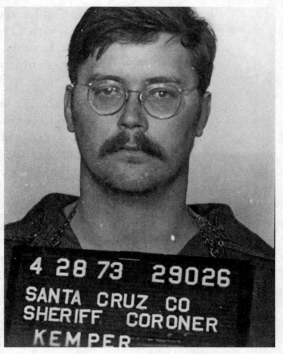

A mug shot of Kemper in 1973, a year after he started to kill young female hitchhikers.

frightened and intimidated Kemper, to the point where he was even incapable of having a polite, casual conversation with one. As he also pointed out, they represented something that was important to his mother, and therefore abusing and killing them provided him with great satisfaction.

In Edmund Kemper's mind, if he could not succeed in violating an attractive young woman, he could at least achieve the next best thing: taking her life. Kemper stabbed Mary Anne Pesce multiple times with a knife he had brought along for just that purpose.

Knowing that he could not leave Anita Luchessa alive to tell the tale, he then did the same thing to her. Both bodies were then placed in the trunk and driven back to the apartment Kemper shared with a roommate. After ensuring that it was empty, he brought the bodies inside and had sexual intercourse with them. He then cut them up, placing the dismembered parts into separate plastic bags. The remains of Mary Anne Pesce and Anita Luchessa were disposed of in the wilderness near Loma Prieta in the Santa Cruz Mountains—with the exception of the heads, which he saved and used as masturbatory aids until they began to decompose. He found the smell off-putting and finally disposed of them too. Although Mary Anne's skull was eventually discovered, no trace of Anita's body has ever been located.

It is telling that Kemper was unable to have intercourse with a living woman but could—with a certain amount of effort—do so with a dead one. "The first time [you have sex with a corpse], it makes you sick to your stomach," he told interviewer Marj von Beroldingen.

Four months later, Kemper picked up another victim, a 15-year-old named Aiko Koo, who was on her way to a dance class but had missed the only bus that would have taken her there. The thought of such a young girl walking along the roadside all alone is almost incomprehensible to us today, but it raised few eyebrows back then. Recognizing that he might be the only way she could get to her dance class on time, Aiko got into the passenger seat alongside the big man and meekly told him where she was going.

> Kemper liked to pop the trunk and stand there, just staring at the decapitated head, admiring it.

According to Kemper's testimony, things started out pleasantly at first, but the situation quickly went downhill when it became apparent that the car was going the wrong way. Night had fallen when Kemper parked in an area where he knew there would be little to no traffic. Instead of stabbing her, as he had done with his two previous victims, he covered Aiko's nose and mouth until she asphyxiated. Kemper had sexual intercourse with the unresponsive girl, both prior to her death and once again with her lifeless body afterward. He then cut up her corpse, just as he had done to his previous two victims, and disposed of the remains at an unknown location (they, too, have never been found). Once again, he kept the head, leaving it in the trunk of his car. Kemper liked to pop the trunk and stand there, just staring at the decapitated head, admiring it. There is a sick irony in the fact that when he attended an obligatory mental health evaluation as part of the terms of his ongoing parole—a test that he passed with flying colors—Aiko Koo's head was still there inside the trunk of his car, which was sitting in the parking lot outside. He would later explain that the ritualistic decapitation of his victims' heads gave him an intense sexual thrill, the feeling of being a hunter who was taking a trophy.

He did not kill again for the rest of the year. Kemper's home life underwent a brief period of turmoil when circumstances forced him to move back in with his mother. In early January 1973, he picked up another co-ed student, named Cynthia Ann Schall. He had stabbed and suffocated his last three victims. This time, he employed the method that he had used to kill his grandparents, shooting her with a .22 caliber gun. Although a relatively small bullet, it proved to be fatal.

Kemper kept Cynthia's body in his bedroom closet overnight. Waiting until his mother left for work the following morning, he had sex with the corpse before cutting it up and throwing the constituent parts into the ocean from a cliff top. Once again, he retained his victim's head, using it for sexual purposes for a time until he ultimately buried it in the garden of his mother's house.

This was the first time that Kemper's handiwork became public. Brought by the tides and currents, a series of body parts began to wash up on beaches along the California coast. Pathologists put them back together as best they could, determining that they all belonged to the same missing woman. While there was no way to use dental records to identify the Jane Doe, due to the lack of a head, her fingerprints were still legible despite several days in the water. Jane Doe's real name was Cynthia Ann Schall.

As more California co-eds began to disappear, an air of generalized fear descended upon university campuses. Some of this was the work of other serial killers, who were committing murders of their own in the same vicinity as Edmund Kemper.

School officials recommended that students—particularly females—only accept rides from people with university stickers affixed to their cars. Nobody could have known that the Co-ed Killer, Edmund Kemper, had one of them on his own car.

"My mother had an 'A' sticker on her car, and obvious access, day and night to the campus. I was picking up some very lovely young women. You know what we were talking about as we were driving around, as often as not? This guy that's going around doing this stuff [murdering young women]. And the second they started talking about it, they didn't realize it, but they were getting a free ride. I couldn't touch that with a ten-foot pole, I swear." One has to wonder just how many women unknowingly courted death by getting into Edmund Kemper's car, only to be spared a grisly fate because they happened to talk about the killer who was also their driver—the very definition of a narrow escape.

Despite the certain knowledge that there was a murderer on the loose, female students kept getting into cars with men like Kemper anyway—men who were complete strangers to them but who also, in the words of Kemper himself, "just didn't look like him." Something about Kemper's appearance and demeanor managed to convince them that he wasn't predator material, proving that most of the time, people really *do* judge a book by its cover. A killer was right there among them on campus, hiding in plain sight.

As time passed and still more women died, Edmund Kemper became increasingly confident. He freely admitted afterward that he "flaunted that invisibility."

Hitchhikers were a common site in the 1970s, and Kemper took advantage of this to prey on young women along the road.

Kemper gives an insight into his state of mind when he describes how he would carry the severed heads of his victims around with him in a bag (he often liked to have sex with decapitated heads). It was very much a fantasy realm, Kemper explained, seeming like a kind of alternate reality—one that went away once the "real" world intruded, such as the time when his landlady knocked on the door to his apartment, or he passed a young couple on the staircase while he was carrying a camera bag owned by his most recent victim—a camera bag that contained her severed head.

During each of those episodes, Kemper claims to have perceived two separate realities at the same time, which may go some way toward explaining how such an outwardly placid and intelligent individual could engage in the atrocities that he did. In a parallel with fellow serial killer John Wayne Gacy, Kemper went out of his way to court the friendship of local police officers. This was not because he truly wanted to have their friendship (it is doubtful that his warped mind truly understood the concept of having friends) but because they provided an open window into the search for the Co-ed Killer. He wanted to know how close he was to being discovered; yet at the same time, he was careful not to seem *too* interested, lest the cops start to question his motivations.

Kemper's mother, Clarnell, had a knack for making her son angry, driving him into fits of rage that only narrowly stopped short of actual violence. All that would change on the night of February 5, 1973, when mother and son had what was the latest in a long series of epic yelling matches.

Sometimes their fights made Edmund stew for days on end, with rage simmering and festering inside him. This time was different. Kemper stormed out of his mother's house and went in search of somebody to take his hatred out upon, a surrogate for his mother upon whom he could vent his rage and disgust. He found not one but two such surrogates in the form of students Rosalind Thorpe, 23, and Allison Liu, 20.

It was raining on the university campus that night, which probably influenced both girls' decision to get into Kemper's car when he offered them a ride. The university access sticker would most likely have reassured them, as would the presence of one another in the vehicle. After all, serial killers only ever picked up lone victims—didn't they?

This false sense of reassurance would not last long. The driver, who had seemed friendly and jovial at first, pulled out a handgun and opened fire on them both. Rosalind, who was sitting next to him in the passenger seat, was taken totally by surprise and had no time to fight back. In the back seat, Allison screamed and tried to duck away from the gunfire, which was deafening in the enclosed space she now found herself trapped in. There was no evading the .22 bullets at such close range. Kemper simply kept on shooting until she was dead.

Parking outside his mother's apartment, Kemper decapitated both women in the trunk of his car *while it was parked in plain sight on the street*. This was an act of foolhardy recklessness almost unparalleled in Kemper's life so far, something he alluded to in the video interview, during which Kemper recalled "severing a human head—*two* of them, at night in front of my mother's residence with her at home, my neighbors at home upstairs, their picture window open, their curtains open, eleven o'clock at night. The lights are on. All they have to do is walk by, look out, and I've had it."

This is a very astute observation by Kemper. Taking extreme risks (though usually nothing as extreme as decapitating women in public) is a hallmark symptom of several behavioral disorders, including bipolar disorder in some instances. There was nothing to be gained for Kemper by doing this and everything to lose. He was walking a knife-edge, practically begging to be discovered; in fact, it is entirely possible that he subconsciously *wanted* to be discovered, that he actually wanted his situation to be forcibly brought to an end.

Parking outside his mother's apartment, Kemper decapitated both women in the trunk of his car *while it was parked in plain sight on the street*.

Once he had despoiled the corpses of the two young women, Kemper dug the bullets out of each one to delay identification, cut them up, and disposed of them. Ten days later, the headless remains of Rosalind Thorpe and Allison Liu were discovered by a horrified road crew, who at first mistook them for the sort of mannequins that stood in the windows of clothing stores. One body was completely naked, while the other wore a bra and panties. From what police could tell, the killer had made practically no effort to conceal the bodies, simply discarding them with as much thought as tossing a piece of litter from the window of a moving car.

Over the Easter weekend, the ever-present tensions between Kemper and his mother finally came to a head. After patiently waiting for Clarnell to fall asleep, Edmund went into her bedroom clutching a hammer, which he used to batter her skull. To make sure that she was dead, he then cut her throat with a knife. In doing so, he had finally fulfilled his one lifelong ambition: to take the life of the woman he believed had made his own such a misery.

After her death, Kemper decapitated his mother and then had sex with the severed head. He then placed the head on a shelf and threw darts at it, all the while screaming in rage. Still not placated, Kemper obliterated her facial features with the hammer, destroying the face that objectified all his accumulated anger and hatred. He exacted retribution for years of nagging and verbal tirades by cutting out the dead woman's tongue, a truly symbolic gesture if ever there was one.

If Edmund Kemper was expecting to feel better after the death of his mother, he was in for a disappointment. The cold rage was still there, even though its primary focus lay dead just a few feet away from where he sat. After going to a bar to mull the situation over with a few drinks, he came back to the house and invited his mother's best friend, Sally Hallett, 59, to come over and join him. If she thought there was anything strange about her friend's son inviting her over for a visit completely out of the blue, it didn't stop her from coming.

Murdering his mother had not brought Kemper any real closure. It may well be that his next actions happened because he wanted to destroy something else his mother valued highly: her best friend. When an unsuspecting Sally Hallett walked into the house, he took her by surprise and strangled her. Kemper told interviewer Marj von Beroldingen, "I squeezed and just lifted her off the floor. She hung there and, for a moment, I didn't realize she was dead.... I had broken her neck and her head was just wobbling around with the bones of her neck disconnected in the skin sack of her neck."

With both women dead, Kemper scrawled a note intended for the police officers that he knew would inevitably come to investigate and placed it next to his mother's headless body.

APPX. 5:15AM SATURDAY. NO NEED FOR HER TO SUFFER ANY MORE AT THE HANDS OF THIS "MURDEROUS BUTCHER." IT WAS QUICK—ASLEEP—THE WAY I WANTED IT. NOT SLOPPY AND INCOMPLETE, GENTS. JUST A "LACK OF TIME." I GOT THINGS TO DO!!!

Edmund Kemper closed the door behind him and never looked back. He did indeed have things to do—in Colorado.

After starting his long interstate drive in Sally Hallett's car, he soon exchanged it for a rental vehicle. All he took with him were guns and ammunition, enough rounds to kill a hundred people if the urge took him.

The urge, however, did not take him. Edmund Kemper had claimed his last victim. When he reached Pueblo, Colorado, he parked the car by a phone box and called a police station back in Santa Cruz. The operator listened with mounting disbelief as he took responsibility for a string of murders that had long baffled detectives. The fact that the caller was a man well known to them, a guy who hung out socially with their off-duty officers and was a self-professed "cop groupie," took them completely by surprise.

At first, the police officers found Kemper's story a little difficult to believe. All it took to convince them was a visit to his mother's house, where her horribly mutilated corpse and that of her best friend provided all the proof they needed. As difficult as it was to believe, the notorious Co-ed Killer had just turned himself in.

Despite the firearms and extensive supply of ammunition stockpiled inside his car, Kemper went quietly when officers arrived to arrest him. Based upon his sheer size, his compliant demeanor came as a great relief. Still, the police officers were taking no chances, approaching Kemper with guns drawn in order to cuff him and take him into custody.

There were no issues with extraditing Edmund Kemper from Colorado back to his native California. The process went remarkably smoothly, with law enforcement personnel escorting him every mile of the long drive west. In fact, Kemper was surprisingly helpful throughout his trial and incarceration. Not only did he confess to the co-ed murders and outline in graphic detail the manner in which he had committed them and then gotten rid of the bodies, he also undertook visits to the various disposal sites to show police where the parts of his female victims had last been seen.

A 2011 mug shot of Kemper, who has been in prison since 1973.

This unusually forthright approach meant that the attorney appointed to defend him could not make the argument that his client was innocent of the murders. The only card left to play was the insanity defense, declaring that Edmund Kemper was not mentally fit to stand trial for his crimes. The members of the jury disagreed, however, and found him both competent to stand trial and guilty on all counts. Despite Kemper's request to be executed, California state law did not permit the death sentence to be applied at that time, so the judge sentenced Kemper to multiple life sentences in a mental institution, with the strong recommendation that he never be allowed to walk free again.

At the time of this writing, Edmund Kemper remains behind bars, serving time without the possibility of release. He is no longer in the business of fooling judges and assessment boards, trying to convince them that he is cured and fit to be paroled. When asked if he will continue to kill people in the event of his release, he answers with a blunt, succinct "Yes."

Men such as he cannot be reasoned with, bargained with, or rehabilitated. They are simply too sick and twisted for that. Kemper proves the point himself, far better than any writer ever could, with one direct quote: "What do you think, now, when you see a pretty girl walking down the street? One side of me says, 'Wow, what an attractive chick. I'd like to talk to her, date her.' The other side of me says, 'I wonder how her head would look like on a stick?'"

THE YORKSHIRE RIPPER: PETER SUTCLIFFE

For the people of the United Kingdom, the word "Ripper" is an evocative one. The British press were fully aware of this when they dubbed the man who was killing women in the north of England during the 1970s "the Yorkshire Ripper." It conjures up images of Jack the Ripper himself, stalking the mist-shrouded streets of Victorian-era Whitechapel in search of victims to carve up with his knife. It also served to instill fear and sold a great many newspapers, which was exactly what the tabloid news editors had intended.

The fact that this modern-day Ripper also often targeted prostitutes made the comparison even easier for the public to accept (though some of his victims were no such thing). When the police finally caught him, the Yorkshire Ripper turned out to be a truck driver named Peter Sutcliffe. Over the course of five years, Sutcliffe had murdered thirteen women and savagely attacked at least seven more.

Sutcliffe was Yorkshire born and bred. After his birth on June 2, 1946, in the town of Bingley, he experienced a relatively unremarkable childhood. The Sutcliffes were a blue-collar, working-class family, and, surprisingly, young Peter showed a strong inclination toward academics while at school, but there would be no university education in his future. Instead, he would leave school at the youngest age the law allowed (15 at that time) and go straight into the workforce.

Those who remember Peter Sutcliffe from his boyhood days almost uniformly describe a quiet, often lonely boy who exhibited none of the obvious red flags seen with some serial murderers. As far as anyone knows, young Sutcliffe did not torture or kill animals or show a tendency toward violent outbursts and irrational behavior. Nothing marked him as someone who would grow up to commit crimes of a horrifically violent nature. He was particularly close to his mother, but there is no indication that what they shared was anything other than a normal, loving mother-son relationship, as opposed to a mutually antagonistic one such as that shared by Edmund Kemper and his mother. If anything, as a child, Peter Sutcliffe was something of a mother's boy, never wanting to be too far away from her at any given moment. Most normal children outgrow this stage of their lives fairly quickly, but Sutcliffe was far from normal.

> Nothing marked him as someone who would grow up to commit crimes of a horrifically violent nature.

In Peter's eyes, his mother could do no wrong—until the day on which his father accused her of cheating on him, calling her out in front of the entire family. John Sutcliffe suspected that his wife was having an affair with another man, so he decided to set a trap for her. Kathleen Sutcliffe went to a hotel with the expectation of having a clandestine meeting with her lover, only to be confronted by her outraged husband and a gaggle of her confused and crying children.

The fact that his mother might be anything less than perfect came as an immense shock to young Peter, and several behavioral specialists have speculated that this incident may have sparked his pathological hatred for women, which only grew stronger as he got older.

As a young man, Sutcliffe liked to visit prostitutes, who were not difficult to find in the Bradford area. His stance toward these women was massively hypocritical: Sutcliffe would speak of their "immoral behavior" in tones of disgust, scream abuse when he drove past them on the street, but would then think nothing of picking one up later on and paying for her sexual services. He objectified and depersonalized women, seeing them as little more than commodities to be abused and humiliated once his own sexual needs had been met. This continued after he had courted and then married his wife, Sonia, who never suspected that her apparently loving husband became an entirely different man once he left the house and went to work.

Before he first began to kill, Peter Sutcliffe started out by targeting women seemingly at random in order to inflict injury upon them. These appeared to be crimes of opportunity—unplanned and completely spontaneous.

One night in September 1969—the witness who testified to the attack at Sutcliffe's trial could not remember the exact date—Sutcliffe was sitting in a van with his friend, Trevor Birdsall, in one of the seedier areas of Bradford, a part of the city that prostitutes were known to frequent. Sutcliffe suddenly opened the van door and stepped out into the street, then disappeared for ten minutes without offering any explanation. When he returned, it was obvious to Birdsall that he had physically exerted himself somehow. The logical explanation would have been a quick, secret dalliance with a prostitute, but Sutcliffe's story was unbelievable: he claimed to have assaulted a woman with a heavy stone that he had stuffed inside a sock, hitting her over the head with the makeshift weapon. To prove what he said, Sutcliffe produced a sock from his pocket and dumped the stone out into the street.

So far as we know, more than five years would go by before Sutcliffe's violent urges would rear their head again. In the early morning hours of July 5, 1975, Anna Rogulskyj, 36, better known as "Irish Annie," was walking home from a nightclub when Sutcliffe suddenly came out of the darkness of an alleyway and propositioned her for sex. Anna was no prostitute, and she turned down the man in no uncertain terms.

Sutcliffe lunged at her, swinging a weapon with his right hand. Before Anna could defend herself, he was battering her with a hammer. In seconds, she was beaten unconscious. That didn't stop him from lifting her blouse and slicing into the soft flesh of her abdomen with a knife. It is likely that Anna Rogulskyj would have been the Yorkshire Ripper's first murder victim had it not been for the shouts of a nearby resident demanding to know what all the noise was about. Sutcliffe ran off, leaving his victim barely alive. Extensive brain surgery was required to evacuate the pressure inside the head of the comatose Anna. A priest even gave her the last rites, but as her name implied, Irish Annie was a fighter. She eventually pulled through, albeit with permanent physical and emotional scars.

Sutcliffe struck again one month later, on August 15, in Halifax. Olive Smelt, 46, was not a prostitute either. Her only "crime" in the eyes of Peter Sutcliffe was that she appeared to be one to him, and he first set eyes on her in a pub that prostitutes were known to drink at. She had been enjoying a social evening out with her friends and wasn't expecting any trouble. Unfortunately, trouble found her anyway.

After the pub had closed for the night, Sutcliffe followed Olive on her walk home, trailing a short distance behind her. Just as he had done with Anna Rogulskyj, he picked a spot in a dark alleyway and struck at her head with a hammer to incapacitate her. When his victim fell to the ground, he used a knife to slash at her body. Her buttocks were severely lacerated during the attack. The only thing that saved Olive's life was the unexpected arrival of a passing car, which spooked her assailant sufficiently to make him run off into the night.

Sutcliffe patrolled the dark alleys of Yorkshire villages, searching for prostitutes. His attacks on hookers would lead to his being compared to Jack the Ripper.

It is clear that Peter Sutcliffe intended to kill his victims rather than just hurt them: repeated blows to the head with a ball hammer are potentially lethal. It was only unanticipated interruptions that saved the lives of Anna Rogulskyj and Olive Smelt. Tracy Browne, just 14 years old at the time of her encounter with the Ripper, was also fortunate to have survived it. Sutcliffe approached the teenager as she was walking home late one evening in August 1975, less than two weeks after his last attack. He seemed friendly and affable enough at first, even charming. The man introduced himself as Tony and asked casual questions about her personal life, such as whether she had a boyfriend.

Unfortunately for her, the car she got into was that of the Yorkshire Ripper.

They had almost reached Tracy's home when he attacked her. She described what she remembered of the horrific ordeal to a BBC reporter:

The first blow sent me crashing down on my knees. I fell into the side of the road. I pleaded with him, "Please don't, please don't," and screamed for help. But he hit me five times with so much force and energy that each blow was accompanied by a brutal grunting noise.

Yet again, a passing car startled Sutcliffe, preventing him from finishing off what he had started. Blinded and covered with her own blood, Tracy somehow managed to get to her feet and stagger home, collapsing into the arms of a neighbor. Although she would require extensive brain surgery, Tracy Browne survived. His next victims would not be so fortunate.

Sutcliffe struck again two months later, this time in Leeds. His chosen victim, Wilma McCann, 28, was intoxicated after having spent the night drinking in several pubs around the town. Wilma was a single mother of four young children who liked to unwind with a few drinks, and on the evening of October 29, she had overdone it. She found herself staggering along the roadside trying to hitch a ride from any passing motorist who would stop to pick her up. Unfortunately for her, the car she got into was that of the Yorkshire Ripper.

We only have Sutcliffe's word for what happened next. In the confession he would later make to the police, he claimed that after she accepted his offer of a ride, she propositioned him with an offer of sex in return for five pounds. According to other motorists who were interviewed by the police, Norma had made similar offers to them, which they had declined.

Sutcliffe parked in a shady spot, well away from any streetlights. Sutcliffe claimed to have been unable to perform as quickly as she wanted him to, which caused her to storm off in anger. He went after her, surreptitiously taking a hammer along with him. He described the incident thusly:

I put my coat on the grass. She sat down on the coat. She unfastened her trousers. She said, "Come on then, get it over with." I said, "Don't worry, I will."

> I then hit her with the hammer on her head. I was stood up at that time behind her. I think I hit her on top of the head. I hit her once or twice on the head. She fell down flat on her back and started making a horrible noise like a moaning gurgling noise.

In one version of events that he described, Sutcliffe went back to the car and rummaged around in his toolbox, exchanging the hammer for a knife with a seven-inch blade. (In another version of the story he told, the weapons were already with him when he followed her.) When he returned to Wilma's supine body, she hadn't moved. Whether she was already dead or had simply been battered unconscious was unclear. In order to make certain, he stabbed her repeatedly, focusing upon her chest, belly, and neck where the majority of the vital organs and major blood vessels are.

In his confession, he claimed to have "pulled her blouse or whatever it was and her bra so I could see where I was stabbing her." This seems like an attempt by Sutcliffe to ignore there being a sexually compulsive component to the frenzied knife attack.

> I was in a blind panic when I was stabbing her just to make sure she wouldn't tell anyone. What a damn stupid thing to do just to keep somebody quiet. If I was thinking logical at the time I would have stopped and told someone I'd hit her with the hammer. That was the turning point. I realize I overreacted at the time; nothing I have done since then affected me like this.

Peter Sutcliffe's statement concerning the murder of Wilma McCann is nothing but more self-serving garbage. Why would he have stopped somebody and told them that he had hit a total stranger repeatedly with a hammer? He did not do so after his attacks on Anna Rogulskyj, Tracy Browne, or Olive Smelt, despite inflicting injuries on each of them that could very easily have been fatal—indeed, were almost certainly *intended* to be fatal. His MO up to that point was to approach a woman with an offer of paying her for sex, or (in the case of Browne) just pounce on her out of the shadows. His disdain for prostitutes, or those women that he simply *perceived* as being prostitutes, plainly applied not just to grown women but to teenage girls as well.

Wilma's body would not be found until the following morning by a milk delivery man

Wilma McCann's lifeless body was discovered by a milk delivery man. The murder immediately launched a manhunt.

making his rounds. An investigation and wide-ranging manhunt were immediately launched by the police, who knew that her murderer had to be an extremely dangerous man, one who had to be caught before he killed again. The victim's state of partial undress suggested the crime was sexually motivated.

Tragically, Wilma's eldest daughter, Sonia, would never get over her mother's loss. After battling chronic alcoholism for many years, a condition directly linked to losing her mother during her childhood, Sonia took her own life in 2007. In an earlier interview, she had made the point that while society usually remembers the names of murder victims, the orphaned children they leave behind are often forgotten.

"After that first time. I developed and built up a hatred for prostitutes in order to justify within myself the reason why I had attacked and killed Wilma McCann," Sutcliffe confessed to detectives after his capture. This may be the closest we get to an explanation for why he continued to kill women—attacks that were motivated by a hatred for "prostitutes" that he deliberately fueled to rationalize Wilma McCann's murder.

Peter Sutcliffe would not kill again for the remainder of 1975. After the Christmas and New Year holidays came and went, his mind turned once again to murder. His first victim of 1976 was 42-year-old Emily Jackson, who, despite assisting with her husband's roofing business, occasionally supplemented her meager income by engaging in prostitution. She kept this secret life under wraps from her neighbors, friends, and family.

The Ripper's attack on Emily, whom he had picked up after promising to pay her five pounds for sex and then driven to an out-of-the-way area, was even more savage than his last. After exposing her breasts and sexual organs, he stabbed her more than fifty times. Rather than using a knife, for this attack

The Millgarth Police Station in Leeds is where much of the investigation for the Yorkshire Ripper would take place.

he elected to use a screwdriver with a Phillips head instead (this particular type of screwdriver tip has a very distinctive cross shape). Her head also bore signs of blunt force trauma that had most likely been inflicted by a hammer, Sutcliffe's preferred method of stunning and thereby incapacitating his victim. This, along with the imprint of a boot, helped police connect Emily Jackson's murder with that of Wilma McCann.

At first, police in Leeds did not connect Sutcliffe's next attack with the murders of Wilma McCann and Emily Jackson, primarily because the victim (20-year-old Marcella Claxton) did not die after he assaulted her with a ball hammer in the early morning hours of May 9. Claxton sustained serious injuries to her skull and brain but was somehow able to make it to a telephone and call for help. When police officers questioned her, she offered up the best description she could muster of the man who had attacked her—who was, of course, Peter Sutcliffe. Despite this, it was only after the Yorkshire Ripper had been caught that they realized her assailant had been the same man they had been hunting for so long.

For reasons known only to himself, Sutcliffe now began keeping a low profile, refraining from any further attacks for the next nine months. For the remainder of 1976, the people of Leeds and the surrounding area began to breathe a little easier. The unidentified individual who had terrorized their community by killing several women appeared to have disappeared as mysteriously as he had first arrived.

Their hopes were dashed on February 5, 1977, when the Yorkshire Ripper struck again in the very same location. A pattern was now beginning to develop: Peter Sutcliffe was hunting for victims late on Saturday nights and early on Sunday mornings, when the pubs, clubs, and bars were packed with weekend revelers and the streets were full of people. The body of Irene Richardson, 28, was discovered early on a Sunday morning by a man jogging across a sports field in Roundhay. Detectives instantly knew that their predator was back. The victim showed signs of blunt force trauma to the head, followed by penetrating injuries inflicted to the abdomen. Yet there was something strangely different about this particular body. In the other murders, the killer had peeled back the victim's clothing, exposing large parts of their body surface area for all to see. In this case, the victim's body had been covered up with her own coat, although beneath it, some of her skin had still been exposed. Her boots had been taken off and placed over her legs, the reason for which still remains elusive—Sutcliffe claims she took them off herself, though he gave no reason why she might have done so.

Sutcliffe would later confess that he had gone out that night with the intent "to find a prostitute, to make it one more less." He claimed that Irene Richardson got into his car without any prompting on his part, and they drove to the same field in which he had assaulted Marcella Claxton the previous May. Irene had needed to use the bathroom, which was locked, and she was not shy about squatting down and urinating in the middle of the dark field. It was at that time, when she was at her most vulnerable, that he hit her on the head with the hammer. She fell onto the ground, and he began slashing at her with the Stanley knife he kept in his pocket for just such a purpose.

Once he was certain that his victim was dead, Sutcliffe checked himself to make sure that he hadn't gotten any blood splatter on his clothes or body, then drove home to his wife and acted as if nothing out of the ordinary had happened.

Rather than walk the streets to pick up her clients, as so many working girls did, Patricia Atkinson worked out of her flat in the city of Bradford, just a short drive from Leeds. Late at night on Saturday, April 23, Sutcliffe stopped to offer her a ride. Patricia had been drinking all night and was very much acting like it, swearing and staggering in the middle of the street. She must have looked like an easy mark to the man who was out to murder prostitutes. Hearing that she had a flat, a private and secure location away from the prying eyes of the public, was too good an opportunity for him to pass up.

His chosen weapon was no longer a ball-peen hammer but rather a hooked claw hammer, which he used to strike Patricia Atkinson on the head. Pulling away her clothes, Sutcliffe used both the claw and the hammer head upon her bare skin, then took out a knife and began to slash and stab the defenseless woman with it.

When I first hit her, she was making a horrible gurgling sound ... and she carried on making this noise even though I'd hit her a few times. She was still making a gurgling noise when I left, but I knew she would not be in a state to tell anybody.

> His chosen weapon was no longer a ball-peen hammer but rather a hooked claw hammer, which he used to strike Patricia Atkinson in the head.

Nor was she. Patricia Atkinson's dead body, wrapped up in a white bedsheet, was discovered the next day by a friend. Police were immediately alerted, and despite the fact that this was the first murder in the series that had taken place inside a building rather than out in the open, they had no doubt that they were dealing with the same perpetrator. Not only did the repeated blows to the head fit with the killer's MO, but he had inadvertently stepped on a bedsheet, leaving a bloody footprint—a footprint that matched one found on the leg of previous murder victim Emily Jackson.

But the "Ripper Squad," a special police unit that had been set up to put an end to the spate of murders, was no closer to identifying the owner of the boot. Until the police did, they knew that the murders would continue. Two months later, the Ripper murdered 16-year-old Jayne MacDonald, a Leeds girl who had no identifiable ties to the world of prostitution whatsoever. Once again, the murder took place in the early hours of a Sunday morning. Sutcliffe approached the teenager from behind, bludgeoned her with his signature hammer, and then dragged her body into a nearby yard, where he proceeded to stab her over and over again in her bare chest and upper back.

This was one of the very few instances in which Peter Sutcliffe showed any signs of remorse after the murder, lamenting the fact that the shock of Jayne's murder had resulted in her father's death.

When I saw in the papers that MacDonald was so young and not a prostitute, I felt like someone inhuman and I realized that it was a devil driving me against my will, and that I was a beast.

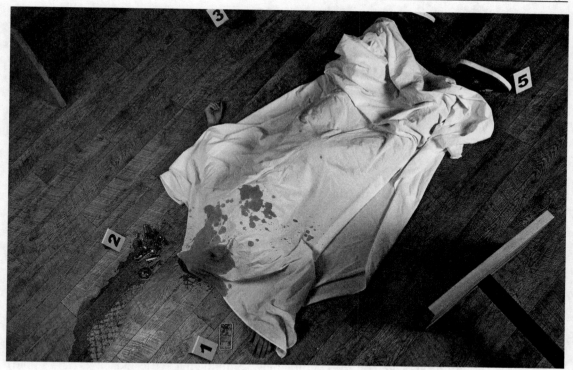

Patricia Atkinson's body was found wrapped in a white sheet and indoors, unlike the earlier murders, which made police wonder if they were dealing with a new killer.

Still, this rare moment of self-awareness (if it was ever actually genuine) did not stop him from killing again. On July 10, he attacked 42-year-old Maureen Long, who had spent the night drinking and dancing in Bradford, on a piece of deserted wasteland. Yet again, after giving his victim a ride in his car, Sutcliffe waited until she squatted down to relieve herself on the ground before striking. Despite a hammer blow to the head and multiple stab wounds to her torso, Maureen somehow survived the attack. She lay there at the scene of the crime until daybreak, when she was finally found by passersby, covered in blood but still alive.

Her would-be murderer learned of her survival later that day. "I thought that I had stabbed her enough when I left her," Sutcliffe would later admit. Had it been the middle of winter, rather than a relatively balmy night in July, Maureen Long would almost certainly have died.

On an even more chilling note, just a few weeks before his capture, Sutcliffe was out with his wife, Sonia, at the Arndale Shopping Centre when he saw Maureen Long coming the other way. She looked directly at him without displaying any kind of visible reaction. She either didn't recognize the man who had given her a lift that fateful night, or she simply didn't remember what had happened after the attack—which is completely understandable, considering the serious head trauma that she had suffered. Until his arrest and subsequent confession, Maureen hadn't the slightest inkling of her close encounter with the man who had tried to kill her.

Sutcliffe made certain to ensure the death of his next victim, 20-year-old prostitute Jean Jordan, on October 1. It was another Saturday night, and the Ripper had traded his usual hunting grounds of Leeds and Bradford for the city lights of Manchester, primarily because things were getting a little too uncomfortable for him in those cities. Sutcliffe picked her up and, after agreeing on a five-pound payment, drove her to an allotment, ostensibly to have sex. (An allotment is the British term for a rented stretch of ground used for growing plants, vegetables, and flowers.) Once there, Sutcliffe employed his standard technique of delivering a hammer blow to the head followed by multiple knife wounds to the abdomen and upper body.

> The bodies of most of the Yorkshire Ripper's victims were found the same day as their death, or at the latest the following day.

The bodies of most of the Yorkshire Ripper's victims were found the same day as their death, or at the latest the following day. Jean Jordan was unique in that her body went undiscovered for more than a week after her murder. Finally, when no word of the killing appeared on the evening news, Sutcliffe made the audacious (and stupid) decision to return to the scene of the murder on October 9. Not only was this the first time he had ever gone back to the location of a murder he had committed, it was also the first time that he mutilated the body of a victim postmortem.

Jordan's body was in the process of decomposing. Sutcliffe used a shard of razor-sharp broken glass to slash open her abdomen, then switched to a hacksaw and attempted to saw her head off. He recalled:

> I forgot to say that before I did this, it was my intention to create a mystery about the body. I felt sure this was the end for me anyway. I had taken a hacksaw out of my car, intending to remove her head. I started sawing through her neck. The blade might have been blunt because I was getting nowhere at all, so I gave up. If I had cut the head off, I was going to leave it somewhere else to make a big mystery out of it. The glass I used was about three quarters of a pane with the corner missing.

Sutcliffe returned to his old haunt of Leeds on December 14 to carry out his next attack, on Marilyn Moore, 25. Like so many of his other victims, she was a prostitute. After Sutcliffe tried to procure her services that night, he bungled a hammer attack on her, causing her to shriek in pain and terror. Concerned that the noise would bring the police, Sutcliffe fled the scene, leaving his latest victim wounded with a depressed skull fracture and several defensive wounds, but miraculously still alive. She was able to describe her attacker to the police with a reasonable amount of detail, painting a picture of a man who called himself "Dave."

As he usually did, the Yorkshire Ripper took the holidays off and returned to killing in the new year. On January 21, Bradford-based prostitute Yvonne Pearson, 21, became his next victim. If Sutcliffe's word is to be believed, she was to be one of the only women he did not deliberately set out to kill. Sutcliffe was driving home that night, when he stopped to allow another car out of a side street. Seconds later, Yvonne Pearson was tapping on the driver's side window. He rolled the window down, and she propositioned him, offering sex for the commonly accepted price of five or ten pounds, depending on the specifics of what he wanted.

After hitting Pearson with a hammer, he dragged her onto a shadowy stretch of ground where a threadbare old couch had been dumped. Throwing her body down onto the couch, Sutcliffe hesitated when the headlights of another car swept by. In order to keep her quiet, he pinched her nose shut and stuffed her mouth full of straw.

In a very out-of-character moment, Sutcliffe suddenly found himself apologizing to Yvonne's lifeless body for having murdered her. He then placed her corpse on the ground and overturned the couch, using it to cover her body from view. It was a simple but effective form of conceal-ment—her remains were not found for two more months. An autopsy revealed that Yvonne's killer hadn't stabbed her. As such, her death wasn't immediately recognized as being part of the greater pattern of Ripper murders.

Ten days later, Sutcliffe killed Helen Rytka, an 18-year-old from Huddersfield. A delivery driver by trade, he had delivered goods to a place in the city earlier that day and had happened to catch sight of several work-ing girls in an area that he correctly assumed was the red-light district. This was another hammer-and-stabbing type of attack and was therefore immediately attributed to the York-shire Ripper when the body was discovered in a timber yard three days later.

According to Sutcliffe, two taxicab dri-vers had been standing no more than 35 yards from the place where he had just committed murder. Both were so engrossed in their con-

After the killing of 18-year-old Helen Rytka, a huge manhunt was organized to capture the monstrous Peter Sutcliff (pictured).

versation that they had failed to notice him bludgeon Rytka to death with a hammer in the back seat of his car. He then claimed to have had sex with her as she lay dying, before stabbing her to death with a knife.

Enlisting the help of the general public, an enormous manhunt was now underway, and the police were deluged with thousands of leads, almost all of which were a colossal waste of time and effort—yet each had to be investigated and run down anyway. The women of Yorkshire lived in a state of constant fear. Many refused to go out alone at night, whereas others made sure they were escorted and stuck to well-lit areas whenever they could. In just the same way that his namesake, Jack, had haunted Victorian London, the Yorkshire Ripper cast an evil shadow over the streets of Bradford, Leeds, Manchester, and Huddersfield. Some people began to wonder if he would ever be caught.

Breaking with his usual form, Peter Sutcliffe murdered Helen Rytka on a Tuesday night. So, too, was Vera Millward, a 40-year-old prostitute from Manchester who made the fatal mistake of getting into Sutcliffe's car late in the evening of May 16, 1978. One of the places that working girls used to ply their trade was a parking lot of the Manchester Royal Infirmary hospital, which is where she suggested they park and get down to business. After making sure that there was little chance of them being seen, Sutcliffe pummeled the head of the unsuspecting Vera with a hammer, then eviscerated her with a knife.

The Ripper then took almost a year off, minding his own business until the spring of 1979. His MO had changed once again. No longer was Sutcliffe restricting his attacks to prostitutes (or at the very least, to women he *thought* might be prostitutes). Now, he would assault any woman who took his fancy, no matter her profession or perceived nature. He said:

> Following Millward, the compulsion inside me seemed to lay dormant, but eventually the feelings came welling up, and each time they were more random and indiscriminate. I now realized I had the urge to kill any woman, and I thought that this would eventually get me caught, but I think that in my subconscious this was what I really wanted.

Sutcliffe may well have been telling the unvarnished truth during this part of his confession. Many serial killers experience this desire to be caught, whether it is a conscious or subconscious one. Even Jack the Ripper begged the police to catch him before he could kill again, which suggests a strong homicidal impulse that may be beyond the killer's ability to tame or suppress. Peter Sutcliffe's pathological hatred of prostitutes had now expanded to encompass any and all women, suggesting that this deep-seated sense of loathing was growing and intensifying.

Josephine Whitaker was no prostitute. The 19-year-old worked in a building society (the equivalent of a U.S. savings and loan institution), helping people withdraw money or pay into their savings accounts. Sutcliffe killed her on April 4, 1979, in Halifax. Far from any sort of red-light area, Josephine was walking alone late at night through a field when Sutcliffe spotted her and engaged her in conversation.

> I realized she was not a prostitute …, but at this time I wasn't bothered. I just wanted to kill a woman.

> She told me that she normally took a short cut across the field. I said you don't know who you can trust these days. It sounds a bit evil now. There I was, walking along with my hammer and a big Phillips screwdriver in my pocket, ready to do the inevitable.

"The inevitable" involved knocking her unconscious with the hammer before stabbing her to death with the screwdriver, then dragging her body further into the field until it was out of sight.

It had been almost a year since the last Ripper murder, and while the police Ripper Squad had been far from idle, some had begun to hope that they had seen the last of the murderer. When Josephine Whitaker's body was found on the morning of April 5, there was absolutely no doubt as to who had killed her.

Peter Sutcliffe's pathological hatred of prostitutes had now expanded to encompass any and all women, suggesting that this deep-seated sense of loathing was growing and intensifying.

For his next murder, which took place shortly after midnight on September 2, Sutcliffe returned to his old habit of stalking and murdering women over the weekend. The social scene in Bradford's city center was buzzing that Saturday night, and there was no shortage of young women for the predatory Sutcliffe to choose from. He finally settled on a 20-year-old university student named Barbara Leach. She also had no ties to prostitution; she was simply a young woman out with her friends for a few drinks and some dancing.

Barbara was walking home alone, totally unprepared when Sutcliffe came out of nowhere on a quiet side street and struck her in the head with a hammer. The blow rendered her semiconscious but did not knock her out. Moving quickly, Barbara's assailant dragged her around to the back side of a house, where he stabbed her repeatedly with a screwdriver.

After he killed Leach, the Ripper went underground again. He would not surface until August 20, 1980, when he killed Marguerite Walls, 47, in Leeds. She was walking home from work late on a Wednesday evening when Sutcliffe abducted her, dragged her into a garden, and murdered her. Her near-naked body was discovered the following day.

Once again, the level of public fear regarding the Yorkshire Ripper had abated over the course of the past year. Many women had gotten used to the idea that it might be safe to walk the streets again, or at least they weren't actively thinking about there being any danger. It might have been expected that the cold-blooded murder of Marguerite Walls, a civil servant who was simply going about her everyday business, would come as a shocking reminder to the people of Yorkshire that there was still a killer on the loose. Instead, it was misconstrued as a one-off killing rather than a Ripper murder, not least because the method used—strangulation—did not fit the Ripper's standard MO.

> After he killed Leach, the Ripper went underground again. He would not surface until August 20, 1980, when he killed Marguerite Walls, 47, in Leeds.

As summer ended and the first leaves began to fall from the trees, Sutcliffe attacked two more women—Upadhya Bandara and Theresa Sykes—in his old haunts, Leeds and Huddersfield. Mercifully, both survived the assaults, though not without having sustained serious injuries.

The last Ripper murder took place on November 17 in Leeds. The victim was a student named Jacqueline Hill, 20, who was heading home for the evening. Peter Sutcliffe followed her at a discreet distance on foot, and when he judged that there was nobody around, he picked up his speed and beat her insensible. It was not particularly late at night—around 9:30—and the crime scene took place close to the city's busy Arndale Shopping Centre, a brazen move to say the least. The murder weapon was again a screwdriver, which Sutcliffe used to stab Jacqueline in the chest and eyeball.

"I pulled Miss Hill's clothes off, most of them," Sutcliffe would later confess. "I had a screwdriver on me.... I stabbed her in the lungs. Her eyes were wide open and she seemed to be looking at me with an accusing stare. This shook me up a bit. I jabbed the screwdriver into her eye, but they stayed open, and I felt worse than ever.

Huge amounts of time, effort, and money were poured into the hunt for the Yorkshire Ripper. Tens of thousands of hours were logged by undercover officers, staking out red-light areas in which prostitutes were known to congregate. Peter Sutcliffe was actually interviewed by detectives and released after being dismissed as a potential suspect. Huge cash rewards were offered as inducements for tips, leading to a torrent of information pouring in from the public, much of it a complete waste of time. But there were exceptions. One such exception was an anonymous letter, stating in clear and simple terms that Peter Sutcliffe was the Yorkshire Ripper. Its author was none other than Peter Sutcliffe's old friend Trevor Birdsall, who had been unable to shake a growing sense of unease over some of the things he had witnessed Sutcliffe do. He even made sure to include Sutcliffe's home address.

What finally got him, ironically, was something simple. On January 2, 1981, Peter Sutcliffe was seen by a police officer talking with a prostitute in one of the seedier areas of Sheffield, a major city that was relatively fresh ground for him. A routine traffic stop ensued, and the constable ran the license plate number on Sutcliffe's car through the vehicle registration database. The results came back quickly. The plates were stolen, and the driver duly arrested. When he was taken to the police station, his resemblance to the composite pictures of the Yorkshire Ripper was not lost on them, and he was interviewed regarding his possible involvement in the murders.

Because he had been picked up while in the company of a prostitute, officers went back to the scene of his arrest the following day to conduct a more comprehensive search. They discovered a knife and a hammer—the hallmark weapons of the Yorkshire Ripper. Back at the police station, Sutcliffe had disposed of another knife by placing it in the cistern of the toilet when he was taking a bathroom break.

Realizing that the game was now up, Sutcliffe confessed during a marathon interview session that took place on January 4, 1981. He declared himself to be guilty—not of murder, but of manslaughter, because although he admitted to having attacked and killed his victims, he said it was God's divine will that he do so. The fault, therefore, lay with the Almighty, not with Peter Sutcliffe.

> Because he had been picked up while in the company of a prostitute, officers went back to the scene of his arrest the following day to conduct a more comprehensive search.

Neither the judge nor the jury at Sutcliffe's trial was buying it, declaring him guilty across the board and sentencing him to life imprisonment twenty times over.

Many of those who have studied the Yorkshire Ripper have concluded that he almost certainly attacked and killed more women than is commonly accepted, victims whose bodies have never been found and most likely never will be. It is certainly possible.

Whether incarcerated behind the walls of a prison or committed to a secure hospital facility for the mentally unstable, Peter Sutcliffe became the target of multiple attacks by other inmates and patients. During one such attack, he was nearly blinded in an assault with a pen wielded by fellow murderer Ian Kay. Few would disagree with the sentiment that, in being exposed to a number of unexpected surprise attacks, Peter Sutcliffe was getting a long-overdue taste of his own medicine.

What does the future hold for the Yorkshire Ripper? A number of the United Kingdom's vilest, most notorious murderers have been sentenced to a whole life order (life imprisonment), which practically guarantees that they will never walk the streets of Britain again. And so it was with Peter Sutcliffe, who passed away on November 13, 2020, while serving his time at Frankland Prison in Brasside, County Durham. He was suffering from several ailments, including COVID-19, and had been hospitalized.

THE ANIME KILLER: TSUTOMU MIYAZAKI

The term "serial killer" evokes a definite sort of mental image. For Americans, the faces of Jeffrey Dahmer, John Wayne Gacy, Ted Bundy, or H. H. Holmes may spring to mind. For the British, there are the Moors Murderers, Harold Shipman, and the ever-mysterious Jack the Ripper. In all likelihood, for most readers of this book, the image of the typical serial killer seems to be a Caucasian male of Western descent.

The serial murderer is not restricted to the Western world, however. Many societies and countries have them. In this chapter, we will look at one who came from the island nation of Japan.

Born in 1962, Tsutomu Miyazaki did not have an easy childhood, due to a rare deformity that prevented him from bending his wrists in a normal way. Children can often be cruel, especially to those who stand out as different, and the young Miyazaki was teased and bullied mercilessly because of his condition, which many believed to be freakish. Whenever photographs were taken, Miyazaki self-consciously kept his hands out of sight.

Quiet and withdrawn, the little boy had few friends to keep him company. Rather than going out to play, he preferred to spend countless hours alone, drawing cartoonish characters from his imagination. It was a lonely childhood, and he found himself escaping into the pages of comic books whenever the opportunity presented itself.

A bookish child who loved to read, Miyazaki's academic performance declined as he grew older. His desire to follow a career path as a teacher was shattered when he failed to achieve the grades needed for university admission. Instead, his plan upon leaving school was to take a job as a printer.

He soon developed an interest in pornography. Tsutomu quickly grew bored with Japanese adult magazines, mainly because they blurred out the genitalia of the female subjects—the parts that he most wanted to see. This was because the publishers could not legally show pubic hair in any of the pictures. Consequently, he sought out obscene material featuring much younger girls who had shaved their genitalia. He also took surreptitious photographs of girls playing tennis, trying to catch as much exposed skin in each picture as he possibly could. The photos were intended to be used as masturbatory aids. Tsutomu's collection of porn grew so extensive that the magazines, photographs, videos, and comic books ultimately numbered in the thousands.

> The loss of his closest family member may well have been the straw that broke the camel's back.

Having little interaction with most of his family, especially his sisters, Miyazaki's closest relationship was with his grandfather. When he died in 1988, Tsutomu was heartbroken, and he soon went into a period of major depression. After his grandfather's body was cremated, the young man hit upon a unique way of maintaining their close bond—he ate some of the ashes.

The loss of his closest family member may well have been the straw that broke the camel's back. While Tsutomu had a well-deserved reputation for strange and bizarre behavior, in mid-1988—the year his closest family member died—he truly went off the rails when he began to abduct and murder young girls.

The first to go missing was four-year-old Mari Konno. Tsutomu snatched the girl while she was playing and drove her to a secluded area on the outskirts of Tokyo that was screened from its surroundings by trees. There he strangled her to death and had sexual intercourse with her corpse. Keeping her clothing as a souvenir, he then dumped the girl's naked body on a remote hillside.

Months later, little Mari's body still had not been found. Despite the danger of being discovered, Miyazaki couldn't stop himself from going back to the place where he had left her. The little girl had been constantly on his mind, with her murder becoming something of a major obsession. Heaping further indignities on her decomposing remains, he cut off what was left of her feet and hands. Like Jeffrey Dahmer, he kept them at home in his room, taking them out whenever he wanted a reminder of the first life he had taken.

As if that wasn't grotesque enough, Miyazaki decided to taunt the dead girl's family. After incinerating her remains, he boxed up the ashes, along with a few teeth, and had them delivered to the Konno family along with a postcard that read, "MARI. CREMATED. BONES. INVESTIGATE. PROVE." Also tucked inside the box were a series of photographs of the clothing that he had stripped from Mari's dead body. Forensic testing proved that they were indeed the remains of Mari Konno. The family received another taunting note that described the postmortem changes that had taken place in their daughter's body and alluded to the pungent smell caused by decomposition. There were also a series of phone calls in which nobody spoke for long minutes at a time, Tsutomu's attempt to turn their world into a living nightmare that would only end when her murderer was finally caught.

Six weeks later, he abducted a second victim. At the age of seven, Masami Yoshizawa was almost twice as old as Mari Konno had been. It is believed that this was a crime of opportunity for Tsutomu Miyazaki; he encountered the girl on an empty stretch of road, and she was naive enough to accept a complete stranger's offer of a ride. Miyazaki murdered her in the same place that he had killed his first victim and did so in almost exactly the same way: first strangling her, then having sex with her dead body once her heart had stopped beating. Her corpse was dumped on the same hillside, and once again, her killer took the little girl's clothes with him to serve as mementos.

Miyazaki took the ashes of his victim and put them in a box, which he then sent to the Konno family to torment them.

Miyazaki changed his MO for victim number three. Erika Namba was four years old and walking home when the serial killer happened to drive by. Pulling over to the side of the road, he dragged the struggling child into the car and took off, driving her to a parking lot. Rather than kill her right away, Miyazaki made the terrified girl slowly remove her clothes while he took photographs of her in various stages of undress.

In a significant break from his established routine, after strangling the girl on the back seat of his car, he then bound her hands and feet before covering her body in a white sheet and locking it in the vehicle's trunk. Rather than keep her clothes for himself, he abandoned them close to the scene of the murder.

As Miyazaki was on the way to dump the body in the usual spot, he accidentally drove his car off the side of the road. When he tried to drive away, he discovered that it was stuck in mud.

Even somebody as mentally disturbed as Tsutomu Miyazaki could tell that this was a bad spot to be in: stuck in an immobile vehicle at the roadside with the body of a murdered little girl in the trunk. If a police patrol car happened to stop and ask any questions, his crimes might easily be discovered. Thinking fast, he decided that he needed to get rid of the evidence as quickly as possible. Stepping out of the car and popping the trunk, Miyazaki lifted Erika's lifeless body out and hiked a short distance into some nearby woods. Removing the bedsheet that had been used to cover the corpse, he left it on the ground and went back to his car—only to find two men standing there waiting for him.

The would-be Good Samaritans had spotted the stuck car and were kind enough to help push it back onto the road. We can only imagine what excuse Miyazaki gave when he emerged from the pitch-black woods holding a sheet, but whatever it was seems to have worked, for he was soon on his way again—and there was to be a fourth victim in the not-too-distant future.

In the meantime, Miyazaki subjected Erika Namba's parents to another of his creepily silent phone calls and sent them a cryptic postcard that read, "ERIKA. COLD. COUGH. THROAT. REST. DEATH."

Then came a six-month period during which he refrained from killing again. Instead, Miyazaki immersed himself in the cartoonish world of manga and video games, in addition to watching hour after hour of pornographic video material and horror movies of the stalk-and-slash variety, further warping his view of humanity to the point where he could finally no longer tell the difference between living human beings and fictional characters. For Tsutomu Miyazaki, the murder of a little girl and defilement of her corpse held no more meaning than killing a character from one of the video games that he loved so much, or the hero of a manga comic book executing his nemesis. For him, there was no longer a line between reality and fantasy.

While the abductions and murders of multiple children had frightened many of Tokyo's parents and put the police on their guard, Miyazaki was still able to find opportunities to prey upon young girls. His victim on June 6, 1989, was five-year-old Ayako Nomoto, who was playing by herself in a park when he chanced upon her. Offering to take photographs of her, he lured the innocent child into his car and strangled her.

After taking Ayako's body back to his apartment, Miyazaki repeatedly had sex with it and took another series of photographs, posing the little girl's body in a variety of different

Miyazaki repeatedly preyed on girls as young as four years old, killing them and having sex with their corpses.

positions for his own personal gratification. In another break with his established MO, he videotaped this macabre process with a movie camera that he had rented expressly for that purpose.

As the body slowly started to decompose, he found it increasingly difficult to have intercourse with it. Deciding to dispose of Ayako's remains, Miyazaki set to work on dismembering the corpse. Up to this point, he had not engaged in any acts of cannibalism—unless one counts his eating the ashes of his grandfather. That changed when he decided to eat several chunks of the dead girl's body, after which he went on to drink some of her blood, which by now was almost three days old.

Ayako's decapitated head was tossed into the woods on a nearby hillside, while the remainder of her body was taken to a graveyard for disposal late one night. As the days passed, Tsutomu started to grow agitated, haunted by his decision to abandon the body parts relatively close to his home. He had gotten lazy, and alarm bells were ringing in his brain. Finally, two weeks after the murder, he could stand it no longer, and he went back to recover them. Bringing the now-rotting human remains back into his house seemed like a safer bet to him than leaving them for a member of the public to find, no matter how bad the smell had now become.

Unbeknownst to him, Tsutomu Miyazaki had just claimed his last victim. Time ran out for him on the 23rd of July. Whether he was completely divorced from reality or had simply grown overconfident after getting away with four murders, his abductions were becoming increasingly blatant. This time, he made the mistake of approaching two young girls together, both of whom were sisters. One of them was sufficiently frightened to run home and fetch her father, but the other went with Miyazaki to a nearby park. If her sister had not returned promptly with her dad in tow, she would undoubtedly have become victim number five. As it was, the enraged father reached her just in time to find Miyazaki in a state of undress, taking photographs of the girl without her underwear on. Justifiably enraged, he slammed the now-naked serial killer to the ground.

Never particularly capable at handling confrontations with those who were his physical equal, Miyazaki turned and fled. He was left with a significant problem, however; his car, which had been used as a convenient place to carry out previous murders and transport the body of his victims, was still sitting in the park where he had just molested the young girl. He knew that he couldn't just leave it there, but when he went back to pick it up, a squad of police officers were lying in wait for him.

The officers met no resistance from Miyazaki. After some preliminary questioning, detectives quickly realized that they had more than just a pedophile and a pervert on their hands. Over the course of the next few

Tsutomu Miyazaki was sentenced to death in 1997 and executed by hanging in 2008.

weeks, their suspect calmly confessed to being responsible for molesting and murdering four other young girls over the course of the past year. The seasoned police officers listened incredulously to stories of drinking blood, dismembering dead bodies, and even the ultimate taboos of cannibalism and necrophilia.

While it was hard for them to believe at first, some basic fact-checking soon bore out the horrific story. When police officers searched Miyazaki's residence, they found an extensive collection of pornographic material with thousands of videotapes and photographs, some of them featuring underage girls. Miyazaki also had a comprehensive library of gory horror movies and a significant amount of anime material. This led to one of the nicknames bestowed upon him by the media: the Otaku killer. *Otaku* is a Japanese term for somebody who has a passionate, borderline obsessive interest in subjects such as manga anime. A Western equivalent would be "nerd" or "geek."

It took close to eighteen years for the judicial process to be completed. Japanese culture places a great deal of emphasis on saving face, and the long, drawn-out trial and appeal process was particularly hard on Miyazaki's parents. Unable to bear the shame that his son had brought upon the family, Tsutomu's father ended up taking his own life.

Miyazaki's lawyer attempted to spare his client from execution by employing the insanity defense. Tsutomu claimed that he hadn't committed any of the murders himself. It was somebody else living inside him who was to blame, a personality that he referred to only as "the Rat Man." After an extensive evaluation, psychological experts concluded that while Tsutomu Miyazaki did indeed suffer from multiple personality disorder, he still understood the difference between right and wrong. In the eyes of the law, he was both competent to stand trial and guilty of his crimes. The judge sentenced him to death by hanging.

Miyazaki went to his death a completely unrepentant man, never once having accepted responsibility for his crimes or expressing remorse over the young lives he had taken. Nor did he apologize to the families of his victims—in fact, quite the opposite. He was a prolific correspondent while in prison, but his attitude toward the killings was summed up in one letter: "There's nothing much to say about them. I'm happy to think I did a good deed."

In another letter, he mused on the fact he was sentenced to be hanged: "Under the current execution method, death row inmates have to suffer great fear at the time of their execution, and therefore won't have a chance to feel regret for what they've done. For this reason, we should switch to lethal injections of the kind used in the United States."

Assuming that the translation of this letter is completely accurate, his turn of phrase is particularly interesting. Miyazaki describes Japanese death row inmates as "they" ("at the time of *their* execution"), but he then switches to "we" when talking about the system overall. It may suggest that he was in denial about his impending execution.

Tsutomu Miyazaki went to the hangman's scaffold on June 17, 2008. He was accompanied by two other men, both of whom had also been found guilty of committing multiple murders. He has gone down in the history books as one of the most warped serial murderers in Japanese history.

THE MILWAUKEE CANNIBAL: JEFFREY DAHMER

Nobody who knew him as a boy would ever have suspected that Jeffrey Dahmer, who was born in the Milwaukee suburb of West Allis on May 21, 1960, would grow up to torture, kill, decapitate, and then *eat* 17 victims.

By all accounts, there was none of the abuse, neglect, or trauma that characterizes the formative years of some serial killers. It was, if anything, an unremarkable childhood, albeit one spent with a slightly distant mother who didn't bond with her son as most mothers tend to do. Perhaps the only point of note was that Dahmer's parents fought often, with their quarrels finally reaching the point where they slept in separate bedrooms. Hardly the stuff of which nightmares are made, though.

Young Jeffrey Dahmer was fascinated with animal anatomy. While there are no reports that he ever tortured or killed any living creatures, he did like to carve dead specimens up and then bleach the bones. With hindsight, this may have been the first sign of his morbid fascination with death. His father, a Ph.D. in the physical sciences, encouraged his son's interest and often helped young Jeffrey develop his bleaching skills. He had no idea that, years later, those same skills would be applied to dead human beings.

Dahmer spent his high school years in Ohio, and while he only had a few friends, he was by no means reclusive. Reports show that he possessed above-average intelligence, was generally polite, and was a little socially awkward. He continued to dissect animals, only now, whenever he did so, he found that he became sexually aroused.

He also developed an addiction to alcohol, getting drunk at school almost every day. He struggled to come to terms with the fact that he was sexually attracted to other boys his age. Being a homosexual in the mid-1970s carried a huge stigma, particularly for a high-school teenager. This was doubly true in a place like Ohio, far from the bohemian cities on the East or West Coast. His only option was to try to suppress his sexual urges and fly under the radar—the alcohol may have been an attempt to do that, but if so, it really didn't help much.

At the age of 14 or 15, Dahmer's daydreams about having sex with other boys started to turn violent. He soon developed a taste for sado-masochism that only grew stronger with time. He didn't just want to have sex with men; he wanted to *hurt* them. To torture them.

But Dahmer needed a victim. It wasn't as though somebody was going to volunteer willingly. He would need to overpower one somehow, get him under his control, and keep him there. There was just the small matter of Jeffrey still living with his parents, which meant he had no private place in which to act out any of his depraved fantasies.

All that changed in 1978 when his parents split up, each of them moving out of the Dahmer household and leaving Jeffrey as the sole occupant.

Dahmer is shown here in his high school yearbook at age 17. By this time, he was already having fantasies of having sex with men and then torturing them.

Suddenly freed from parental oversight, the 18-year-old Dahmer began to drink more heavily. While making a liquor store run one day, he picked up a shirtless hitchhiker named Steven Hicks. The easygoing Hicks agreed to go home with Jeffrey for a few beers.

At first, all went well. After a few drinks, Hicks said he wanted to get back on the road. Dahmer didn't want him to leave. Hicks was insistent and made for the door. Dahmer snatched up a dumbbell. Hicks never even saw it coming. Ten pounds of cast iron struck Steven Hicks in the back of the head. He fell to the ground, dead.

This was a defining moment in Jeffrey Dahmer's life. He felt no sense of remorse at having taken a human life for the first time. After contemplating Steven Hicks's dead body for a while, he unzipped his pants and began to pleasure himself. He had realized part of his sickening fantasy: committing murder and, so far at least, getting away with it. All that was missing were the acts of sadistic torture, the idea of which had so greatly tantalized him. Those would come later.

For now, Jeffrey's attention was focused on the corpse that lay on the floor in front of him. He dragged Hicks's lifeless body into the bathroom and heaved it into the tub. After spending countless hours cutting up animal remains during his childhood, it now seemed only natural to him that he would do the same to a dead human being. He worked slowly and methodically, cutting the body open with great care and exposing various anatomical compartments and organs one by one. Dahmer not only found the process fascinating but also realized that it was a massive turn-on for him.

Once he was finished, Dahmer took the remnants of his twisted experiment down into the crawl space beneath the house and concealed them there. If his parents ever came back to visit, as they did occasionally, it was highly unlikely that they would ever go down there.

Steven Hicks's remains sat undiscovered for a few more weeks. Finally, realizing that they might be discovered at some future time, Dahmer used a strong acid solution to dissolve the bones and then pulverized the remnants with a hammer. He disposed of what was left in the woods.

> **D**ahmer's alcoholism soon began to degrade his job performance. He often showed up for duty drunk.

After enrolling in and quickly dropping out of college (his perpetually drunken state didn't help), Jeffrey had to make a living somehow. Finding little in the way of job prospects, he instead enlisted in the U.S. Army.

Following boot camp, Jeffrey underwent advanced training as a medic and shipped out to a base in Germany. While not exactly the life and soul of the platoon, on the surface Dahmer seemed to get along well with his fellow soldiers. Yet there were reports that he had assaulted and raped some of his fellow soldiers, accusations that either emerged long after they took place or were not taken seriously by command staff.

While it's difficult to procure alcohol during basic training, mostly because new recruits are under intense and constant scrutiny, conditions are usually somewhat more lax in the line units. Dahmer's alcoholism soon began to degrade his job performance. He often showed up for duty drunk. Before long, it was impossible for him to maintain even the basic appearance of professionalism. In the end, the army threw him out and shipped him back stateside.

He wound up in Florida. At first a warm and sunny paradise to him, Dahmer spent every spare moment getting drunk, funded by the last vestiges of his army pay. Once that was gone, he was evicted and forced to move back in with his father, who flatly refused to tolerate his drunken behavior. Hoping that a change of scenery might help the situation, Dahmer's father sent him off to Milwaukee, where his grandmother had a spare room available in her home. But things did not go quite as expected.

It quickly became apparent that Jeffrey's already borderline mental state was starting to unravel. A visit to the Wisconsin State Fair ended in his arrest for unzipping his pants and exposing himself to a crowd of horrified onlookers. Doubtless those who knew him wrote this off as being a symptom of Dahmer's worsening alcoholism, but in reality, it was a warning sign of far worse things to come.

He became a regular in several of Milwaukee's gay bars. Although he had no problems finding willing partners to have sex with, the act itself failed to satisfy Dahmer's lusts. It wasn't enough for him just to have intercourse; he wanted to inflict pain and suffering while he did it, to totally control everything that his partner—or, more accurately, his victim—said and did. For Jeffrey Dahmer, consent was the ultimate turnoff. Frustrated, he broke a store window and stole a mannequin, the sort that are used to display clothing outfits.

As strange as it may sound, in some ways, this new acquisition was the perfect sexual companion for him. Keeping it in his bedroom, he used it to help pleasure himself, enjoying the way that the dummy lay perfectly still and never talked back to him.

Nine years had gone by since Jeffrey Dahmer had committed his first murder. In interviews given after his capture, he would claim that he had spent those years trying to control the perverse desires that ended up taking him over. Whether that is true or not, on November 20, 1987, he finally gave in to those murderous impulses.

As with many serial killers, Dahmer could be charming when he wanted to be, and he used that charm on Steven Tuomi, whom he picked up in a gay bar and took back to a room in one of Milwaukee's higher-end hotels. We only have Dahmer's word for what happened that night, but he spoke very candidly during interviews while in prison and had no reason to lie. According to Dahmer, once the two of them went to the hotel, Jeffrey's goal was to drug Tuomi and then molest him while he slept; it was never, he maintained, to kill him. Nonetheless, that's exactly what happened. When Dahmer sobered up

Dahmer became a regular at gay bars, and although he had no trouble finding sex partners, hooking up did not satisfy his lust for violence.

sometime the following morning, the sheets were soaked with Tuomi's blood. Based upon the signs of blunt force trauma visible upon the body, Dahmer guessed that he must have battered his victim to death at some point in the middle of the night.

He had killed for the second time in his life. It would not be the last.

Now, Dahmer found himself with a problem: he was stuck in a hotel room with a dead body. He couldn't leave it to be discovered; his name and personal contact details were on file with the registration desk. No, Dahmer decided, he needed to move Tuomi's body somewhere more secure, where he could dispose of it in privacy. After mulling it over, he finally hit on the idea of buying the biggest suitcase he could find and bundling the corpse inside it. Dahmer was in decent shape, but there's a reason for the term "dead weight." Straining with the exertion, he manhandled the suitcase out of the room, down the hallway, and into the street outside, where he hailed a taxicab and loaded it into the trunk. One can only imagine how the poor cab driver would have reacted if he had known about the grisly contents of the case, but there was no reason for him to suspect that anything strange was afoot—unless the bowels and bladder are voided, it usually takes a few hours for a corpse to start emitting any kind of discernible odor.

After paying the taxi driver, Jeffrey carried the suitcase into the house, taking care not to wake his sleeping grandmother. Once he got it down to the basement and closed the door behind him, he felt elated. He was going to get away with it again.

Unzipping the suitcase, he rolled its contents onto the floor. The sight excited him so much that he repeated what he had done with the remains of Steven Hicks, first masturbating over them and then getting down on the floor to quietly lay alongside them. This time, however, he went a step further and had intercourse with the body before chopping it up and disposing of it. Once again, his fascination with anatomy and dissection came to the fore. Secure in the privacy of his grandmother's basement, Dahmer lingered over the body parts for hours before he finally threw them out—apart from the head, which he intended to keep as a trophy and masturbatory aid. The head was boiled in a bleach solution and stored in a closet in his bedroom until it became brittle, causing him to throw it out.

Two months later, Dahmer killed again. This time, his victim was a 14-year-old male prostitute named James Doxtator. He was hanging around outside one of the gay bars that Dahmer frequented and agreed to go back with him to his grandmother's house in order to have sex and pose for some naked photographs. The older man promised Doxtator that he would be well paid for his trouble.

> Secure in the privacy of his grandmother's basement, Dahmer lingered over the body parts for hours before he finally threw them out—apart from the head.

Although it seemed risky to bring a potential victim home while his unsuspecting grandmother went about her everyday business upstairs, that's exactly what Jeffrey did, quietly sneaking the teenager downstairs into the house. Drunk and drugged, Doxtator was incapable of putting up a fight when Dahmer strangled him. Dahmer had sex with the corpse, much preferring its flat affect and total compliance to that of a living, breathing person. After the dismembered body spent a week down in the basement, Dahmer disposed of it in the same way as he had the others.

Gay bars proved to be a target-rich environment for Jeffrey Dahmer. He began to develop a characteristic MO. First, he would use his charm to ingratiate himself with a young man; next, he would lure them to a private place with promises of money, sex, and alcohol; and then murder them before having sex with their corpse.

Things did not always go smoothly. One of the victims, Ronald Flowers Jr., was taken in by Dahmer's offer to fetch a car that could be used to jumpstart his own car's dead battery. Once they were both back at Dahmer's place, he succumbed to the drug-laced coffee that was given to him, but before Dahmer began to strangle him, his grandmother's voice interrupted him, calling out that Jeffrey wasn't permitted to have visitors over at the house so late at night. Rather than run the risk of discovery by going through with the murder, he took the semicomatose young man to a nearby hospital's emergency department instead, where he woke up the following day, covered in bruises and with his underwear turned inside out.

He had greater success with Richard Guerrero, 22, whom he met in a gay club, brought home, then strangled with a leather belt. Dahmer performed fellatio on Guerrero's dead body, cut it up into several parts, and tossed out everything except the head.

Finally, Jeffrey's grandmother ran out of patience. The basement was beginning to stink, and the constant stream of young men accompanying her grandson home finally got to be too much. Jeffrey was no longer even bothering to hide the fact that he was bringing them back to her house. The tensions with his grandmother resulted in Dahmer moving out of her house and getting an apartment of his own. Free from any kind of oversight, his pathologic behavior, exacerbated by his chronic drinking problem, grew even worse. He came to the attention of the police after luring a 13-year-old boy back to his apartment and drugging and groping him. Before Dahmer could harm him further, the teenager left his apartment and went home. He came back with a police escort.

The trial was short and conviction came quickly. It was January 1989, and it looked as if the game was finally up for Jeffrey Dahmer, but the police investigation uncovered no trace of his murderous activities. Sentencing would take several months. While he was waiting, Dahmer moved back in with his grandmother. Rather than keep his nose clean, he instead took the opportunity to kill again.

Twenty-four-year-old Anthony Sears was the latest to fall for Dahmer's "cash for nude photos" scam. Quietly sneaking his latest conquest back into his bedroom while his grandmother slept upstairs, Dahmer had sex with him and then took his life. He disposed of the body in the usual way, keeping the head and genitalia as trophies. Rather than risk leaving them at home, he took them to work and secured them in his personal locker. He was employed at a chocolate factory at the time.

Dahmer received a surprisingly light sentence for committing sexual assault on a child, which would see him committed into a work release program for one year. In addition, he was placed on parole for five years, and his name was entered into the Register of Sex Offenders. He went to work during the daytime, reported back to the prison at night, and kept his nose clean enough for the next ten months that he was able to petition the judge for early release.

> **I**t was January 1989, and it looked as if the game was finally up for Jeffrey Dahmer, but the police investigation uncovered no trace of his murderous activities.

One of the benefits of serving ten months in jail while simultaneously working full time was that there was little to spend his money on. Jeffrey had socked away enough cash to get himself a new apartment, this one a little closer to his place of employment. It wasn't the nicest or safest of neighborhoods, and when the full extent of his crimes finally came to light, Jeffrey Dahmer would put the area surrounding 924 N. 25th Street, Apartment #213, on the map for all the wrong reasons.

He spent the first week scoping out and growing accustomed to his new environment. Dahmer soon felt comfortable enough to retrieve the head and genitals of Anthony Sears from his locker at the chocolate factory and bring them home. Then it was time to find a new victim.

At 32 years of age, Raymond Smith was older than the others Dahmer had targeted thus far. Smith was a prostitute, and he willingly came back to #213 for sex. Dahmer then strangled him and, once he was dead, took photographs of the body in a series of different positions.

His body disposal MO was beginning to change. Rather than simply dismember the corpse, pulverize the bones, and either scatter the remains outdoors or put them out with the trash, Dahmer instead immersed the body in acid, with the intent of dissolving as much of it as possible. He kept the skull, placing it next to that of Anthony Sears. He would regularly stand in front of the two and admire them side by side.

One month later, in June 1990, he murdered Edward Smith, 27, and froze the remains. Dahmer was beginning to conduct bizarre experiments on his victims after their deaths and was still taking a perverse sexual interest in

Dahmer would often use a sleeping pill concoction to subdue his victims before strangling them.

the dissection and dismemberment process, trying out a number of different methods for preserving the skulls.

Usually, Dahmer prepared a concoction of sleeping pills before heading out to hunt his next victim. It would be ready and waiting when they both came back to Apartment #213; these pills made strangling the victim much easier for him. In the case of Ernest Miller, 22, Dahmer had gotten just a little too lax. The drug mixture was too weak and failed to adequately subdue him. Dahmer improvised, slashing Miller's neck with a knife and restraining him until he bled to death.

Jeffrey then removed the dead man's heart and set it aside. He was about to venture into an even uglier realm: that of cannibalism. Dahmer indulged in a long-held fantasy taboo, beginning to eat chunks of Ernest Miller's heart. His biceps, which Dahmer had found particularly attractive, were also treated as food. After he was caught and interviewed, he explained that eating the muscles and organs of his victims made him "feel they were a part of me." The skull went alongside the others. Dahmer took to painting them in order to make them look more decorative.

Now, killing the men he brought home, having sexual intercourse with the corpses, and then eating parts of them was no longer enough for him. Yes, he was able to murder them into a state of compliance—no thrashing, struggling, or movement of any kind—but Jeffrey Dahmer craved more. He wanted total control over his victims, and the more he thought about it, the more he came to believe that what he wanted wasn't a dead victim at all—it was a living, breathing slave, one whose mind and will were completely subservient to his own. In other words, he needed to create a zombie.

Dahmer kept on killing throughout 1991, and he kept on getting away with it. He was growing overly confident, and his mental state was starting to deteriorate even faster. After overcoming one victim, Errol Lindsey, 19, he drilled a hole in the man's head and introduced hydrochloric acid into it. This did not have the anticipated effect. Rather than render the young man into the submissive slave that Dahmer so desperately craved, or even kill him outright, the acid did little more than make him wake up with a severe headache. A frustrated Dahmer strangled Lindsey and disposed of his body in the usual manner. It was time to go back to the drawing board.

Even under the best of circumstances, cutting up a corpse isn't exactly a quiet process. It wasn't long before Jeffrey's neighbors started to complain about the odd noises coming from Apartment #213. Then there was the stench: it was starting to smell as if something had died in there. Dahmer made a series of vague excuses to the building manager, tales of broken freezers and dead pets that averted suspicion—for a while, at least. In order to mitigate the smell, he purchased an industrial-sized drum filled with hydrochloric acid to help break down the moldering body parts.

Things finally started to fall apart for Dahmer when he targeted a 14-year-old boy named Konerak Sinthasomphone, whom he saw in the street while he was out taking a walk. In a cruel twist of fate, Dahmer's victim was the brother of a boy he had sexually assaulted three years earlier, although there is no way that Konerak could have known of Dahmer's identity.

Completely taken in by the serial killer's charming facade, the police officers canceled the ambulance that was already on its way to the scene.

After slipping his victim a spiked drink that rendered him unconscious, Dahmer repeatedly raped him. Once again, he drilled a hole in the helpless boy's head and injected hydrochloric acid directly into his brain. Then, apparently in need of a drink or two, the serial killer locked his apartment and decided to hit one of his favorite gay bars. He had mis-judged the potency of the sedatives that he had given to the young man, how-ever, and when he got back home a few hours later, Dahmer found himself answering to the police.

Two women had found Konerak Sinthasomphone staggering through the streets, naked and rambling. Although he had several scrapes on his body, of greatest concern was the blood that streamed from his anus. Jeffrey went into full damage control mode with the cops, ratcheting up the charm and explaining that the 14-year-old boy was in fact his 19-year-old lover.

This should have been the end of Jeffrey Dahmer's reign of terror. After responding to the scene, police officers quickly separated them both to get their side of the story. Konerak was borderline incoherent, but Dahmer smoothly explained that away by claiming that he'd just had a few drinks too many. Completely taken in by the serial killer's charming facade, the police officers canceled the ambulance that was already on its way to the scene. Had they just allowed the paramedics to conduct a medical assessment, it is almost certain that the boy would have been taken to the hospital, where the reason for his altered mental status—almost certainly brain damage, secondary to the hydrochloric acid—would have been found.

As it was, the police officers went along with Dahmer's cover story, taken in by his claim that this was just a domestic dispute between two homo-sexual men. They gave Dahmer's apartment a cursory look and failed to find anything suspicious about the strange background smell or the nude photographs of Konerak that were scattered about the place. Had they made any kind of thorough search, they would almost certainly have found skulls and other body parts. Finally, over the objections of the women who had discovered Konerak in the street, they handed him over to Jeffrey Dahmer once more and cleared the scene. In doing so, they effectively signed his death warrant.

Once the door to Apartment #213 was closed and locked behind him, Jeffrey Dahmer set out to finish what he had started. He injected a second dose of hydrochloric acid into the same hole he had already drilled in the boy's skull. This time, the injection was lethal, leaving Dahmer with yet another body to dispose of. The cops had nearly gotten him, but rather than being terrified at the possibility of discovery and capture, his narrow escape served only to further excite Dahmer. This near-miss did nothing to stop him from killing again, but it *did* make him a little more cautious about picking up men and boys locally. He decided to snare his next victim a little further from home.

Chicago's annual Gay Pride festival and parade was huge, attracting tens of thousands of people each year. Jeffrey took the two-hour bus ride with the intention of getting drunk, having a good time, and enticing a fresh prospect back to Milwaukee with him. Despite his best efforts, however, none of the men he met at the parade were willing to take him up on his offer. Dejected, Dahmer went back to the bus station, where he met Matt Turner, 20. Dahmer promised Turner photo shoots at Dahmer's apartment in exchange for money. What awaited Turner, of course, was death. Dahmer killed him, then stored his organs and head in the freezer, alongside the frozen, decapitated head of Konerak Sinthasomphone.

Less than a week later, Jeffrey went back to Chicago in search of another victim—this time Jeremiah Weinberger, 23. Unlike most of the men Dahmer killed after he'd spent some time having sex with them, Weinberger survived the first night in Apartment #213. The day after, when he told Dahmer he wanted to go home, the serial killer mixed up another of his potent knockout cocktails. This time, once his victim was rendered unconscious—Dahmer proved it to his satisfaction by raping him—he injected boiling water into the young man's brain. He had given up on the hydrochloric acid at this point and hoped that injecting something "cleaner" would have the effect he sought—turning Weinberger into a zombie.

Needless to say, it did nothing of the sort. Instead, the hot water caused widespread brain damage, rendering Jeremiah Weinberger completely catatonic. Dahmer lost his patience two days later and killed him.

He continued to kill throughout 1991. As more body parts, muscles, and organs went into the refrigerator and freezer, Dahmer turned increasingly toward cannibalism. Just as it had in the army, his increasingly erratic behavior eventually got him fired from his job at the chocolate factory. Dahmer didn't care. Being without a job just gave him that much more time to stalk, kill, and dismember more men. He was working on a macabre shrine that was composed of the skulls and assorted bones of his various victims. His refrigerator and acid-filled industrial drum, which he used to break down torsos and other leftover body parts, were beginning to get crowded.

On the night of July 22, Jeffrey used the tried-and-tested offer of cash for naked pictures and managed to coax 32-year-old Tracy Edwards back to his apartment. As soon as the door closed behind him, alarm bells began going off for Edwards. The place stank to high heaven, and something just seemed terribly off-kilter. Before the hapless Edwards knew what was going on, Dahmer had locked a handcuff about his wrist and began brandishing a knife.

> As more body parts, muscles, and organs went into the refrigerator and freezer, Dahmer turned increasingly toward cannibalism.

"I'm going to eat your heart," Dahmer told him matter-of-factly. Edwards believed him. Knowing that he was in the presence of somebody who was, at the very least, mentally unhinged, he decided to play it cool and bide his time, waiting for the perfect opportunity to escape. That time came when his captor was momentarily distracted. Edwards punched him in the face as hard as he possibly could, then lunged for the door. Making for the street, he flagged down the first police cruiser he encountered.

Had Jeffrey Dahmer possessed any kind of survival instinct whatsoever, now would have been the time to flee. He did not. Instead, he waited calmly until Tracy Edwards returned to his apartment in the company of two police officers. One of the cops asked where the key to the handcuffs locked around Edwards's wrist could be found. Responding that it was in his bedroom, the serial killer stood docilely by while one of them went to go find it. He returned moments later clutching a handful of Polaroids, all of which had clearly been taken in that very same apartment. They documented scenes of utter carnage, human bodies in various states of dissection and dismemberment. Just from looking at them, the experienced police officers could tell that the photographs were authentic.

Now that the game was up, Dahmer tried to fight back. It was too late. The officers overpowered him easily. Now it was Jeffrey Dahmer's turn be placed in handcuffs against his will. One of the officers kept him pinned to the ground while his partner called for backup and started to search the apartment. What he found in the refrigerator nearly made him throw up: a decapitated human head looking back at him with sightless eye sockets. At long last, Jeffrey Dahmer's killing spree was at an end.

Dahmer made no attempt to hide the nature of his crimes. Now that forensic investigators were searching his apartment and cataloging every grue-

Dahmer's 1991 mug shot taken at the Milwaukee Police Department.

some discovery they made there, what was the point in him telling more lies? Dahmer offered up a full confession, admitting to all of the murders and to sodomizing the victims both before their death and afterward, then gave graphic details of how he had attempted to create zombie sex slaves and his techniques for disposing of the human remains.

He confessed to a total of seventeen killings—his first murder, that of Steven Hicks, in Ohio, and sixteen more after he moved to Milwaukee. He held nothing back, sharing everything with the horrified homicide detectives down to the last nauseating detail. There was absolutely no question of his guilt. When it came to the trial, the issue was never: "Was Jeffrey Dahmer innocent or guilty?" It was: "Is Jeffrey Dahmer criminally insane?" In other words, was he capable of understanding the nature of his crimes, and could he ever have stopped himself from doing what he did? Was he sick … or simply *evil?*

The insanity defense didn't wash with the jury, who found Dahmer guilty on sixteen counts (he would later be tried separately for the single murder he had committed in Ohio). They believed the argument put forward by the prosecution that he knew exactly what he was doing and, despite his depraved and twisted nature, knew the difference between right and wrong—and deliberately chose wrong. The same thing happened in Ohio, where a seventeenth murder conviction was added to the rest. Jeffrey Dahmer was sentenced to just short of 1,000 years behind bars. Rather than a relatively more comfortable state mental health hospital, he would serve out his time in a maximum-security prison.

During his time as an inmate, Dahmer underwent what he claimed to be a religious conversion, adopting the faith of Christianity. It should be borne in mind that he had always been a master manipulator and was never above using his charm and charisma to get what he wanted. We will never know how genuine his remorse and desire for forgiveness truly were.

Some people felt that life in prison wasn't nearly sufficient punishment for Jeffrey Dahmer, believing that the only fitting response was for him to be put to death. The death penalty hadn't been a sentencing option for the judges at the conclusion of either of his murder trials. Those people would get their wish on November 28, 1994, however, when a fellow inmate bludgeoned

Dahmer spent the final years of his life at the Columbia Correctional Institution and was murdered by a fellow inmate in 1994.

Dahmer repeatedly about the head with an iron metal bar. Another prisoner on the same work detail got similar treatment. Despite the efforts of medical providers, Jeffrey Dahmer died in the hospital shortly afterward due to massive brain trauma—an eerie synchronicity, when one considers the damage he had inflicted upon the brains of some of his victims.

After the cremation of his body, Jeffrey Dahmer's ashes were divided up evenly between his mother and father, for disposal or retention, however they saw fit. The few material things he possessed were destroyed or buried to keep them out of the hands of ghoulish collectors. For the same reason, the apartment building in which he had committed so many murders was also demolished. As much of his physical legacy as possible was methodically wiped out.

Yet Dahmer's place in the public consciousness lives on. He has appeared in books, movies, TV documentaries, and even comic books. Few serial killers have engendered such a macabre fascination as the man dubbed by the media "the Milwaukee Cannibal." There are many possible reasons for this, but the most likely seems to be that Jeffrey Dahmer broke two of the ultimate taboos: he engaged in sex with the dead and then ate their flesh. Few things have the ability to disgust to the extent that necrophilia and cannibalism do, and to think of them taking place in the heart of a modern-day American city is enough to make even the most hardened person's skin crawl.

KILLER AT LARGE:
THE ZODIAC

With the obvious exception of Jack the Ripper, few serial killers have struck fear into as many people as the Zodiac Killer has. Indeed, there are several close parallels between the two men.

Each enjoyed taunting the authorities, sending written correspondence (and in the Zodiac's case, making phone calls) to the media, providing information about the murders that only the killer could possibly have known.

Each loved to outwit the detectives who were hunting him, often by offering up information in a hidden form. Part of the Ripper's modus operandi was his use of certain cryptic phrases, such as "The Juwes are the men that will not be blamed for nothing," which was found painted on a wall close to one of the murder sites. To this day, Ripper experts still debate its meaning.

The Zodiac Killer, on the other hand, preferred to send encrypted messages, which required significant time and mental effort to decode. At least one of those codes remains unbroken more than forty years later.

Neither man claimed a particularly large number of confirmed victims, although in each case, the exact number of victims is unclear. Jack the Ripper is believed to have murdered somewhere between five and eleven people; Zodiac is known to have killed five, with an additional two victims surviving their ordeal at his hands, but if the killer's claims are correct, he may actually be responsible for up to thirty-seven murders in total.

Despite the relatively small (in comparison to some other serial killers) number of victims attributed to each of them, both the Ripper and Zodiac occupy a disproportionately prominent place in the public consciousness even today. The reason for this is simple: we still don't know who they were, and there is no guarantee that we ever will.

It was five days before Christmas Day of 1968. To the people of Benicia and nearby Vallejo, California, one particular turnoff on Lake Herman Road was well known as the kind of place where young couples would go to make out. It was dark and isolated enough to afford them a little privacy, set well away from prying eyes. Usually, when two star-crossed lovers wanted to get to know one another a little better, that kind of privacy was a good thing.

David Faraday, 17, and Betty Lou Jensen, 16, however, would prove to be a tragic exception to the rule. Their first date was also their last and marked the first appearance of the Zodiac Killer.

Sometime between ten and eleven o'clock that night, a man approached their parked car in his own vehicle, pulled up alongside their station wagon, then got out and opened fire on the two unsuspecting teenagers. Faraday was shot once, just above the left ear. Jensen was hit five times in her back on the right side, then twice more from the front.

Both victims had gotten out of the car, probably having been forced out at gunpoint. Faraday was shot while just a few feet away from the passenger door. He would be pronounced dead on arrival shortly after an ambulance crew transported him to a nearby hospital. His date for the evening, Betty Lou, had made it some twenty-eight feet from the car before dying, most likely shot while she fled, and was then finished off at the killer's leisure.

> **Their first date was also their last and marked the first appearance of the Zodiac Killer.**

The homicide detectives working for the Solano County Sheriff's Department were aware that the majority of murder victims tend to have some kind of personal tie to their killer, so that's where they started. One promising avenue of inquiry, a bitter and jealous ex-boyfriend of Betty Lou's, turned out to be a dead end when the boy in question had a cast-iron alibi. Both Betty Lou Jensen and David Faraday were clean-cut American kids without any known criminal connections or shady history. Who could possibly have wanted either of them dead?

As the investigation went on, the motives behind the double homicide remained completely opaque. No cash or personal items had been stolen from either victim. Neither victim had been sexually molested. Although a number of passersby had reported seeing an unoccupied white car parked in the vicinity of Lake Herman Road that night, nobody was able to identify the driver.

Unbeknownst to the detectives working the case, the deaths of Jensen and Faraday heralded the first known appearance of a serial killer—one who would eventually go by the nickname Zodiac. Based upon ballistic tests conducted by the police department, it was determined that the Zodiac's weapon of choice was almost certainly a .22-caliber handgun.

When seven months passed without further incident, talk turned to other things. The double murder was written off as an inexplicable tragedy, and few people gave it much thought—until the killer struck again.

Summer had arrived, bringing with it the hot, sunny weather for which the San Francisco Bay area is well known. It was July 4, 1969, and waitress Darlene Ferrin, 22, was taking a drive with a male companion, Mike Mageau, 19. They found themselves a secluded spot, which happened to be just a few miles away from the scene of the first two murders, at a place called Blue Rock Springs. Another Independence Day was coming to an end, with the clock reading just a few minutes before midnight. Another car pulled up close to them, switched off its lights, and just sat there, its driver presumably watching them. Then it drove off.

> He used a powerful hand-held flashlight to light up the interior of Darlene's car. Then he opened fire.

A few minutes later, it returned—at least, Mike Mageau *believed* it to be the same car. This time, its occupant got out, approaching their vehicle on foot. He used a powerful hand-held flashlight to light up the interior of Darlene's car. Then he opened fire.

Darlene and Mike were both hit several times. Satisfied that his work was done, the shooter walked away. Unfortunately, Mike was unable to contain a cry of pain, which caused their assailant to return and put two more bullets into each of them.

As the shooter took off again, Mike lay on the ground, bleeding heavily from multiple gunshot wounds. He had tried desperately to escape but only made it a few feet before collapsing. Darlene hadn't even made it out. By the time emergency medical services providers got them both to the hospital, she had died; Mike, miraculously, would pull through and go on to describe their assailant to the police.

According to Mike, the man who had killed Darlene and tried to do the same to him was 5' 8" tall, beefy—though not fat—and somewhere around 26 to 30 years of age.

In the aftermath of the first murder, little was known about the killer. He seemed content to have simply gotten away with it, hanging back and avoiding the police. Now he seemed to have gained confidence, as a telephone call some thirty minutes after he had shot Darlene and Mike was to prove. An incredulous 911 Vallejo Police Department dispatcher named Nancy Slover listened as a male caller claimed to have killed "two kids in a brown car." In addition to providing the location, the caller also revealed that they had been shot with a nine-millimeter Luger. "I also killed those kids last year," he went on, before finishing with an eerie "Goodbye." With a click, the line went dead.

More than forty years later, Nancy Slover could still recall the Zodiac's voice. She described it as having been monotone in pitch, sounding as if he was reading a speech that had been rehearsed in advance.

> In the aftermath of the first murder, little was known about the killer. He seemed content to have simply gotten away with it, hanging back and avoiding the police.

When the call was finally traced, the phone booth from which it had been made turned out to be just a mile away from the police station. Clearly, the caller enjoyed the idea of playing games with the authorities. However, the killer was also unaware that one of his victims had survived.

Detectives tracked down every lead they could find, but once again, each one of them ultimately led nowhere. The trail was going cold, but just as it began to seem that the investigation had completely stalled, a series of envelopes arrived in the mail rooms of three newspapers, all of which were located in the San Francisco Bay region.

Each letter had been mailed on the 31st of July. They contained intimate details of the two shooting incidents, details that could only be known by somebody who had been present at the time—or somebody with insider knowledge of the ongoing investigation. This included the type of ammunition used, the position of the victims' bodies, and the number of shots that were fired.

The unidentified author of the letters went on to introduce an intriguing twist. Each of the three letters contained a coded cipher, which, he claimed, contained the secret to his identity. These ciphers were to be printed on the front page of each of the three newspapers no later than Friday afternoon (August 1), or else, he wrote:

> I will go on a kill rampage fry [Friday] night. I will cruise around all weekend killing lone people in the night, then move on to kill again until I end up with a dozen people over the weekend.

Rather than a signature, the letters ended with an image: a circle surrounding a set of crosshairs.

While it was theoretically possible that the letters had been written by a crank, it was clear that they had been written by *somebody* with inside knowledge of the crimes. The bottom line was that the police dared not run the risk of angering the killer, so the ciphers ran in each of the newspapers—but not on time. One paper printed its cipher on Friday, another on Saturday, and the last waited until its Sunday edition. Despite this, the threat of a murderous rampage never materialized. Either the killer was mollified by the newspaper coverage, or he had never intended to make good on his threat in the first place.

Now that the ciphers were out there in the public domain, everybody with an interest took a crack at decoding them. This ranged from professional agencies that broke ciphers on a regular basis to talented amateur code breakers working from their own homes. Incredibly, it wasn't the pros who made the great breakthrough—it was a couple named Donald and Bettye Harden.

The Hardens were able to decrypt what is now known as the 408 cipher (so named because it contains 408 symbols). When the police put all three parts of the cipher together

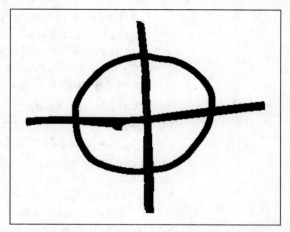

Instead of signing a name, the Zodiac Killer ended his letters with a crosshair symbol.

and decoded them, they found that the author—surprise, surprise—had lied about his identity being part of the revealed message. What they found instead was an insight into a truly sick and twisted mind.

I like killing people because it is so much fun. It is more fun than killing wild game in the forest because the man is the most dangerous animal of all. To kill something gives me the most thrilling experience. It is even better than getting your rocks off with a girl. The best part of it is that when I die I will be reborn in paradise and all that I have killed will become my slaves. I will not give you my name because you will try to slow down or stop my collecting of slaves for my afterlife.

Until now, the killer had no identity and little in the way of a description. A handwritten letter sent to the *San Francisco Examiner* on August 4 changed at least part of that. It began:

Dear Editor,

This is the Zodiac speaking.

And just like that, the predator who had been stalking the Bay area, killing victims at random, had been given a name.

The letter went on to describe specific details of the attack on Darlene Ferrin and Mike Mageau, and it even answered some open questions about the murders of David Faraday and Betty Lou Jensen, including how he had been able to hit his victims with accuracy on such a dark night.

What I did was tape a small pencil flashlight to the barrel of my gun. If you notice in the center of the beam of light, if you aim it at a wall or ceiling, you will see a black or dark spot in the center of the circle of light approximately 3 to 6 inches across. When taped to a gun barrel, the bullet will strike exactly in the center of the black dot in the light. All I had to do was spray them as if it was a water hose. There was no need to use a gun-sight. I was not happy to see that I did not get front page coverage.

Already, the Zodiac's desire to make the headlines was beginning to rear its head.

On September 27, the Zodiac struck again, and this time, he would change his MO slightly. He picked the scenic Lake Berryessa, Napa County's biggest lake, and once again, his victims were a relatively young couple— Cecelia Shepard, 22, and her companion, Bryan Hartnell, just 20. They had parked their car quite some distance away from the shore before walking down to a knoll that had a great view. As they were enjoying an evening picnic and the pleasure of each other's company, they noticed a man approaching them.

The couple knew immediately that something was wrong. *Very* wrong. The man's head was concealed beneath a black hood, with clip-on sunglasses

The Zodiac attacked a young couple near the scenic Lake Berryessa in Napa County. Incredibly, one of the two survived multiple stab wounds and lived to tell the tale.

covering his eyes. Emblazoned on his chest was a set of white crosshairs surrounded by a circle—the sign of the Zodiac killer.

Most worryingly of all, the man was armed with a handgun, which was aimed squarely in their direction.

The hooded man claimed to be an escaped convict, now on the run after killing a prison guard in Montana. If they did everything that he said, everything was going to be fine. He needed their vehicle to make good his escape by crossing the border into Mexico.

Unfortunately, this turned out to be nothing more than a cruel ruse to keep his victims from panicking. Handing Cecelia a short length of clothesline, the Zodiac covered her with his pistol while she bound Bryan's hands behind his back. Within minutes, both were face down on the ground and hog-tied, completely helpless in the face of what happened next.

Up until then, the Zodiac had killed exclusively with firearms. Holstering the .45-caliber pistol, he pulled out a long knife and began stabbing Bryan repeatedly in the back.

After stabbing Bryan six times, the killer started on Cecelia. Tied up and prone, his victims could do nothing but scream as they endured the savage assault. Despite her best efforts to escape, twisting and rolling as much as her bound hands and legs would allow, the Zodiac stabbed Cecelia ten times, half in the front of her body and half in the back. Mercifully, she soon lost consciousness.

For his part, Bryan knew that his one chance to survive was to play dead. Despite having suffered horrific wounds, he managed to stay quiet and limp. Apparently satisfied that he had dispatched both of his victims, the killer walked away.

After a park ranger found them, police officers soon descended upon the scene, but the Zodiac was long gone. Incredibly, both Cecelia and Bryan were still alive and were able to recount what had happened to them in considerable detail. Along with this came a description of the killer, which was of little practical use considering the precautions that he had taken to conceal his identity. The best they could come up with was that he had been at least six feet tall and weighed around 200 pounds.

Unbeknownst to the officers who had responded to Lake Berryessa, while they were desperately trying to render first aid to both victims, the man responsible was standing in a phone booth, speaking to a police dispatcher. It was 7:40 P.M., just over an hour after the attack.

"I want to report a murder," said an eerie male voice, before the speaker corrected himself. "No, a *double* murder." After describing the victims' vehicle and giving the location, the man closed with: "I'm the one who did it."

The description exactly matched Bryan Hartnell's Volkswagen. When detectives examined the vehicle, they found the crosshairs symbol of the Zodiac drawn on the passenger side door in black ink. Beneath it were scrawled the words:

VALLEJO
12-20-68
7-4-69
SEPT 27-69-6:30
BY KNIFE.

The meaning was clear. The killer was listing his first two crimes, followed by the date, time, and weapon of the attempted murder that he had committed the same night. If the similarity between the three crimes hadn't made it clear that they had been committed by the same perpetrator, this message spelled it out, quite literally, in black and white.

Detectives saw that a pattern was starting to develop. The Zodiac liked to target couples who were enjoying a little alone time in isolated, out-of-the-way areas. The reason behind the switch from a gun to a knife was still unclear. He may simply have felt like changing things up. Some speculated that the killer didn't want to attract attention by firing a pistol. It is every bit as likely, however, that the knife was chosen to appease the killer's sadistic streak. Quite often, it takes longer for a victim to die from knife wounds than from gunshots. In this case, both Bryan and Cecelia made it to the hospital alive. Bryan ultimately survived the ordeal, but Cecelia succumbed to her injuries two days later, dying in the hospital.

The note written on the door of Bryan Hartnell's Volkswagen.

The fourth attack took place two weeks later, on October 11, and saw yet another change in the Zodiac's behavior. This time, the Zodiac's target of opportunity wasn't a young couple but rather a lone taxicab driver named Paul Stine. Instead of staking out an isolated country road, the killer became more brazen, choosing a location right in the heart of San Francisco. The unsuspecting driver was shot in the head at close range by his fare, never knowing that he had picked up a serial killer that night.

Watching from the window of a house across the street, several teenagers failed to witness the murder itself but did see enough suspicious activity to make them call the police. They saw a man cleaning the inside of a parked taxicab, and at one point they thought that the driver's head may have been in his lap. It looked to them as if a robbery was in progress.

By the time the first police unit arrived, the suspect—a white male in his 20s or 30s—was gone, having disappeared on foot. While wiping down the interior of his murder scene, the Zodiac also took the time to cut off a blood-soaked piece of Paul Stine's shirt. The witnesses described the killer as being a stocky white male with a crew cut, who also wore glasses.

Crime scene photographs clearly show the cab driver's body sprawled across the passenger-side seat, with his arms and head extending out through the open door. A careful search of the taxi revealed one spent casing from a nine-millimeter handgun, a pair of leather gloves from an unidentified owner, and what may have been the Zodiac's bloody fingerprint.

With no hood to obscure his features this time, the Zodiac's face now appeared in the form of a police sketch artist's depiction. Flyers were sent out far and wide. He responded via another letter, this time to the *San Francisco Chronicle*. When the envelope was opened, the small piece of Paul Stine's shirt, stained with dried blood, fell out.

The murderer who became known as the Zodiac Killer was described as a man in his late twenties, having a heavy build but not fat, a crew cut, and wearing glasses as shown in this sketch artist's depiction.

After admitting to killing Stine and offering up a few smug tips as to how the San Francisco Police Department could have caught him on the night of the murder, the handwritten letter concluded with another horrific threat:

> Schoolchildren make nice targets. Okay, I think I shall wipe out a school bus some morning. Just shoot out the front tires and then pick off the kiddies as they come bouncing out.

The writer signed off with the by now-familiar Zodiac crosshairs.

Although the Zodiac never made good on his threat in real life, it *did* play out on thousands of cinema screens around the world. The crimes of Scorpio, the antagonist in the 1971 Clint Eastwood thriller *Dirty Harry*, are based heavily on those of the Zodiac. The movie culminates in a confrontation between Eastwood's Detective Harry Callahan and the Scorpio killer, as portrayed by Andrew Robinson, on a hijacked school bus, and helped firmly cement the Zodiac case in the public consciousness. It is also, one suspects, a major case of wish fulfillment.

Another cipher was mailed to the *San Francisco Chronicle* in November. This 340-character cipher has not, at the time of writing, been decoded, despite the best efforts of hundreds of people and some extremely advanced computer software. A second letter followed the next day, this one longer and rambling. In it, the Zodiac accepted responsibility for seven murders so far (recall that not all of the victims of his known attacks actually died) and taunted the "blue pigs" once more. He elaborated on his plans for destroying a school bus, stating that he would use an ammonium nitrate fertilizer bomb— something akin to the explosive used in 1995 by Timothy McVeigh in the Oklahoma City bombing.

The Zodiac was now threatening to carry out a terrorist attack on the city of San Francisco, and yet by the time the Christmas holidays came around, there had been no such explosion. Well-known attorney Melvin Belli received a handwritten plea for help from the Zodiac in the mail on December 20. It had been mailed precisely one year after he had killed his first two (known) victims. "I will lose control again and take my nineth + possibly my tenth victom," the killer wrote, with several spelling mistakes that were characteristic of his letters. "Please help me I am drownding."

The cipher letter sent by the Zodiac to the *San Francisco Chronicle*.

He went on to claim that he was struggling to keep control of himself, unable to reach out for help because "this thing in me won't let me." Just how much of this is genuine and how much was simply the Zodiac playing more games with the authorities is impossible to tell. Genuine or not, the letter certainly paints the picture of a truly twisted and tortured mind.

The remainder of 1969 passed without any more murders, but if the public and the authorities were hoping that they had seen the last of the Zodiac Killer, they were gravely mistaken. On March 22, 1970, Kathleen Johns was nearing the end of an eight-hour road trip to visit her mother in Petaluma, when the car behind her began flashing its lights, trying to get her to pull over. It was close to midnight, and there wasn't a lot of traffic on the highway. Naively, Kathleen complied and was told by the male occupant of the car that one of her tires appeared to be coming loose. He offered to fix the problem for her, and Kathleen accepted. She had Jennifer, her ten-month-old daughter, in the car and wanted the drive to be as safe as possible.

Grateful for the offer of help, Kathleen sat and waited while this apparent Good Samaritan knelt down and tightened the lug nuts on one of the rear tires. As soon as he was finished, she thanked him and drove off. She had gone no further than a few feet when the wheel came partially free, rendering the car undrivable.

The man had not yet driven away and offered to drive Kathleen and her daughter to the nearest gas station. With her only other choice being to stay stranded at the side of a dark and lonely stretch of road, she reluctantly climbed into his car, keeping a tight hold on baby Jennifer.

As time passed, the investigation began to stagnate. Although a number of potential suspects were identified, none of them ultimately turned out to be credible.

When he drove straight past several gas stations, alarm bells began sounding in Kathleen's head. They grew louder when he refused to answer when she asked him why he wasn't stopping to drop her and her daughter off.

The bad feeling in the pit of her stomach intensified. Finally, after more than an hour had passed, Kathleen screwed up her courage and jumped out of the car. Afraid for her life, she ran off into the darkness and hid, waiting for the creepy man to drive away.

Fortunately for Kathleen and Jennifer, the next driver to happen along the road was genuinely willing to help them and drove mother and daughter to the closest police station. Her sense of dread went off the charts when she saw a wanted poster tacked to one of the walls: the face that stared back at her was the man who had stopped to interfere with her wheel. She had spent nearly two hours in a car with the Zodiac Killer.

The next day, police officers went out to the place where she had broken down. Kathleen's car had been torched, its interior completely gutted by fire. Yet some things don't quite add up. For example, Kathleen's description of her abductor varies from those provided by the Zodiac's victims; she said that he was about 40 pounds lighter, although it could simply be the case that she was a poor judge of the man's weight—especially in the dark. Neither was the mother and daughter mentioned in any of the Zodiac's future letters to the newspapers, the next of which was sent to the *Chronicle* some three weeks later.

As time passed, the investigation began to stagnate. Although a number of potential suspects were identified, none of them ultimately turned out to be credible. More letters emerged, some of which appeared to be fakes—with emphasis on *appeared*, because many experts could not agree on whether they were authentic or not. There were also a number of copycat killings, which only served to further muddy the waters.

The San Francisco Police Department has essentially given up on ever finding the Zodiac. At the time of writing, the current status of the case is "inactive." Barring some major break, which seems highly unlikely, it seems that the mysterious killer has successfully evaded justice.

Yet the Zodiac lives on in the public consciousness, and thanks to the current popularity of serial killers, he has successfully entered the pantheon of pop culture. In addition to the *Dirty Harry* connection, director David Fincher (*SE7EN*, *Mindhunter*) placed the killer firmly back in the spotlight with his movie *Zodiac*, fictionalizing the hunt for this enigmatic killer.

At the heart of the fascination we have with the Zodiac lies the sense of this case being an unsolved, and most likely unsolvable, mystery. Did he really kill as many as 37 people, as he once claimed? Why did he suddenly stop killing—did the Zodiac perhaps go to jail for some other crime, as happens with some serial killers?

Perhaps the killer has long since gone to his grave, the victim of a heart attack, cancer, or some other medical malady; or maybe Zodiac is spending the last years of his life in a retirement home.

We will almost certainly never know, but one thing is for certain. Along the West Coast of America, millions of people can rightfully wonder whether their friend, neighbor, mailman, bartender, or any number of other people could have been the Zodiac. *Somebody* knew him—and perhaps they still do.

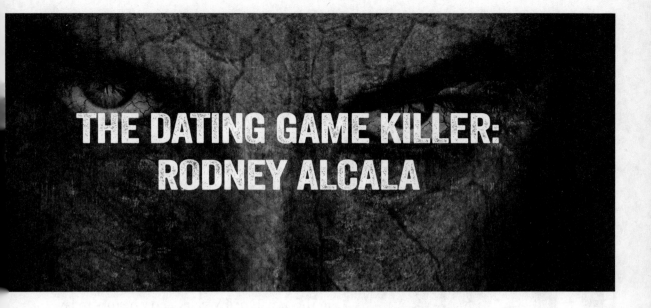

THE DATING GAME KILLER: RODNEY ALCALA

Predators by nature, serial killers are known to stalk their prey in a wide variety of locations. Some simply pick a stranger at random or seize upon an unforeseen moment of opportunity: an unlocked door or open window, a car broken down on a lonely stretch of road, a hitchhiker thumbing a ride to the next town or truck stop. Others target coworkers, friends, or acquaintances—occasionally even family members.

Ego and the need for its gratification also plays a significant role, and narcissism is a well-documented trait among serial murderers. Many of them prefer the social scene as their hunting ground of choice, picking up their victims in bars and nightclubs. What at first appears to be a charming, erudite, and well-dressed gentleman sitting across the table from you may actually be someone altogether different when he finally gets you behind closed doors.

The "handsome stranger" stereotype does have a certain degree of truth to it. The poster child for this type of serial killer is Ted Bundy, who was often described as being extremely charismatic by those who knew him. Yet there is arguably no more bizarre backdrop for a serial killer plying his charms than that of "Bachelor Number One"—Rodney Alcala.

With his long, dark hair and undeniably good looks, Alcala had seemed like a natural fit to the casting department for the TV game show *The Dating Game*. The show's format was a simple one: three contestants would compete with one another for the affections of a member of the opposite sex. Most commonly, this would mean that three men were vying to win a date with an attractive young lady. The catch was that all three were hidden from her view, meaning that she had to decide which one she wanted to go out with based purely upon their answers to a few basic questions.

The Dating Game was a popular television show in the 1960s and 1970s that featured a woman asking three hidden men questions before she picked one for a date. In a 1978 episode, one of the hidden men was Alcala.

When Alcala was chosen to appear on the show, nobody could ever have known that he was actually a cold-blooded serial killer, one who had already murdered a number of young women and who would go on to kill several more.

The Dating Game's formula was simple, raunchy, and undeniably effective, making it one of the more popular shows to air on American TV during the 1970s. This was long before political correctness ruled the airwaves, and some of the contestants' answers would today be considered inappropriate. The show was nevertheless rather unremarkable and would probably be little more than a footnote in the annals of TV game show history today were it not for the events that took place on September 13, 1978.

Sitting in the hot seat was a young, single brunette named Cheryl Bradshaw, who was presumably looking forward to solving an entertaining dilemma: selecting one of the three bachelors who would take her out on a romantic date. A screen emblazoned with the show's logo separated Cheryl from the three potential suitors, and as the cameras rolled and host Jim Lange fired off a few nudge-nudge, wink-wink quips, she wasted no time in asking the men a few questions.

Alcala preened like a peacock showing off his feathers. He sat perched on a stool that was positioned closer to Cheryl than those of the other two contestants. Host Lange had introduced him as being a photographer, and he looked every inch the part. His shirt was unbuttoned, showing off his tanned skin, a modicum of chest hair, and a shiny gold necklace. Each time he smiled—which was often—Alcala's teeth gleamed. His relaxed posture radiated pure confidence. To him, this was no contest. The end result was a foregone conclusion: Cheryl was going to pick him.

A few minutes of verbal frolicking followed. Cheryl Bradshaw fired off questions at each of the three men, every one of which held some degree of sexual innuendo. Rodney Alcala was in his element, pretending to be "a dirty old man" when requested to do so, and grinning that if he was to be a type of food that Cheryl happened to be serving up for dinner, then it would be a banana—would she care to peel him?

Apparently, Cheryl would. At the end of the segment, she chose Bachelor Number One without any hesitation whatsoever. When he stepped out from behind the screen to embrace her, Cheryl saw exactly what she had expected to see: a handsome and debonair-looking young man, one who would soon be her companion on an adventure-filled romantic date.

It was only afterward that she began to have second thoughts. Rodney Alcala's bizarre behavior backstage after the show raised her hackles to the point where she refused to go on a date with him, a case of intuition quite possibly having saved her life. "I started to feel ill. He was acting really creepy," she would later state in an interview with the *Herald Sun*. The other male contestants also got weird vibes from Alcala and were put off by his excessive alpha-male behavior.

It's highly unlikely that the producers of *The Dating Game* carried out any kind of background check on their contestants. If they had, they would have made the awful discovery that Bachelor Number One had spent several years in prison for the heinous crime of raping a young girl in 1968. The assault was brutal by any standard. After luring the unsuspecting child into his car with flattery and promises, Alcala had taken her back to his apartment and smashed in her head with an iron bar before forcing himself upon her.

> It's highly unlikely that the producers of *The Dating Game* carried out any kind of background check on their contestants.

The child was just eight years old. Rodney Alcala had beaten her to within an inch of her life. Had the police not intervened just in the nick of time, kicking down the door and bursting their way into the crime scene, the child would almost certainly have bled to death. Detectives identified the chief suspect as a UCLA photographic art student named Rodney Alcala. He was the quintessential "nice guy," according to faculty and fellow students, but for some reason, nobody could find him. This was because, unbeknownst to them, Alcala had moved across the country, enrolling in classes at New York University.

In the summer of 1971, airline stewardess Cornelia Crilley was found dead in her Manhattan apartment. She had been beaten, bitten, strangled, and raped. An article of her clothing had been stuffed into her mouth to act as a gag.

A police investigation ensued, but despite the best efforts of law enforcement officers, it appeared as though the perpetrator had gotten away. Justice was, however, about to catch up with Rodney Alcala, who had taken a job as a summer camp counselor under the pseudonym of "John Berger."

Shortly afterward, thanks to an FBI 10 Most Wanted poster, two campers recognized his face and figured out that "John Berger" was in fact

Rodney Alcala. They wasted no time in turning him in, and Alcala was soon behind bars, where he belonged.

He didn't stay there for long, however. Collectively traumatized by the attack, the little girl and her family had left the country. Without their testimony, there was no way to secure a water-tight conviction. Bearing this in mind, prosecutors reluctantly agreed to a plea deal. Despite the severity of his crime, Rodney Alcala would spend just a little over two years in jail before becoming eligible for parole in 1974.

After his release, it was not long before he struck again, plying a teenage girl with marijuana and attempting to force her into having sex with him. Were it not for the timely intervention of a passing park ranger, the situation may have ended tragically. Rodney served time in jail until the summer of 1977, when 23-year-old New Yorker Ellen Hover suddenly went missing.

A police search of her apartment revealed nothing obviously amiss, but an entry made in her diary on the day of her disappearance gave them their only solid lead. It was the name of one John Berger, and beneath it was written the word "photographer."

John Berger was, of course, Rodney Alcala, and true to form, after committing the murder of Ellen Hover, he fled across the country, finally turning up in Los Angeles. Here, he took an office job with a newspaper and began looking for his next victim. It didn't take long for him to find her.

Jill Barcomb, 18, was raped, brutally beaten, and strangled. Her body was dumped at the side of a road near Mulholland Drive, up in the Hollywood Hills. The fun-loving girl from New York had come to California to make what she thought would be a better life for herself.

The police officers who discovered Jill's body were sickened by what they saw. She had been posed on her hands and knees in the dirt, with her chin to her chest and her head making contact with the ground. The killer had used one leg of her trousers to strangle her. A blood-slicked rock found at the scene appeared to have been used to bludgeon her to death, inflicting massive blunt force trauma to Jill's skull. Bloodstains were found all over her body and also on the ground alongside her, some coming from the wounds on her head, and the remainder having bled from her vagina and rectum—the result of her having been forcibly sodomized.

Petechial hemorrhage, a by-product of the massively increased pressure in the blood vessels that occurs when a person is strangled, had turned the whites of her eyes red with thousands of pinpoint dots. The coroner would later discover during the autopsy that, in addition to the victim's pant leg, the killer had also used a belt and a pair of knotted stockings to strangle her.

The assault to which she was subjected had been nothing short of horrific, betraying a level of brutality and sadism that is difficult to comprehend.

When field agents from the FBI's New York office figured out that John Berger and Rodney Alcala were the same man, he was immediately brought in for questioning by the Los Angeles Police Department, who were still unaware of his connection with the Jill Barcomb case. He was their prime focus for the disappearance of Ellen Hover, and based on his track record, he seemed like a reasonable suspect. A smirking Alcala made no attempt at denial when asked whether he knew Ellen, even going so far as to admit having spent some time with her on the day she disappeared, taking a few pictures—but after that, he shrugged, who knew what had happened to her? (Almost a year later, what was left of Ellen Hover would be found buried in a shallow grave north of New York City).

As with many serial killers, it was all a game to him. He delighted in thumbing his nose at the authorities, hiding in plain sight as they attempted to put the pieces of the puzzle together.

> As with many serial killers, it was all a game to him. He delighted in thumbing his nose at the authorities....

Rodney Alcala walked out of the police station at complete liberty to kill again, which is exactly what he did a few days before Christmas of 1977, murdering a nurse named Georgia Wixted in her apartment on the Pacific Coast Highway. With each successive murder, the killer's contempt for and loathing of his female victim was becoming increasingly apparent.

Left on the floor of her home, Georgia Wixted's naked body was badly contused and surrounded by congealed blood. She had been viciously raped, tortured, strangled, and finally bludgeoned to death with a hammer, which the murderer left behind at the scene. She had been deliberately posed with her legs spread apart, one final indignity heaped upon so many others.

The similarities between her murder and that of Jill Barcomb were impossible to miss. Perhaps the most disturbing fact was that in both cases, according to the coroner's office, the victims had still been alive when most of the wounds had been inflicted. Injuries that are caused postmortem look different to those that occur when the patient is still alive because the tissues are still adequately supplied with blood. The only rational conclusion was that the killer had *wanted* his victims to suffer as much as humanly possible, simply because he enjoyed inflicting pain and degradation upon them.

In the summer of 1978, Rodney Alcala murdered 32-year-old Charlotte Lamb, leaving her naked body in the laundry room of an apartment complex. Once again, the victim's brutalized body had been posed in a sexually suggestive way. She appeared to have been strangled with a shoelace.

Detectives had never stopped looking for the missing Ellen Hover, and once her connection with Rodney Alcala had been established, they began to question his friends, colleagues, and acquaintances. When they announced the location at which Ellen's human remains had been unearthed, a female acquaintance of his came forward and said that she had once accompanied Rodney to that same area for a discreet photo shoot. (In hindsight, she was extremely lucky to have survived the experience.) Increasingly, the evidence was beginning to point toward him as the murderer.

> **What started out with a series of naked pictures ended in violence, as Rodney beat the girl unconscious, tied her up, and repeatedly raped her.**

Rodney's string of murders should have ended when he picked up a 15-year-old homeless girl and took her out into one of the wilderness areas of Riverside County for another of his photography sessions. What started out with a series of naked pictures ended in violence as Rodney beat the girl unconscious, tied her up, and repeatedly raped her.

Showing an incredible amount of self-discipline, the girl somehow managed to not only endure the horrific sexual assault but also to befriend Alcala, convincing her attacker that rather than turn him in to the cops, what she actually wanted was to get to know him better. Ever the narcissist, he was flattered enough to believe her. Carefully biding her time, the girl waited until he had driven them both back to civilization again, and then she made a break for it. She ran to a nearby hotel, where the staff and guests sheltered her and called the cops.

It took no time at all for her to ID Rodney from a series of pictures that detectives showed to her. With positive identification now in place, they arrested him at his mother's home on suspicion of rape. Under questioning, he finally admitting to having raped his victim, but despite this and his extensive criminal background, he was still somehow allowed to post bond and be released on parole. The criminal justice system had failed again, and more innocents would pay for that failure with their lives.

One year after the murder of Charlotte Lamb, Alcala killed 21-year-old Jill Parenteau. When detectives examined the crime scene at her Burbank apartment, they were met by a gruesome scene that was similar to all of Alcala's other crimes: a female victim who was naked, strangled, beaten, raped, and posed in a manner intended to shock and degrade her, even in death.

A few days later, on June 20, 1979, Alcala abducted and murdered a 12-year-old girl named Robin Samsoe. Unbeknownst to him, however, Alcala had been seen taking photographs of the young girl and her friends down at the beach. Police sketch artists were able to assemble a reasonably accurate composite drawing of his face based on eyewitness testimony. A hotline was set up, and soon multiple calls were coming in, all of them describing a long-haired photographer who had been seen taking pictures of girls in the vicinity of Robin's disappearance. One of those who recognized the composite turned out to be Rodney Alacala's parole officer.

By the time Robin Samsoe's skeletal remains were finally found, they had been picked clean by animals. They were also in a state of advanced decomposition and could only be identified by means of the remaining teeth. A wider search turned up several discarded items, the most telling of which were knives—at least one of them stained with blood.

Detectives kept Rodney Alcala under round-the-clock surveillance, slowly building and solidifying their case. On July 24, having at last obtained a search warrant, they made their move, arresting him at his mother's home in the early hours of the morning. The detectives knew that they had finally caught their man.

His trial lasted for three months. Despite Alcala's protestations of innocence, the jury wasn't taken in. They handed down a guilty verdict in the murder of Robin Samsoe. Rodney Alcala was sentenced to death.

As with so many cases in which the death penalty is involved, the wheels of justice turned slowly. Alcala was convicted twice and had the finding overturned twice, based on the jury and one of the key witnesses being biased against the defendant. Sitting on death row for years, which ultimately stretched into decades, Alcala steadfastly maintained his innocence, despite there being strong material evidence against him. DNA-matching techniques had advanced considerably, and semen had been found upon the bodies of the murdered women.

In 2010—some thirty years after his arrest for the murder of Robin Samsoe—Rodney Alcala received his third, and definitive, trial. The police

had not been idle during this time, and based upon the results of their investigation, he now stood accused of having tortured and killed not only the 12-year-old girl but also Jill Barcomb, Georgia Wixted, Charlotte Lamb, and Jill Parenteau. Such was his sheer arrogance and narcissism that Alcala chose to defend himself, with predictable results. His defense was, surprisingly, both organized and somewhat coherent, but he largely failed to address vast quantities of the evidence that the prosecution put forward. Much of it boiled down to his assertion that he just couldn't remember having killed any of the five victims.

Neither judge nor jury was convinced. Five death sentences were duly handed down, and Rodney returned to death row. He wouldn't stay out of the courtroom for long, however; in 2011, a New York-based court

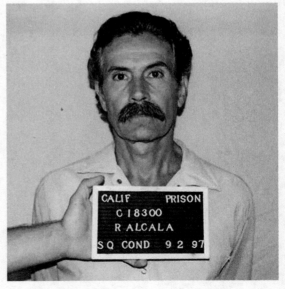

Rodney Alcala is shown here in a 1997 photo. As of 2020, he remains on death row.

convicted him of the murders of Ellen Hover and Cornelia Crilley. Due to the lack of a death penalty in the state, the judge awarded him the maximum permissible sentence: 25 years to life. This time, he pled guilty.

It is likely that there are other victims, both unexplained disappearances and cold case murders, that can also be attributed to Rodney Alcala. Detectives in several different states have linked him to possible victims, one of whom was identified via one of his photographs. The authorities released 109 pictures that he had taken, most of them containing women and girls posed in a variety of different ways and locations. Their identities are currently unknown.

The public domain pictures are only the tip of the iceberg. Hundreds more were not released because they were of a sexually explicit nature. One can only wonder who they are and how many of them fell victim to the charms of a serial killer.

At the time of writing (2020), Rodney Alcala remains on death row, awaiting execution. Dementia is said to be slowly robbing him of his mental faculties, and it is impossible to say whether his death will ultimately come at the hands of the criminal justice system or of natural causes.

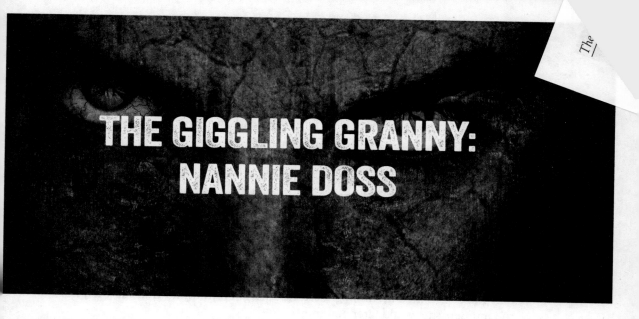

THE GIGGLING GRANNY: NANNIE DOSS

As we continue our study of serial killers, one question accompanies us on the entire journey, from start to finish. That question is: *why?* We keep asking why it is that these men and women do the things that they do. Are they simply "born bad"? Are they somehow fundamentally wired wrong when compared to the rest of us? Alternatively, could it be that such people are shaped by their environment and upbringing?

In some cases, a possible explanation might come from the medical field. As a medical professional myself, I have always found the link between severe head trauma and homicidal behavior to be particularly fascinating.

Does suffering significant head trauma truly make one prone to becoming a serial killer? Indeed, there is serious scientific evidence to support that contention. The authors of a landmark study titled "Neurodevelopmental and Psychosocial Risk Factors in Serial Killers and Mass Murderers" studied 239 serial killers, scrutinizing their backgrounds for such conditions as autistic spectrum disorder and closed head injury or concussion. Of those 239 individuals, 51 of them had sustained (or were strongly believed to have sustained) a serious head injury during their lifetime. That's 21.34 percent, more than a fifth. This was subdivided into the categories of *possible* head injury (the subject suffered an impact to the head but no documented loss of consciousness) and *definite* head injury (a brain scan indicated that the subject's brain had definitely suffered physical ill-effects).

Four serial killers who are covered in this book were part of the study: Richard Ramirez, Andrei Chikatilo, Aileen Wuornos, and Fred West. West suffered several head injuries and concussions as a young man, once after falling from a balcony and knocking himself unconscious.

There are relatively few female serial killers, particularly those who act alone, without a male accomplice. Male murderers tend to prefer violent methods, such as shooting, stabbing, beating, and strangulation; females, on the other hand, often employ less-violent techniques such as poisoning. (Aileen Wuornos, who shot her victims to death, was an exception.)

One female serial killer who *did* act alone (and also was not included in the aforementioned study) is the little-known Nannie Doss, who was also known by the more colorful moniker of "The Giggling Granny." She was born in 1905 as Nancy Hazel, the product of an Alabama farming family. At the age of seven, she was a passenger on a train that stopped too quickly, throwing the unprepared little girl out of her seat and slamming her head against a hard surface. The aftereffects of this head injury plagued Nancy (or Nannie, as she also liked to be known) for the rest of her life. In addition to the headaches and mood swings that would plague her, there has also been speculation that she may have sustained an undiagnosed traumatic brain injury that factored into the murders she would later commit.

She married at the relatively young age of 16, as many did in the 1920s, but the relationship was turbulent and relatively short-lived. The young man's name was Charley Braggs. Friends and family members were deeply sympathetic when two of their four children died unexpectedly of food poisoning—at least, that was what everybody believed when the tragedies took place. In light of later events, it is entirely possible that her two daughters were the first of many murder victims to die at Nannie's hands.

There is some speculation that Nannie Doss's homicidal behavior could have been the result of a brain injury suffered when she was seven years old.

Nannie's husband left her, taking the eldest of the surviving children, Melvina, with him and filing for divorce. She was left alone with their one remaining daughter to care for. Charley would ultimately return the child he had taken to her, and he wasted little time in finding himself another paramour. It would be decades before he realized just what a narrow escape he had, for Charley Braggs would turn out to be the only husband who ever survived being married to Nannie.

By 1929, she had married again, this time to an unsuspecting beau named Frank Harrelson, whom she had met through the local newspaper's "Lonely Hearts" column. This marriage was to last much longer than her first—16 years—despite the fact that her husband was a violent, sometimes physically abusive alcoholic. During their marriage, Nannie became a grandmother when Melvina had two children of her own. The second child passed away roughly an hour after being born, dying under what can only be described as questionable circumstances; Nannie was seen to be holding the baby girl shortly before she died, making this the third child to die who was part of her immediate family circle. Melvina had been semidelirious in the hours after having given birth, for it had been a prolonged and difficult delivery, and one that had been overseen by her mother; yet she had a dim recollection of seeing Nannie puncture her newborn daughter's skull with a long, sharp pin and could never be sure if this was real or some kind of awful daydream. When the local doctor attended upon the family and certified the infant's death, no specific cause was found to account for it. Nannie certainly owned such a pin, Melvina knew, but had she *really* seen what she thought she had seen?

There could have been no further doubts when, just a few months later, Melvina's firstborn child, Robert, also died ... once again while being looked after by his grandmother. The physician believed he had stopped breathing somehow and did not raise the possibility of foul play—despite the fact that Nannie had taken out a life insurance policy on young Robert a few months before his untimely death.

By 1945, Nannie's marriage to Frank Harrelson was turning sour, due in no small part to his increasingly drunken and aggressive behavior. Having gotten away with murder at least twice, if not four times, already, she had no compunction in seeking a way out that would be quicker, easier, and more convenient than a divorce: she administered a fatal dose of poison into his drink. The death was not deemed to be suspicious, and Nannie got away with murder yet again. She took the opportunity to leave Alabama and move to North Carolina, where she met and married husband number three, a man named Arlie Lanning.

The marriage lasted less than three years and ended when Arlie died suddenly of unexpected heart failure. The fact that he had earned a reputation for womanizing, and thereby embarrassing his wife, was apparently not taken into consideration by the authorities, who saw nothing suspicious in the man's unanticipated demise. No autopsy was carried out, which meant that the contents of Arlie Lanning's bloodstream were never analyzed by a toxicologist. And nobody was perceptive enough to connect the dots: a twice-widowed woman whose past two husbands had both died while she was ostensibly taking care of them, plus two children *and* two grandchildren who had also died while in close proximity to her. Nannie's personal orbit was proving to be a dangerous place indeed, and she wasn't done yet.

Nannie was quite the actress, however, and played the role of the grieving spouse perfectly. Those who knew her—or at least, *thought* they knew

Nannie's personal orbit was proving to be a dangerous place indeed, and she wasn't done yet.

her—had nothing but sympathy for her. Nobody suspected that she was a cold-hearted murderess.

Now husbandless, Nannie moved in with her infirm sister, with the expressed intent of taking care of her. The result: her sister died, again unexpectedly. She married her fourth husband, Richard Morton, in Kansas. The year was now 1952, and the change of state put still more distance between Nannie and the trail of dead bodies she had left in her wake. One more victim would be added to the list when Nannie's mother, Louisa, came to stay with the recently married Mr. and Mrs. Morton. Louisa did not live long. Neither did Richard Morton, for when his wife found out that he too was an adulterer, Nannie fatally poisoned him.

Her fifth and final husband was named Samuel Doss. The pair married in 1953, in Tulsa, Oklahoma, just a few short months after Richard Morton's funeral. Unlike her past husbands, Samuel was a straight arrow, a pious man who didn't drink to excess or chase other women. Doss offered her financial security and little drama, yet Nannie was still not satisfied. For his part, Samuel Doss was taken in by Nannie's act, totally falling for her performance as a respectable, kindly widow who had experienced a rough life.

Nannie managed to convince her new husband to take out multiple life insurance policies on himself, which unfortunately raised no red flags. No sooner was the ink dry on the policies than she struck, using her tried and trusted method for ridding herself of a bothersome problem: arsenic, with which she liberally laced Samuel's food and drink.

When he passed away after complaining of excruciating stomach pain, Samuel's doctor smelled a rat. He could think of no reason why his patient's condition—which he had diagnosed as a gastrointestinal infection—ought to have killed him, for Samuel Doss was a clean-living and healthy man. An autopsy was immediately called for. The findings clearly showed that Doss had been poisoned with arsenic, and the list of potential suspects was rather short. His wife had been the one with ready access to his food supply, after all, and in addition to having both the means and the opportunity, she also had a strong motive, in the form of the life insurance policies Nannie had insisted he get.

The police promptly arrested her. Nannie denied everything. She had spent the last few years honing her acting skills and was experienced in putting up a near-flawless facade as a harmless old grandmother. She deflected all questions and accusations with a playful, singsong laugh, one that suggested that the very idea of her being a murderess was patently ridiculous.

Despite her light-hearted denial, the detectives knew they had their woman. Nannie Doss had a checkered past. Many people, of all ages, had died while in her care or her company, far more than mere chance would account for. Under repeated and persistent questioning, they finally ground her down. Nannie finally confessed to having murdered her past four husbands, though she adamantly refused to admit killing her mother.

In some states, Nannie would likely have received the death penalty for her crimes. But in Oklahoma, the most she could be given was life imprisonment (it was considered unseemly to execute a woman, particularly a relatively senior one).

Nannie Doss would spend ten years behind bars before finally developing leukemia in 1965 and ultimately dying of the condition. Experts still debate her primary motives for having committed so many murders, particularly of those who should have been near and dear to her. It is easy to see why she might have chosen to kill her husbands; there was an element of extricating herself from an unhappy (some would say abusive) marriage, and also the financial incentive of collecting on life insurance policies to motivate her. If those four grown men were her only victims, then the case of Nannie Doss would be a relatively

A 1954 mugshot of Nannie Doss.

straightforward one. But what about her two young daughters? What about her grandchildren, one of whom was two years old and the other less than two *hours?* There was no material gain to be had from such killings.

Perhaps two of her four daughters had become an annoyance to Nannie, though if so, killing them would have been an extreme reaction, to say the least. Even if that *had* been the case, what of her infant grandson, who had barely drawn breath before Nannie—his own grandmother—snuffed out his life. What benefit was there to her?

It is hard to avoid the conclusion that Nannie Doss was far more than a cold-blooded opportunist, somebody who killed simply to remove those people who she saw as obstacles standing between her and her own happiness. That would have been somewhat understandable, at least, though no more forgivable. But the infanticide she committed, alongside the murder of three other children—all her own flesh and blood—paint a far darker picture of her emotional state. It is my belief that she was compelled to kill because of a pathological part of her personality, which may have originated when Nannie was just a young girl riding on a train.

THE ROSTOV RIPPER: ANDREI CHIKATILO

Of the many countries that endured cruelty and devastation during the Second World War, Russia and its territories may have suffered the most. German divisions swept across the frozen steppes of the Ukraine, driving hard through the bitterly freezing winter as they sought to capture Moscow. Along the way, they burned, butchered, raped, and murdered the civilian populace indiscriminately.

Every able-bodied man was conscripted into the armed forces and sent to the front in a desperate attempt to hold the line. One such man was Roman Chikatilo, a farm laborer who lived with his wife, Anna, in the rural Ukraine village of Yabluchne. When Germany launched a surprise attack and declared war on Russia, Roman was taken away to swell the ranks of the military struggling to defend the Soviet Union. Unfortunately for Roman's wife and young son, Andrei, that left nobody behind to defend *them*. While there is no direct evidence to prove it, it has been contended by some that Anna Chikatilo was one of the countless women who were raped by German soldiers during their occupation of Ukraine. Anna gave birth to a daughter in 1943, while her husband was still away serving with the Red Army. Clearly, Roman Chikatilo could not have been the father. Had the sexual assault taken place inside the family residence, a single-room hovel, then it is entirely possible that Andrei would have witnessed it.

If so, it would not have been the first atrocity that the young boy saw. Born in 1936, Andrei Chikatilo grew up during a famine in which people fought over every scrap and morsel of food. His mother told him a story, possibly apocryphal, of an older brother he had never met named Stepan. As the story went, starving neighbors had captured Stepan, killed him, and then

Life was cheap indeed, a lesson that the boy would learn all too well, and one that would color his attitude toward his fellow human beings in later life.

eaten the still-warm flesh from his bones. We will never know if this was a genuine case of cannibalism or simply a horror story told by a mother to frighten her son. Both are disturbing in their own way and serve to illustrate the harsh times in which Andrei Chikatilo grew up.

Cruel and domineering, Anna Chikatilo was far from the ideal of a caring, loving mother that every child deserves. Despite having been captured by the Germans and spending time in a prisoner of war camp, Roman Chikatilo was easily the kinder and more nurturing parent of the two. When her son began to wet the bed (a trait not uncommon in developing serial killers), Anna wasted no time in scolding him for what she perceived as a moral weakness. Compounding his humiliation, such scoldings were usually accompanied by a thrashing from Anna, which in turn only made Andrei wet the bed more frequently. It was a vicious cycle from which he was unable to escape for many years.

Corpses of both humans and animals, along with dismembered human body parts, were everywhere to be found during the German occupation. Life was cheap indeed, a lesson that the boy would learn all too well, and one that would color his attitude toward his fellow human beings in later life.

Psychologically speaking, Chikatilo's childhood experiences had already done a great deal of damage. The regular stream of humiliation from his mother was exacerbated by that of the local bullies, who constantly picked on him because of his diminutive build. His physical stature became a running joke at school. Children can be remorseless at the best of times, and the Soviet Union during the 1940s and 1950s was far from the best of times. It was a harsh, uncompromising time and place in which to grow up. Nobody could have known that for the perpetually picked-on child, each insult would be repaid in blood and pain inflicted upon strangers a few years down the line.

Young Andrei's only real escape came in the pages of books, especially the classic works of Russian fiction and those that covered national history. With the onset of puberty, things changed. The bookish teenager sprouted into a strong and muscular young man practically overnight. Now the worm had well and truly turned. Nobody dared push him around anymore, yet the sense of hatred that his tormentors instilled in him had left a permanent emotional scar that would never heal.

A fervent communist, Chikatilo immersed himself in political theory and activism while still a young man. There are parallels with John Wayne Gacy here, another serial killer who used politics to his full advantage. Despite Chikatilo's involvement with the Communist Party, the popularity he craved continued to elude him. He was awkward, a loner with exceptionally limited social skills. Girls instinctively avoided him, and he found himself unable to make the effort to even approach a female, let alone court one.

By the time he reached adulthood, Andrei Chikatilo already fit the classic profile of a serial killer. He was a chronic bedwetter with an emotionally distant, physically abusive, overbearing mother; and he was lonely, awkward, and socially ostracized by other children. His inability to approach the opposite sex or connect with them in any way led inevitably to sexual frustration and repression. He would begin to see women not as human beings but rather as objects to be seized, possessed, and ultimately destroyed. By the time he finally did manage to find a consenting partner, Chikatilo had developed a serious case of sexual dysfunction. No matter what he did, his own body betrayed him. This was just the latest in a long line of humiliations that he had endured since childhood. It affected him badly enough that he tried to commit suicide, attempting to hang himself. His savior came in an unlikely form: that of his mother, Anna, who probably wanted to avoid the shame of having a son kill himself while under her roof.

An intelligent and disciplined student, Chikatilo opted to pursue training as an engineer. There was always work available in the field of telephony, he reasoned, and so he spent two years becoming qualified to work on various telecommunications systems. A brief spell in the military followed—he followed in his father's footsteps, joining the army and serving well but without particular distinction for three years, until his honorable discharge in 1960.

In 1963, after a little unasked-for matchmaking by his sister, Andrei married a young woman named Fayina. Even with the pressure of having to woo a partner now gone, his impotence was still a problem for the newlyweds. In spite of this, however, the Chikatilos conceived two children: a son and a daughter.

Andrei had always been an overachiever, which was probably a result of subconsciously compensating for his awkwardness and sexual dysfunction. His education had initially been in telecommunications, but now he changed focus, choosing to pursue a degree in Russian literature, one of his boyhood passions. He had always excelled academically, and this was to be no exception. After devoting all of his free time to study, Andrei excelled and graduated from the program.

Andrei then took a teaching position at the local school. The experience was not a happy one for him. His pupils were less than kind, never passing up an opportunity to make fun of their new teacher, who seemingly lacked for confidence and decisiveness when it came to handling a class full of children. It was here that a number of early warning signs of Andrei being a sexual predator began to surface. Rumors began to circulate that he had forced oral sex on an unwilling boy. He also molested a teenage girl while she was swimming, holding her in a tight grip to restrain her struggling.

Chikatilo taught at Technical School No. 33 in Shakhty, Russia. He was harrassed by his students, who took advantage of his lack of self-confidence.

By 1978, the Chikatilo family was living in a small mining town, where Andrei was once again working as a teacher. His habit of sexually abusing children and teenagers, which had cost him at least one teaching position already, was not in the least bit abated—if anything, it had only grown stronger. Without his wife's knowledge, he paid cash to purchase a run-down shack in one of the poorest parts of town. Rather than live there, he used it primarily as a private place for him to bring back sexual partners—whether willing or otherwise.

A few days before Christmas, Andrei took his first human life. Yelena Zakotnova was just nine years old, and when what appeared to be a kindly adult suggested that they take a walk together, she wasn't worldly enough to refuse or cry out for help. It was cold and dark, and she badly needed to use the toilet. No problem, Chikatilo told her with a smile, she could use the one at his place. It was on the way home.

Once the front door had slammed shut on Chikatilo's covert shack, the poor girl was never seen alive again. The interior was dark and dingy. Yelena immediately knew that something was not right, but it was too late. Andrei leapt on her and began ripping the clothes from her body. No matter how much she fought, a physical struggle between a nine-year-old girl and a grown man could only have one outcome. Yet when she had been overpowered, Chikatilo's impotence prevented him from following through with his intentions. Frustrated at his inability to penetrate his victim, he pulled out a pocketknife and stabbed her repeatedly. Yelena was screaming, so he put his hands around her throat and choked her to death.

It was only after he released the dead girl from his grip that Andrei Chikatilo came to a horrifying realization: the act of ending her life had somehow cured him of his impotence. With the benefit of hindsight, we can see that this discovery would lead to the death of scores of other victims.

After first poking his head around the front door and making sure that nobody was around, he picked up Yelena's body, which by now was covered in blood, carried it across to the nearby river, then dumped it unceremoniously into the inky-black waters. That, Chikatilo hoped, would be that. The corpse should never be found, and even if it was, how could it possibly be traced back to him? Her personal effects (the clothes she had been wearing and a satchel) were thrown in after her, removing any last trace of Yelena Zakotnova from Andrei Chikatilo's life—or so he thought.

Two days later, on Christmas Eve, he was proven wrong. The lifeless body of Yelena Zakotnova washed up against the riverbank, where it was seen and reported to police. As they began their search, officers found her soaking-wet satchel further upstream, close to the shack of Andrei Chikatilo. They started to pay closer attention to the ground surrounding that particular section of the river and were rewarded with the discovery of a drop of blood, no doubt shed from her body when her killer had taken her to the edge of the water.

Talking to everybody who lived along that stretch of water, detectives soon learned of the odd man who occasionally frequented the run-down structure numbered 26. He came and went at sporadic intervals, they said, and he was very rarely there, but a direct neighbor recalled that the light had been left on all through the night of December 22. That had been odd enough to make it noteworthy and stick in the neighbor's memory. Unbeknownst to the neighbor, Chikatilo had gone straight home after disposing of his victim's body, but in his haste to leave the murder scene, he had forgotten to turn out the light.

Circumstantial evidence was beginning to point to him as a good fit for the little girl's murderer. If the police had only pursued this lead a little more diligently, many more lives could have been saved in the future. Unfortunately, a "better" prime suspect popped up, and the police latched onto him, setting aside the strange man who used number 26 as a sex den. To be fair, it is easy to see why. This new suspect had already spent time in jail for the rape and murder of a different girl, and the more the police looked at him, the more they saw what they wanted to see. Despite a lack of evidence, a confession (most likely extracted after the careful application of boots, fists, and night-sticks) sealed the deal. The accused man, Aleksandr Kravchenko, went to the firing squad. Andrei Chikatilo remained free—and would kill again.

    The urge to violently rape and murder girls and women to sexually gratify himself grew steadily within Chikatilo, but he was somehow able to keep his twisted impulses under control for almost three years. He would not kill again until 1981, his victim being 17-year-old Larisa Tkachenko. Andrei's reputation as a man not to be trusted around young people had caught up with him, and so he sought his next victim in the much bigger city of Rostov, where there would be a greater selection of girls to choose from and he could more easily maintain his anonymity.

    Larisa and the much older Chikatilo were taking a walk together in a secluded spot when he suddenly forced her into the cover of some nearby trees

Yelena Zakotnova's body was found under a bridge by the Grushevka River.

and attempted to rape her. While she was stronger than his last victim had been, he was still more than capable of overpowering her. The attack was savage. Chikatilo punched and choked her to the edge of consciousness. In a grisly parallel with one of the Ted Bundy murders, he ripped off one of Larisa's nipples with his teeth. True to form, he was incapable of sustaining an erection until after she was dead, at which time he used the sight of Larisa's body as a masturbatory aid.

When serial killers are interviewed (usually a number of years after the fact), most of them recall that the first murder was usually the most difficult. They may have spent months, years, or even decades fantasizing about taking a human life in cold blood, but the experience itself can induce any of a wide range of emotions and physical reactions. Nausea, vomiting, and breaking out in a cold sweat are commonplace, as the visceral reality of what they have just done finally begins to sink in. Some claim to experience a feeling of intense elation, akin to a state of ecstasy or the relief of a great weight being lifted from their shoulders; this sensation can intensify in the period after the murder, when the murderer finally comes to accept that they have actually gotten away with it.

> Andrei's reputation as a man not to be trusted around young people had caught up with him, and so he sought his next victim in the much bigger city of Rostov.

For Andrei Chikatilo, escaping justice for the killing of Yelena Zakotnova had been a sheer fluke. He must surely have known that he came very close to being caught and executed for his crime; yet he had also learned that he would never be able to satisfy his sexual urges in a conventional way, without brutally dominating his victim before ultimately taking their life. With that discovery, his worldview completely changed. There was no going back.

During the next few years, Chikatilo continued to kill regularly. He simply couldn't stop himself, and when the police failed to catch him, he no longer bothered to try. At first, his victims were young girls, but as time passed, he felt confident enough to begin killing adult women (but not adult men) and young boys.

Chikatilo's preferred MO was to choose an out-of-the-way spot, preferably with woods or trees nearby. He liked to surprise his unwitting target and drag them into the cover of the trees and foliage, where others were less likely to hear their cries for help. There was almost always some degree of penetrating physical trauma, most likely inflicted with a blade, which reflected the fact that Chikatilo found the sight of blood to be an erotic stimulant. Without it, he had great difficulty achieving climax.

As the number of victims increased, the police at first had no idea that they had a serial killer on their hands. Whether by design, happenstance, or both, Andrei Chikatilo primarily preyed upon outcasts such as the homeless,

A 1990 mugshot of Andrei Chikatilo, who would soon confess to murdering 55 people.

substance abusers, and prostitutes—those who were unlikely to be missed and less likely to be looked for by the police. This is common among serial killers. It is small wonder that the detectives assigned to track down the perpetrator of what, at first, seemed like a series of tenuously connected murders initially had difficulty seeing the bigger picture.

There were some commonalities. Because many of the crimes took place in woodlands, the bodies of the victims were found to have had their mouths crammed full with dirt, which their assailant had used as a means of keeping them quiet. Others had been blinded, their eyeballs either cut or gouged out of their sockets with a sharp implement. Frenzied stabbing was the most frequent cause of death, although injury patterns suggestive of strangulation were also sometimes found. Some of the victims bore as many as 40 or 50 stab wounds. Many had gone missing from train stations, bus stations, and other busy areas of transit where a large number of people would be passing through at any given time.

Throughout the remainder of the 1980s and into the next decade, Chikatilo continued to murder with impunity. His luck would finally run out in 1990. Frustrated with the ongoing series of killings and under immense public pressure to bring the perpetrator to justice, police chiefs signed off on a plan to flood all train stations with undercover police officers. They were aware that these stations were where the killer seemed to be picking up his victims. Hundreds of officers were involved in the ongoing operation, mounting round-the-clock surveillance and watching the comings and goings of tens of thousands of commuters.

Their patience and perseverance finally paid off when one particularly observant officer spotted a shifty-looking man emerging from the woods and immediately heading to a well to wash his face and hands. The red stains that marked him had made the policeman suspicious, and with good reason: Andrei Chikatilo was returning from the scene of yet another vicious murder.

Apart from a minor wound to Chikatilo's hand, nothing was obviously amiss when the officer stopped the man and questioned him. Having no probable cause to make an arrest, the officer allowed Chikatilo to go on his way—but he made a point of jotting down his name for future reference. One week later, on November 13, that name would prove to be extremely useful when the mutilated, decomposing body of a woman named Svetlana Korostik was found abandoned in the woods.

Officers covertly tailed Chikatilo as he went about his daily routine and found the way that he approached seemingly random children and women (though never men) suspicious enough to warrant an arrest.

The interrogation process lasted for days. At first, Chikatilo maintained his innocence. Finally, he broke down and told them everything: 55 people had died at his hands, he said, many of them children. When asked directly what his motivation had been, he simply mumbled that it was impossible for him to explain.

Chikatilo's trial was far from simple. Some of his confessions were recanted, only to be replaced by accounts of other crimes that he had not even been charged with. Sometimes Chikatilo would testify; sometimes he would refuse to speak or otherwise participate in his own defense. It did not matter. He was found guilty of all but one of the murder charges levied against him. The presiding judge had no hesitation in sentencing him to death.

While the Russian equivalent of the death row appeals process is not quite as convoluted as that of the United States, it took more than three years for the sentence to be carried out. For his part, Chikatilo seemed to have resigned himself to his fate, acknowledging that there was no possible way to rehabilitate or cure him. By his own admission, he was simply too sick to live.

On February 14, 1994, 15 years after an innocent man took a bullet for a crime that Andrei Chikatilo had committed, Chikatilo finally met the same fate: not a firing squad, but a single, well-aimed bullet fired into his head at close range. The most prolific serial killer in Russian history was dead; the long nightmare was over.

KEEPING IT IN THE FAMILY: THE SAWNEY BEAN CANNIBAL CLAN

History is replete with legends that contain more than a kernel of truth, such as Robin Hood and King Arthur. One of the lesser-known tales—outside of Scotland, at least—is that of Alexander "Sawney" Bean. Even today, it is unclear just how much of the story is true and how much of it is folklore. It certainly makes for a compelling mix of history and fantasy; if the story did indeed happen as it was told, then the notorious Sawney Bean clan represents one of the first documented cases of a *family* of serial killers.

One of the earliest iterations of the story comes to us by way of *The Newgate Calendar*. Newgate was one of London's oldest (and nastiest) prisons, and a number of prisoners were publicly executed directly outside its gates while crowds of onlookers bayed and hooted at them. Witnessing an execution was a popular public pastime, one that entire families often turned out to attend. Broadsheet publications were sold as souvenirs, cheaply designed rags containing stories of crime, punishment, and execution in gruesome and lascivious detail. Street entrepreneurs would collect different copies of these broadsheets and bundle them into an omnibus edition, which was then called *The Newgate Calendar*. It was one of the most popular "true crime" publications of its day, although the word "true" was sometimes a stretch.

According to the *Calendar*, the tale of Sawney Bean begins like this:

An incredible monster who, with his wife, lived by murder and cannibalism in a cave. Executed at Leith with his whole family in the reign of James I.

Young Sawney's parents made their living by digging ditches and trimming hedges, and they encouraged their son to follow in their footsteps, but an

An entrance showing Sawney Bean with a victim. In the background is Agnes Douglas carrying body parts.

honest day's work was not in his nature. Having had his fill with manual labor one day, Sawney ran away from home, absconding alongside a woman known as Black Agnes Douglas, who was similarly lazy and antisocial. The two set up home in a series of networked caves along the southwestern coast of Scotland.

Sawney and Agnes lived in total isolation for 25 years, completely shunning the company of other human beings and raising a brood of children, who in turn grew up and began to sire children of their own. They were breeding incestuously with their own kin—brothers with sisters, fathers with daughters, and mothers with sons—leading to what we can only assume were some truly hideous genetic grotesqueries.

Rather than farm the land, the Beans took to supporting themselves by waylaying passing travelers, who they would rob and then murder. Animal meat was in short supply, but that didn't bother Sawney and his family. They took to cutting up the bodies of their victims and eating them. Once the last shreds of flesh and muscle had been stripped from them, the victims' bones were discarded inside the cave and tunnel network. With the passing of time, the Beans got to be complacent, and along with complacency came carelessness. Rather than eat the entire body of each victim, they were said to favor the hearts, livers, kidneys, and other soft organs and viscera over the tough and stringy limbs and sinews. Gnawed-off arms and legs were tossed into the ocean without a second thought, sometimes washing up on beaches further up the coast, where they were discovered and remarked upon.

This gruesome state of affairs couldn't go on forever. People were disappearing far too often, or so the story goes, and parts of what could only have been their bodies were now turning up on beaches at low tide. Something was very obviously terribly wrong, and the public wanted something done about it. A few brave souls volunteered to patrol the region in which the disappearances were taking place, but most never returned alive to tell the tale.

A wave of terror swept over the countryside, and people began to look for somebody—*anybody*—to blame. Innocent travelers who had somehow managed to pass safely through Bean territory were falsely accused and strung up, as were a number of innkeepers whose only crime was that some of the missing people had spent a night as residents under their roof. Unsurprisingly, the innkeepers began leaving the area in droves, unwilling to run the risk of being killed for something they hadn't done.

Fanciful conspiracy theories abounded, but nobody seemed to suspect that a family of 45 incestuous cannibals might be to blame. Although they were a little too cavalier when it came to disposing of human remains, the Beans took great care when it came to planning and laying an ambush, setting out multiple groups in order to cut off any victims who might try to escape.

According to *The Newgate Calendar*, in the quarter of a century for which they remained undetected, the Bean family "had washed their hands in the blood of a thousand, at least, men, women and children."

They couldn't get away with it indefinitely, and Sawney's luck finally ran out when a man and his wife, completely oblivious to the danger they were in, rode blithely into one of their ambushes. The trap was sprung, and the husband and wife found themselves fighting for their lives against a mob of snarling cannibals. The woman was ripped out of the saddle and torn apart before her husband's disbelieving eyes, shredded and eaten right there in front of him. This drove the man into a rage. He used his sword to lash out at everybody within range and would have been killed just as his poor wife had if not a party of 30 people who happened along, coming from a nearby fair. The Beans made a tactical withdrawal, making for the sanctuary of their cave network.

> Fanciful conspiracy theories abounded, but nobody seemed to suspect that a family of 45 incestuous cannibals might be to blame.

In a state of shock because of what had just befallen him, the survivor nevertheless told his saviors exactly what had happened. The disemboweled, half-eaten body of his dead wife would certainly have made for a convincing piece of corroborating evidence. Now that the mysterious disappearances of so many people in the region had an explanation, it wouldn't have taken long for the mood of the crowd to turn ugly.

Word of the cannibal band soon reached the ear of King James I himself, who wasted no time in marshaling a formation of soldiers and putting them on the coastal road with orders to bring the family of Sawney Bean to justice at any cost. The king himself is said to have ridden at the head of this force, numbering some 400 men and a pack of hounds, who began to alert when they passed the entrance to the caves. With swords drawn and bayonets fixed, the soldiers made their way inside.

What the soldiers found inside the Beans' subterranean lair horrified and disgusted them—the remains of countless butchered human bodies, caked in dried blood, scattered around the caves in readiness to be eaten. The valuables that had once belonged to these unfortunate victims were heaped in piles. As for the Beans, they put up little in the way of resistance against the heavily armed king's men and were soon taken prisoner and bound up. The king ordered what body parts remained in the cave to be buried, and he then marched Sawney, Agnes, and the rest of their brood to Edinburgh to be executed. No trial was necessary. On the king's order, the grown men had their arms and legs cut off, causing them to bleed to death; the women and children were cast into fires and burned alive.

> It is a chilling and disturbing tale, but the question remains—just how much, if any, of it really happened?

It is a chilling and disturbing tale, but the question remains—just how much, if any, of it really happened? The matter is still debated to this day. The historical records of the time do not show any traces of hundreds, let alone thousands, of people disappearing along the coast of Scotland. Some historians have made the case that the entire story was nothing more than a political hit piece, written by an unknown eighteenth-century English author who wanted nothing more than to defame the Scottish people and portray them in a sinister and abhorrent light.

"The Sawney story was a dig at Scots—a people so barbarous, they could produce a monster like Sawney, who lived in a cave and ate people," says Dr. Louise Yeoman, a Scottish historian, in a BBC interview. She also makes a compelling point about the supposed involvement of King James: "If James had successfully led an expedition to face down a well-armed group of bloodthirsty cannibals—we would never have heard the end of it." Kings had stopped fighting their own battles back in the Dark Ages. There were now generals to take care of that for them.

In popular culture, the tale of Sawney Bean, meant to have taken place in the sixteenth century or so, has endured well into the twenty-first century, thanks to the work of filmmaker Wes Craven, director of *A Nightmare on Elm Street*. Craven was familiar with the story and used it as an inspiration for his horror movie *The Hills Have Eyes*, featuring a very Bean-like family of mutants who hide out in the desert and prey upon unsuspecting passersby.

In 2013, the low-budget film *Sawney: Flesh of Man* relocated the Sawney Bean story to modern-day Scotland, transferring Sawney into the position of a taxicab driver who prowls the city for potential victims.

Although there are different accounts of the story on record, the caves at Ballantrae Bay are the most commonly accepted location for the Bean family's lair. The local people take great delight in keeping the legend alive, and some insist that the caves are still haunted by the specters of Sawney and his victims to this day.

Cannibalistic serial killer, figment of rural folklore, or something in between? You can decide for yourself.

THE RESURRECTION MEN: BURKE AND HARE

The year was 1827, and the science of anatomy was still in its infancy. Although human bodies had been dissected in an attempt to learn their inner workings ever since the days of the ancient Greeks, a great deal remained to be discovered, and some of the keenest minds in British medical schools thirsted for still more knowledge.

Unfortunately, there was a catch. Knowledge meant dissection, and dissection in turn meant bodies. A constant stream of fresh human cadavers was needed to feed the insatiable appetite of the schools and academies. Yet people were understandably reluctant to allow themselves or their loved ones to be cut open after death, laid on a table and subjected to the indignities of the knife and the bone saw. Leaving aside the sheer squeamishness of it all, those who followed the Christian faith believed that they would rise from their graves on Judgment Day, and for that, they would need their bodies to be intact and whole—an unlikely prospect, once the anatomists had plied their trade upon them.

Enter the so-called Resurrection Men. These included William Burke and William Hare, the two most notorious examples of what some came to see as the ultimate service industry: bodysnatching. They were also serial killers.

Although their paths would converge in Edinburgh, Scotland, both were Irish by birth. Skilled in no trade, the two men decided that, rather than make an honest living, there was more money to be made dishonestly. They had tried menial labor in the past, but neither had particularly liked it.

On moving to Edinburgh, they soon learned that medical schools such as the Royal College of Surgeons would pay handsomely for corpses, the fresher the better. Recent legal reforms had meant that fewer and fewer miscreants were being sentenced to dance at the end of the hangman's rope, which in turn led to a bottleneck in the supply chain of dead bodies. To make matters more difficult still, some people went to great lengths to protect their earthly remains, installing sturdy iron grilles and cages over their graves or constructing strong stone enclosures in which to be buried. Both were effective measures of stymieing the Resurrection Men. So were the tall stone watchtowers that began to appear in cemeteries seemingly overnight, a vantage point from which relatives of the deceased or paid night watchmen could keep a close eye on the graves and ensure that they went undisturbed.

Dismayed by the increasing challenges that came along with obtaining dead bodies, Burke and Hare would hit upon a novel (if grisly) solution to the problem. In their view, there simply weren't enough cadavers to go around, and so they decided to make a few of their own.

Hare had been running a boarding house, and when one of the tenants who rented a room from him died suddenly (with, as far as we can tell, no foul play involved this time), he and Burke sold the dead man's body for the princely sum of seven pounds to an Edinburgh-based anatomist, Sir Robert Knox.

The second death at Hare's boarding house was a little more nefarious in nature. While the man in question had fallen seriously ill, he showed no signs of actively dying. Burke and Hare lurked around him like a pair of vultures, anxious for the tenant to shuffle off this mortal coil so that they could exchange his body for another financial windfall. Finally, when they could stand to wait no more, the two men turned to murder, employing a very specific technique.

William Burke

After getting the unsuspecting victim roaring drunk, one man would apply pressure to their chest by kneeling on it, while the other plugged his (or her—Burke and Hare didn't discriminate based upon gender) nose and mouth, cutting off the victim's air supply and slowly suffocating them to death. So successful was this method of murder that it subsequently became known as "Burking."

Burking left few signs of physical trauma on the cadaver, which meant that it was easier for Burke and Hare to downplay the manner of the decedent's death (it's harder to cover up foul play when the victim is bruised) and also that the cadaver fetched a much better price because it was still in relatively "mint condition."

In a pattern that was (and still is) common to serial killers the world over, once they ran out of sick people to help across death's doorway, Burke and Hare turned their murderous attentions upon the homeless, the indigent, and prostitutes. The streets of Edinburgh were teeming with such people, men and women who would almost certainly not be missed if they happened to disappear, only to turn up dead a few days later on the dissection table of an anatomy lab. Few, if any, questions would be asked by the students or faculty whose education and livelihood depended upon them.

The two men soon fell into a routine: gain a stranger's confidence, ply them with drink, and then pounce, "Burking" them to death. Burke and Hare murdered sixteen victims in this way, cashing in on each death by selling the bodies to Sir Robert Knox and his students for dissection. Ultimately, their greed turned out to be their undoing. After murdering a female lodger at the boarding house, they were foolish enough to leave the body unattended in bed, where it was later found by two other tenants. Horrified at their discovery, the tenants went to the police and reported the crime. Burke and Hare's cover was blown.

Closer scrutiny on the part of detectives showed a string of suspicious cadaver sales to Knox, who claimed that he had not found them to be questionable in any way. Nevertheless, when the newspapers printed the story, the public viewed him as villainous. To give Burke and Hare a small amount of credit, when they confessed, Burke insisted that Knox had not known anything about how they obtained bodies. The court evidently believed them, because Knox was not indicted for the crime. Instead, the book was thrown squarely at William Burke and his lover, Helen McDougal, who was believed to have assisted him with the killings. William Hare had accepted the Crown's offer of immunity from prosecution in exchange for testifying against his former partner in crime, and his testimony was enough to send Burke to the gallows (due to insufficient evidence, however, McDougal walked away a free woman).

Executions in nineteenth-century Scotland were the equivalent of a big sporting event such as the Super Bowl. The trial had been a massive public spectacle, but it was nothing when compared to the actual hanging, which took place on January 28, 1829. A crowd of thousands turned out to watch

William Hare

William Burke swing by the neck until he was dead. So popular was it that local people sold tickets to view the event from the windows of their homes. Once the lifeless body was taken down from the scaffold, it was carted away from the eyes of the jeering onlookers and given to the anatomy school for educational dissection—the same school to which Burke and Hare had sold the bodies of their victims (sometimes karma can be very quick). If you go to the University of Edinburgh Medical School today, it is still possible to see William Burke's skeleton, which is kept in a locked glass case as a grisly reminder of the school's connection with the world's most infamous and notorious body snatchers.

THE GRIM SLEEPER: LONNIE FRANKLIN

Although it isn't unheard of, it is rare for a serial killer to stop killing for long periods of time. Some struggle with their murderous urges, trying to suppress the impulse to kill. They succeed for a time, but usually the compulsion wins out in the end. One exception is Lonnie Franklin, who ceased killing for so long that he was given the macabre nickname of "The Grim Sleeper."

With the benefit of hindsight, a number of red flags indicated that Lonnie Franklin had a tendency toward violent and predatory behavior. As a military cook stationed in Stuttgart, Germany, he was part of a three-man group of soldiers who gang-raped a teenage German girl in 1974. The men took turns holding the teenager down and sexually assaulting her, using the threat of a knife to ensure her compliance. As if that wasn't bad enough, they also took a series of photographs of the girl's ordeal, which Franklin would revisit later in his life during his spree of solo crimes.

Franklin wasn't particularly bright. Showing remarkable presence of mind, the rape victim feigned an interest in him and managed to talk him into giving her his phone number, which she immediately gave to the police. Franklin and his two cronies were all arrested and charged with rape, based largely upon her court testimony. (In an extraordinary act of courage, the victim faced off against Franklin in court for the second time, some 40 years later, when she attended the sentencing phase of his murder trial.)

By all rights, Franklin should have served three to four years in prison, but for reasons that were never documented, he was freed after spending just one year behind bars. Following his discharge, he returned to civilian life, taking his sadistic appetites for rape and violence along with him.

According to an article in the *Los Angeles Times*, Lonnie Franklin was by all accounts well-liked in his South Los Angeles neighborhood. He was known as a good neighbor, if a little volatile sometimes, especially where his interactions with women were concerned. The father of two children, he was also a good provider. Nobody who knew him would have thought to connect him with the disappearances of young black women that were taking place throughout South L.A. He was a little on the crooked side, sure—dealing in some stolen goods here and there, the guy who could get you a bargain that had fallen off the back of a truck every once in a while—and a bit of a dirty old man, but hardly a killer.

> By all rights, Franklin should have served three to four years in prison, but for reasons that were never documented, he was freed after spending just one year behind bars.

Yet there were signs that all was not right, for those who knew where to look. One acquaintance told reporters that he had chanced upon a stack of photos of naked women in the glove box of Franklin's car (chillingly, these may have been pictures of some of his victims); another was nonplussed when Franklin showed her a box of women's underwear that he kept in his garage.

"He was always talking about prostitutes," said a female neighbor interviewed by the *Los Angeles Times*. "He said they were no good."

A *Rolling Stone* article described a disturbing interaction that Lonnie Franklin had with one of his targets, Enietra Washington, who was the only known victim fortunate enough to have lived to tell the tale:

> In taking the stand to testify against the man who shot and raped her in 1988, Washington noted how Franklin pulled up alongside her in an orange Ford Pinto, offering her a ride. After she initially declined the offer, Franklin fired back "that's what's wrong with you black women. People can't be nice to you," according to Washington.

Against her better judgment, Enietra had gotten into the car alongside him. Suddenly, her supposed Good Samaritan had shot her repeatedly, raped her, and dumped what he thought was her lifeless body on the ground. During the process, he had taken several photographs of her struggle. When he drove away, Franklin had no idea that one day he would have to face the woman he believed to be dead, as she stood across from him at the witness stand during his murder trial.

Lonnie Franklin's first murder was committed on August 10, 1985. Debra Jackson, aged 29, was shot three times at close range with a .25 caliber pistol before her body was dumped in a back alley in South Los Angeles. Although a qualified beautician, she had been making a living as a waitress around the time she encountered Lonnie Franklin. Henrietta White, 36, followed one year later, on August 12, 1986. She, too, had been shot multiple times, and her body was stuffed beneath an old mattress that had been abandoned in an alley.

Franklin continued killing two or three black women a year for the next couple of years, committing the last murder in the initial sequence on September 11, 1988, before stopping for no apparent reason—at least, that's what he *appeared* to do. His botched attack on Enietra Washington took place on November 20, and it may be that when Franklin heard that his victim had survived, he decided to fly under the radar for a while to avoid police scrutiny.

For whatever reason, the Sleeper appeared to go dormant for the next 14 years, only to return with the murder of Princess Cheyanne Berthomieux, who was just 15 years of age when Lonnie Franklin battered and strangled her to death. This was a departure from his usual MO of shooting his victim repeatedly with a small-caliber handgun. Her naked body was found in yet another alleyway. She had been missing for the past three months.

The following year, in 2003, the body of 35-year-old Valerie McCorvey was discovered by a crossing guard.

Nearly four more years passed without an apparent murder, until on New Year's Day of 2007, the body of Janecia Peters, a bubbly 25-year-old, was found by a homeless man searching through trash bags. She had been shot to death.

It is entirely possible that if it hadn't been for a twist of fate, Lonnie Franklin may never have been caught. His son, Christopher, was arrested in 2008, when officers found that he was in possession of an illegal firearm. They conducted a DNA test on him, entering the results into a criminal records database, and came back with a partial DNA hit for some of the unsolved murders, meaning that although Franklin's son had not committed the crime himself, a close member of his family almost certainly had. The method, known as a familial search, was relatively new to law enforcement, but it paid off significantly in the case of the Grim Sleeper. Progressing on from the match with his son's DNA, the police quickly refined their search and put 57-year-old Lonnie Franklin under the microscope. An undercover officer managed to snag a DNA sample from a piece of leftover pizza, conclusively tying the elder Franklin to the murder of 23-year-old Barbara Ware.

A 1998 mugshot of Lonnie Franklin.

The Los Angeles Police Department did not seem to pick up on the Grim Sleeper's activities very quickly, possibly because his victims were all people living on the fringes of society.

Knowing that the game was finally up when uniformed officers knocked on his door, Franklin came along quietly.

The so-called Grim Sleeper also murdered teenage runaways as young as 15. All of his victims were either on the fringes of society or had fallen off the grid completely, which may explain why the presence of a serial killer operating in Los Angeles may have gone undetected for so long—although it has also been suggested that the Los Angeles Police Department kept quiet about their suspicions for too long. Nor did the press pick up on the fact that somebody was quietly stalking and murdering women in the city.

Another frequently seen trend is that serial murderers normally prefer to kill those within their own racial group—not exclusively, but generally. White men tend to kill white victims. Lonnie Franklin killed black women and black girls. In that respect, he was quite conventional. Some have raised the possibility that if the people who were disappearing and subsequently turning up dead had been white, the killer might have been apprehended sooner.

Some serial killers like to grandstand in the courtroom, perhaps recognizing the fact that once they have been caught, the game is up, and little else remains but to enjoy the fame and notoriety their crimes have brought. The theatrics of Theodore "Ted" Bundy constitute one such example, as does the darkly brooding menace of Night Stalker Richard Ramirez, who clearly enjoyed the Satanic image he had so carefully cultivated.

Lonnie Franklin, on the other hand, remained mute throughout the entire duration of his trial, apart from the occasional mutter. He appeared to be completely placid, totally unaffected by the turn of events that would ultimately lead to his being sentenced to death for the murder of ten women. When the niece of one of his victims confronted him in the courtroom, saying, "You are one cold-hearted dude," Franklin did nothing more than nod in agreement. He showed no signs of remorse, guilt, or acceptance of responsibility. The only emotion he expressed was a single explosive outburst of anger, declaring that one of the women who claimed to have recognized him was telling "a bald-faced lie."

He had been an uncooperative prisoner, refusing to assist the detectives who were trying to piece together the full extent of his crimes. It is believed that the actual number of victims could have been significantly higher than ten, based on the fact that a search of Franklin's home turned up over 1,000 photographs and videotapes of 33 women, the identities of whom were never established. Disconcertingly, many of the women in the pictures were either naked or partially unclothed, and some appeared to be either unconscious or dead, hinting at the possibility that serious harm may have befallen them. Others were posing in a sexually suggestive way, although whether this was done voluntarily or under duress is impossible to say.

The subjects of other photographs found there proved to be some of Franklin's already-identified victims, such 25-year-old Janecia Peters, whose body had been disposed of in a trash dumpster and found on New Year's Day of 2007. In addition to photographs and videos, police officers also found identification cards from other women, some of whom had already been reported missing. Franklin flatly refused to accept responsibility for murdering them or to give detectives any information concerning their whereabouts.

> Lonnie Franklin earned his nickname, the Grim Sleeper, because of the apparent lull in his murderous activities that took place between the late 1980s and 2002.

A commonly held belief concerning serial killers is that they tend to keep on killing until they either die, become too ill or feeble to continue, or end up behind bars. One prime example is Jack the Ripper, another prostitute-hating killer whose murder spree abruptly ended as quickly and unexpectedly as it had begun. The reason behind the Ripper ceasing to kill has been hotly debated among Ripper-ologists for decades and shows no sign of being solved any time soon. Lonnie Franklin earned his nickname, the Grim Sleeper, because of the apparent lull in his murderous activities that took place between the late 1980s and 2002. Not everybody is convinced that he actually stopped killing, however.

Interviewed by a reporter from the *Toronto Sun*, Detective Daryn Dupree said, "I don't think he stopped because he was getting away with it. I think he slowed down, but I don't think that big gap was as much as we thought it was." In other words, some of the unidentified females whose pictures turned up in Franklin's photograph collection were probably killed and disposed of during that time period.

Many serial killers like to keep trophies of their victims, such as an article of clothing or a personal item. Lonnie Franklin had kept pieces of jewelry from some of his victims at his home, no doubt using them to vicariously relive the murders he had committed whenever he felt the urge to do so. This proved to be a mistake, as it usually does, because the small hoard of personal items tied him to the missing and deceased women in a way that neither Franklin nor his attorney could satisfactorily explain.

The search had also turned up the weapon that he had used to murder most of his victims, a .25 caliber handgun. He had been too arrogant or careless to dispose of it, and now the ballistics evidence would be a huge help in nailing a conviction.

On the evening of March 28, 2020, just as this chapter was being completed, Lonnie Franklin was found dead in his cell. At the time of writing, his death does not appear to be suspicious.

KING OF THE MURDER CASTLE: H. H. HOLMES

"**I** was born with the devil in me," H. H. Holmes famously said. When we look back at the horrors that this seemingly mild-mannered man was believed to have perpetrated, it is hard to disagree. Also nicknamed "the Beast of Chicago," Holmes is described by many as being America's first ever serial killer—a false claim, since other serial killers are documented prior to his string of murders in the 1890s. A great deal of confusion, exaggeration, and sometimes outright fiction surrounds his story, making it difficult to tell where the truth ends and the fantasy begins.

Much of what we know of Holmes's childhood comes from his own accounts. Since he found it almost impossible to tell the truth, one must be skeptical of this information. It is a measure of the man's ego that, while he was imprisoned and awaiting his ultimate fate, Holmes wrote his autobiography (it was titled *Holmes' Own Story*).

Some have claimed that H. H. Holmes murdered more than 200 people. In fact, the number is more likely closer to fewer than ten people. And yet the twisted story of Holmes and his so-called murder castle continues to gnaw its way into popular culture, a Victorian-era equivalent of the *Hostel*-style torture-porn horror movie.

As with so many serial killers, Holmes was a liar and a charlatan, happy to tell a tall tale if it suited his need for self-aggrandizement. He personally laid claim to having committed 27 murders, a number that once again is not borne out by the facts.

Few things fascinate us as much as serial killers who come from a medical background. The field of medicine is arguably the most trusted vocation in the world. Doctors minister to us when we are at our weakest, at our most vulnerable, and they have the power of life and death over their patients. Members of the medical profession are afforded great respect and are held in the highest esteem. All of this makes the betrayal so much deeper when one of them turns out to be capable of inflicting harm on the innocent, rather than healing.

The American Civil War began on April 12, 1861, when Confederate artillery batteries opened fire on the Union-held Fort Sumter, not far from Charleston, South Carolina. A little over a month later and a thousand miles away, a baby boy named Herman Webster Mudgett was born in New Hampshire on May 16. He would later become infamous under the name of H. H. Holmes.

Researchers who retrospectively analyze the childhood of serial killers in search of red flags often look for things such as chronic bedwetting, antisocial behavior, and a propensity for torturing and killing animals. If there was anything of this nature in Holmes's boyhood, no evidence of it survives today. He seems to have been an ordinary boy in a hardworking, rather religious family. There are very few stories of note that might explain why he became a serial killer when he grew up.

H. H. Holmes was born Herman Webster Mudgett in New Hampshire. He appeared to have a normal childhood and gave no indication that he would grow up to be a killer.

One story goes that young Holmes was frightened of a skeleton that stood in the local doctor's office. One day, a group of local children lay in wait for him as he walked home. Then they pounced, dragging him kicking and screaming into the building, where the terrified boy was pushed into a cold and unfeeling skeletal embrace. This experience supposedly set him on the road to practicing medicine in later life and may have scarred him psychologically.

Holmes apprenticed with a New Hampshire doctor named Nahum Wight for a year before carrying on his medical studies at a school in Vermont. Holmes was comfortable around dead bodies, which were dissected to teach medical students the intricacies of anatomy. On one occasion, a woman cleaning Holmes's room in the boarding house in which he lived was shocked to find the corpse of a baby under his bed. He often took home amputated body parts—arms, legs, hands, feet—for his own purposes.

It soon became apparent to those who knew him during his medical school days that Holmes could not be trusted, particularly when it came to women, money, or property. He would say anything to get a woman into bed, including making promises of marriage that would be revoked or denied when he tired of the lady in question, and he began to display the attributes of a thief and a swindler. The words "schemer," "liar," and "scoundrel" were frequently used to describe him. One thing that many people agreed upon after Holmes's eventual capture and trial was his seeming inability to look somebody in the eye, especially while he was talking to them. It was assumed that this was due to his fundamentally untrustworthy nature.

After a spell working with the mentally ill, he surfaced in Chicago during the summer of 1886 and took an examination that would allow him to practice as a licensed pharmacist. The name he chose to work under, for reasons best known to himself, was not Herman Mudgett: it was Harry H. Holmes.

Under these auspices, he began working in the Chicago neighborhood of Englewood at a drug store owned by a married couple. Holmes eventually purchased the store from them. It was located on a spot that was just across the road from what would one day become the scene of his infamous Murder Castle, the plans for which were being drawn up the following year. The ground floor was intended for commercial/retail purposes (primarily a drug store, Holmes's primary business venture), while the floor above would be residential. Holmes and his wife would move in there, and there was plenty of space to sublet to other tenants if he chose to. Much has been made of the fact that Holmes had the architects incorporate hidden spaces and passageways into the plans prior to construction, which has added greatly to the building's mystique.

Holmes's second wife, Myrta, gave him a daughter in 1889. It is believed that he was still bigamously married to his first wife, Clara. As his new family grew, Holmes found that he needed more income than running a drug store could provide. His solution was to engage in a variety of schemes and shenanigans—some legal, some outright fraudulent. Holmes seemed to have little to nothing in the way of personal ethics; if lying, cheating, and stealing would get him what he wanted, he did so without hesitation or compunction. Predictably, he was sued and taken to court many times.

A man named Icilius "Ned" Conner ran a jewelry store on the ground floor of the building. It wasn't long before his wife, Julia, began having an illicit love affair with Holmes. Julia had started working closely with Holmes, serving as a cashier, which gave them both ample opportunity to spend time together. Having both his wife and mistress living under the same roof may well have excited him at first, but it soon became tiresome. Ned grew angry with the situation and moved out in 1891, ultimately filing for divorce. Julia and her daughter, Pearl, remained behind under Holmes's roof.

Neither of them would leave the Murder Castle alive. They were last seen on Christmas Eve or early on Christmas Day—nobody is entirely sure— but then they both simply disappeared. None of their possessions had been

Holmes called the mixed-use building he owned in Chicago his "Murder Castle." He ordered architects to add secret passageways and spaces to the structure. Part of the building was the World's Fair Hotel, although the space was never used as a hotel.

taken with them, so it is unlikely that they "just moved out," as Holmes claimed. It was as if mother and child had vanished into thin air. To this day, it is not known precisely what happened to either of them, although the remains of a young girl that detectives would later discover in the cellar most likely belong to Pearl. Holmes later claimed that Julia had died on the operating table during a botched abortion procedure.

Julia and Pearl were a threat to H. H. Holmes's marriage and social standing and, therefore, to his livelihood. Threats like that had a habit of disappearing without a trace when Holmes was around.

His next romantic conquest was a young lady named Emeline Cigrand, who sometimes spent the night at the castle. She, too, disappeared without a trace after falling for Holmes. It is believed that she was murdered within the castle. More victims would follow.

When it came to swindling, Holmes liked to cast a wide net. He and his accomplice, Benjamin Pitezel, often traveled to such places as Denver, Fort Worth, and St. Louis. It was in the latter city that Holmes's luck ran out: he was arrested for fraud and sent to jail. While imprisoned, Holmes made the mistake of telling a fellow inmate of his plan to scam an insurance company.

The idea was a simple one: after taking out the biggest life insurance policy possible on Pitezel, they would fake his death, using a cadaver that Holmes would somehow obtain especially for that purpose. This was a con that he claimed to have successfully pulled off before, and he was confident that he could make some big bucks by doing so again. For a trained medical professional such as himself, Holmes boasted, it would be child's play to doctor up a corpse to make it look as if his partner in crime had suffered a fatal accident.

This "criminal master stroke" was to be pulled off in Philadelphia, just as soon as Holmes was released from jail. There was just one catch: in an ironic twist of fate, Holmes ended up actually killing Pitezel for real, chloroforming him to death. To make it look like a freak occurrence rather than foul play, it was necessary for him to burn Pitezel's body and position it in a very specific way.

The reasons for Holmes's sudden change of heart and killing the person we now know to have been his accomplice are murky at best. It may simply be that Pitezel had too much dirt on Holmes for him to be comfortable with, and that the murderous doctor callously removed another threat to himself. Alternatively, Pitezel may have said something to Holmes that sent him into a rage, and the killing took place in a fit of anger. We will never know for sure.

Once Pitezel was dead, Holmes wasted no time in making good his escape. Displaying an unbelievable level of brazen confidence, his first stop was to visit Mrs. Carrie Pitezel. Employing all the charm of a master criminal, Holmes told her that her husband was still alive and that his death had been faked, then enlisted her help in pulling off the insurance swindle.

The life insurance company required a family member to identify the body of the deceased before they would pay out on a policy. Although Mrs. Pitezel would have been the natural choice, the task fell to Alice Pitezel, Benjamin and Carrie's teenage daughter. Benjamin's body had already been interred by the time Holmes and Alice arrived in Philadelphia and had to be exhumed. The process of decomposition had already taken hold. Despite the gruesome appearance of her father's corpse, Alice agreed before a supervising physician and a representative of the insurance company that yes, this was indeed the body of her father. Holmes solemnly concurred. The insurance company duly issued a check for a significant lump sum of money. It went straight into Holmes's pocket.

For reasons best known only to himself, Holmes wanted a number of Pitezel's children to be placed into his care. Still believing that her husband was not really dead and was just lying low, Carrie Pitezel consented to letting two of her daughters, Alice and Nellie, and her young son, Howard, accompa-

Holmes's accomplice, Benjamin Pitezel, was a carpenter by trade.

ny Holmes on his travels across the country. The police were on his trail—primarily for some of his many frauds and swindles—and so he kept moving, traveling from state to state with the three children in tow.

As is the case with so many criminals, Holmes wasn't quite as smart as he liked to think he was. He had now painted himself into a corner: to fool the insurance company, it had been necessary for the 15-year-old Alice Pitezel to be shown her father's mouldering body so that she could positively identify it. Alice knew without a doubt that her father was dead. Her mother, on the other hand, was still under the illusion that he was alive and well, hiding out from the authorities so that the insurance fraud wouldn't come to light.

What if the two compared notes when they next saw one another? Obviously, Holmes couldn't allow that to happen. The Pitezels knew far too much—more than enough to put him in prison for murder if the police started asking questions about Benjamin's death. There was only one solution: they had to die. Not only Carrie, but all of her children too.

The first to be killed was Howard. Holmes had stashed Nellie and Alice in a hotel in Indianapolis while he and the young boy took up residence in a cottage some distance outside of town. We can only speculate as to how the boy was murdered, for Holmes never said during any of his confessions, but Adam Selzer states in his excellent biography *H. H. Holmes: The True History of the White City Devil* his belief that Holmes used poison (most likely cyanide) to kill Howard, then chopped his remains up and burned them in the cottage stove, which Holmes had installed in the cellar for this exact reason. Howard's heavily burned bones were left behind inside the chimney, and his feet were discovered buried in the bare earth of the cellar floor, alongside a can of coal oil that had presumably been used to set fire to his body.

The next killings took place in Toronto, at a house that Holmes had rented expressly for that purpose. He is said to have employed a most unusual murder weapon this time out: a large trunk, of the sort used to carry clothes and personal belongings. The story goes that Holmes made both Nellie and Alice climb into the trunk, closed and locked the lid, then gassed them to death by means of a pipe that he pushed inside. Selzer refutes this idea, pointing out that the property in which the murders were carried out had no gas supply during the time of Holmes's very brief tenancy, and substitutes his own very plausible theory that the girls were poisoned. Whichever turned out to be the case, the bodies of both girls were buried in the cellar of the house. By the time their naked remains were unearthed, each was too decomposed to yield much in the way of insight as to the nature of their death.

When Holmes was arrested on November 17, 1894, it was because his life as a swindler had caught up with him—not that of a murderer. Insurance fraud was a costly business for companies such as Fidelity Mutual, and therefore it liked to make a strong example out of anybody found perpetrating it. Now that Fidelity Mutual suspected Holmes to have ripped off the company with the Pitezel case, it pushed for a speedy trial.

> When Holmes was arrested on November 17, 1894, it was because his life as a swindler had caught up with him—not that of a murderer.

Ever the con man, Holmes confessed to having defrauded the insurance company but maintained that his former partner in crime, Benjamin Pitezel, was still alive and free. After all, he reasoned, better to go to jail for fraud than for murder. He began denying the whereabouts of any of the Pitezel children, slowly moving to distance himself from having been seen in their company for weeks on end.

As H. H. Holmes sat behind bars, his so-called confessions began to change, twisting and turning on a regular basis. Whether he was genuinely trying to distort the facts into some form of story that would get him acquitted or simply enjoyed spinning a tale to further muddy the waters is impossible to say. The more he talked, however, the less the detectives believed him.

No matter what he said, once the remains of the two murdered Pitezel girls were unearthed in a Toronto cellar, the game was up for Holmes. He knew it. "Well, I guess they'll hang me for this," contemporary newspaper accounts quoted him as saying. As things turned out, he would be right.

Newspaper reporters picked up the story and ran with it. There was nothing that a nineteenth-century reading audience found quite so titillating as a juicy murder story, complete with a dastardly villain. H. H. Holmes fit the bill nicely. It wasn't long before he became infamous as the man who had murdered two little girls in cold blood—and who knew how many others? A media frenzy ensued. Back in Chicago, the eyes of the press turned to the large property Holmes had owned at the corner of 63rd and Wallace. Although the upper part of it had been damaged in a fire, the building still stood and operated as a business. What grisly secrets might it hold?

One thing that was *not* unearthed were the buried remains of Minnie Williams, a wealthy young lady whom Holmes had met in Boston, and those of her sister. After joining him in Chicago in 1893, it's believed that Holmes, never one to let something as trivial as having a wife get in the way of his plans, married her bigamously. Although he enjoyed the company of attractive young women, he liked getting his hands on their money even more. Once he tired of the complication such a relationship brought, the woman in question had to go. Things became even more complex in the case of Minnie Williams when her sister came to town and decided to stay. Holmes felt that he had no choice but to kill them both. It's likely that the murders took place inside the Murder Castle, although historians aren't entirely sure of that. The bodies remain missing to this day.

Despite being locked up, Holmes granted interviews to reporters in which he told his own version of the story—a mess of half-truths and outright lies, with a liberal sprinkling of the truth thrown in for good measure. A book soon followed, giving him the chance to spin the narrative entirely in his own favor.

As time wore on, even somebody as delusional as H. H. Holmes could see that his murder trial was not going well. There was no way he was going to get away with his crimes, Holmes realized. Despite the smokescreen of lies he put up and hid behind, there was little doubt that the jury would convict him of murder. Under his real name of Herman W. Mudgett, he was sentenced to be hanged by the neck until he was dead. Holmes tried every trick in the book to dodge his impending execution. Nothing worked.

Holmes was executed by hanging at Moyamensing Prison, Philadelphia, in 1896.

With seemingly nothing left to lose, Holmes came forth with a complete confession. A very different picture of the man would emerge in the pages of this document, painting him as somebody who was essentially born evil—a monster in human form who was compelled to kill and acted on that compulsion whenever the mood took him.

He admitted to having killed Julia Conner, his erstwhile lover, while in the middle of aborting her unborn baby. Once the mother was dead, Holmes claimed, her daughter Pearl could not be allowed to live. She had been the next to die at his hands.

As if that wasn't extraordinary enough, Holmes then listed close to 30 victims he claimed to have killed inside the walls of the

Murder Castle. They had supposedly died by a wide variety of methods, including starvation, poisoning, and blunt force trauma.

If H. H. Holmes's written confession is to be believed, he took the lives of 27 people. The question is, how much of it was truth, and how much was the fictitious ramblings of a sick and egotistical mind?

What was his motivation for making up a large part of his confession? From a purely mercenary point of view, H. H. Holmes hoped to make a lot of money from publishing his version of events. Based on the timeless journalistic principle of "if it bleeds, it leads," the potential readership would presumably want to hear all the grisly details; his confession had better contain blood and death, and as much of both as possible, in order to please the crowd.

For somebody who liked to think of himself as being very detail-oriented, Holmes made a lot of sloppy mistakes while recording his alleged crimes for posterity. For one thing, not everybody he claimed to have murdered was actually dead; some "victims" turned up alive and perfectly well, seemingly oblivious to the hoopla of which they were part. This should all have come as no surprise when one considers Holmes's propensity for swindling; the man was a proven con artist, after all, and not even a particularly good one!

Much of what H. H. Holmes said had happened turned out to be lies. Experts today generally agree that he killed no more than nine people at most; that's still an awfully high number, but nowhere near the 100 to 200 murders claimed by some sources. A great deal of the mystique surrounding Holmes was an invention of the media, including the fanciful tales surrounding the unusual architectural nature of the so-called Murder Castle. The notion of Holmes constructing the place in order to ensnare visitors to the Chicago World's Fair and torture them to death had little, if any, solid evidence to support it.

In true Holmesian form, there was one final reversal. The condemned man went to the hangman's scaffold and asked permission to give a short speech. Holmes declared to the large crowd that had assembled that he had never committed a single act of murder. He remained a habitual liar to his very last breath. Following his comments, a hood was placed over his head and a noose secured about his neck, and with the pull of a lever, H. H.

Holmes's "full confession" was published in the April 12, 1896, issue of the New York *Journal*. Illustrated here are the faces of some of his alleged 27 victims.

Holmes dropped, dangled, and twitched at the end of the rope until all the life had been squeezed out of his body. He was as theatrical in death as he had been in life. As no autopsy was performed, we do not know whether his neck had snapped, killing him instantly, or if he had instead been strangled, which would explain much of the spastic twitching those present reported seeing.

Due to his fear of having his corpse stolen by body snatchers, Holmes had stipulated that he be buried ten feet beneath the ground in a coffin filled with cement. Surprisingly, this wish was granted; the authorities showed more consideration to a convicted murderer than he had to any of his victims. The coffin was so heavy that it would have been impossible for anything less than a large gang of grave robbers to steal it.

> Holmes's infamy grew over the following years. Rumors began to circulate that he wasn't dead at all....

That should have been the end of the story, but it wasn't. Holmes's infamy grew over the following years. Rumors began to circulate that he wasn't dead at all; rather, he had supposedly eluded the hangman, slipping out of prison and escaping to a new life, presumably under a new identity. Some wondered whether the grave truly contained the body of H. H. Holmes.

Matters finally came to a head in 2017, largely because of a TV show named *American Ripper*. The premise of the show, fronted by Jeff Mudgett, Holmes's great-great grandson, was to investigate a supposed link between Holmes and Jack the Ripper—could they have been one and the same man? (Short answer: possibly, though highly unlikely).

A judge gave permission for Holmes's grave to be unsealed and the body within it exhumed. Although those who opened the grave reported that it stank to high heaven, they were surprised to discover that thanks to the unique layering of cement around the coffin, parts of Holmes's corpse had rotted far less than would normally be expected. His body had decomposed significantly, but his mustache was still there, and the suit he had worn to the gallows was in remarkably good shape.

After examining the dental records carefully, forensic anthropologists concluded that, yes, this really *was* the body of H. H. Holmes. Claims that his death were faked were untrue.

The question still remains: Was H. H. Holmes a true serial killer, as we understand the term today? We can reasonably conclude that he killed up to nine victims, nowhere near the 27 to which he would ultimately lay claim (several of whom were demonstrably not dead). But we must also wonder: Did he kill because he liked it and was compelled to do so, as many serial killers do, or was it simply a matter of pragmatism—a cold, calculating man murdering those who simply got in the way of his plans? Were the H. H. Holmes murders the case of a shrewd businessman coldly removing obstacles from his path?

Over a century after his death, we are still fascinated with the case of H. H. Holmes. There is a ghoulish mystique attached to the man, due in no small part to his infamous Murder Castle; yet researcher Adam Selzer has done a superb job in demolishing tales of acid vats, torture rooms, and gas chambers, most of which appear to have been concocted by the active imaginations of those seeking to sell newspapers.

We may never know the final tally of Holmes's victims. It is entirely possible that there are other victims for whose murders he was never tried or convicted. H. H. Holmes was a con man and a liar to the bitter end—so why would he have told the truth about that?

BUSTED BY THE INTERNET: MAURY TRAVIS

The things that those who knew him said about Maury Travis were similar to those we have heard about many other serial killers: a variation on the "he was such a nice guy, he wouldn't harm a fly" theme. He "didn't have a violent bone in his body," said a longtime friend when interviewed by the *St. Louis Post-Dispatch*. "He's a robber, not a murderer." Despite having a criminal record for holding up shoe stores, nobody who knew him suspected that he was also abducting, torturing, and then murdering prostitutes by strangling them.

Born on October 25, 1965, in St. Louis, Missouri, there was no evidence that Maury Travis had had a troubled childhood. He appeared to have come from a normal, well-adjusted family home with loving parents, although they did divorce when he was 13 years old. Growing up, he was an introvert—unremarkable to friends, family members, acquaintances, and teachers.

In his early 20s, Travis turned to petty crime to support an expensive cocaine habit, finally running afoul of the law and accepting his arrest meekly when it came. The presiding judge accepted Travis's explanation that the drugs were responsible for his short-lived robbery spree, a decision no doubt influenced by a letter supporting Travis's moral character written by a local congressman. Nevertheless, he served five years behind bars before being released in 1994.

Neighbors described him as being a good neighbor, polite, considerate, and respectful. One referred to him as "the perfect gentleman." Yet there was a backslide in 1998 when he spent another year in jail on drug charges. He was released in 1999, but he found himself back inside for the same reason on November 29, 2000, for another three-month stretch. In between these stints, he is believed to have murdered 62-year-old Mary Shields.

Following his release from jail in March 2001, police believe that Travis began to kill new victims every few weeks. He targeted those within his own racial group—African American—and preferred to kill sex workers and drug abusers (though not exclusively), bringing them back to his house under the pretense of having sex with them. Once the women were in his basement, Travis dropped the nice-guy act and beat, raped, and murdered them. Sometimes he would film the sickening assaults, hiding the videotapes inside a wall cavity.

> Once the women were in his basement, Travis dropped the nice-guy act and beat, raped, and murdered them.

The best estimate of the St. Louis police is that Maury Travis carried out most of his murders between the spring of 2001 and 2002. When a serial killer is caught, it can be for a variety of reasons. Sometimes, their luck runs out—they happen to be in the wrong place at the wrong time, or the police officers who are hunting them catch a lucky break. More often than not, however, the reason is that the killer simply got careless.

In the case of Maury Travis, a compulsion to taunt detectives, coupled with a lack of understanding about how computers and the internet work, proved to be his undoing.

On May 21, 2002, Travis mailed an anonymous letter to *St. Louis Post-Dispatch* reporter Bill Smith that read:

Dear Bill, nice sob story about Teresa Wilson. write one about Greenwade write a good one and I'll tell you where many others are to prove im real here's directions to number seventeen search in a fifty yard radius of the X put the story in the Sunday paper like the last.

The X in question appeared on a printed map that accompanied the letter. Smith immediately turned the map and letter over to the police for analysis. It was obvious to the detectives that both documents had been printed from a computer, rather than drawn by hand or cut out of a book. The letter could simply have been written by a crank, but when detectives went to the position indicated by the cross and dug, they unearthed the remains of a woman. But the letter turned out to be real. It had been sent by the unidentified victim's killer. Now all that remained was to find him.

Thankfully, this was the internet age. There was no such thing as true anonymity when it came to things like this. Computer experts scrutinized the map and determined that it came from the website *Expedia.com*, one of the more popular travel sites on the Web. FBI agents immediately subpoenaed records for all of the maps generated on *Expedia.com* for that area in the days before the letter was mailed and quickly came up with a hit in the form of an internet protocol (IP) address.

Temporary IP addresses are assigned to every device that is connected to the World Wide Web. Today, that means telephones, tablets, and all manner of home devices, but in 2002, half of those items didn't exist yet; the only devices that needed an IP address were network devices such as routers and desktop computers. An IP address is a unique identifier, as individual as the home address of your house or apartment, though it is only issued for a specific period of time—sometimes as little as a few hours, but sometimes for as long as a day or two. A skilled computer technician can track one to its physical location with relatively little effort. The engineers at Microsoft, which hosted *Expedia.com*'s website and monitored its traffic, determined that only one computer had requested maps of that particular part of the country in the past few days. The user in question had logged on under the name */MAURYTRAVIS*.

Travis did not understand that he could be tracked using his IP address, and that was how police caught him.

Now that the name Maury Travis was on their radar, the man himself wasn't difficult to find. He was 36 years of age and a waiter. Travis was arrested and taken to jail, saying only, "I'm toast. I'm toast."

Travis appeared cold and unrepentant when a detective asked him to cooperate in order to help provide closure for the families of his victims. "Hmmph, victims," the serial killer responded, and that was the end of that. The detective who interviewed him concluded that Travis saw his victims as less than human.

The search warrant that police obtained for his home turned up enough evidence for them to conclude that they had apprehended the killer of a number of missing and dead St. Louis women. The basement was transformed into a makeshift torture chamber. Present were tools that Travis had used to inflict severe pain upon his victims and various restraints such as handcuffs that were stained with human blood. There was also a stun gun, which was presumably used to keep them compliant.

One of the more horrifying discoveries was a videotape on which Travis was seen to torture and then apparently break the neck of a naked young woman, who had been bound and brutalized prior to her death. The kidnapped subjects of his abuse were stripped and cuffed to a wooden beam in the basement. There was also a series of newspaper articles concerning the murders he had committed, a sort of souvenir scrapbook that chronicled the law enforcement agencies' hunt for him. In addition, several bodily fluid samples linked him to the bodies of two victims.

One of the dead women had a tire track imprinted on her leg, indicating that her killer had driven over her lower body at one point. In something similar to a vehicular "fingerprint," the track matched precisely with the tread on Maury Travis's personal vehicle.

> One of the dead women had a tire track imprinted on her leg, indicating that her killer had driven over her lower body at one point.

It should have been a slam-dunk case for the prosecution. Detectives knew that their man had killed at least two women but felt confident that he could be associated with many more murders—perhaps as many as 20. Sullen and uncooperative, Travis sat in his cell at the St. Louis County Jail until June 10, three days after his arrest, saying nothing to anybody and admitting nothing despite the overwhelming amount of evidence that was stacking up against him.

The closest he ever came to confessing was during his initial interview, when a police officer asked him whether murders carried out by serial killers were "inherent" or "learned" behavior. Travis told the cop that he had been born that way, had been like it for as long as he could remember, and that the police officer simply wouldn't understand.

Despite being placed on suicide watch, a standard precaution when a prisoner is accused of murder, Maury Travis was not as closely watched as he perhaps ought to have been. He waited until the patrolling guard had looked in on him while making welfare checks on the block, and then he hanged himself. When the guard returned for the next round of suicide watch, the serial killer's body was limp and lifeless. He had escaped the reach of justice.

The precise extent of Maury Travis's crimes will likely never be entirely clear. Educated estimates on his final number of victims range from 12 to 20. Just like Herb Baumeister, the I-70 Strangler, Travis was never convicted of a single murder.

There is another disturbing parallel between Maury Travis and Herb Baumeister. Just as Fox Hollow Farm, the residence of the Baumeister family in which Herb murdered his victims, was left standing (and remains a private residence to this day), so too was the house in St. Louis where Travis tortured and killed his victims.

The St. Louis Fox affiliate reported on the awful experience of tenant Catrina McGhaw, who leased the house without having the slightest idea of its grisly history. According to McGhaw, the landlord didn't disclose this information to her—possibly because the landlord was the mother of Maury

Travis. (It should be pointed out that the landlord claims to have fully disclosed to McGhaw the nature of the crimes committed in the home.)

So how did Catrina McGhaw find out about the events that had taken place in her new home? By watching a true crime show about the Maury Travis murders *while sitting in that very same home*. Going downstairs into the basement with the full knowledge of what took place there must have been nauseating, to say the least. The beam to which Travis chained his victims was still standing.

The final straw came when a young family member was playing downstairs in the basement and suddenly became upset by something near the pole. The crying little girl said she was scared, though there was nothing for anybody to be visibly scared of.

Surprisingly, the law does not require realtors and landlords in St. Louis to disclose the fact that murders have occurred at a specific property before leasing or selling it. The ethical question, on the other hand, is an entirely different matter. Fortunately, the local housing authority decided to break the deadlock between tenant and landlord in this case, and McGhaw was allowed to get out of her lease early. Who could possibly blame her?

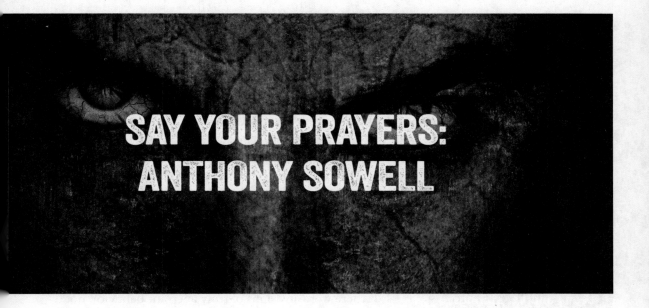

SAY YOUR PRAYERS: ANTHONY SOWELL

Born in 1959, Anthony Sowell grew up in East Cleveland, Ohio, during the 1960s. There are conflicting accounts of precisely what happened in the house that was presided over by his single mother, Claudia "Gertrude" Garrison, but all of them include some degree of physical and sexual abuse of the children in the household from a very early age.

Testifying at his trial for murder, Sowell's niece, Leona Davis, gave a heart-rending account of a childhood spent under constant physical, emotional, and sexual assault. Sowell's father, Thomas, a construction worker, abandoned his family when Sowell was little more than a baby. According to Leona, much of the abuse was carried out at the direction of his mother, Claudia, who sometimes had the young girl stripped naked, tied to a bannister, and whipped with an electrical cord until she bled. After running away from home and being returned by police officers, Leona recalled being smacked about the head with a high-heeled shoe by her enraged great aunt.

Leona's mother had been Sowell's sister. After she died of an illness, her orphaned seven children were forced to move in with Gertrude and her own brood of seven children. In court, Leona maintained that Gertrude's children watched while Leona and her own siblings suffered regular humiliations and beatings.

The 11-year-old Sowell was a year older than Leona and physically stronger, capable of overpowering her with ease. She was unable to fight back. After seeing that the naked Leona was beginning to enter puberty and starting to develop the physical characteristics of a grown woman, he began taking her to an isolated room in the house, where he would rape her.

This demonstrated a pattern of physical violence and forced sexual intercourse that would continuously recur in Sowell's adult life. Despite Sowell's claims that he himself had also been molested as a child, Leona and her siblings insisted that they had never once seen him be abused as they had been—but they had definitely seen him *be* the abuser.

After leaving school, Anthony Sowell enlisted in the U.S. Marine Corps in January 1978. After attending boot camp at the Parris Island Recruit Depot in South Carolina, he received specialized training as an electrician and served at various different postings during his seven years of service, before being discharged in 1985. He was an average Marine with a somewhat patchy service record, earning a number of commendations and a Good Conduct Medal but also going absent without leave (AWOL) for two months and being busted down in rank because of it.

> Despite Sowell's claims that he himself had also been molested as a child, Leona and her siblings insisted that they had never once seen him be abused.

If there were any signs of truly aberrant behavior, none of them made it into his personnel file or were spoken of by his platoon mates. During his term of enlistment, Sowell married a fellow Marine, but the marriage didn't work out and was legally dissolved when he left the Marine Corps.

It is not unheard of for some of those who leave the structure and security of the armed services to have difficulty adjusting to civilian life, and Anthony Sowell was no exception. He used alcohol to cope; he was a very heavy drinker and would regularly pass out. Alcohol stoked his temper and made him violent. It may also have loosened his inhibitions, making it easier for him to do things to others that would have been more difficult for him to do while sober.

Sowell managed to put on a convincing "everyday Joe" facade, but lurking just beneath the surface was the same vicious boy who had raped his niece over and over again, threatening her with violence if she resisted. In 1989, four years after his return to civilian life, Sowell's true nature finally came to the fore. After luring Melvette Sockwell back to his house under false pretenses, he repeatedly raped her, tying her up and choking her during the assault.

"You might as well say your prayers," Sockwell claims Sowell told her while holding her at knifepoint, "'cause I'm gonna feed you, and then I'm gonna kill you." Had she not fled from her captor by climbing onto the roof, Melvette Sockwell likely would have been Anthony Sowell's first murder victim. Fortunately, a bystander saw Melvette's plight and called 911. Sowell was arrested, tried, and given 15 years imprisonment for his crime. He was released in 2005.

In 2007, the murders would begin.

A free man again (albeit now a convicted sex offender), Anthony Sowell moved into a modest home at 12205 Imperial Avenue, in the Mount Pleasant neighborhood of Cleveland, Ohio. It was here that he would commit the atrocities for which he would become notorious. A white house with a pitched roof that was sandwiched between two neighboring brick properties (one of which was a sausage shop), number 12205 looked mundane and safely anonymous, certainly not the sort of place in which a serial killer would rape and murder his victims. Sowell liked it that way. He did nothing to tip off his neighbors that something truly ugly was going on inside.

Posting on an internet fetish site just a month after his release from prison, Sowell advertised for a submissive sexual partner to help him fulfill his fantasies, stating:

> IF YOUR SUBMISSIVE AND LIKE TO PLEASE, THEN THIS MASTER WANTS TO TALK TO YOU. SO GET YOUR *** ON OVER HERE NOW!

Sowell included a photograph of himself staring blankly into the camera, his face expressionless, with a computer monitor in the background.

Posting on an internet fetish site just a month after his release from prison, Sowell advertised for a submissive sexual partner to help him fulfill his fantasies.

When it came to ensnaring victims, Sowell often used the promise of crack cocaine to entice them back to his home. Drugs were a huge problem in Mount Pleasant, as were prostitution and other forms of crime. It was a rough neighborhood, where shootings and stabbings were not uncommon. As African American women started to disappear, the police put minimal effort into tracking them down. These were poor black women (at least one of whom lived in a homeless shelter), vulnerable and ripe for exploitation, and Anthony Sowell had selected them for that exact reason.

In a documentary film about Sowell (*Unseen*, 2018), one resident of Mount Pleasant—a man who had known Sowell personally, often selling him things such as ice cream—voiced his wish that the world had a million Anthony Sowells, because "he took out the garbage." By *garbage*, he meant the female victims. It is almost unbelievable to hear such a thing said by one human being about others, but it provides valuable (if distasteful) insight into the attitude of some local residents toward Sowell and his activities.

There are parallels here with the case of Lonnie Franklin, the so-called Grim Sleeper. Here was another African American serial killer who preyed upon vulnerable women from his own ethnic group. The Grim Sleeper murders also took a long time to garner police attention, and some believe that this is because the disappearances of black women, many of whom were sex workers or drug users, were not treated as seriously as those of "respectable" white victims would have been.

Anthony Sowell's MO was to bring women back to his home, tie them up, rape them, and then kill them, usually by strangulation. Their bodies would then be disposed of either in the house or in the garden outside.

Neighbors reported "a terrible smell" in the vicinity of 12205 Imperial Avenue, but nobody thought for one minute that it might be the rotten stench of decomposing bodies.

An opportunity to bring Sowell to justice was botched in December 2008. Gladys Wade, 40, had been approached by Sowell in the street and physically attacked. He attempted to drag her inside his home, but she was able to overpower him and get away. When they took her report, police officers knew that a registered sex offender named Anthony Sowell lived at that address, which could only have made Wade's story all the more credible. There were also bloodstains on the outside wall and steps leading up to the entrance of the house.

But Gladys Wade did not want to press charges, so the investigation went no further. Sowell was arrested and subsequently released after a detective questioned Wade's credibility. As a result, the prosecutor decided that the case against Sowell was too flimsy, and the matter was dropped.

Eleven women had died inside the house at the hands of Anthony Sowell before he finally made a crucial mistake. Latundra Billups, 37, went back to Imperial Avenue with Sowell to drink a few beers and take some drugs. When she was high, Sowell pounced on her, punched her in the head, and raped her. He used a power cord to strangle the defenseless woman, but when she survived the ordeal, Sowell told Billups that he was going to kill her to keep himself out of jail.

The photo used for the arrest warrant poster on Sowell in 2009.

Latundra Billups was able to use her powers of persuasion to convince him that she was not going to turn him in to the cops. Believing her proved to be a bad call for Anthony Sowell. Although reluctant at first to involve the police, she knew that unless she did something to help stop him, there was a strong likelihood that he would do the same thing to other women, and so she gathered her courage and spoke with a sex crimes detective about the attack she had endured at Sowell's hands. Latundra's story was similar enough to that of Gladys Wade that it could not have been mere coincidence. A judge agreed and promptly issued a search warrant on October 29, 2009. Officers could not possibly have been prepared for what they found upon entering Sowell's home.

Decomposing human remains were everywhere. One set of body parts was hidden behind some drywall in a crawl space. More were found in the living room. A severed head, later identified as that of Leshanda Long, was wrapped up in paper and kept down in the cellar, and another set of remains was buried beneath the cellar steps. Bodies were also interred in shallow graves less than two feet below the surface in the backyard. Still more were discovered up on the third floor. One body had been stuffed into a trash bag, apparently forgotten.

It seemed as if the tenant had gone to great lengths to hide them, wrapping them in plastic (perhaps to contain the by-products of decomposition). All of the victims were black women. The state of decomposition of some of the bodies was so advanced that it was difficult to tell which body parts were which. How Sowell had been able to live in the house for so long in the face of such an odor was almost beyond belief. Even the coroner could not immediately tell whether some of the bodies had been there for weeks, months, or perhaps even years.

> Sowell was picked up when a police unit saw him walking casually down the street, acting as if nothing out of the ordinary had happened.

Those who lived and worked nearby were horrified. Some had perceived Anthony Sowell as being a respectable man. Others had seen him drunk from time to time, loafing in front of his house, but few had anything truly bad to say about him. He just wasn't all that memorable, one way or the other. When questioned by police, some local residents recalled seeing him wandering the streets from time to time, usually looking for old junk to sell.

Sowell was picked up when a police unit saw him walking casually down the street, acting as if nothing out of the ordinary had happened. He went along without putting up a fight, as if resigned to what was about to happen next. "I'm Anthony Sowell," he said. "I'm the guy you're looking for." Despite his having raped and murdered 11 women, he would go on to claim that he was not a bad guy—he was just somebody who needed a little help.

In the courtroom, Sowell claimed to have incomplete memories of the murders. The women he had killed were drug addicts and needed to be punished, he explained to detectives. Laying the groundwork for his eventual defense, Sowell painted a fanciful picture of the murders taking place in some sort of dreamlike state, implying that he had diminished mental capacity during each killing. In truth, there were few other cards that he could have played. He was already a convicted violent rapist, and the presence of the human remains in and around his home were impossible to explain away.

Sowell's story revolved around a drug-addicted ex-girlfriend who he said had dumped him after he "put a lot of time and effort into helping her turn her life around." The women he brought back to the house on Imperial Avenue reminded him of her, Sowell maintained, particularly as many of them had a history of substance abuse issues. This realization caused him to enter a fit of irrational rage, during which he "somehow" strangled them to death.

The detectives who interrogated him maintained a respectful attitude toward him, but they didn't find his story to be even the least bit convincing. After all, even if it *was* true that Sowell became briefly unhinged while committing the murders, then why did he make only a half-hearted effort to conceal the victims' bodies around the house? He just went about his daily business for at least two years in the full knowledge that the remains of those women were all around him, and he kept on adding to their number whenever the urge took him. At no point did he ever seek help from the authorities.

The parallels with Scottish serial killer Dennis Nilsen are striking. Nilsen, whose case is covered elsewhere in this book, murdered at-risk young men at his residence and stashed their bodies beneath the floorboards. He was widely believed to have been "killing for company." He was a lonely, antisocial man who took a perverse comfort in being permanently surrounded by the dead, sometimes draping their corpses over his own body while he lay in bed at night.

> The entire 12-person jury unanimously determined that Anthony Sowell should receive the death penalty for each one of his murders.

Sowell's defense attorneys challenged many aspects of the police investigation but were ultimately unsuccessful. Of the 85 crimes that their client was charged with, he was acquitted of just two. Still, his attorney, John Parker, did his thankless job to the very last and tried to prevent his client from being executed. "What the State is asking you to do is eliminate this man from the face of the Earth. But what you need to keep in mind is that when you execute a person, you are killing their entire life. You are executing the abused child. You are executing the honorable Marine. You are executing the well-behaved prisoner. You are executing the man who held down a job."

He neglected to mention that they would also be executing the serial rapist, physical abuser, and murderer. Regardless, his efforts were unsuccessful. The entire 12-person jury unanimously determined that Anthony Sowell should receive the death penalty for each one of his murders.

With some light finally shed upon his murderous activities in the Mount Pleasant neighborhood, detectives began to look back at a number of unsolved cold case files, killings that had taken place in Sowell's vicinity when he left the Marines. He could potentially have murdered several other women long before his "official" start date in 2007, though it is unlikely that his involvement will ever be conclusively proven or disproven.

Even though several years have passed since the last murder took place, one burning question remains: How much more could have been done to track down the killer of "the Imperial Eleven"?

Sowell was a Tier-3 sex offender, the highest and most dangerous rating the justice system can assign. As such, police patrols stopped by 12205 Imperial Avenue to perform random spot checks from time to time. These sheriff's deputies did not enter the house (something for which they lacked permission) but did speak to Sowell and walk around the exterior of the property. There is no record of them ever finding anything amiss, despite the fact that the bodies of murder victims were decomposing in the yard behind the house and that an increasing number of locals were complaining about the smell.

In the fall of 2018, the City of Cleveland agreed to pay one million dollars to the family members of six of Anthony Sowell's victims—though it did not admit to any wrongdoing on the part of the police department. The case hinged on the way that the report of Gladys Wade was handled in 2008. When a grand jury reviewed the evidence, Sowell was indicted on rape and assault charges, vindicating Gladys Wade and in some small way redressing her poor treatment immediately after the attack.

At the time of writing, Anthony Sowell remains on death row, where he has been awaiting execution since September 2011.

The house at 12205 Imperial Avenue was demolished in 2011, the only fitting response to the atrocities that had occurred inside. At the time of writing, a memorial to the victims of Anthony Sowell that has long been planned for the site has not materialized. In its place is a humble sign, which serves as a temporary epitaph for those poor women.

GONE, BUT NOT FORGOTTEN

The victims of Anthony Sowell were:

- Crystal Dozier (age 35)
- Tishana Culver (age 31)
- Leshanda Long (age 25)
- Michelle Mason (age 45)
- Tonia Carmichael (age 53)
- Nancy Cobbs (age 43)
- Amelda Hunter (age 47)
- Telacia Fortson (age 31)
- Janice Webb (age 49)
- Kim Yvette Smith (age 44)
- Diane Turner (age 38)

May they all rest in peace.

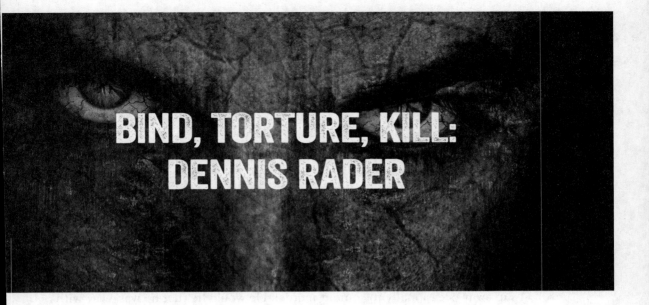

BIND, TORTURE, KILL: DENNIS RADER

He didn't look like a murderer. The man seemed far too ordinary for that. He lacked the psychotic stare of Manson, the clean-cut handsomeness of Bundy, or the pouting scowl of Ramirez. Kansas native Dennis Rader looked like the guy next door, the sort of middle-aged man who worked in a bank or an office and went home to a wife and kids at the end of the day.

That perception wasn't too wide of the mark. It was the mask he wore, day in and day out, in order to hide his true face: that of a serial killer with a penchant for torture.

Dennis Rader was born on March 9, 1945, into a Lutheran Christian household. He would continue to attend a Lutheran church throughout his life. His family life growing up was ordinary; he does not appear to have been abused, either physically or emotionally. If his own anecdotes are to be believed, however, something very unusual was going on inside young Dennis Rader's psyche.

Rader would later claim to have tortured and hanged domestic animals while he was growing up. Much like Richard Ramirez, he liked to peep into windows in the hope of catching women undressing, and he did his best to snatch underwear whenever the opportunity presented itself.

Rader had served a four-year hitch (1966–1970) in the U.S. Air Force as a young man and then worked various civilian jobs after his discharge, including a position with a security alarm company. Ironically, there was an increased demand for his services when his own murder victims started to be discovered.

While still an airman, he would give life to his depraved sexual fantasies by drawing sketches on paper and then destroying them when it was time to move on to the next posting.

In 1971, he got married, subsequently fathering a son and a daughter. The Raders were always a churchgoing family, and Dennis was sufficiently respected by the other members of the congregation for him to rise through the ranks to sit on its council. His facade as a pillar of the community was further bolstered by his status as a leader with the Boy Scouts of America. Dennis Rader could have given a master class on the subject of hiding in plain sight.

Rader's daughter, Kerri, who would go on to write a book about her experiences as the child of a serial killer, spoke of a childhood mostly spent in a warm and loving family environment. "I was born in '78. My dad murdered a young woman when my mom was three months pregnant with me. Most of the time, [my father] was even-keeled, kind and warm," she told ABC News reporters. "At times, he could be very firm or have flashes of anger or outbursts that you weren't expecting."

Yet despite this seemingly normal environment, Dennis Rader would slip away occasionally to commit murder. He would lie that he was away with the Scouts on a camping trip—a dangerous alibi that would not stand up to close scrutiny if it was ever questioned.

Rader's first murders took place on January 15, 1974. He entered the home of the Oteros, a Wichita family. Joseph, 38, and his wife, Julie, 33, were home, as were two of their children—Joseph Jr., 9, and Josephine, 11.

In anonymous letters that he sent to the authorities, Rader described the events that took place inside the Otero residence at the time of the killings. The detectives investigating the case were acutely aware that taking the word of a serial killer could be unwise. Meanwhile, Rader was immensely ego-driven and enjoyed the feeling of imparting knowledge to the police that they could not have obtained by any other means. He liked to feel privileged, and he got off on the idea of his crimes being in the spotlight while he himself remained safely hidden in the shadows—or so he thought.

Rader had expected Julie Otero and the children to be home, but he had not anticipated the presence of her husband. Rader had cut the phone lines before entering the house through an already-open door, ensuring that they could not call for help.

Dennis Rader looked for all intents and purposes like an ordinary, middle-aged family man. He had a family, went to church, and was a Boy Scout leader.

Pulling out a knife and a pistol, Rader held the Oteros at gunpoint and lied to them, saying that all he wanted was to steal their car and then he would be on his way. Herding them all into one of the bedrooms, he tied the family up with their hands behind their backs. Realizing that the family dog could be something of a wild card, he had it put out into the yard first.

Joseph Otero was the greatest threat, and Rader, a natural coward but a shrewd one nevertheless, tried to kill him by putting a plastic bag over his head and tying it at the neck in an attempt to asphyxiate him. He then moved over to the bed and began strangling Julie. Unbeknownst to Rader, however, he had only succeeded in rendering her unconscious, and she would soon recover, making it necessary for him to strangle her a second time.

> **P**ulling out a knife and a pistol, Rader held the Oteros at gunpoint and lied to them, saying that all he wanted was to steal their car and then he would be on his way.

Rader returned to Joseph and strangled him to death. Taking Joseph Jr. into a nearby bedroom, he did the same thing to him.

Josephine Otero was killed last. Rader took her down to the basement, claiming at first that her parents and brother were simply sleeping, but then telling the girl, "You [sic] be in heaven tonight with the rest." Rader hanged her from a sewer pipe, watched her die, and then masturbated over her body.

Once the entire family was dead, Rader went from room to room tidying up, stole their car, and drove it away. The Oteros' bodies were discovered by their son Charlie when he came home from school later that day, a shocking discovery that quite understandably scarred him for life.

Although he wanted to safeguard his identity, it chafed Rader that he wasn't getting the recognition for his killings that he thought he was entitled to. One attempt to address this was a letter that he typed, detailing the way in which he had murdered the Oteros. Rather than mail it to the police or to the media, he had instead tucked it inside an engineering textbook that was shelved at the Wichita Public Library. When it wasn't immediately discovered, Rader called the library and told them of its existence. The library staff wisely contacted the Wichita Police Department and allowed them to retrieve the letter safely, safeguarding its integrity as evidence:

OTERO CASE

I WRITE THIS LETTER TO YOU FOR THE SAKE OF THE TAX PAYER AS WELL AS YOUR TIME. THOSE THREE DUDE [sic] YOU HAVE IN CUSTODY ARE JUST TALKING TO GET PUBLICITY FOR THE OTERO MURDERS. THEY KNOW NOTHING AT ALL. I DID IT BY MYSELF AND NO ONES HELP. THERE HAS BEEN NO TALK EITHER. LET'S PUT IT STRAIGHT.

He then proceeded to outline, in precise and exacting detail, the location in which each Otero family member was found, what they had been wearing, and how they had been bound at the time of their death. This was proof positive that the letter had indeed been written by the murderer, or at the very least, somebody who had been present at the crime scene. The note concluded:

I'M SORRY THIS HAPPEN TO SOCIETY. GOOD LUCK WITH YOUR HUNTING.

YOURS, TRULY GUILTILY

P.S. SINCE SEX CRIMINALS DO NOT CHANGE THEIR MO OR BY NATURE CANNOT DO SO, I WILL NOT CHANGE MINE. THE CODE WORDS FOR ME WILL BE … BIND THEM, TORTURE THEM, KILL THEM. B.T.K., YOU SEE ME AT IT AGAIN. THEY WILL BE ON THE NEXT VICTIM.

The name by which he would become notorious—B.T.K.—was thus self-christened.

Less than three months later, on April 4, 1974, Dennis Rader committed his next murder after breaking into the home of 21-year-old Kathryn Bright. The home was empty, leaving Rader time to wait in ambush. When Kathryn and her 19-year-old brother, Kevin, came home, Rader sprung his trap. Walking past the bedroom, the Brights saw a man standing in the doorway with a gun leveled at them both.

Rader used the same routine that had worked to pacify the Oteros, claiming that if they handed over a car and some money, everything would be okay. Understandably, the Brights bought into this and chose not to resist. Still at gunpoint, Kevin tied up his sister, and then turned his back to allow the intruder to tie his hands behind his back.

Separating the brother and sister into two different rooms, Rader disappeared for a few minutes. When he came back, it was with a stocking that he looped around Kevin Bright's neck and began to strangle him. Kevin attempted to fight back. Rader shot him, then went away for a short time while Kevin lay on the floor bleeding. He was shot a second time and had the presence of mind

Unhappy that he wasn't getting enough attention for his murders, Rader typed out a letter about killing the Oteros and placed it in a book at the Wichita Public Library (pictured).

(not to mention incredible willpower) to play dead until his would-be killer had left the room again. Then he went for help.

Unfortunately, help came too late for Kathryn. She fought her assailant courageously, but Rader finally managed to overpower her and repeatedly stabbed her in the torso with a knife. Then he went back to make sure that Kevin was dead and found the door open. He hurriedly cleaned up as best he could and fled the scene. Kevin Bright remains the only victim to have survived an assault by the B.T.K. killer. Tragically, his sister was not so lucky.

B.T.K. would not kill again for another two and a half years, striking again on March 17, 1977. Shirley Vian was a mother of three. Knocking on Vian's door, Rader pretended to be a detective when Vian's young son answered. Completely taken in, the boy opened the door and allowed Rader to come inside. Once the door was closed behind him, Rader took out his .357 magnum and used it to forcibly compel Shirley Vian into being compliant with his wishes.

> Kevin Bright remains the only victim to have survived an assault by the B.T.K. killer.

According to Rader's own account of events, he told her that he "had a problem with sexual fantasies" and might have to tie her and her children up. She was understandably nervous, but like all of Rader's victims, believed it when he told her that everything would be okay if she would only cooperate. She even assisted Rader in corralling her children, who began to scream and cry when Rader attempted to tie them up. Put off by the screaming, he locked the children in the bathroom, giving them toys to play with as a distraction while he set about murdering their mother in an adjacent room.

Still the children would not stop crying. Distracted and concerned about somebody coming to check on them, Rader strangled Shirley Vian and left the residence in a hurry. One is forced to wonder whether he might have killed them too if they had not been quite so loud. He had betrayed no qualms about killing a child as young as nine in the Otero household, after all; the man quite clearly had no conscience to prevent him from doing it again. In a future letter, Rader alluded to this by saying that he had been startled by a ringing phone, which had prevented him from killing all three of Shirley's children.

Twenty-eight years later, Shirley Vian's young son, Stephen Relford, spoke about his recollections of that awful day. He had been just five years old at the time, but he still remembered it very clearly, the memories doubtless burned into his brain because of the emotional trauma he and his siblings sustained.

"It's been 28 years, and I hope I meet this ******* face to face," Relford said during an interview with KAKE-TV. At the time of the interview, Rader had not yet been caught and unmasked.

Despite the facade of courtesy and normality that Rader put on in the courtroom, his true nature came out when young Stephen watched B.T.K. tying up his mother and said that he was going to undo the knots. "You better not … I'll blow your ******* head off," the killer had told him. The chances are good that he wouldn't have pulled the trigger, but if time had allowed, Rader would have been only too happy to kill the child by suffocation or strangulation.

KAKE-TV was the recipient of its own letter from B.T.K. in 1978, following the murder of 25-year-old Nancy Fox. On December 8, 1977, Rader had forced his way into her home while she was out, after once again cutting the telephone line first. He had staked out the property and knew when to expect her to come home. When Nancy walked through the door, Rader was waiting. He told her the same story about having "a sexual problem" that made him have to tie her up and rape her.

Rader forced her to undress, handcuffed her wrists, and had her lie down on the bed. He then climbed on top of her and strangled her to death with a belt. When she was dead, Rader masturbated, leaving a D.N.A. sample at the scene that would constitute evidence later. Rader left the scene and then phoned the police to let them know what he had just done.

> The tone of the letter is by turns petulant and condescending, practically oozing "why won't you recognize my genius?"

Two months later, Rader was apparently feeling underappreciated. He typed another missive, this one much longer, and mailed it to the KAKE-TV newsroom. As one reads the letter—full of the usual grammatical and spelling errors—it is almost possible to hear Rader pouting and sulking like a child due to a lack of attention:

"HOW MANY DO I HAVE TO KILL BEFORE I GET A NAME IN THE PAPER OR SOME NATIONAL ATTENTION," Rader writes. He goes on to bemoan the lack of critical thinking shown by the police, and he claims responsibility for killing Shirley Vian and Nancy Fox and laboriously lays out the connections between the two murders. The tone of the letter is by turns petulant and condescending, practically oozing "why won't you recognize my genius?" from every line. Rader places himself in the same context as the Son of Sam, Jack the Ripper, H. H. Holmes, and other serial killers who he clearly feels are his peer group.

Rader signs off with "MAY YOU NOT BE THE UNLUCK [sic] ONE!" but cannot resist adding a postscript in which he insists that he needs some type of nickname beyond B.T.K. ("IT'S TIME. 7 DOWN AND MANY MORETO [sic] GO.") He even adds a list of potential names, such as the Wichita Strangler, the Poetic Strangler, the Wichita Hangman, and the Wichita Executioner. The sheer amount of narcissism and depth of insecurity on display are staggering. ("Poetic Strangler" refers to a poem that Rader had sent to a local Wichita newspaper in January.)

B.T.K. then went dormant for the next seven years, returning to kill again on April 27, 1985. His depraved urges had not gone away; they had merely lain fallow. This time, things took a somewhat different path.

Fifty-three-year-old Marine Hedge came home to find Dennis Rader waiting for her. Rader strangled her to death and then, in a break from his usual MO, drove the corpse back to the church at which he worshiped, Christ Lutheran, where, earlier, he had stored such materials as plastic sheeting and bondage restraints. Once there, he posed Marine's dead body in various sexualized positions, tying it up and snapping some Polaroid pictures for his personal collection. He had planned this particular assault meticulously, even going so far as to draw out a diagram of her home prior to gaining access to it. Rader knew the floor plan because she lived just a few doors down from his own home, in a house that was laid out in almost exactly the same way as his. This was a turning point for Rader because he now felt comfortable—or cocky—enough to kill one of his own neighbors, knowing full well that the police would soon be conducting a full-blown homicide investigation near his own house.

Predictably, this overconfidence would be what eventually got him caught.

Once he had sated himself with Marine Hedge's body, he disposed of it by laying it in a ditch and covering it up as best he could with some leaves and plants.

A year and a half passed before the next B.T.K. murder. On September 16, 1986, Dennis Rader killed 28-year-old Vicki Wegerle. Rather than force his way in, Rader instead went with guile. Trying to pass himself off as a telephone repair technician, he was surprised when she allowed him into her home without any apparent suspicion or asking him to present any credentials.

Once inside the home, Rader pulled a gun on his victim and forced her into the bedroom. He attempted to tie her up. She fought back. Rader managed to get a nylon stocking around Vicki Wegerle's throat, tighten it, and then strangle her. Believing her to be dead, he exposed parts of her body by readjusting her clothing and took some photographs, then fled the scene.

Vicki's husband came home moments later to find his wife in the bedroom. Fortunately, B.T.K. had not had the time to harm the Wegerles' two-year-old child (we will never know if he would have done so, if time had allowed). Paramedics transported Vicki Wegerle to the hospital. Resuscitation was attempted, but she was ultimately pronounced dead in the emergency room.

The night of January 19, 1991, saw the next B.T.K. murder. At 62, Dolores Davis was Dennis Rader's oldest victim. She would also be his last. It

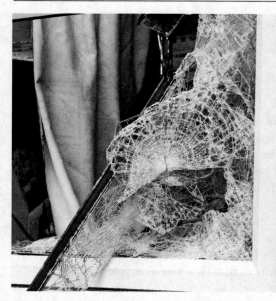

Rader broke the window with a concrete block and climbed inside Dolores Davis's home, where he strangled her with a pair of pantyhose.

was cold outside, so Rader didn't want to waste any time getting inside her house. He simply threw a concrete block through one of the windows and climbed inside.

According to Rader, Dolores Davis emerged from her bedroom because his entrance had been so loud. She had actually thought that a car had driven into her house. Overpowering her, Rader tied his victim to her own bed and slowly strangled her with a pair of pantyhose. He also went through her home and stole some personal items to keep as trophies, something he occasionally did.

Just as he had done with Marine Hedge, he stuffed Dolores's body into the trunk of her own car, drove to a bridge, and disposed of her body beneath it.

Over the course of the next fourteen years, B.T.K. did not kill again—but he *did* continue to taunt the police and the media with letters and photographs. He also included some of the personal items he had taken from the crime scenes for which he was responsible, which confirmed to the detectives who were hunting him that this really *was* their killer, rather than simply a hoaxer. It was the equivalent of constantly raising his hand and saying, "Hey, I'm still here!" before disappearing back into the shadows again.

Dennis Rader was not the first murderer to be caught thanks to a lack of savviness with computer technology (see the case of Maury Travis elsewhere in this book), nor will he be the last. Lieutenant Ken Landwehr of the Wichita Police Department had been working on establishing a rapport with the unidentified killer, who had been communicating with the department via secretive messages. Without realizing the risk that he was placing himself under, the murderer asked if it was safe for him to send further messages by means of a floppy disk—could he be traced by the police using that method?

Quite why Rader expected an honest answer from the detectives trying to hunt him down is unclear, but he was evidently reassured when Lt. Landwehr replied that it was okay for him to send in a floppy disk. Rader did just that, sending his next taunting message to a TV news station in the belief that it could not be connected to him. He was wrong.

Rader had used a desktop computer at his Lutheran church to compose the message and then write it to a disk. Along with the disk, he had included the cover of a bondage-themed novel about a murderer (*Rules of Prey* by John

Camp) and several index cards. All that the floppy disk contained was a single text file declaring itself to be a test and directing the reader to look at one of the enclosed index cards.

The disk's sender was oblivious to the fact that every computer file ever created, no matter what its format, contains a series of associated properties. These included the file type, the date it was last created, and, sometimes, the name of the individual who last modified it. In this case, when detectives examined the file properties, the modifier's name was listed as DENNIS, and it had been modified at the Christ Lutheran Church, which just so happened to be the place of worship of one Dennis Rader. Lt. Landwehr knew this because punching the name of the church into a search engine brought up its web page, which listed Rader as the president of the congregation.

Rader had tried to be clever by deleting all but the text file from the floppy disk. He hadn't known that deleting data doesn't mean it's actually *gone*. Unless the floppy is wiped and its file structure overwritten, the 1s and 0s are all still there, just waiting to be recovered by somebody with the proper know-how.

> **R**ader had tried to be clever by deleting all but the text file from the floppy disk. He hadn't known that deleting data doesn't mean it's actually *gone*.

Still, more was needed before an arrest warrant could be issued. With Dennis Rader in the frame as the most probable B.T.K. suspect to date, the police officers were very aware that they could not afford to slip up now. One simple mistake could undo their entire case, and they had worked too hard to let the B.T.K. killer escape on a technicality.

Knowing that Kerri Rader had undergone a medical screening procedure at a student clinic, Landwehr obtained a subpoena to test a sample of her tissue. DNA from B.T.K. himself was already on file, and the two were cross-checked. A familial match came back, indicating that she must be the daughter of the B.T.K. murderer.

Now they had their man. A warrant was issued for detectives to search the Rader family home. Although the house itself was clear, a search of Rader's outdoor shed turned up pairs of women's underwear, duct tape, pantyhose, and a variety of ropes and cords. Rader would sometimes dress in the clothes of his dead victims, tie himself up as best he could, and take BDSM-themed pictures of himself in what seemed to be a perverse attempt to re-create the murders he was responsible for.

On February 25, 2005, Dennis Rader was arrested on the grounds that he was the prime suspect for being the B.T.K. killer.

Surprisingly, Dennis Rader confessed to his crimes, walking the judge through his recollection of each one of the murders to the best of his memory. He had waived his right to a trial by jury. The judge awarded him ten life sentences, the maximum allowable under the law at that time because the death penalty had only been reinstated in Kansas in 1994—three years after the last B.T.K. murder. Dennis Rader was therefore not eligible for execution, and so at the time of writing he is currently serving a 175-year life sentence at the El Dorado Correctional Facility in Kansas.

Since his arrest, some police officers and criminal profilers have suspected that Rader was responsible for more than the ten murders to which he confessed. They point to the fact that few serial killers have such large gaps between killing victims as Rader had. Typically, when there is a long gap, the killer was imprisoned, hospitalized, or otherwise rendered incapable of murdering. To all appearances, Dennis Rader just stopped, then started killing again when the urge took him.

It may well be that we will never know the full extent of his crimes.

THE TIP OF THE ICEBERG: SAMUEL LITTLE

Although he is now a frail 80-year-old man, Samuel Little is believed by some in law enforcement to be one of the most prolific serial killers—if not *the* most prolific—in U.S. history. For decades, he flew below the radar, murdering victim after victim without arousing any suspicion as to his existence, let alone his identity.

As with so many of the serial killers covered in this book, Little tried wherever possible to choose victims who were unlikely to be missed, such as sex workers, drug users, and transients. In many instances, the deaths were not even classified as homicides at all—they were only ever considered as such once Little confessed to them after his eventual capture and questioning.

"I'm not going to go into the white neighborhoods and pick up the teenage girls," Little, who is black, told interviewing detectives. "I'm not going to go to the shopping centers and get the housewives, who would start screaming. Them are the kind that get you busted."

Samuel Little was born on June 7, 1940, in Georgia, but raised in Ohio by his grandmother. Although not a great deal is known about his childhood, his criminal track record began with an arrest for breaking and entering in 1957, when he was just 17. It was a habit that he never grew out of. There are inmates like Little incarcerated in prisons all across America, long-term lawbreakers who know no other way of living than the criminal way and aren't particularly inclined to try to break out of that cycle.

Over the course of his long lifetime, Little was arrested over 50 times in at least 24 different states. He made a living as a petty criminal, robbing stores, stealing items, and then selling them to other minor crooks. There were crimes of violence too, such as assault and battery, and drug-related offenses,

Arrested over 50 times for theft, assault and battery, and drug offenses, Little still only spent about ten years in jail for his crimes.

including the possession of a crack pipe. In his early 20s, Little did time in prison for burglary, but shoplifting—which had a lower gain but also a lower risk—was more his forte. That, and murder.

Remarkably, despite his almost ridiculous number of brushes with the law, Samuel Little spent less than a decade behind bars. In an Associated Press article, Los Angeles deputy district attorney Beth Silverman said, "It's the craziest rap sheet I've ever seen. The fact that he hasn't spent a more significant period of his life (in custody) is a shocking thing. He's gotten break after break."

There can be no denying that he was extraordinarily, almost freakishly, lucky. He was charged with murdering women twice but was not convicted for either death.

As he drove back and forth across the country over the years, Samuel Little used the opportunity that a change of scenery brought with it to help him sexually assault and then kill the various women that he picked up. It took decades for law enforcement to finally catch on, and when they did, police departments across the United States were forced to take a long, hard look at their cold case files in order to see how many of them could have been attributed to him.

A powerfully built man, Samuel Little was once a proficient boxer, and he used that to help overcome his victims. He took a perverse desire in beating them aggressively, punching and choking them with no advance warning. Little punched one victim so hard in the belly that her spine broke under the impact. Much like Dennis Rader, the B.T.K. Killer, he got sexual gratification from slowly strangling a woman and would often masturbate while doing so.

During an interview with journalist Jillian Lauren, Samuel Little recalled his first victim. "She was a big ol' blonde. Round about turn of the new year, 1969 to 1970. Miami. Coconut Grove. She was a ho. A prostitute. She was sitting at a restaurant booth, red leather, real nice. She crossed them big legs in her fishnet stockings and touched her neck. It was my sign. From God."

Experts probing Little's motivations, trying to develop a profile to understand what makes him tick, were confident that he was sexually driven, which he made no attempt to refute. Unusually, Samuel Little was a serial killer who murdered victims outside of his own ethnic group, seemingly paying little or no attention to the color of their skin. He confessed to selecting many of his victims purely based upon the size and shape of their neck, the smoother the better as far as he was concerned. Referring to him as a rapist often drew angry denials. Little liked to masturbate while strangling his victims rather than forcibly penetrate them much of the time, but both are a crime of control and dominance no matter how he chooses to think of it. He was also ignoring the fact that a number of his victims demonstrably *had* been raped. Little had his own personal reality distortion field at times, the ability to blind himself to what was true and substitute a faux reality of his own.

> He did not deny having beaten Smith, but he maintained that he had not raped her. In a shockingly light piece of sentencing, he was jailed for just three months.

Although Little is believed to have begun killing in 1970, when he was 30 years old, he did not attract significant police attention until 1976 when he attacked Pamela Kay Smith in St. Louis County, Missouri. The distraught victim was naked and terrified, and her wrists were bound with electrical cord when she staggered up to the door of the closest house and screamed at the residents for help. She had also been brutally beaten and sodomized.

She was able to give a good description of her attacker, and patrol officers picked Samuel Little up and brought him in for questioning. He did not deny having beaten Smith, but he maintained that he had not raped her. In a shockingly light piece of sentencing, he was jailed for just three months. It has been theorized that because his victim was a known heroin addict, her testimony was considered to be questionable, and therefore Little's lawyer was able to cut him a sentencing deal.

When choosing potential victims, Little steered clear of his hometown and its local environs, instead finding the streets of Cleveland, Ohio, to be more to his liking. He deliberately selected some of its poorer and more violent neighborhoods on the East Side, assaulting and killing one victim in 1984 and another in 1991. In both cases, he was not connected to the crimes until more than two decades later.

If his word is to be believed, Samuel Little's 35 years of killing ended in 2005 with one final murder. He was 65 years old at the time and was living in Mississippi.

When the police finally caught up with Samuel Little in 2012, his place of residence was a homeless shelter in Kentucky. He had been living on the streets, with little in the way of documentation to provide a paper trail. Still, the police were tenacious. The detectives looking for him were not local; they hailed from Los Angeles, on the opposite side of the country. Nor were his crimes recent. The detectives were attempting to clear up a couple of cold cases dating back to the 1980s.

The murders of three women, all similar in their MO—death by strangulation, with the bodies being left partially naked in a sexually suggestive way—had been linked to Little, thanks to a computerized search of the DNA database. He was found guilty of three murders and given three life sentences. There was no way he would ever get out of prison alive.

Now that it was obvious the game was up, it soon became apparent that there were more than the three murders with which he was charged. Because he was no longer free to murder, the serial killer began working with detectives to identify some of the more than 90 victims he was believed to have killed. He formed an unlikely bond with a Texas Ranger named James Holland, which would help clear up a swathe of cold case murders. Pulling from 35 years' worth of memories, Little made sketch drawings of as many of the victims' faces as he could remember, perhaps in an attempt to jog the memories of family members or to try to match them against unknown Jane Does across the United States. Little liked to sketch, a fun pastime that detectives were now using to help fill in the cold case blanks.

Although a captured serial killer would normally be considered to be an unreliable historian, the detectives found him to be credible, noting that he

Sketches by Samuel Little based on his memories of two of his victims. He made the drawings to cooperate with the FBI on cold cases and get a more lenient sentence.

admitted to murders that other men had been convicted for when there was no tangible benefit to him. On the other hand, when it was suggested that he might be guilty of other murders that he insisted he was not responsible for, Little would get angry, as if his "good name" was somehow being besmirched.

When the police followed up on his claims, most of the time they turned out to be true and verifiably accurate. He had just one condition before offering his help to the authorities: under no circumstances would any of the jurisdictions in which his victims were found be allowed to charge him with a capital crime. In exchange for Samuel Little's cooperation, he could not be given the death penalty.

At the time of writing, Samuel Little is still cooperating with the FBI and various local law enforcement jurisdictions, helping to identify women from his back catalog of victims. Most recently, in March 2020, he confessed to being involved with two cold cases in Indiana. In 1980, Little murdered 18-year-old Valeria Boyd, whose body was abandoned in a field, and 31-year-old Mary Ann Porter, left at the side of the road. Forty years after their deaths, there is at least some hope of closure for their families.

Samuel Little is now wheelchair-bound, suffering from both diabetes and cardiovascular disease. While he has contrived to evade the death penalty, this seems like a hollow victory. Rather than die relatively quickly in an electric chair or by lethal injection, the final years of Samuel Little's life are spent in a state of painful dwindling as his health slowly but surely ebbs away. His passing, when it finally comes, is unlikely to be either pleasant or peaceful.

This may be the closest thing to justice that he will ever face.

THE BOSTON STRANGLER: ALBERT DESALVO

Albert DeSalvo was born on September 3, 1931. From a very young age, he showed signs of being abnormal. DeSalvo said that he liked to kill and wound animals, particularly cats, firing arrows at them from a bow. During his trial, his defense attorney would speak of young Albert's childhood having taken place in "warped and perverse" conditions and that he thought nothing of shoplifting from convenience stores. Much of this information came from DeSalvo himself as part of a prolonged confession he would make after his arrest. The man who taught him to steal from stores at just five years old was his own father, who had a lengthy criminal record.

DeSalvo's childhood was antisocial and lonely. Unlike many boys of his time, he always went out of his way to avoid a fight. This contradicted the example set by his father, an alcoholic and a violent domestic abuser who brutally pummeled his wife in front of Albert and his siblings. This extreme disrespect for females, which he witnessed at such a young and impressionable age, may go some way toward explaining Albert's deviant behavior in later life. It also left him with a lifelong aversion to liquor.

DeSalvo also claimed to have had sexual encounters with older women when he was no more than ten years old. As a teenager, he sought out opportunities to be a Peeping Tom, pleasuring himself while he watched others having sex or undressing.

As a boy, he was his mother's favored son. DeSalvo's father had no apparent favorites, showing his children little other than violent disregard. His method of instilling discipline or correcting his children—whether they had done anything wrong or not—was a thick leather belt, which he applied liberally to his offspring. Whether son or daughter, it made no difference to Frank

Albert DeSalvo, shown here in a 1967 photograph, was already a petty criminal by the time he was 12.

DeSalvo. Just like his wife, his children were an outlet for his anger.

DeSalvo's penchant for theft landed him in reform school at the age of 12 for the crimes of breaking into a home and stealing. His first spell in an institution seemed to do little toward reforming his behavior. As an adult, he further developed his interest in breaking and entering for the purposes of theft.

DeSalvo enlisted in the military and soon earned a reputation for being a decent enough soldier, though not exactly an exemplary one—he was court-martialed once for insubordination. In spite of this, he would go on to attain the rank of sergeant. He married German native Irmgard Beck during an overseas posting and had two children with her. She would soon discover, to her chagrin, that her new husband was a sex addict, with a libido far beyond that which most people would consider to be normal.

This abnormally high sex drive would manifest in an extremely ugly way when DeSalvo and his family were posted back to the United States, to Fort Dix in New Jersey. Albert entered the home of a nine-year-old girl when she was left without adult supervision and sexually molested her. Although the girl positively identified him, her mother refused to press charges. Regardless, it provides insight into the disgusting behavior of which he was capable. He left the army in 1956, taking his wife and two children with him to Massachusetts. Irmgard became increasingly resistant to his persistent sexual demands, which he perceived as a slight and a rejection. He would go on to seek sexual gratification elsewhere.

At this point, it is important to note that Albert DeSalvo and the Boston Strangler are referred to as though they are two separate and distinct entities. The reason for this is that, while we know that DeSalvo killed at least one of the victims attributed to the Strangler (thanks to DNA evidence), he cannot definitively be tied to them all. Even today, controversy still rages over whether they were one and the same.

From the summer of 1962 to January 1964, women were turning up dead inside their homes all across Boston. For 18 months, the city's female population lived in fear of an intruder breaking into their home, assaulting them, and murdering them.

The case took on a life of its own in the media, as such things still tend to do today. In a somewhat unusual move, *The Atlantic*, a widely circulated magazine, retained the services of the notable crime writer Erle Stanley Gardner, who was perhaps best known for creating the literary legal eagle Perry Mason, to visit Boston on its behalf and try to get to the bottom of the killings. At that time, the press had given the unidentified killer been given the nickname "The Mad Strangler of Boston."

As far as we are aware, the first victim of the so-called Strangler was killed on June 14, 1962. She was a 55-year-old Latvian seamstress named Anna Slesers. Her adult son, dropping in on the way back from work to take her to church, discovered his mother's dead body lying in the hallway of her third-

Crime author Erle Stanley Gardner was hired by *The Atlantic* to research and investigate the murderous goings-on in Boston.

floor apartment on Gainsborough Street, apparently strangled by the belt from a dressing gown she was wearing.

At first glance, it was believed to have been a possible suicide, but a closer look soon revealed that this was in fact a murder scene. Too many things were out of place, including the way that the body was positioned and its nakedness exposed. It would subsequently be determined that Anna Slesers had been sexually assaulted. Twelve more victims would follow her.

Mary Mullen, the Strangler's second victim—*if* his confession is to be believed—was also the oldest, at 85 years of age. On June 28, two weeks after Slesers's murder, Mary died inside her apartment on Commonwealth Avenue. Her death was not connected to the murder that had taken place on Gainsborough Street because the police had no reason to link the two events together. Mary Mullen had died of a heart attack, and her body showed no signs of strangulation or other foul play. It was only when Albert DeSalvo finally told his story almost a decade later that a closer look would be taken at her case. DeSalvo claimed to have entered Mullen's apartment, presumably with the intent of killing her, only to have her drop dead in front of him before he could assault her.

Whether Albert DeSalvo truly was in Mary Mullen's apartment that day can never be proven. We can be more confident, however, that the Boston Strangler was responsible for the death of 68-year-old Nina Nichols just two days later. Once again, the murder took place on Commonwealth Avenue. After Nichols was late for an appointment, an attendant used a master key to unlock the door of her apartment. Inside, he found Nichols sprawled naked on the floor. She had been strangled with her own nylon stockings, and once again, there was evidence of sexual assault. Part of a wine bottle had been inserted into her vagina.

Not satisfied with taking one life on June 30, the Strangler had killed another woman that same day. His victim was 65-year-old Helen Blake, a former nurse who was also strangled with her stockings in her bedroom. Her nude body was positioned in an equally suggestive way to that of Nina Nichols.

By now, the police department was aware that a serial killer was at large on the streets of Boston. It was deemed prudent that women keep their doors and windows locked at all times and not allow strangers into their home, no matter how trustworthy they might seem. It didn't help.

> It was deemed prudent that women keep their doors and windows locked at all times and not allow strangers into their home, no matter how trustworthy they might seem.

One unusual characteristic of the Boston Strangler murders was the way in which the killer managed to gain access to each of his crime scenes. He did not force doors open, break glass windowpanes, or slip in through open windows. Detectives investigating the murder scenes typically noted that there were no signs of forcible entry or evidence of damage to the building. Perhaps the killer knew each woman personally, although there was never any evidence to link all the Strangler victims with one another. Maybe he used a gun or a knife to terrify them into allowing him access into their homes. Or perhaps he was simply so charismatic that he was able to charm his way inside. No matter the answer, the people of Boston found the lack of breaking and entering to be disturbing. It didn't matter how many locks, chains, or safety bars you put on your doors and windows if a homicidal maniac was somehow able to easily bypass them. How was anybody supposed to feel secure, knowing that such a dangerous man was out there and could make his way inside an average home—perhaps even *your* home—without any apparent struggle?

People began to look at tradesmen in a suspicious light. That TV repair guy suddenly found it harder to get inside the home of his clients. Police officers were asked to show proper identification. When the technician who came to repair the heating or air conditioning arrived, the client had to call the company to have his description verified by the company before he was allowed inside to do his job. If the murders were teaching Bostonians anything, it was that you could never be too careful about who you chose to let inside your safe space.

More frightening still was the fact that the Strangler seemed to have a knack for killing his victims quietly. Whenever there were neighbors living either next door to, above, or below the victim, police asked whether anybody had heard the sounds of screaming, breaking objects, or physical altercations.

They never had. Occasionally there would be muffled thumps and thuds, but nothing that prompted neighbors to call for help.

The Boston Strangler never targeted men. Some theorized that he was a less-than-muscular physical specimen himself and was therefore incapable of overpowering a male, which was why he restricted his attacks to female victims. Another explanation, and a far more likely one, was that he simply enjoyed raping and murdering women. Killing a man would have given him no sexual gratification and little in the way of satisfaction.

Gun sales went up as more women sought a means with which to defend themselves. Yet police received few reports of women having to defend themselves from a home intrusion, and those reports that did take place were soon ruled out from being the work of the Boston Strangler.

Because the killer managed to get inside homes without breaking anything, people speculated that perhaps the Strangler was a tradesman who knew how to pick locks.

The Strangler then took a few weeks off from killing, emerging again on August 19, 1962. The body of 75-year-old Ida Irga was discovered two days later in her fifth-floor apartment. This time, the murder weapon was a pillowcase, rather than a nylon stocking, but the coroner found signs of manual strangulation as well. The killer had partially strangled her with his bare hands. Sexual assault had also taken place.

With the exception of Mary Mullen, the Strangler had always left the bodies of his victims positioned in a sexually suggestive way, seeming to take a perverse desire in exposing their nakedness. In Irga's case, he placed her exposed body in the supine position, with each leg elevated and resting atop one of two chairs that were placed there for just that purpose. Her killer had made sure to use both chairs in order to keep her legs spread apart.

This was the mark of a murderer who wanted to stress to the police the sheer ugliness of what he had done. It was as though he sought to emphasize the fact that he could kill and degrade women—in this case, a harmless grandmother who had been going about her own business in her own home—with complete impunity. The police had no real leads on his identity. Staging such a grotesque tableau was theatrical, perhaps an attempt to taunt the detectives who were hunting him.

His next victim was a nurse. Jane Sullivan, 67, was strangled on August 20 or 21. Her body went undiscovered for somewhere between a week and ten days, forcing the coroner to make an educated guess on the day of her death. Once again, the killer had taken great pains to position the body of his victim in a humiliating and sexually suggestive manner after her death. She had been either dragged or carried into the bathroom and put into the tub, kneeling with her head down and her buttocks in the air.

The sense of hysteria that held Boston in its grip grew with each new murder, stoked by newspaper headlines and the lack of any real suspect for law enforcement to chase down. Extra police patrols were assigned, to provide reassurance to the public as well as to increase the chances of catching the Strangler. Few of the citizens of Boston felt safe.

> With the exception of Mary Mullen, the Strangler had always left the bodies of his victims positioned in a sexually suggestive way....

Perhaps because of this heightened sense of public and police awareness, the Strangler went underground for the next few months. Between the end of August and early December, there were no further murders. Slowly, hesitantly, people began to relax just a little. The Boston Strangler seemed to have disappeared. Perhaps he had moved on, died, or gone to jail for something else.

All that changed on December 5, with the murder of Sophie Clark. It was here that the Strangler broke with his established pattern of victim selection. Up to this point, his victims had been older, in their sixties, seventies, or eighties. Sophie Clark was just 20 years old and African American. A hospital technician and student, she lived alone in an apartment and was found gagged and strangled to death with her own stockings. She was found in a state of partial undress, wearing stockings and a garter belt, lying on her back in a similar manner to that of the other Strangler victims. Detectives found something unique to this murder: semen stains on the carpet.

Everybody in the apartment building was questioned. One tenant recalled answering the door earlier that afternoon to find a stranger standing there. He claimed to have been sent to assess the need for her apartment to be painted and walked inside, giving the place a cursory looking-over. The man changed his tune and began to compliment the woman, asking her whether she had ever thought about doing a little modeling. (There are shades of Rodney Alcala here.) Fortunately, the tenant was able to get the man out of her apartment by claiming that her husband was in the bedroom. If she had not, it is entirely possible that she would have been the next victim of the Strangler.

Fear descended on Boston again, just in time for the holiday season. Christmas came and went without any more murders, but the Strangler would take one more life in 1962. On New Year's Eve, 23-year-old secretary Patricia Bissette was killed in her apartment, not far from that of Sophie Clark. Medical examination proved that Patricia had been sexually active before her death by strangulation, but it was impossible to determine if she had been sexually assaulted, due to the fact that she had been engaged in a relationship at the time.

Breaking with the Strangler's pattern again, Patricia's killer had covered her up with a bed sheet. Rather than pose her in a sexually explicit condition, the murderer had placed her feet together in bed and put her arms by her side. Detectives were forced to ask themselves whether the Boston Strangler had truly changed his MO, or if they were in fact dealing with some kind of copycat killer.

On March 6, 1963, 69-year-old Mary Ann Brown was found strangled and sexually molested in her apartment. At first, she fit the profile of a Boston Strangler victim, but on closer examination, a degree of physical trauma was inflicted upon her body that had not been seen in the other murders. Not only had she been beaten by her assailant, but she had also been stabbed repeatedly in the chest with a fork. The utensil was still sticking up out of her chest when police officers arrived on the scene.

> Christmas came and went without any more murders, but the Strangler would take one more life in 1962.

The next murder attributed to the Strangler, carried out on May 6, involved 25-year-old graduate student Beverly Samans. It, too, had atypical aspects to it. After she failed to keep an appointment, her fiancé used a key that he kept to her apartment to gain access. He found Beverly's naked body lying on the bed. Her legs were apart, her hands were bound behind her back, and she was covered in blood. The blood came from multiple puncture wounds to her chest and neck that appeared to have been inflicted with a knife. A nylon stocking was knotted tightly about her neck.

Up until the murder of Mary Ann Brown, the Strangler had restricted himself to choking his victims and had avoided inflicting penetrating trauma. Now came two sequential murders in which he had not only strangled but had also stabbed the victim. In the case of Beverly Samans, the stabbing proved to be fatal. The killer had left the blood-stained murder weapon in the kitchen before leaving.

After this murder, the killer dropped off the grid again, returning on September 8 to rape and strangle 58-year-old Evelyn Corbin in Salem. Evelyn was found on her bed, with stockings wrapped tightly around her throat. Her killer had made a point of exposing her breasts and genitalia and had pushed a pair of her own underwear into her mouth. The obscene body positioning was back, and this time there were no stab wounds. Death had been due to strangulation.

The same was true of Joann Graff, 23, who was killed on November 23—one day after the assassination of President John F. Kennedy in Dallas, Texas. Yet again, there was the same spread-eagled positioning. Her stockings

A number of the Strangler's victims were found dead in their beds, their bodies posed in suggestive ways, with stockings wrapped around their throats.

had been the murder weapon. They were tied in a huge bow around her neck. With the exception of one breast having been bitten, there was no other evidence of trauma.

Still, the police had no leads to go on. The search for the Boston Strangler continued up through the end of the year. Christmas and New Year passed uneventfully.

There would be one last murder before the Boston Strangler finished his run. The nude body of Mary Sullivan, 19, was found lying on the bed in her third-floor apartment on January 4, 1964. Even by the standards that had already been set, she had endured a particularly cruel and brutal death. Not only had she been strangled to death, but a broom handle had also been inserted into her vagina. A Happy New Year card was propped up against her body, one last sick gesture presumably aimed at those who discovered her. Two colorful scarves were looped around her neck, covering up the stocking that had been used to end her life.

Much debate has taken place concerning the reasons the Boston Strangler chose his specific victims. There were definite sexual overtones to the way he posed the women once they were dead, making sure to position them with their legs open and their private parts exposed. It wasn't enough for him to kill them. He had to degrade and humiliate them too, in order to obtain gratification from the act.

Nor, at first, did he choose females who were young and conventionally attractive. The Strangler targeted older women for his initial block of killings, possibly because he thought them easier to overpower. During the second phase of killings, however, he switched to murdering women in their twenties (with two exceptions). It may be that he had gained sufficient confidence in the early stages to begin attacking women who were better able to fight back. There was little evidence of a struggle at any of the early Boston Strangler crime scenes, but some of his younger victims, such as Sophie Clark, had put up what fight they could.

> One common factor in the cases was that they were all women, and most (though not all) lived alone.

Some of the apartments had been ransacked, giving the appearance that a burglary took place. Once the Strangler's classic murder pattern became well-known, detectives saw right through the possibility of the crimes being a robbery/home intrusion gone bad. The primary motive was not theft.

If Albert DeSalvo was indeed the Strangler, he did not stick to killing victims within his own racial type. One common factor in the cases was that they were all women, and most (though not all) lived alone. The victim had usually been strangled with their own nylons, and often they had been tied using the same type of butterfly knot.

There was no shortage of doubters. Albert DeSalvo's brother, Richard, led the charge to his defense, claiming that while Albert may not exactly have been an angel, there was no way he was capable of carrying out the Boston Strangler murders.

DeSalvo was a powerfully built man, his natural strength enhanced even further by a period of enlistment in the army, during which he boxed at the championship level. As a military policeman by specialty, he would have been taught various methods to quickly restrain and take down another human being, gaining control over them quickly by employing pressure points and choke holds. It is likely that after leaving the army and returning to civilian life, that training would have been so ingrained that he would have had little difficulty in subduing the average female victim.

DeSalvo certainly had the physical capacity to kill, and the DNA evidence connects him strongly to the Mary Sullivan murder, the final killing in the string attributed to the Boston Strangler. But it does not necessarily follow that just because DeSalvo killed one of the victims, he killed them all. Some of the murders did not quite fit the established pattern, raising the question of whether DeSalvo truly was the Boston Strangler and was simply making exceptions, or there was another killer at work, patterning his crimes on those that had already taken place.

It's fair to say that most police departments dislike unsolved cases, particularly murders, and the more high-profile the crime, the more pressure is placed upon them to break the case and bring the perpetrator to justice. Before he was arrested for unrelated crimes, Albert DeSalvo was not considered a suspect in the Strangler killings. The police department was not watching him or investigating his background. His confession came as a complete surprise to everybody. By the same token, it helped mollify an angry and frightened public who wanted to see the Strangler taken off the streets and put behind bars. The loved ones of the dead victims would be given some form of closure. The police no longer had to spend time and resources looking for a suspect, so the confession worked out well for them, too.

> Richard DeSalvo believed that his brother assumed responsibility for the Boston Strangler crimes in the hope of making money.

The confession even had an upside for Albert DeSalvo himself. Richard DeSalvo believed that his brother assumed responsibility for the Boston Strangler crimes in the hope of making money by either selling the media rights to his story or otherwise cashing in on the notoriety that came with being an infamous serial killer.

When 29-year-old Albert DeSalvo was arrested in the spring of 1961, it was because patrol officers caught him red-handed during a breaking and entering attempt. He fled but was caught after a brief foot chase and held at gunpoint. The fact that he had equipment commonly used for burglary in his possession at the time did not help his case. He was taken to the police station and booked.

Rather than refuse to speak and demand a lawyer, DeSalvo did exactly the opposite. If he had simply admitted to attempted housebreaking, DeSalvo would probably have gotten away with minimal jail time, if any at all. Instead, once he started talking, he simply wouldn't shut up. He confessed to the interrogating officers that he had recently been going around to the houses of strangers, knocking on doors, and when a female resident answered, spinning tall tales of being a talent scout for a modeling agency. He dangled the possibility of a lucrative modeling job in front of them, with just one preliminary requirement to satisfy first: Albert DeSalvo had to be permitted to take their measurements personally, right then and there.

Surprisingly, a number of women had fallen for his door-to-door scam and acquiesced, allowing him to pull out a tape measure and run it along the various dimensions of their body. According to DeSalvo, he got his kicks from this not in a sexual way but rather from the idea of hoodwinking those he believed were more attractive or more successful than he was. The idea came from a TV show that he had once watched.

Although the Boston Strangler killings had yet to start, with the bene-fit of hindsight, this brings to mind the murder of Sophie Clark, in which an unidentified male tried to pull the same routine on a female resident in the same apartment building. It's an extremely specific connection and seems highly unlikely to be pure coincidence. It is likely that the man in question was indeed Albert DeSalvo.

Looking at the timeline of events, there is another very telling piece of information. Albert DeSalvo was tried and sentenced to prison time for breaking and entering, spending a little under a year behind bars. He was released in the spring of 1962, just two months before the first Boston Strangler murder took place.

Following the death of Mary Sullivan on January 4, 1964, there were no further Strangler murders that year. In late October, Albert DeSalvo found himself in trouble with the law once again after breaking into the apartment of a 20-year-old woman while she lay alone in bed. Holding the terrified woman at knife point, DeSalvo gagged her with her own panties, tied her to the bed, and raped her. When he was fin-ished, he did not kill her; instead, he told her that he was sorry for what he had just done, as if that made everything okay, and walked out.

> The drawing looked like somebody the officers already knew, a housebreaker and pervert who had been nicknamed "The Measuring Man"....

Even though DeSalvo had worn dark glasses to disguise himself, the young lady was still able to describe his face quite accurately to a police sketch artist. The drawing looked like somebody the officers already knew, a housebreaker and per-vert who had been nicknamed "The Measuring Man"—one Albert DeSalvo.

Showing great courage, DeSalvo's victim came into the police station when officers brought DeSalvo in for an interview, and she positively identi-fied him as the man who had assaulted her. His picture was distributed widely among law enforcement officers, and it wasn't long before detectives from the neighboring state of Connecticut recognized him too. This was the face of a man who had tied up and raped a number of women over the past few months, posing as a tradesman in order to gain access to their home. A significant number of those women also came forward and positively identified him. The game was finally up for Albert DeSalvo.

The detectives were shocked. They believed they had a serial rapist in custody—a significant enough catch by itself, but they had no idea at first that their prisoner would turn out to be something even worse.

Now in custody, DeSalvo confessed to having committed rape after rape, admitting to using weapons sometimes in order to get his way. The more he talked, the more the detectives realized that he was a prime candidate for the Boston Strangler homicides. The longer he remained in custody, the more they noticed that DeSalvo exhibited episodes of bizarre behavior, strongly suggesting that he had mental health problems. Clinical evaluators at Bridgewater State Hospital, where DeSalvo was now an inmate, concurred, diagnosing him as a paranoid schizophrenic.

As 1965 wore on, Albert DeSalvo became friends with a fellow inmate, an accused murderer named George Nassar. The two men got along well and confided in one another. For DeSalvo, this turned out to be a mistake. He told Nassar that he was the Boston Strangler. Nassar promptly relayed the information to his attorney, F. Lee Bailey. Bailey interviewed DeSalvo himself and listened intently as he spoke of murdering 13 women between the years 1962 and 1964.

> So, the prosecution team decided it was safer to grant him immunity for the Strangler murders, secure his confession, and then try him for the sex assaults rather than the murders.

Albert DeSalvo had just admitted that he was the Boston Strangler. Bailey dutifully reported this fact to the police and then began courting DeSalvo as a potential client of his own.

DeSalvo spent much of 1965 and 1966 being interviewed and psychologically assessed. In an attempt to determine whether he truly was the Boston Strangler, the interrogators peppered him with questions from every angle, getting him to speak about each of the Strangler murders in as much detail as he could possibly recall.

After DeSalvo had answered questions about all 13 of the killings to the best of his ability, officials determined that there might not be enough of a case to try him for murder. Key to that decision was that the Boston Strangler had left behind no living witnesses to any of his crimes.

Yes, he had described carrying out the murders, but DeSalvo would not make a *formal* confession unless he was guaranteed immunity from prosecution. He knew that it would likely lead to a death penalty sentence. He could still disavow everything he had admitted as far as his involvement was concerned.

The whole case was a mess. If the state prosecutors went ahead and tried Albert DeSalvo for murder, only to have him acquitted, they ran the risk of very publicly exonerating a serial killer of his crimes—if, that was, DeSalvo even *was* the Boston Strangler. Based upon his testimony, prosecutors believed he was—but belief counts for little in a court of law. What truly matters is what can be proven.

While there was some uncertainty about whether Albert DeSalvo was the Boston Strangler, there was absolutely no doubt that he committed rapes and assaults. So, the prosecution team decided it was safer to grant him immunity for the Strangler murders, secure his confession, and then try him for the sex assaults rather than the murders. A conviction would serve to keep him off the streets and prevent him from harming any more women. A skilled prosecutor is, by necessity, something of a realist and will not go to trial without there being at least a reasonable prospect of a conviction. Such an attorney will also look at alternative solutions—Al Capone, for example, went to jail for tax evasion.

DeSalvo's trial began in January 1967. Ultimately, he confessed to the murders of 13 women in Boston—he was the infamous Boston Strangler. The courtroom erupted into pandemonium.

A consulting mental health clinician named Dr. James Brussel explained that Albert DeSalvo was a paranoid schizophrenic who had developed a second personality that was completely separate from that of his ordinary, everyday self. He painted a picture of a man who killed because a mental health condition led to a compulsion that was completely beyond his control.

The court was then reminded that DeSalvo had used several different objects to strangle the women he killed, most often choosing their own nylon stockings. He would then position them in a very specific manner, legs akimbo and arms up, before having sexual intercourse with their bodies, no matter whether they were unconscious or dead.

Albert DeSalvo's defense attorney put it in plain and simple terms: "Thirteen acts of homicide by a completely uncontrollable vegetable, walking around in a human body."

There were some reasonable doubts about the validity of the confession. For one thing, DeSalvo's recollection of the murders was somewhat lacking. He got some of the details jumbled up in more than one instance, claiming to have assaulted several victims who weren't assaulted at all. Whether this was because his memory failed or because he hadn't really committed them remains open to interpretation. On the other hand, he also seemed to know things that only somebody who had been inside those apartments with the murder victims could possibly have known.

If Albert DeSalvo was not the Boston Strangler, then he must have read and internalized a great deal of information about the case. Although much was written about the murders in the press, police kept some facts out of the public record. DeSalvo knew some of these facts, but others he either did not know or got wrong when questioned about them. During his confession, he was either recalling as much as he could about all 13 deaths, or he was working hard to concoct an elaborate false narrative, a tale spun from hundreds of different data points covered in newspaper articles.

Chronic fantasist, financial opportunist, or serial killer? DeSalvo certainly had the opportunity to kill every one of the 13 Strangler victims. A painstaking check of his movements and whereabouts demonstrated that he had been away from home at the time of each murder and therefore could conceivably have been responsible for each one.

After weighing the evidence, the jury found Albert DeSalvo guilty of the sexual assault charges. The judge imposed a sentence that guaranteed he would spend the rest of his life incarcerated. He was not tried (and therefore could not be found guilty) for the Boston Strangler murders, despite having confessed to them. Yet the public had their public enemy number one, and even though the murders would officially go unsolved, there was a certain sense of closure. Still, many believed there was much more to the story, and some thought that although he may have been responsible for some of the killings, not all of the murders could be attributed to him.

DeSalvo had originally intended to cash in on his ownership of the Boston Strangler mantle. He had dreams of a book deal, associated movie rights, and making a small fortune on the back of his newly found fame. Although he knew he would likely never walk free or be able to enjoy the proceeds, his wife and children would be set for life. That was his only available option of trying to make amends for having destroyed their lives.

None of the deals, however, came to much of anything. By 1973, DeSalvo still had not made any money from his story. Immensely frustrated, he started to claim that he never had been the Boston Strangler. Quite why anybody should believe him now, after he had staunchly maintained the opposite for so many years, was unclear. The man was a proven liar and opportunist, and he had told so many untruths and half-truths that it was difficult to separate fact from fiction.

On November 25, 1973, an unidentified assailant went into Albert DeSalvo's jail cell and stabbed him multiple times in the chest. He bled to death during the night. His corpse was discovered the following morning, covered in a blanket and lying in a pool of congealed blood. He was 42 years old. To this day, his murder remains unsolved.

The controversy surrounding DeSalvo's culpability for the murders never quite went away, and they flared up again as soon as he retracted his confession. By then it was too late for him. He went to his grave with the unshakeable reputation as a serial murderer and rapist. His name will forever be associated with that of the Boston Strangler.

Albert DeSalvo was buried in a plot at the Puritan Lawn Memorial Park in Peabody, Massachusetts. His body would lie undisturbed for 40 years, until July 2013. Criminal investigators attempted to shed more light on the murky question of whether Albert DeSalvo truly was the Boston Strangler by exhuming his body. DNA sampling and analysis techniques were used to corroborate DeSalvo's claim that he had murdered 19-year-old Mary Sullivan, confirming that he had killed at least one of the Boston Strangler victims. Traces of semen taken from her underwear were also subjected to DNA—testing that would later determine that it belonged to Albert DeSalvo.

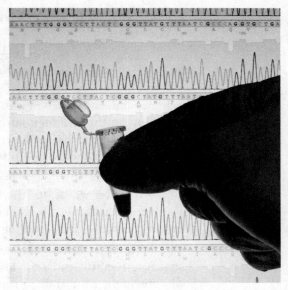

DNA testing confirmed that DeSalvo had, in fact, killed Mary Sullivan, but many of the others who were murdered may never be satisfactorily verified as being his victims.

With no remaining DNA from DeSalvo on file, the testing couldn't occur unless crime lab technicians obtained DNA from a male relative of Albert DeSalvo who shared a near-identical genetic makeup with him. Fortunately, such a relative existed, and police officers tailed him without his knowing it. Finally, DeSalvo's cousin happened to be drinking from a disposable plastic water bottle. When he threw away the empty bottle, officers waited for him to walk away and moved in and snagged the bottle. It contained more than enough DNA to tie DeSalvo to Sullivan's murder.

Questions still remain about the other ten victims. There is a school of thought among detectives and students of the Boston Strangler case that claims it is highly unlikely that one man committed all of the murders alone. Although each of the victims was a female and home alone at the time of the assault and murder, they varied in age from 19 to 85 years old. This was somewhat unusual for a sexually motivated type of murderer, many of whom typically prefer a specific type of victim to focus on.

Did Albert DeSalvo commit some, but not all, of the remaining murders? Was somebody else involved, a copycat who stayed off the police radar and has never been caught? Just who *was* the Boston Strangler? Unless there is a significant break in the case, those questions may never be answered. The only man who can answer them definitively took them with him to his grave.

There is an unsavory coda to the Albert DeSalvo story. In addition to the criminal charges that had been brought against him in the past, DeSalvo has a unique legacy in the world of state law. On April 1, 1971, a member of the Texas House of Representatives, frustrated at the apparent unwillingness of his colleagues to thoroughly read the bills they were passing into law, decided to play an April Fool's Day prank on them—a prank that was in particularly poor taste.

Tom Moore Jr., representing Waco, submitted a request for commendation on behalf of a man whose compassionate dedication to his work, the resolution claimed, had "enabled the weak and lonely throughout the nation to achieve and maintain a new degree of concern for their future." The proposed recipient of the commendation was one Albert DeSalvo. As if that wasn't going far enough, the resolution also stated that its nominee had been "recognized by the state of Massachusetts for his noted activities and unconventional techniques involving population control and applied psychology."

In other words, for the first time in its history, an accused serial killer was being commended by governing authorities for having helped with "population control"—and terrifying an entire city full of people.

To say that this "joke" was made in poor form is understating the matter significantly. Still, once the legislature passed the commendation without any disagreement or abstention, Rep. Moore explained what he had done and immediately had it withdrawn. One suspects that his fellow representatives were far from amused.

THE ACID BATH MURDERER: JOHN GEORGE HAIGH

John George Haigh was one of the most notorious serial killers of mid-twentieth-century Britain. Born in 1909, Haigh was raised by extremely religious traditionalist parents. They were strict disciplinarians, and their son did not have an easy childhood.

If Haigh's parents thought that this upbringing would keep their son on the straight and narrow during his adult life, they were sorely mistaken. After getting married at the age of 25, Haigh turned to forgery to support himself and his bride. This backfired spectacularly, and he was soon caught and jailed. When he was released, he returned to an empty home, for his wife had left him.

Although he attempted to make an honest living, he could never keep it up for long. Haigh was in and out of prison for various criminal offenses, mostly related to fraud. None of this particularly endeared him to his parents, who turned their backs on him after his first imprisonment. If they had known how their son's life would turn out, they would have realized that their decision to cut him off was more than justified.

By the late summer of 1944, with the Second World War finally moving toward its end, Haigh was living at 79 Gloucester Road in the South Kensington neighborhood of London. On September 9, he invited a former employer named William McSwan to visit him there. During one of his periods of incarceration, Haigh seemed to have undergone an epiphany: whenever one of his schemes failed, it was because somebody had seen right through it and had gone to the police. But what if he committed a crime where there was nobody left alive to talk?

Up until that point, there had been no indication that John George Haigh might have homicidal tendencies. While his childhood might have

Haigh disposed of McSwan's body by dissolving it in a drum full of sulfuric acid. The process took several days, leaving only the victim's teeth behind.

been on the harsh side, there's no evidence that he was physically abused (at least, not beyond what passed for corporal punishment in turn-of-the-century Britain).

Haigh had known McSwan for a few years and was aware that he came from a wealthy family. So, he saw an opportunity to make some easy money. He beat the unsuspecting McSwan to death in the cellar of number 79, then stuffed his body into a drum that he filled with industrial-grade sulfuric acid. Haigh dressed in protective clothing to safely handle the volatile chemical, donning Wellington boots, thick rubber gloves, and an apron to act as a splash guard. To offset the noxious acidic fumes, he wore a gas mask throughout the entire body-disposal procedure.

It took just a few days for what remained of William McSwan to dissolve into its constituent chemicals, a viscous sludge that Haigh disposed of by pouring it into the drain. All that remained were the teeth.

There was now no witness to report him and no body for the police to discover. It was, Haigh thought with no small measure of satisfaction, practically the perfect crime. He was now able to live on the money that McSwan had earned as the landlord of several different buildings. There was just one small snag: William's parents, Donald and Amy McSwan, quite understandably wanted to know how and why their son had suddenly disappeared.

Introducing himself to them and turning on the charm, Haigh smoothly explained that their boy William had been forced to go into hiding. There was a war on, as the saying went, and every able-bodied man had been called up to serve in the military. Dodging the draft, their son was keeping a low profile so that the police would not catch him. This made some sense considering William's background. At the outbreak of World War II, when an entire generation of British men were putting on uniforms, William McSwan had registered as a conscientious objector. This bought him a little time, but the government wouldn't be put off forever. William stayed on the move, making it harder for him to be tracked down and forcibly enlisted.

The occasional letter or postcard from "William" (convincing enough, due to Haigh's forgery skills) kept his parents believing this fantasy for the next year, but when the armistice came in 1945 after the fall of Japan, they realized that there was no compelling reason for William to remain hidden anymore—so where was he?

On July 2, 1945, Donald and Amy finally got their answer—and it was not the one they had expected. Invited over to 79 Gloucester Road on the pretext of a reunion with William, Haigh murdered them by using the same method he had employed on their son. Neither of the too-trusting McSwan parents ever saw it coming, and shortly afterward their bodies were also liquefying in 40-gallon acid drums down in Haigh's cellar.

With two generations of the McSwan family now dead by his hand, Haigh was in a position to take full advantage of the situation. He forged the proper signatures on all the right documents. Now, William McSwan stood to inherit his parents' estate—but he no longer existed as anything other than a name on a set of legal documents. The real beneficiary was John George Haigh, who started raking in the cash income of three deceased people.

> **With two generations of the McSwan family now dead by his hand, Haigh was in a position to take full advantage of the situation.**

If he had been smart and had possessed even a small measure of self-control, Haigh would have left London quietly and without any fanfare, moved to a different part of the country, and started a new life in which to enjoy the proceeds of his ill-gotten gains. What he *actually* did was move into a ritzy London hotel and start living the high life, getting out into the social scene of the postwar capital. He had a penchant for gambling but neither the skills nor the run of luck a professional gambler requires. In just a couple of years, the sizable windfall he had gotten from the McSwans was severely depleted. Haigh needed funds if he was to maintain his comfortable lifestyle, and he needed them fast.

Supporting himself by putting in an honest day's work just wasn't in Haigh's nature. He had seen how easy it could be to profit from murder and, using acid to remove the evidence, keep his hands relatively clean. He began casting about for another wealthy mark just waiting to be fleeced and found it in the form of a couple named Archibald and Rosalie Henderson.

Passing himself off as an inventor/engineer, Haigh had rented a private workshop in Crawley, a town in Sussex. He talked the Hendersons into paying him a visit there, and before they arrived, he prepared the necessary acid-filled drum and protective clothing.

For these, his fourth and fifth killings, which took place on February 12, 1948, Haigh altered his MO slightly. Rather than beat the couple to death, he shot them with a .38 pistol instead. Their bodies were disposed of in the usual manner, and once again, Haigh fraudulently inserted himself into their legal affairs and began to milk their estate for cash. John George Haigh was financially solvent again, and all it had required was two more deaths.

The lesson was clear: killing wealthy people, disposing of their corpses, and defrauding their estate could keep him in money for a very long time, with relatively minimal effort on his part. Far from being a frugal man, Haigh would probably have killed many more victims over the course of his life if fate had not intervened.

Instead, he would take just one more life before his entire world fell apart. Olive Durand-Deacon, 69, lived in the same Kensington hotel as Haigh and was clearly not short of a few pounds to spend. Haigh could be a charmer when he wanted to be, and when money was at stake, he wanted to be. On February 18, 1949, he talked Olive into visiting him at his workshop in Crawley. While we will never know what she expected to find there, when she arrived, Haigh shot her with the same .38 Webley pistol that had been used to murder the Hendersons. After stripping the dead woman's body of its jewelry and whatever money she carried, Haigh pushed it into the acid drum to begin the process of dissolution.

Once again, Haigh believed that he had committed a near-perfect crime. But Durand-Deacon had at least one friend who missed her, someone who found her disappearance both worrisome and out of character. This was soon reported to the police, who began to make enquiries at the hotel where she and Haigh were guests. When personal items of hers turned up in a pawn shop, foul play was suspected.

John Haigh shown here shortly after his arrest in 1949.

It didn't take long for detectives to realize that John George Haigh was almost certainly their man. His criminal record (for fraud and theft, rather than murder) made them instantly suspicious. They arrested him and took him into custody. His workshop was searched, along with the surrounding area. Behind it, police found the mostly liquefied remains of Olive Durand-Deacon, dumped there because the workshop had no drain plumbed into the floor.

Haigh's laziness had finally gotten the better of him. If he had just taken the acid drum to another location and disposed of its contents into the sewer, he might not have gotten caught—or at least, not gotten prosecuted. As it was, he had handed the police a veritable smoking gun. After detectives investigated in greater depth, the entire pack of lies began to fall apart.

In court, nobody on the jury bought Haigh's defense, and the judge wasted no time in sentencing him to death. Capital punishment was still on the books in 1949. On August 10, John George Haigh, 40, was hanged. His sole "achievement" in life was to gain notoriety as the infamous Acid Bath Murderer.

That legacy survived in British pop culture for many years. As a young boy, I distinctly remember being taken to Madame Tussaud's waxworks in London and walking wide-eyed through its Chamber of Horrors, in which some of history's most evil men and women had been immortalized as wax sculptures. There, my five-year-old self came face to face with John George Haigh for the first time. His sculpture was clad in the actual clothes of the man himself, which he had bequeathed to Tussaud's in his last will and testament, with the stipulation that they always be kept meticulously clean and pressed. A few days before his arrest, Haigh wandered into Madame Tussaud's and walked through the Chamber of Horrors himself, with no idea that in just a few months' time he would be dead, and his effigy would be taking its place among the ranks of the murderers.

John George Haigh's motive for murder remains unclear. On the surface, one may assume he killed for cash, a perfunctory, businesslike method of murder to sustain his comfortable lifestyle. But Haigh offered a different explanation in his private correspondence, writing that he was involved in a car accident, after which he began to crave the taste of human blood. Although that would make for a great story, it doesn't really fit with the timing of Haigh's murders, which seemed to track closely with the amount of money that was left in his bank account. Haigh was far from being one of the thrill-killers that would emerge in the second half of the twentieth century. Nor did he murder for the sake of sexual gratification, so far as we can tell, or because he was lonely and wanted the company. He wasn't trying to make his mark in the media or incite fear in the general public. Had he been born a millionaire, he might never have killed at all.

Many high-profile serial killers have their copycats, individuals who are inspired by media accounts of their murders to re-create them themselves. This may be done out of admiration, a misplaced sense of hero worship, or simply because their method of killing seemed to work effectively.

Long after Haigh's death, another would-be murderer was surfing the internet, searching for inspiration. He found it in the form of John George Haigh.

In London, in July 2017, 33-year-old itinerant construction worker Mujahid Arshid had developed a pathological obsession with his 20-year-old niece, Celine Dookhran, and another woman who remains anonymous. Four years

Long after Haigh's death, another would-be murderer was surfing the internet, searching for inspiration. He found it in the form of John George Haigh.

prior, while texting an undercover police officer, Arshid had said that "these kinds of girls deserve rape—LOL." That comment wasn't enough to have him put in jail. His case was never prosecuted, and Arshid walked free. Had the case been taken further, a tragedy might have been prevented.

Both women had gotten boyfriends, which pushed Arshid into a jealous rage. He kidnapped them both and took them to a property that he had been working on, assaulted them, and cut their throats. Celine died of her wounds. Police officers later found her body crammed inside a freezer. A sock had been stuffed into her mouth, which had then been taped shut, presumably to keep her quiet.

The second victim only survived because she had the courage and immense presence of mind to play along with her attacker, telling him exactly what he wanted to hear. Even though she was wounded and bleeding, she was able to escape and call for help. Testifying against Arshid in court, she provided testimony that helped get him put away for the rest of his life.

Mujahid Arshid was arrested at a hotel. He insisted that he had nothing to do with attacking either victim, claiming instead that the unnamed female had been responsible for the murder of Celine Dookhran. Detectives found this somewhat difficult to believe, particularly when they took his computer into custody and accessed its browser history.

Arshid had obviously been planning the attack for quite some time. Internet searches focused upon the best way to cut up and dispose of a body, which included dissolving it in acid, just as John George Haigh had done. Arshid had browsed Haigh's entry on Wikipedia and done follow-up research on the man and his life.

His research wasn't thorough enough; if it had been, Mujahid Arshid would have learned that John George Haigh did not get away with it. He was caught, tried, and executed—and while Arshid won't dance at the end of the hangman's rope as Haigh did, he will have at least the next 40 years to think about that.

THE KILLER AT 10 RILLINGTON PLACE: JOHN CHRISTIE

John Christie was born on April 8, 1899, in the sleepy English hamlet of Northowram. He would grow up to become one of the most infamous British serial killers of the twentieth century. Immortalized in the movie *10 Rillington Place* (1971; remade as a BBC-TV miniseries in 2016), the soft-spoken Christie was played by actors Richard Attenborough and Tim Roth.

As a boy, Christie had six other siblings, five of whom were older sisters. He would later claim that their domineering behavior crushed his sense of self-worth and led to lifelong psychological issues, although we only have Christie's word for that.

He was an extremely intelligent child, one who had the mental capacity to excel academically at practically anything he set his mind to. Although he is not known to have tortured or killed animals during his childhood, the young John Christie did meet the classic serial killer criterion of being lonely and introverted, largely isolated from his fellow schoolboys. That may have been partly due to his inherent intelligence, which other children can find intimidating and will therefore shun. Growing older, he was remorselessly teased by other young men, mostly about his lack of sexual prowess, which engendered a great sense of hostility within him.

When his grandfather died, young Christie saw him lying in his open coffin. Rather than being frightened by the sight of a dead body, as many children would have been, Christie instead felt an odd sense of detachment. He would later claim that the sight of a corpse never frightened him again for the rest of his life.

He served in the British Army during the World War I, seeing action on the front lines and suffering wounds in a poison gas attack. This is the reason he usually gave for his being so softly spoken. On returning to civilian life, Christie married Ethel Simpson in 1920. The marriage was not a happy one, fraught with infighting and lasting for just four years. At one point the couple separated, only to get back together again in 1934. Tragically, this decision would ultimately cost Ethel her life.

Even before their separation, Christie engaged in a number of criminal activities, ranging from the relatively minor (stealing from the post office) to the rather more serious (attacking a female acquaintance with a cricket bat, striking her so hard on the head that he could have killed her). Plainly, John Christie's soft-spoken demeanor did not extend to his violent temperament. Just *how* violent that streak was, would only surface later. He spent time both on probation and going in and out of prison.

> He felt a need to dominate and control the women with whom he had sex, something he could not do with his wife.

With a high IQ and the mental capacity to master a wide range of skills, Christie could have been successful in life had he chosen to be. Instead, he took the path of least resistance, preferring a life of crime over making an honest living. (He wasn't even a *good* criminal, as his arrest and imprisonment record clearly attest.) It would not turn out well for him in the end, but the real tragedy is that so many others would suffer because of him.

Christie had deep emotional issues involving the opposite sex, perhaps rooted in his boyhood emasculation by his older sisters and his mother. He struggled with impotence even as a young man, finding it a challenge to engage sexually with his wife. His answer to this problem was a pragmatic one: whenever he felt the need, Christie engaged the services of prostitutes, turning what should have been a pleasurable experience into a cold, businesslike transaction that was completely devoid of emotion.

He felt a need to dominate and control the women with whom he had sex, something he could not do with his wife. This may have been why he finally turned to murder. Christie would also engage in extramarital affairs behind his wife's back, although this backfired on him at least once when the husband of the woman he was sleeping with found out about it and gave Christie a serious beating.

The Christies lived at 10 Rillington Place, a three-floored terraced house (what Americans might call a townhouse) in Notting Hill, one of the less prosperous parts of London at that time. Constructed primarily out of brick, number 10—like the majority of its neighboring buildings—was something of a tenement, in dire need of renovation and cleaning up. They moved in to the ground-floor flat around Christmas of 1938, having already spent some time living in one of the flats above.

Incredibly, despite his extensive criminal history, John Christie was somehow able to secure a job as a police officer. Either the need for law enforcement personnel was dire at that time, with the onset of another world war, or nobody carried out a diligent background check on him. Whatever the explanation, Christie patrolled the streets of London as a special constable for a time, a position of some small authority and minor prestige that must have gone some way to assuaging his feelings of deep insecurity and inadequacy.

In the summer of 1943, Christie brought a young woman named Ruth Fuerst home to Rillington Place. We only have his word for what happened during the encounter, which is still believed to have been his first murder. Christie claimed to have been suddenly overcome by the urge to strangle the 21-year-old. Her body was the first to be buried in the back garden of number 10. It would not be the last.

A year would pass before he killed again, on Saturday, October 7, 1944. His second victim was another female, 31-year-old Muriel Eady, whom he had met while working in a London factory. When she was absent from work the following week, nobody thought much of it. But as the days went on without any word from Muriel, her friends and family grew worried. It took almost a month for her to be formally declared a missing person, and by that time, there were no obvious clues as to where she might have gone. There was no link between her and the affable John Christie.

Back at 10 Rillington Place, he had devised an unusual way of rendering his victims unconscious. Christie would use a rubber tube connected to the gas pipes to knock them out, after which he would murder them. Motivated primarily by sexual perversity and a desire to exert complete control over the women he killed, he would usually wait until after their heart stopped beating before having intercourse with their newly dead body.

Over the next ten years, John Christie would continue to kill, disposing of his victims' bodies inside the walls, under the floor, and in the backyard of 10 Rillington Place. There were often lengthy gaps between murders. After 1944, Christie would not kill again until the autumn of 1949, when he murdered 20-year-old Beryl Evans and her 13-month-old daughter, Geraldine. Beryl's husband, Timothy, was developmentally challenged and eagerly manipulated by the cunning Christie. The Evanses were new residents at Rillington Place, and it wasn't long before John Christie was contemplating Beryl as a potential sexual conquest.

The Evanses' marriage was far from idyllic. Beryl was not the most diligent housekeeper, which sometimes drew her husband's ire. Timothy also drank too much, and the presence of a young child in their home caused tension. When Beryl became pregnant for a second time, both she and her husband were less than enamored with the idea of adding another mouth to be fed.

Christie claimed to be knowledgeable in the performance of so-called back-street abortions, a dark business that was not uncommon in the days

John Christie was a policeman in London when he began committing murders. His victims were women, and he would have intercourse with their lifeless bodies.

when the procedure was still illegal throughout Great Britain. The abortions were risky, often performed in dark and dingy places by people who were not trained medical professionals. It was not unheard of for the recipient to bleed to death, but nonetheless, illegal abortions still took place. Often, unwed pregnant women took the chance rather than live with the shame of giving birth while they were unmarried.

What happened next was both convoluted and mysterious. We know for certain that the pregnant Beryl Evans suddenly disappeared, as did her daughter, Geraldine. Timothy Evans told police that he gave his wife a liquid concoction to drink, which was intended to terminate her pregnancy. Instead, he claimed, it had killed her. In a state of shock, Evans had buried his wife's body. Police officers duly accompanied him back to 10 Rillington Place and searched the house, but Beryl's body was nowhere to be found. It also raised the question of just what had happened to young Geraldine.

Police did not thoroughly search outside. If they had, they likely would have found the femur bone of either Ruth Fuerst or Muriel Eady, which in a show of almost staggering nonchalance, Christie had long been using to support a wooden structure in plain sight of anybody who looked. (This would also have included Christie's wife, Ethel, whose degree of involvement in her husband's murders has long been debated.)

Challenged by detectives about the absence of a body at the place where he said he had buried it, Timothy Evans abruptly changed his story. What *really* happened, he now said, was that fellow tenant John Christie had offered to perform an abortion on his wife, while he, Timothy, only had to give his tacit permission. Evans said that he had then left, and when he returned, both his wife and his daughter were gone. The abortion had gone catastrophically wrong, he continued, and Beryl had not survived. As for Geraldine, Christie had placed her in the care of a friendly couple that he knew.

The police understandably found Evans's reversal of story to be suspicious and went back to search 10 Rillington Place again. This time, they searched the wash house at the back of the property, a small room (usually locked) that was primarily used for cleaning laundry. Inside they found the bodies of both Beryl and Geraldine. A coroner's report would later state that each of them had been strangled. Beryl had indeed been pregnant at the time of her death.

Things turned strange when, after being taken into police custody, Timothy Evans confessed to the murders of his wife and daughter. The police seemingly took this confession at face value, although there is some conjecture that his confession may have been embellished or forcibly extracted. Since Evans was not an intelligent man, it is possible that he was coerced into confessing to the crimes.

Some 70 years later, there are still plenty of questions about the case. Despite contemporary reports that he drank heavily and had a volatile temper, Timothy Evans had no real motivation for murdering his wife—let alone his young daughter. Debate has raged about whether Evans or John Christie killed Beryl and Geraldine. An autopsy of Beryl's body revealed no signs of sexual assault, unlike several other victims of John Christie. While this might suggest Christie was not the killer, we must ask what the likelihood was of there being two killers coincidentally living at 10 Rillington Place at the same time. Certainly unlikely.

> Things turned strange when, after being taken into police custody, Timothy Evans confessed to the murders of his wife and daughter.

There is no dispute that John Christie was a serial killer. At the time of the Evans murders, he had already killed two other women, usually when his wife was away from the house. What's curious is why he felt the need to kill the child in addition to her mother. If Timothy Evans was to be believed, he had left London and taken a trip to his native Wales. Could it be that once Beryl Evans was dead, Christie simply could not be bothered to care for the child and did not want to answer any questions about her—and so, he took the path of least resistance and killed her? That seems to be the likeliest explanation.

What's known is that Timothy Evans was arrested and charged with murder. Throughout the entire criminal investigation and trial, his story was never completely consistent. Both large and small contradictions always crept in. The biggest by far was a retraction of the confession he had made earlier. Evans replaced it with a new claim: John Christie had killed his wife and daughter. The court didn't take this seriously; it believed Christie's testimony over that of Evans, and in just three days, it found Evans guilty of murder. In 1950, a conviction of this nature typically led to a capital sentence.

From the moment he withdrew his confession until his dying day, Timothy Evans maintained that the guilty man was John Christie. It did not save him. He was hanged on March 9, 1950.

Three more years would go by between the double murder of Beryl and Geraldine Evans (triple, if we factor in her unborn child) and John Christie's next murder. It may be that he tried to restrain his urges, wary of what others would think of Evans's courtroom accusations. Nevertheless, on December 12, 1952, he could no longer help himself.

This time, however, his victim was not an outsider; it was his own wife, Ethel. Christie strangled her while she was lying in bed, presumably waiting until she was asleep and at her most vulnerable. An autopsy of Ethel Christie's body would reveal that she had not had sexual intercourse with anybody immediately prior to her death, a reflection of the Christies' mostly sexless marriage. John Christie saved his limited sexual capabilities for other women, usually prostitutes. He pulled up the floorboards in the front room of the house and secreted his dead wife's body beneath them.

> The house was beginning to stink of death. On March 20, two weeks after the death of his final victim, Christie made a fatal mistake: he moved out.

Now that Ethel Christie was dead, her husband had free rein to kill whenever he chose to, as he was no longer restricted to when his wife wasn't home. Within the three months after he murdered his wife, Christie killed three young women: Rita Nelson, 25; Kathleen Maloney, 26; and Hectorina MacLennan, 26. Christie strangled all three and had intercourse with them, then placed the bodies inside a hidden alcove at the back of the kitchen, adjacent to the wash house.

The house was beginning to stink of death. On March 20, two weeks after the death of his final victim, Christie made a fatal mistake: he moved out. The next tenant to move in was granted access to the ground floor kitchen and soon discovered the alcove—and the three decomposing bodies it contained. There was no sign of John Christie. Yet even in a city as large and populous as London, it is impossible to disappear forever. He was finally caught during a random police stop, shortly after news of the grisly discovery at 10 Rillington Place became public.

At his trial, John Christie tried to use an insanity defense, claiming impairment at the time of the murders and therefore diminished responsibility. The jury didn't believe him; their deliberations were quick and the verdict was unequivocal: guilty. The judge sentenced him to death.

On July 15, 1953, John Christie was hanged by Albert Pierrepoint, the same executioner who handled the hanging of another London-based serial killer, John George Haigh, as well as Christie's dupe, Timothy Evans. A crowd of 200 people gathered outside the walls of Pentonville Prison for the event, which took place at 9 A.M. The mood was one of cheerful excitement, rather than respectful introspection and remembrance of his victims, as would have been more fitting.

"Death was quite clearly instantaneous," said Dr. Francis Camps, who certified Christie's death. "He was a healthy man."

It was a quick, clean, and efficient ending to a mean and sordid life. Yet tantalizing questions still remained. As part of his MO, Christie often shaved off a small amount of his victim's pubic hair and kept it as a trophy. The hairs were examined by pathologists, who could not determine the source of it all, because not all of it could be matched to the victims who were unearthed at 10 Rillington Place. Had John Christie killed other women, possibly while away from his home, and disposed of their bodies elsewhere? While it is certainly feasible, this would represent a significant deviation from his usual method of murder, something rather unusual for a serial killer like Christie, who seemed to take comfort not only in killing women at home but also in keeping their remains close to him after their death.

Three years after he was hanged, the execution of Timothy Evans began to look like a grave miscarriage of justice. John Christie had confessed to murdering Beryl Evans, but a new inquiry initially upheld the guilty finding against her husband by casting aspersions on Christie's reliability—why should the court believe a man who had been angling for an insanity plea?

As time passed, a groundswell of support began to build for Timothy Evans's claim of innocence. It was buttressed by a pair of books that were published that analyzed the case in greater detail. (Neither book looked upon the actions taken by police officers very favorably). The British public was increasingly coming to believe that Timothy Evans could have been railroaded.

During the days when capital punishment was the law of the land, it was not unusual for the bodies of executed prisoners to be buried inside prison walls. When Timothy Evans was finally exonerated of his crime and issued a pardon, his remains were exhumed and buried in a civilian cemetery—unfortunately, the closest thing he will ever get to justice.

Times have changed in Notting Hill since the days of Christie's tenancy, largely for the better. The residential district has gone from slum to sought-after and fashionable, helped in no small part by the release of the movie *Notting Hill*, starring Julia Roberts and Hugh Grant.

Both Christie's murder house and the street on which it was located were demolished in the 1970s. But some local residents believe that Christie's crimes placed a curse on the land, blaming episodes of misfortune on the murderer and his legacy. It has left a scar of sorts on the landscape. The house may be gone, but the rumors remain—and probably always will.

Christie's home on Rillington Place, now demolished, was in Notting Hill. Now considered an upscale neighborhood, during the murders there it was a place for struggling, lower-class occupants.

A memorial garden now covers the spot where 10 Rillington Place once stood. It is beautifully kept, picturesque, and above all, peaceful, the sort of place where those who live in St. Andrews Square (as the street is now called) might go to enjoy some peace and quiet in the sunshine. If one didn't know the history of the place, which sits between three different houses, one might never know that the freshly cut grass on which they were standing covered the same ground in which John Christie had once buried the bodies of his victims.

Today, children play in the garden quite regularly. When the weekend weather is nice, families go there to enjoy a picnic. While some might find this morbid, I prefer to think of it as a prime example of turning a negative into a positive. The evil deeds that once festered at 10 Rillington Place have been blotted away, to be replaced by the sounds of laughter and happiness. Good has grown out of the bad.

JACK THE RIPPER

In all likelihood, if the average twenty-first-century person is aware of the existence of just one serial killer, it is going to be Jack the Ripper.

Jack's story is so well known, and his character has reached such a wide audience, that those who express strong interest in the Ripper and his crimes have been given their own name: Ripperologists. Ripperologists run the gamut from credulous peddlers of their own pet theories all the way up to serious researchers with a professional background in criminology and in-depth historical research.

We have a tendency to think of the Ripper as being the father of the serial killing phenomenon, despite there being plenty of evidence to the contrary. Serial murderers have been with us throughout the span of human history, and one is forced to wonder just how many of these predators escaped with their crimes going unrecorded. But the Ripper came along at just the right moment in history for him to become not just famous but *infamous*.

Much of this had to do with the location itself: London, the vibrant, beating heart of the all-powerful British Empire, on which it was said that the sun never set. The image of a black-cloaked figure wearing a top hat emerging from the fog to cut down Whitechapel's "ladies of the night" is a striking one, made even more so by the fact that his crimes took place in the same city in which the monarchy lived and ruled.

Another part of the Ripper's eternal fascination lies with the fact that he was never positively identified, let alone caught and brought to justice. There are several credible candidates, and many more outliers, but despite the fact that every once in a while a new theory will gain traction and its author will claim to have solved the mystery of the Ripper's identity once and for all

ASPINALL'S ENAMEL.

PERFECTION
COLOURS EXQUISITE

SURFACE LIKE PORCELAIN
SOLD EVERYWHERE

PUCK

JACK THE RIPPER.
WHO IS HE?   WHAT IS HE?
WHERE IS HE???

One of the intriguing parts of the Jack the Ripper case is that he was never identified. As this cover of *Puck* magazine depicts, there were many suspects, however.

(such as bestselling crime novelist Patricia Cornwell in her *Portrait of a Killer: Jack the Ripper—Case Closed*), the mystery still endures: Just who was Jack the Ripper, and why did he do the awful things that he did?

During the late 1880s, the Whitechapel district of London suffered from chronic overcrowding. It was primarily the home to the poor or completely destitute. Most of Whitechapel's slum housing was packed full with large families crammed into relatively small living spaces; seven or eight people to a room was not unusual.

It could also be a violent place, with plenty of muggings and fistfights. To make matters worse, racial tensions often ran high, a consequence of the mass immigration that had been taking place on the British mainland at that time. More often than not, the police constables who patrolled the streets and back alleys of Whitechapel turned a blind eye to the many prostitutes who plied their trade both in the shadows outdoors and in one of the hundreds of brothels that were scattered across the district. Some have described Whitechapel as a cesspool. If so, it was a cesspool that was perfectly suited for a serial killer to stalk and murder his victims.

August 31, 1888, was a Friday night, which meant that the pubs and streets were busier than usual. Forty-three-year-old prostitute Mary Ann Nichols (who also went by the name Polly) was plying her trade. It's fair to say that she had not lived an easy life. The mother of five children, she was separated from her husband, a situation that left a nineteenth-century woman in a very precarious place. Having no skills with which to support themselves, such women were often forced to turn to prostitution to keep a roof over their head. To complicate matters even further, Polly was an alcoholic and often drank away what money she made from selling herself to men.

At 3:30 in the morning, two delivery men found her severely mutilated body lying in the street on Buck's Row. Her skirt was hiked up around her waist, and out of a sense of common decency, the men covered her back up again before fetching the police.

The trail leading to Polly Nichols's killer was cold before the first officers ever arrived on the scene. Police questioned those who lived and worked nearby; nobody admitted to having seen or heard anything strange. While the residents of a place like Whitechapel tended to keep to themselves, nobody was going to cover up for a criminal who would do something so monstrous. Patrol officers making their nightly rounds had seen and heard nothing unusual.

The initial police report said that Polly Nichols's throat had been sliced open from ear to ear, so deeply that the blade had penetrated completely through the trachea and esophagus before slicing into her spinal cord—a feat that would have required considerable strength. With just a little more force, she would have been decapitated. The carotid arteries and jugular veins were also sliced clean through, which would have resulted in extremely rapid blood loss. Her body was taken to a nearby mortuary to be examined under better lighting conditions.

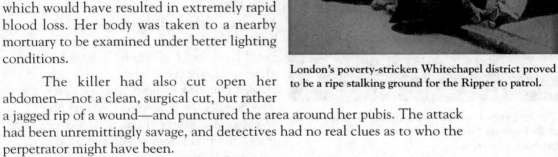

London's poverty-stricken Whitechapel district proved to be a ripe stalking ground for the Ripper to patrol.

The killer had also cut open her abdomen—not a clean, surgical cut, but rather a jagged rip of a wound—and punctured the area around her pubis. The attack had been unremittingly savage, and detectives had no real clues as to who the perpetrator might have been.

Eight days later, the killer struck again. It was a busy Saturday night in Whitechapel, and once again his victim was a prostitute. Forty-seven-year-old Annie Chapman's throat had been cut in almost exactly the same manner as that of Polly Nichols. Her body was discovered in the backyard of 29 Hanbury Street at six o'clock in the morning. In addition to the severe neck trauma she had sustained, Chapman had also been eviscerated, her intestines having been pulled out of a deep incision in her abdomen and then tossed across both sides of her torso in a ghoulish anatomical tableaux.

It wasn't until an autopsy was completed that it became apparent that part of her womb had also been cut out. Its whereabouts were never determined.

Like Polly Nichols, Annie Chapman was husbandless and working as a prostitute to pay for her bed, board, and beer. A key difference with the Chapman case was that an eyewitness had seen a man who was, it seemed likely, her killer; in his 40s, with dark hair, the man looked "like a foreigner," according to the police report. He had been seen speaking with Annie, though it isn't known about what, shortly before her death. Most likely he was posing as a

The lifeless body of Annie Chapman was discovered at 29 Hanbury Street. Her throat had been cut and her body eviscerated.

prospective customer, haggling for her sexual services, before escorting her away for an entirely different reason.

The description, while better than nothing, described tens of thousands of male Londoners. The police dutifully pulled in several potential suspects, casting a wide net, but none of them fit the bill, and all were ultimately released after questioning. They were no nearer to ascertaining the identity of the killer.

On September 27, a letter arrived at the offices of London's Central News Agency, addressed to "Dear Boss." Written in a cursive hand, the letter's red ink was evocative of blood—likely as the author had intended.

Dear Boss,

I keep on hearing that the police have caught me but they wont fix me just yet. I have laughed when they look so clever and talk about being on the right track. That joke about leather apron gave me fits. I am down on whores and shant quit ripping them till I do get buckled. Grand work the last job was. I gave the lady no time to squeal. How can they catch me now. I love my work and want to start again. You will soon hear of me with my funny little games. I saved some of the proper red stuff in a ginger beer bottle over the last job to write with but it went thick like glue and I cant use it. Red ink is fit enough I hope ha ha. The next job I do I shall clip the ladys ears off and send to the police officers just for jolly wouldnt you. Keep this letter back till I do a bit more work, then give it out straight. My knife's so nice and sharp I want to get to work right away if I get a chance.

Good luck.
Yours truly,
Jack the Ripper.
Dont mind me giving the trade name.

PS wasnt good enough to post this before I got all the red ink off my hands curse it. No luck yet. They say I'm a doctor now. Ha ha.

Initially, there was some doubt in the minds of detectives as to whether the "Dear Boss" letter really had been penned by their man. The closing reference to "they say I'm a doctor now" did indeed allude to one of their working theories, which held that the man they were looking for may have had some anatomical knowledge of the sort usually gleaned from a medical education. However, it is equally possible that Jack the Ripper, as he now liked to be called, was a butcher by trade, or even just an interested amateur with access to the right kind of books. (Of course, it was also possible that the Ripper truly *was* a doctor and had deliberately written the "Dear Boss" letter in pidgin English and without proper punctuation to make himself appear to be uneducated, thereby throwing the police off the scent.)

To this day, experts and amateur enthusiasts disagree as to whether Jack the Ripper truly did write the "Dear Boss" letter. At least one self-styled hoaxer would later step forward and claim to have written it himself, for reasons of financial gain.

The murderer took most of the rest of September off, but when he resurfaced at the end of the month, he killed two women on the same day. The early morning of Sunday, September 30, saw the murders of Elizabeth Stride and Catherine Eddowes, both prostitutes.

Of Swedish descent, Stride, 44, had come to London as a young woman for reasons that remain unclear. Her body was found at 1 A.M. in Duffields Yard. Stride's throat had been slit, but her corpse bore none of the visceral trauma that was associated with the other Ripper victims. The commonly accepted explanation for this is that the killer fully intended to cut her open but must have been interrupted partway through the act and been forced to flee, which is why he killed his fourth victim almost immediately afterward. Whatever perverse need it was that drove him went unfulfilled, and so the Ripper targeted 46-year-old Catherine Eddowes.

> To this day, experts and amateur enthusiasts disagree as to whether Jack the Ripper truly did write the "Dear Boss" letter.

Eddowes's body was discovered less than an hour after Stride's was found, in nearby Mitre Square, as a police constable went about his regular patrol beat. Once again pointing to a sexual motivation, Catherine's murderer had pulled up her skirt to expose her lower body. As with the other Ripper murders, the cause of death was a slit throat. Eddowes had also been eviscerated, her intestines pulled out of the abdomen and tossed up and over her shoulder. A blade had been taken to her face, slicing off the tip of her nose and cutting the flesh into gaping flaps; in the unlikely event that she had survived the attack, Eddowes would have been brutally scarred for life. The killer had also mutilated her sexual organs and the surrounding anatomical areas. Her left kidney had been completely cut out, as had portions of her intestinal tract and reproductive organs. Perhaps most tellingly, part of her ear was also cut off,

A police sketch of the corpse of Catherine Eddowes, showing the characteristic disembowelment that was a Ripper trademark.

which the author of the "Dear Boss" letter had threatened to do with his next victim. Did this murder help support the notion that the letter was genuine?

Public fear and speculation regarding the identity of the killer who roamed the streets of Whitechapel ran rampant. A piece of graffiti found on a wall later that day, in close proximity to a piece of Catherine Eddowes's clothing that was stained with her blood, caused even greater speculation: "The Juwes are the men that will not be blamed for nothing."

The streets were ripe with tension at the time, much of it racial in nature, and so the chalked graffiti was hurriedly removed for fear of sparking an outraged uprising. To this day, Ripperologists still disagree about whether the killer wrote the cryptic message or not. Some believe that it was used to taunt the police and attempt to inflame public emotions.

One thing is for certain: the murderer was not beyond taunting the authorities in print. Following the "Dear Boss" letter, a handwritten postcard was sent to the offices of the Central News Agency on October 1, the day after the latest murders. It read:

I was not codding dear old boss when I gave you the tip, you'll hear about saucy Jack's work tomorrow this time number one squealed a bit couldn't finish straight off. Had not time to get ears off for police thanks for keeping last letter back till I got to work again.

Jack the Ripper.

Was this postcard truly written by the perpetrator of the murders? Detectives were of two minds about it. On the one hand, the style of prose and handwriting was sufficiently close to that of the "Dear Boss" letter to suggest that the two could easily have been written by the same author. The unidentified writer offered no information that was not already known to the police and those who lived in the area of the murder scene, however, so the "Saucy Jacky" postcard, as it came to be called, could also conceivably have been a hoax.

Forensic handwriting analyst Dr. Andrea Nini painstakingly scrutinized both the "Saucy Jacky" postcard and the "Dear Boss" letter in 2018 and concluded that they had probably been written by the same person—but not necessarily the Ripper himself. Another possibility was that both documents were written by Central News Agency employees, who recognized that as terrifying as Jack the Ripper could be, he was also a genuine boon to newspaper sales. They therefore had a vested interest in stringing the case out for as long as possible and stirring up public furor.

Detectives used valuable time and resources to sift through the many hoax letters and false leads they received. Although some confidently declared that the police were on the right track, in reality they most assuredly were not.

Throughout October, the residents of Whitechapel and nearby Spitalfields held their collective breath. There was a unified fear that Jack the Ripper would soon strike again.

The Ripper's next murder was November 9. Twenty-five-year-old prostitute Mary Jane Kelly was was killed inside the room she co-rented at 13 Miller's Court, an area in which a number of working girls lived. The rent was due, and the landlord sent a proxy to go and collect it. When he reached Kelly's abode at 10:45 A.M. and knocked loudly on the door, there was no answer. Peeking in through a window, the landlord's assistant saw the blood-splattered remains of the tenant sprawled on the bed.

Mary Jane Kelly had been killed sometime during the early morning hours. Police officers found no signs of a struggle in her room. Kelly's clothing had been folded neatly and set aside, along with her boots. Of all five Ripper murders, this was undeniably the most gruesome. Because he was operating behind closed doors—the previous murders had all been outside—the killer had plenty of time to carry out his mutilation of the dead victim—and it showed.

What had been done to Kelly's body could not have taken place in just a few minutes, or even half an hour. Medical experts brought in to examine the body said the level of mutilation inflicted would have taken at least an hour. So much blood had soaked into the bedding that the mattress was saturated, and a large pool of blood had spread out across the floor beneath. Portions of Mary's internal organs had been cut out and placed alongside her body and underneath her head. Her breasts had been sliced off. Her face had been

A police photo of Mary Jane Kelly, whose body was discovered on November 9, 1888.

horribly disfigured, sliced apart in an irregular pattern of slashes, which left her almost unrecognizable. Her thighs, belly, and groin had been filleted wide open, exposing the underlying musculature, tendons, and other anatomical structures. In one final indignity, Mary's chest cavity was open and her heart was missing. It would never be found.

These five victims are known today as the Canonical Five. Police at the time (and many Ripperologists today) believe that they represent the full extent of the Ripper murders. There are others, however, who believe that later killings that took place in Whitechapel and its surrounding areas in the following months and years could have been linked to Jack the Ripper. While a handful are somewhat plausible, most simply do not hold water.

Following the killing of Mary Kelly, the Ripper murders simply stopped. Why? It is most likely that the murderer either died, was imprisoned, or left the country. Despite the claims of certain authors, the identity of Jack the Ripper has not yet been discovered, nor will it likely ever be. More than 100 individuals have been put forward as potential Rippers.

The suspects have included Prince Albert (consort to Queen Victoria, the monarch of the British Empire), several doctors and other medical men, butchers, merchants, and working tradesmen. Men at all of levels of society from the highest to the lowest have fallen under the microscope of suspicion. Not one has been satisfactorily proven to be Jack the Ripper.

This may well explain the enduring hold that the Ripper still has on us today. The iconic image of the top-hat-wearing cloaked figure walking through the swirling mists of Whitechapel, clutching a knife or a scalpel in his hand, has irrevocably entered popular culture. The Ripper has appeared in everything from graphic novels (such as Alan Moore's *From Hell*, and the motion picture adaptation that followed it) to TV shows, even popping up in the science fiction epic *Babylon 5*, acting as an agent of alien powers.

Even now, over a century after his last murder, Jack the Ripper has lost none of his power to fascinate and repulse us. Each generation discovers the Whitechapel murderer anew and asks themselves one question: just who, exactly, was Saucy Jack, and where did he go?

THE HOUSTON MASS MURDERS: DEAN CORLL

People disappear. In the United States alone, over 609,000 people have gone missing between 1990 and 2019. In 2019, more than 14,000 people were reported missing—many were grown men and women, but there was also a disturbing number of children. Sometimes, the missing person eventually comes back, surprised to learn that their absence was even noticed. Maybe they wanted to unplug from the stresses of the wired world we live in and get away from it all for a while. But sometimes, they never come back at all.

Between the years 1970 and 1973, young men were disappearing in Houston, Texas. The number eventually reached into double digits. The reason was a serial killer named Dean Corll.

All signs point to the childhood of Corll being completely unremarkable. He was born on Christmas Eve of 1939 in Indiana. There was some stress and bickering between his parents, which culminated in them getting divorced—not just once, but twice. The breakup of a family is an unfortunate situation that thousands of children find themselves in each year. Although his parents went their separate ways, no evidence suggests that the young Dean Corll took it particularly badly. He was the apple of his mother's eye, and as the men in her life all ultimately left her, her son remained a constant source of pride and adoration.

The introverted, loner type holds true to form in this case, but those who knew Corll as a child had no recollection of him being particularly angry or aggressive. As far as we know, he did not harm animals or derive pleasure from inflicting pain on others. There were none of the classic warning signs of him being a future serial killer—or if there were, nobody caught them. People described the adult Dean Corll as polite, respectful, warm, and friendly. This was, of course, just a mask to cover up a deeply sadistic and vicious persona that he managed to keep hidden for much of the time.

Although he had occasional dalliances with girls as a young man, Corll would ultimately come to the realization that he was gay. When he began to kill, his sexual preference would influence his choice of victims, all of whom were relatively young men.

A stint in the military taught Corll how to handle a weapon, but there were no reported disciplinary issues or notable infractions in his service record. Army life didn't agree with Corll, and when the opportunity arose for him to leave the service early—after putting in less than a year—he took it.

Back in the civilian world and living in Houston Heights, Corll was working in the family business—the Corll Candy Company, a small local out-fit his mother had started up. He ended up being responsible for much of the company's day-to-day operation. It was this connection that would lead to him being given the nickname of "the Candy Man," as he gained a reputation for giving away candy to people he liked. It wasn't long before people began to notice that Dean was much more likely to favor young men with free candy than he was women.

The Corll Candy Company shut its doors in 1968. Dean's mother moved out of state. Her 29-year-old son chose to remain in Houston Heights, picking up a steady day job as an electrical worker. From 1970 onward, he also developed a taste for murder.

In one respect, Dean Corll was a somewhat atypical serial killer: he liked to use accomplices, typically younger males who also fit his preferred victim profile. The boys, David Brooks and Elmer Henley (who often went by his middle name, Wayne), were targeted by Corll as potential lovers first. The older man used money and gifts to gain their trust and then moved on to paying the boys for sexual favors, trading cash for oral sex. After his arrest, Brooks told detectives that he had first met Corll when he was 12 years old and that their first sexual encounter took place two years later. Brooks turned up at Corll's place unexpectedly one day and walked in on him molesting two teenage boys who had been stripped naked and were tied down on his bed. Corll would later admit to having murdered the boys after he finished abusing them.

A photo of Dean Corll from his days in the military.

When they learned that he was abducting, torturing, raping, and murdering older boys and younger men from around their neighborhood, Brooks and Henley agreed to keep quiet in exchange for keeping the stream of money and gifts flowing. From there, they went on to become active participants in luring potential victims. Dean Corrl was in his early 30s at the time of the murders, but Brooks and Henley were 18 and 17 years old, respectively. This made them seem a little more trustworthy to the unsuspecting youths. The going rate of payment for each victim they brought back was $5 to $10.

Corll's preferred type of victim was young (the vast majority were under age 20, with some as young as 13) or, at the very least, youthful in appearance. His two accomplices took Corrl's car or van and cruised the streets, searching for the right type of boy to approach with an offer of hanging out

> The going rate of payment for each victim they brought back was $5 to $10.

and partying a little. They had a place of their own, the boys said, and there was plenty of free beer and marijuana. Many of Corll's soon-to-be victims were taken in by what appeared to be a harmless offer of a good time.

When they reached whichever place of residence Corll was currently living at (he moved around a lot but always remained within the same general Houston area), the killer would be there waiting for them. With the help of his accomplices, Corll would quickly overpower the unsuspecting young man they had brought home with them. He kept a large wooden board expressly for the purpose of restraint and torture and liked to tie his victims to it. No matter how hard they struggled, the victims were unable to break free of their bonds. Corll bit them in sensitive places and plucked out their pubic hair, sometimes forcing them to fellate him. He also inserted foreign objects into some victims' urethra and sex toys into their anus—the more humiliating, degrading, and painful it was, the better, in his view. Some survived for up to 72 hours, undergoing repeated periods of physical and emotional torture before Corll finally tired of them and ended their life.

There are obvious parallels between the sexually sadistic practices of Dean Corll and those of John Wayne Gacy, although Gacy acted alone. Both serial killers derived pleasure from forcibly sodomizing their victims once they had been rendered helpless. It was the rape and torture, rather than the act of killing itself, that motivated Corll to keep on doing what he did. The act of murder wasn't his primary reason for killing. Some would be shot, others strangled to death. To Corll, the method of death wasn't important; he got off on the suffering he caused, first and foremost, though he was not beyond mutilating the bodies when he felt the urge to do so. One victim, for example, was castrated with a knife.

Before they were killed, Corll forced his victims to write brief letters to their parents and loved ones. The messages went somewhere along the lines of

"Hey Mom and Dad, I'm doing great, moving out of town for a while because I got a job. Don't worry! Love, your son." Corll would then mail them in an attempt to diffuse suspicion when the victim's disappearance was finally noticed.

The family of 15-year-old William Ray Lawrence received a message in the mail purporting to be from their son. It read:

> I'm sorry I decided to leave. I just had to go. I hope you under-stand that I had to go. Daddy, I hope you know I love you.

Corll strangled Lawrence to death with a cord, but only after the youth had endured 72 hours of sadistic torture. His ordeal had been particularly long, it would be revealed later, because Dean Corll "had liked him."

Some victims were even forced to make phone calls to their parents. One managed to scream on the line at his family before Corll made him hang up.

Corll's first victim, killed on September 25, 1970, was an 18-year-old named Jeffrey Konen, who was hitchhiking and accepted an offer from the older man. Emboldened by the fact that he had killed without getting caught, Corll went for two victims next. James Glass and Danny Yates, both 14, disappeared after leaving church on December 13. Abducting two victims at the same time bordered on the reckless. Despite the fact that the families of both boys reported them missing, they did so separately, so the police didn't realize that two teenagers had vanished on the same day in the same neighborhood. Although reports were filed, the police did not launch an active search for James Glass and Danny Yates.

Six more victims died in 1971, including two siblings, Donald Waldrop, 15, and his 13-year-old brother, Jerry, who were taken on the same day.

When it came to disposing of the bodies, Corll buried them at several different sites, including in the ground beneath a boat shed, and on a beach some 60 miles south of Houston. Some of the bodies would later be found buried and stacked one atop the other.

Ten victims died in 1972, and by August of 1973, there were another nine that we know of. There is every reason to believe that Dean Corll would have kept on killing, but his own accomplices would put an end to his streak of killings.

Before killing them, Corll would force his young victims to write letters to their parents saying that they were running away. On other occasions, Corll had them make a phone call.

Corll's demeanor had been getting more aggressive with each new murder, or so Brooks and Henley would later claim. Finally, on August 8, 1973, he turned on them. The night before, Wayne Henley had brought Corll what was supposed to be his next victim, 19-year-old Timothy Kerley. Another friend of Henley's, a 15-year-old girl named Rhonda Williams, had been assaulted by her abusive father earlier that evening, and she gratefully accepted Henley's offer to come back to Corll's place and hang out there with Kerley and Henley, who said they were going to have an intimate little party with the owner. Rhonda and Wayne Henley were friends. He had supported her in the past when she'd needed it, and she trusted him.

Corll, for his part, was not remotely pleased to see a teenage girl turn up at his apartment at three o'clock in the morning, no matter what the reason. In fact, he was livid. It put a damper on his plan to rape, torture, and murder Timothy Kerley. Now that she was in his living room, however, there wasn't much he could do about it. Throwing her out into the street would attract too much attention. Corll went to bed, leaving Rhonda and the two boys to drink and sniff paint fumes out of a paper bag until they all passed out. When he emerged from his room again, Corll set to work handcuffing the trio and tying them up, slapping a length of duct tape across each of their mouths to prevent them all from screaming. He was dead set on killing all three of them. He kicked Rhonda back to consciousness.

Corll took Henley out of the room. The two men came back bearing weapons. Henley was holding a knife. Corll was armed with a handgun. Rhonda had had every reason to trust Wayne Henley up to that point, but now she had to be wondering what the young man she thought was her friend intended to do with the weapon.

> Rhonda was shocked to see that a stark naked and terrified Timothy Kerley was secured to the big wooden board that, unbeknownst to her, Corll liked to use for torturing his victims.

Leaning in close and keeping his voice low enough that only she could hear it, Henley whispered that everything was going to be alright. When a naked Dean Corll lifted her up and carried her into the bedroom, it certainly didn't look as though that would be the case. Rhonda was shocked to see that a stark naked and terrified Timothy Kerley was secured to the big wooden board that, unbeknownst to her, Corll liked to use for torturing his victims. Until now, all of them had been boys or young men. Now, Rhonda Williams was forcibly stripped of her clothes and tied down to the board along with Timothy Kerley.

Corll's main focus was on Kerley. After grabbing his crotch, Corll began hitting the helpless young man. Caught in a rage, however, the serial killer had made a big mistake—one that would prove to be fatal. He put down the pistol that he was using to threaten his three victims.

Finally, Wayne Henley lost it. He went for the gun and pointed it it Corll. "You've gone far enough, Dean!" he yelled.

Corll turned and came at him, screaming "Kill me, Wayne! Kill me!"

Henley obliged. He pulled the trigger over and over until every last round was gone, putting six bullets into Dean Corll. He was dead long before the first police units arrived.

All three survivors were arrested and held there while detectives tried to unravel the entire sordid story. Wayne Henley and David Brooks confessed their involvement in the murder of some of Corll's victims. Brooks denied having caused the victims any direct physical harm, whereas Henley admitted to having pulled the trigger himself and personally killing a number of the young men. In both cases, it could not be disputed that each man been present at the time of some of the deaths, and the fact that they had also helped lure the victims along to Dean Corll's residence made them both accessories. They had also aided him in burying the bodies.

Despite her protestations of innocence, Rhonda Williams also went to jail until the facts could be sorted out.

Henley and Brooks cooperated with the authorities, leading detectives to the burial sites where they dug and uncovered body after body, many of which were wrapped in plastic and liberally coated with lime. The ground beneath the boathouse alone yielded 17 sets of human remains. Stacked above it were the personal effects of Dean Corll's victims, everything from clothing to the bicycles some of them had been riding at the time of their abduction. The deeper they dug, the more decomposed the remains were. The smell rising from beneath the floor of the boathouse became so bad that respirators were necessary to prevent the men digging from throwing up.

Other burial sites were unearthed. Boys had been buried in the woodland close to a place where Corll had vacationed once. Others were recovered from shallow graves that had been dug along a stretch of beach some 80 miles away from where Corll had killed them.

Dean Corll was beyond the reach of justice, but his accomplices weren't. Wayne Henley had not one but two trials, primarily because the first became such a media circus that it was no longer considered to be a fair and objective process. He had been found guilty on multiple counts of murder. In the second trial, he was also found guilty. He showed little remorse for his crimes, and despite his defense attorney's argument that Henley had been the one to finally put a stop to Corll's reign of terror, the jury was not swayed.

Despite his having a young wife (who was pregnant with his daughter) present in the courtroom, David Brooks fared no better during his own trial in 1975. The jury took less than two hours to find him guilty of murder.

Four of the boys whom Corll murdered were found near the shore of Lake Sam Rayburn, which is about 70 miles north of Beaumont in east Texas.

Under normal circumstances, Texas is one of the easier states in which a convicted criminal can receive the death penalty. Brooks and Henley were not executed, however, due to a suspension of the death penalty that was in place at the time of their respective trials. Had this not been the case, the district attorney would almost certainly have pressed the judge to send both to the electric chair. As things stood, each was sent to prison and will almost certainly never be released.

Brooks has made multiple unsuccessful attempts to get paroled. His last was in early 2018. He will not be eligible again until 2028, at which time he will be 72 years old. It is likely that both he and his fellow accomplice Wayne Henley will die in prison.

Rhonda Williams had her name legally changed at the order of a juvenile court judge, to give her a fresh start in life. It was an opportunity to leave behind the horror of nearly becoming another of Corll's victims. Many of the details of what happened on the night of August 7 and the early morning of August 8, 1973, came from her willingness to speak to the *Houston Press* many years after those traumatic events. She now has a family of her own but will never be entirely free of what happened that night.

It is speculated that the total number of boys killed by Dean Corll is between 30 and 40. Not all of them have been found, and of the dead boys whose remains have been found, not all have been positively identified. The families of many young men who went missing in the vicinity of Houston Heights while Dean Corll lived there may never experience any real sense of closure.

The reasons behind Dean Corll's transformation from a seemingly ordinary young man into a homicidal, sadistic rapist are difficult to fathom. The lack of any evidence of trauma or abuse in his childhood or early adult life leaves us with little to go on. It is difficult to avoid the conclusion that Dean Corll was simply "wired wrong" and was somehow able to exert sufficient control over two easily influenced teenagers to have them join him in a series of mass murders that has lost none of their ability to shock and horrify almost five decades afterward.

RAMPAGE AND SPREE KILLERS

Up to this point in the book, we have focused our attention on the serial killer; that is, somebody who murders multiple victims, usually one at a time, but occasionally killing two people during the same incident. As we have seen, the serial killer's crimes can span the course of many year or, in some cases, decades.

In most instances, the serial killer wants to avoid detection. They care about not getting caught and go to great lengths to cover their tracks and try to divert attention from what it is that they are doing. This is the primary reason that so many of them prefer to choose victims whose disappearance will go unnoticed and unquestioned.

Few serial killers have a death wish. Their goal is to survive in order to keep on killing while going about their everyday lives.

Spree, or rampage, killers, however, are different. They tend to want to go out in a "blaze of glory" (it may be glorious to them, but to the rest of us, it is abhorrent). The majority do not expect to survive. For them, the endpoint is going to be either a confrontation with the police, during which they will either be shot dead or taken into custody, or suicide. A great many of them choose the latter. Their revenge has been taken; their point has been made; and the idea of a trial and spending years or decades on death row, followed by execution, holds little appeal. It is far easier for them to simply shoot themselves dead and be done with it, going out on their own terms and doing their best to leave a black mark on the pages of history.

We live in an age when it hardly seems possible for a week to pass by without word of another mass murder. In the United States, which holds the unenviable record of leading the world in rampage killings, the majority of such incidents involve firearms. This is by no means a uniquely American phenomenon, however, and in countries where guns are harder to come by, vehicles, explosives, and knives are just some examples of the means used to inflict horrific injuries upon an unsuspecting public.

The rampage killer is generally categorized differently from the terrorist, whose purpose is to inflict as much suffering and trauma as possible in the furtherance of a political goal or agenda. Timothy McVeigh, the Oklahoma City bomber, was an urban terrorist, whose intention was to make an antigovernment statement by detonating an ammonium-nitrate fertilizer bomb in close proximity to a federal building. The 9/11 hijackers were also terrorists, rather than rampage killers. Rampage killers do what they do in alignment with a personal desire, such as the need for revenge on their fellow human beings in return for some perceived slight, whether real or imagined. Some simply feel compelled to kill, as in the case of the Villisca Axe Murders, a killing spree that left eight innocent victims dead. This was a rare instance of a rampage killer wanting to get away with it and successfully achieving that aim and was an exception to the rule. Most rampage killers are giving the middle finger to the rest of humanity. They judge their level of success based upon the sheer number of people they kill or injure and the amount of media coverage they get for committing atrocities.

In the twenty-first century, both serial killers and rampage killers often have cult followings. James Holmes (see the chapter on him below), the man who killed 12 people and wounded many more in an Aurora, Colorado, movie theater on July 20, 2012, received hundreds of letters while he was in jail, most of them from adoring female fans who wanted to establish some kind of relationship with him. There were even some marriage proposals. Many sent photographs of themselves (or at least, of women the correspondents *claimed* to be themselves), some of which were scantily clad and highly explicit.

Arguably the most disturbing form of rampage killing is the school shooting. Schools should be safe places of learning, but increasingly they are providing the setting for active shooter events. The situation has now grown so bad in the United States that students and teachers must be regularly drilled on how to react to such a catastrophe in case it occurs at their own school.

We tend to think of the school shooting rampage as being a relatively new thing. Ask most Americans about the subject, and the majority will point to the Columbine High School shooting in Colorado (April 20, 1999) as the earliest example of such an incident. The truth is that there are isolated instances of such massacres going back many more decades before that.

THE BATH SCHOOL MASSACRE

On May 18, 1927, in Bath Township, Michigan, a 55-year-old farmer named Andrew Kehoe went on a rampage at the local school, killing 45 people (including himself). Most of the dead were children. Kehoe was not particularly well liked by those who knew him. He was prone to outbursts of anger and had little tolerance for those who disagreed with him, or for those he didn't like.

Kehoe served as the town clerk for a short period in 1925. After the office went up for election and Kehoe was defeated, he began to seethe with rage. He took the loss as an insult, a personal rejection by the community he had been serving. That anger would go on to manifest itself with tragic and deadly consequences.

For many spree killers, tension and stress build up over months and years before finally bursting in a tragic event. In this case, it was more of a continuum than a single event. Kehoe's wife was terminally ill, business was not going well, and he found himself in dire financial straits, with no ability to cover mortgage payments on the farm. He faced the prospect of losing his wife, his home, and his livelihood, all at the same time.

The new township school had become a focal point for his growing sense of rage. A significant tax had been levied on residents to pay for it. Kehoe was heard to say, "If it hadn't been for that $300 school tax, I might have paid off this mortgage." Instead, his inability to pay set him on the road to possible foreclosure on his farm. His response was a very blatant threat: "If I can't live in that house, no one else will."

Rather than simply snap one day, Kehoe carefully planned his attack well in advance. He purchased large amounts of explosives, surreptitiously moving them into position over the course of many months. After the attack, police officers would determine that he was responsible for the theft of dynamite supplies from a bridge construction site. At least 500 pounds of it went beneath the school, without any of the teaching staff realizing it. By the time he had finished, the entire basement of the school was wired to explode, as was the farmhouse in which he lived and all of its outbuildings. This would have presented no significant challenge to Kehoe, who was a skilled and experienced electrician.

Rampage murderers are, sadly, nothing new. Andrew Kehoe (shown here in 1920) went off the rails and blew up Bath Consolidated School in Michigan, killing himself and 44 others, mostly children.

Kehoe turned his own truck into a moving bomb, loading it up with any spare scrap metal that he could find, along with nails and sticks of dynamite. When it exploded, the truck's contents would blast out at high speed like the fragmented casing of a hand grenade.

The first person to die was Andrew Kehoe's own wife, Nellie. Her husband beat her to death and left her body outside. The exact time of her death is unknown, though it had to have been within two days of the attack on the school. By 8:30 in the morning on May 18, school was in session. Kehoe blew up his farm and its buildings at around 8:45, killing nobody in the process. Then he drove to the school.

The truck went up in a huge fireball, spraying shrapnel in all directions. More victims were killed and injured by the blast wave and the flying metal fragments.

Before he arrived, a massive explosion tore through the school. The detonation had been set on a clock timer. The north wing was completely destroyed, taking the full brunt of the blast. Classes were already in session, which is exactly what Kehoe had intended. Seated at their desks, many of the children were crushed beneath the falling structure as it collapsed in upon itself. Bodies and body parts were flung from the wreckage. Although the majority of victims were pupils, teachers died too.

When Andrew Kehoe arrived at the school, nobody knew that he was the one responsible for the disaster. While he parked his truck, the superintendent, E. F. Huyck, approached him. Eyewitnesses saw Kehoe raise a gun and, rather than shoot Huyck (with whom he had a very adversarial relationship), instead fired a shot into the dynamite stored in the back of his truck.

The truck went up in a huge fireball, spraying shrapnel in all directions. More victims were killed and injured by the blast wave and the flying metal fragments. Kehoe himself was killed instantly, as were Huyck and others.

Every emergency responder in the area came to the disaster site, along with hundreds of volunteers. The race was on to rescue as many victims from the rubble as they possibly could, and after that, human remains would have to be recovered. It required a massive effort with the entire community pitching in. Nellie Kehoe's body, charred almost beyond recognition, was discovered when a search was made of the ruined Kehoe farm.

Andrew Kehoe had finally gotten his revenge, and it had come at a terrible cost. Forty-five people had been killed, including Kehoe and his wife; there were also many injuries, ranging from minor to mortal (one victim died later at the hospital). Thirty-eight of the dead were children, three were teaching staff, and two more were citizens of the town.

There was one tiny ray of sunshine on an otherwise black day. Mercifully, hundreds of sticks of dynamite had not detonated, due to shoddy wiring by Kehoe. They were discovered during a search of the schoolhouse and safely removed. Had they gone off as planned, many more children would have perished.

Why did Andrew Kehoe commit such a senseless act of violence? Earlier in his life, Andrew Kehoe had sustained a major closed head injury. The connection between such brain trauma and an increased propensity for carrying out acts of violence has been seen repeatedly throughout the pages of this book. Perhaps the long-lasting aftereffects of this injury, coupled with the hopeless financial situation Kehoe found himself in, combined to make him carry out one of the worst school massacres in American history.

An article that was published in the *Buffalo Evening News* on May 20, 1927 (two days after the massacre) titled "Children Hated by Dynamitard, Neighbors Say" offered some additional insight into why Kehoe targeted the school: "The Kehoes had no children. It was said by neighbors that Kehoe was bitter against children. He was extra bilious and turned vinegary because of his difficulties. Apparently, he blamed the school for his troubles, and he wanted to do away with the school."

PACIFIC FLIGHT #773

Not all rampage killings take place on the ground. On May 7, 1964, one of the more unusual mass murders on record took place. A suicidal man

Seen here in 1962, this Pacific Air Lines Fairchild F-27A crashed near San Ramon, California, when the suicidal Francisco Gonzales shot the pilots.

named Francisco Gonzales boarded Pacific Air Lines flight 773 in Reno, Nevada. The plane, a Fairfield F-27A, was bound for San Francisco. It would never reach its destination.

One day prior to traveling, Gonzales had purchased a .357 Smith & Wesson revolver, which he was able to smuggle on board the flight. Airport security was practically nonexistent at the time.

It was an early-morning flight, and there were at first no signs of anything being amiss. Suddenly, air traffic control received a radio transmission from Pacific 773 that was difficult to decipher but sounded like "Skipper's shot! We've been shot! I was tryin' to help!" The voice was that of the first officer. No further radio transmissions came in from the aircraft, which then went into a dive and crashed into the side of a hill.

When crash investigators combed through the wreckage, they found the .357, which had been fired six times. It was subsequently traced to Francisco Gonzales. After the crash, friends and family members of Gonzales who were interviewed revealed that he suffered from severe depression and had openly stated that he would be dead by either May 6 or May 7. He was said to be having difficulties with his finances and with his personal relationships. Tragically, nobody had taken him seriously when he pulled out the pistol *at the airport* and said that he would soon shoot himself. He had also taken out life insurance policies on himself totaling more than $100,000.

Despite these obvious red flags, Gonzales was able to board the plane. It was determined during the crash investigation that he had gotten out of his seat, walked up to the cockpit, and shot both the pilot and the copilot. All three members of the crew and all 41 passengers on board the aircraft were killed.

It is a sad truth that many people who feel they have nothing left to live for choose to take their own lives. In the case of Francisco Gonzales, we are forced to wonder why he felt compelled to end 43 other lives along with his own.

THE SAN YSIDRO McDONALD'S MASSACRE

On July 18, 1984, James Huberty took his wife, Etna, and daughter to the zoo. Afterward, he kissed Etna and walked out the door for the last time. When his wife asked him where he was going, he casually responded that he was "going to hunt humans." True to his word, he went to a nearby McDonald's restaurant and gunned down as many people as he could.

According to Etna, Huberty would beat both her and their daughters. He also heard voices in his head but had ignored her pleas for him to seek professional psychiatric help. At one point, he had placed the muzzle of a loaded gun to his forehead and came close to killing himself—but Etna had stopped him.

Huberty was raised in a strict and devoutly religious Ohio family. This led to him getting bullied while growing up, which is seen in the background of many serial and rampage killers. Beginning as a youth, one of his favorite pastimes was shooting and developing his marksmanship skills.

As an adult, he worked in the embalming trade, moved on to train as a welder, and then began work as a security guard after relocating to California. He had lost his job a week before launching his killing spree in the San Ysidro district of San Diego. The loss had delivered a huge blow to his sense of self-worth.

Huberty had a deep interest in firearms of all different types and considered himself to be a survivalist, often wearing camouflaged military surplus clothing despite never having served in the armed forces. He was also a conspiracy theorist who believed that the end of American society was imminent and was buying copious amounts of firearms and ammunition to prepare himself for it.

In an interview with United Press International reporter Leon Daniel, Etna Huberty claimed that her husband blamed the government for most of the difficulties in his life, and she added that his political beliefs might best be described as being "Nazi."

He had few friends and quarreled with his neighbors. By all accounts, James Huberty was not a nice man. Quick to anger, mean-spirited in nature, he was an easy person to get on the wrong side of. A colleague who had worked with him in Ohio said that "he was always talking about shooting somebody." The same coworker added that when he lost his job, Huberty made threats to "take everyone with him."

The victims that 41-year-old Huberty finally did take with him were the staff and diners of the McDonald's restaurant located near his apartment on San Ysidro Boulevard. It was late in the afternoon, and the restaurant was busy, with over 40 people eating or waiting to be served. Huberty was armed with a shotgun, an Uzi submachine gun, and a Browning Hi-Power automatic pistol, once the preferred handgun of the British Army. He also carried a bag full of replacement ammunition.

Huberty opened fire without warning, showing absolutely no regard for the age or sex of his victims. He killed several 11-year-old children and a nine-year-old girl, screaming incoherently as he did so. Customers and staff members alike were shot. His shooting pattern varied wildly. Some victims received upwards of

A plaque at the San Ysidro, California, McDonald's restaurant memorializes the 21 victims shot by James Huberty on July 18, 1984.

50 gunshot wounds, whereas others were killed with a single bullet. The shooter was not acting methodically; he was simply venting his rage at the world.

Incredibly, despite the sounds of extremely loud gunfire and damage done to the restaurant, at first customers continued to approach. Huberty gunned them down as they came in, then turned his attention to people outside the restaurant. A young couple and their infant baby were shot with nine-millimeter fire from Huberty's Uzi. In an almost miraculous stroke of good fortune, the baby girl—who was taken to a nearby hospital by a bystander—survived, as did both of her parents.

> To this author, it seems most likely that his ingrained paranoia and rage issues had built to such a crescendo that it set him off.

The first police units on the scene came under heavy fire from inside the restaurant. It wasn't long before Huberty believed he had incapacitated or killed everybody inside the McDonald's (though he had not), and so he focused his attention on those outside. The closest available SWAT team was called to the scene. Snipers were deployed but found it difficult to get a clean shot at first because many of the tall glass windows were damaged. All they could do was bide their time until, finally, a kill shot presented itself to one of the snipers who was sighting in from an elevated position.

Sniper Charles Foster had at last gotten an unobstructed line of sight on the shooter. He did not hesitate, putting a round squarely in Huberty's chest. Huberty died instantly. Officers immediately stormed the restaurant and began to take stock of the carnage.

James Huberty had murdered 21 people and wounded 19 more before he himself was killed. Many theories exist as to why he went on a rampage. To this author, it seems most likely that his ingrained paranoia and rage issues had built to such a crescendo that it set him off. Being let go from his job and losing the ability to support himself and his family pushed him over the edge, and an entire restaurant full of innocent people paid the price.

More mass shootings followed San Ysidro. On August 20, 1986, in Edmond, Oklahoma, Patrick Sherrill went on a rampage, murdering 14 of his fellow post office colleagues and wounding six more before turning the gun on himself. He had been given a verbal warning by a supervisor the day before, felt insecure about his employment prospects, and finally snapped. It was the first in a series of post office–related killing sprees that ushered the phrase "going postal" into the common lexicon.

LUBY'S CAFETERIA

Another restaurant rampage took place in 1991 in Killeen, Texas. The perpetrator was an unemployed 35-year-old man named George Hennard. Screaming that women were all "vipers," he drove his pickup truck straight through the front window of a Luby's Cafeteria and started shooting.

Hennard was armed with two pistols and fired well-aimed, single shots, killing 23 people and wounding 27 more before responding police officers shot him. The wounds were not fatal, and Hennard kept on shooting until he ran low on ammunition. He shot himself before the police could take him into custody.

Those who knew him said that Hennard was a sexist, a racist, and a homophobe, and generally despised females. His unbridled hatred of women was evidenced by the casualty list, as he had killed more female victims than males, and intentionally so—several of those who survived told police that he had passed up the opportunity to shoot men in favor of targeting women and was shouting derogatory terms for them as he fired.

Killeen was to suffer future mass killings when the nearby military base Fort Hood was the scene of two more active shooter episodes. In 2009, an active duty army officer killed 14

The memorial near the Killeen, Texas, Luby's restaurant, where George Hennard shot 23 people dead and wounded another 27 in 1991.

people and wounded 32 before finally being taken into custody. The officer, Major Nidal Malik Hasan, was a psychiatrist. Due to his being a follower of the Islamic faith, there was much speculation about the killings being an act of terrorism. There is no doubt that the act was ideologically motivated by Hasan's religious beliefs.

A second, unrelated shooting at Fort Hood followed in 2014, when Army Specialist Ivan Lopez shot three people dead and wounded many more before fatally shooting himself in the head. It would later emerge that Lopez had been dealing with mental health issues and was recently bereaved.

THE HUNGERFORD MASSACRE

Most firearm-driven rampage killings have taken place in the United States, but the United Kingdom saw its own tragedy on August 19, 1987. Michael Ryan, a 27-year-old firearms enthusiast, put on black clothing and walked through the small English town of Hungerford, shooting indiscriminately with a semiautomatic, Chinese-made copy of the ubiquitous AK-47 rifle, an M1 carbine (once widely used by the U.S. Army), and a pistol. Ryan was a member of a gun club and had acquired his weapons legally.

The entire police force that covered Hungerford and its surrounding villages was composed of just 14 unarmed officers, only four of whom were on duty the morning of the massacre.

To this day, Michael Ryan's reasons for committing a rampage-type mass killing remain unknown. He did not have a history of diagnosed mental illness, nor did he have a criminal record of any kind. Those who knew him would later describe him as an introvert bordering upon an isolationist, who kept to himself. He lived with his mother and had few friends, fitting the lone-wolf archetype.

One possible clue involves Ryan's tendency to fantasize. He would construct elaborate scenarios that involved him associating with a high-ranking military officer who was supposedly teaching him to fly a light aircraft and planned to buy him a house. Whether he truly believed this or not is difficult to say, but he managed to convince his mother that they were real. He would also claim to have served in an elite Special Forces unit, though he had never been in the military at all.

August 19 started out as just another ordinary day in Hungerford. But shortly after noon, Michael Ryan shot 35-year-old Susan Godfrey. She had taken her two- and four-year-old children for a picnic in the woodlands a few miles west of town when a gun-toting Ryan appeared and led her some distance away. Her body would be discovered later with 13 gunshot wounds in her back. All had been fired from a pistol.

From there, Ryan got into his car and drove back to Hungerford. He stopped at a gas station along the way, filling up a container with gasoline. Rather than pay for it, Ryan opened fire on the cashier with the M1 carbine. Even at short range, he missed. The cashier took cover and was somehow able to avoid all of Ryan's incoming gunfire. Ryan then headed into the village, knowing he would find many more targets there.

Ryan's first stop was at his own home to load up his car with his arsenal of weapons. When he tried to drive away, his car refused to start. Frustrated, Ryan got back out and began shooting at it. Before heading for Hungerford on foot, he took the time to kill the family dog, splash the gasoline he had just obtained all over the house, and set the house on fire. The flames quickly took hold, and the house, along with several neighboring properties, burned to the ground.

The first two fatalities were a married couple who were shot in the garden of their home. Michael Ryan then followed a footpath toward the town common, an open stretch of land that many villages have, shooting almost everybody he encountered along the way. This included some who were trying to surrender.

Constable Roger Brereton, the first arriving police officer, was shot and killed shortly after encountering Ryan. He didn't even have a chance to get out of his patrol car before the shooter put 24 rounds into it, four of which hit the constable. Ryan then opened fire on another car that contained two village residents; mercifully, the driver was able to speed away, though not before she sustained wounds from the AK-47.

Ryan resumed walking along the street, shooting at every person he saw. Despite the sound of gunfire, some of the villagers were still outside in their gardens. They were shot down where they stood.

As part of the 999 emergency response, paramedics had been called to the scene, despite the fact that it was still an ongoing active shooter situation. The first ambulance to arrive drew fire and immediately pulled back, with one of its crew members sustaining injuries in the process. Another car drove past the scene. Ryan shot the driver dead and wounded the passenger, causing him to crash into Constable Brereton's patrol car.

Constable Roger Brereton, the first arriving police officer, was shot and killed shortly after encountering Ryan.

The center of Hungerford was by now a scene of complete chaos, all of it centered around Michael Ryan. In the United Kingdom, police officers did not carry firearms. It would take a long time before an armed response unit was dispatched to the scene. In the meantime, there was just one person who might stand even the slightest chance of stopping the carnage: the shooter's mother, Dorothy Ryan. She had spent the morning shopping, completely oblivious to the havoc being wreaked by her son. As she was returning through the center of the village, she saw him standing on the sidewalk with a gun in his hand, surrounded by his dead and dying victims.

It is impossible to know what must have been going through Dorothy Ryan's mind when she realized just what her son had done, but she attempted to do the right thing by approaching him and trying to talk him down. Her efforts to end the massacre before any more innocent people were killed received a hostile reception. Her son shot her dead in cold blood, just as he had done with complete strangers and those he personally knew, waiting for his mother to fall to the ground and then shooting her again to make sure that she was dead.

His longer-ranged weapons were now out of ammunition. Ryan switched to his pistol. He kept walking, firing upon motorists and pedestrians alike, inflicting still more casualties along the way. At some point, he changed tactics, blasting the front doors to some of the houses he passed with the semi-automatic rifle, then went inside and murdered whoever he found there. One victim was wheelchair-bound. Her husband jumped in front of her in a vain attempt to shield her. Ryan, cold-blooded to the last, shot them both.

More police officers descended upon Hungerford, but without any means of returning fire, there was little they could do to counter Ryan. They set up roadblocks to prevent more civilian motorists from driving into the village and adding to the number of victims. Thirty-five minutes after Michael Ryan had first opened fire, armed police officers began to deploy on foot, doing their best to hunt him down. A police helicopter flew overhead, coordinating the ground search and helping the marksmen close in on their target.

The rampage had lasted for almost an hour. As law enforcement personnel continued to pour into the town, they directed the people of Hungerford to shelter in place, taking cover in their own homes as best they could. At 4:40 P.M., gunshots were heard coming from the direction of the school. There were no civilians in the vicinity, so it is possible that Ryan was taking pot shots at the police helicopter circling overhead. Armed officers moved to contain the school inside an armed cordon. One way or another, there was no way they would allow Michael Ryan to harm anybody else.

Officers began talking to Ryan. He was trapped inside the school and tossed the empty AK-47 from an open window. Ryan called out that he was still armed and had a hand grenade at the ready in case they tried to make entry. "It's funny," Ryan said at one point. "I've killed all those people, but I haven't the guts to blow my own brains out."

> More police officers descended upon Hungerford, but without any means of returning fire, there was little they could do to counter Ryan.

Yet that is exactly what he did. When armed officers entered the school, they found Ryan dead. He had been killed by a single self-inflicted gunshot wound to the head. As night fell on Hungerford, the cleanup work was already underway. Sixteen people had been killed (in addition to the man who had murdered them), and 15 more had been injured.

Hungerford was forever scarred by the events of that day. Local people remembered the eerie silence that descended on the village in the aftermath of the mass shooting, observing that for several days afterward even the birds did not sing.

The long-term effects were profound. Some couples split up, unable to bear the reminder of what they had been through in Hungerford. Some villagers left and never came back. Post-traumatic stress disorder was rife, not only among the victims and eyewitnesses but also the first responders who had tried their best to manage a living hell that day.

One of the few positives to emerge from the Hungerford tragedy was a tightening of the U.K. laws regarding firearm ownership, removing the right for citizens to own semiautomatic weapons. Despite being one of the worst firearms-related massacres to take place in the British Isles, it was not the last.

In 1997, Dunblane, Scotland, experienced its own nightmare when 43-year-old Thomas Hamilton opened fire inside the local primary school gymnasium, murdering 16 five-year-old children and their teacher before fatally shooting himself in the head. Hamilton had an inappropriate interest in young boys, and during his short tenure as a supervisor in the Boy Scouts, he had been the subject of several complaints concerning his behavior toward them. Hamilton carried out the murders entirely with handguns, two of which were semiautomatic.

INTO THE TWENTY-FIRST CENTURY

Rampage killings were once a relatively rare occurrence. School shootings, such as those that took place at Columbine High School in Colorado (13 dead, in addition to both killers) and Sandy Hook Elementary in Connecticut (27 dead, in addition to the murderer), have now become commonplace in the United States. A mass shooting at Virginia Tech in 2007 claimed the lives of 32 victims, with almost as many injured, before the perpetrator took his own life.

None of these was intended to further a political agenda. Each was the act of one or more crazed individuals, seeking to inflict pain on others for their own personal reasons—usually some twisted form of revenge.

Over the course of the next two chapters, we will look at two such cases in more detail.

One of the few positives to emerge from the Hungerford tragedy was a tightening of the U.K. laws regarding firearm ownership.

THE TEXAS TOWER SNIPER: CHARLES WHITMAN

The drill instructor stands ramrod-straight, with one hand tucked into the small of his back. His uniform is immaculately pressed, the creases razor-sharp. In front of him, sitting on a series of tiered bleachers, is a cohort of U.S. Marine Corps recruits. They hang on the senior man's every word.

"Do any of you know who Charles Whitman was?" A pause. Nobody answers. The gunnery sergeant sounds exasperated. "None of you dumbasses knows."

A hand goes up from among the recruits. "Private Cowboy," he acknowledges.

The recruit, a Texan, stands to attention. "Sir, he was that guy who shot all those people from that tower in Austin, Texas."

"That's affirmative. Charles Whitman killed 12 people from a 28-story observation tower at the University of Texas, from distances up to 400 yards." Gunnery Sergeant Hartman, played to perfection by former real-life drill instructor R. Lee Ermey, takes an almost perverse pride in the fact that a spree killer who actually killed 15 people, fatally stabbed two members of his own family, and wounded 31 others, learned how to handle a rifle in his own beloved Marine Corps.

The movie is Stanley Kubrick's masterpiece *Full Metal Jacket,* and it follows a batch of USMC recruits on their journey through boot camp to the conflict in Vietnam. Charles Whitman was once one of them and did indeed learn to shoot on the gunnery ranges at Parris Island, the Corps's infamous recruit training depot.

Whitman showed a solid, if unspectacular, aptitude for marksmanship while serving in the Marine Corps, earning himself the distinction of "sharp-

A 1963 photo of Charles Whitman, three years before the Austin massacre.

shooter" on his qualification assessment. This was the second highest of three attainable rankings for a Marine, the highest being "expert."

Tragically, he would put those skills to deadly use against unarmed civilians in Austin on August 1, 1966. It was not long before noon, and already shaping up to be a hot day, as most summer days are in Texas. Encumbered by a heavy footlocker filled with firearms and ammunition, along with food and water supplies that would have sustained him throughout a prolonged siege, the 25-year-old former Marine made his way to the 28th-floor observation deck of the 300-plus-foot tower that looked out over the University of Texas at Austin campus.

Reaching his vantage point, Whitman set out the array of rifles, shotguns, pistols, and spare rounds, then began scoping out potential targets.

This wasn't a random, spur-of-the-moment event. Whitman had put some planning into it, purchasing some of his supplies (including, crucially, a set of binoculars) the day before. Nor was it his first time at the tower. He and his brother had visited a little over a week before. It is unclear whether his shooting spree was inspired by that trip, or whether he was scouting it out as a potential location in advance. We will almost certainly never know.

He also sat down and typed out something akin to a suicide note on the night of July 31, a few hours before taking the lives of his wife and mother.

I don't quite understand what it is that compels me to type this letter. Perhaps it is to leave some vague reason for the actions I have recently performed. I don't really understand myself these days. I am supposed to be an average reasonable and intelligent young man. However, lately (I can't recall when it started) I have been a victim of many unusual and irrational thoughts. Those thoughts constantly recur, and it requires a tremendous mental effort to concentrate on useful and progressive tasks. In March when my parents made a physical break I noticed a great deal of stress. I consulted a Dr. Cochrum at the University Health Center and asked him to recommend someone that I could consult with about some psychiatric disorders I felt I had. I talked with a doctor once for about two hours and tried to convey to him my fears that I felt some overwhelming violent impulses. After one session I never saw the doctor again, and since then I have been fighting my mental turmoil alone, and seemingly to no avail. After my death I wish that an autopsy would be performed on me to see if there is any visible physical disorder. I have had some tremendous headaches in the past and have consumed two large bottles of Excedrin in the past three months.

The "physical break" Whitman refers to was the separation of his parents. After suffering years of abuse, Margaret Whitman finally had enough. She left her husband, aided by her son, Charles. The emotional trauma of watching his mother and father separate, their marriage having been one of the few constants of his life, should not be discounted.

Unbeknownst to him, when it came to his request to have an autopsy carried out, Whitman would ultimately get his wish. The results would prove to be unexpected, to say the least. His letter continues:

It was after much thought that I decided to kill my wife, Kathy, tonight after I picked her up from work at the telephone company. I love her dearly, and she has been as fine a wife to me as any man could ever hope to have. I cannot rationally pinpoint any specific reason for doing this. I don't know whether it is selfishness, or if I don't want her to have to face the embarrassment my actions would surely cause her. At this time, though, the prominent reason in my mind is that I truly do not consider this world worth living in, and am prepared to die, and I do not want to leave her to suffer alone in it. I intend to kill her as painlessly as possible.

"I cannot rationally pinpoint any specific reason for doing this." Assuming that he was writing what he earnestly believed to be the truth—and there was no reason for him to lie, for Whitman must have known that he was going to die the next day—then this is, perhaps, the most chilling part of the entire message. After acknowledging that his wife had been good to him, extolling her virtues, and declaring his love for her, Whitman then plainly declares that he is nevertheless going to murder her anyway, basically saying, "I don't know why, but I am going to do it anyway."

There is considerable introspection and self-examination on display here, with Whitman holding up his motivations for assessment and turning them this way and that, trying to figure out just why he is going to do the things he is planning to do. If Charles Whitman's primary reason for killing his wife was to spare her any further pain—pain that would be inflicted on her directly because of him—then it is difficult to square such a compassionate approach with the cold-blooded acts of murder he was also planning to commit.

The last typewritten section of Whitman's letter reads:

Similar reasons provoked me to take my mother's life also. I don't think the poor woman has ever enjoyed life as she is entitled to. She was a simple young woman who married a very possessive and dominating man.

Once again, Whitman betrays a sympathy and sense of compassion for a loved one he intends to murder in cold blood (note the past tense of the letter, with the author writing as if the murders of his wife and mother have already been carried out). From this, we can glean that Charles Whitman was fully aware of his father's negative character traits, and we can infer that he did not approve of them. This is further supported by the fact that Charles helped his mother move when she decided to leave. He hated his father and, it would later be revealed, was mortified at the prospect of turning out to be anything like him.

> **Whitman murdered both Kathy and his mother while each of them slept, stabbing each woman multiple times in the chest.**

Yet true to his word, early the next morning, he went on to kill both his wife and his mother, the two women with whom he was closest in all the world.

Also of note is the fact that the letter mentions none of the specifics of what Charles Whitman was planning. There are only veiled hints.

Whitman finished his letter by asking for his dog to be given to his in-laws and re-emphasizing his desire for an autopsy, followed by a cremation of his own remains.

It's unclear exactly how he spent the rest of the night of July 31. At some point, his wife, Kathy, went to bed. In the early hours of August 1, Whitman murdered both Kathy and his mother while each of them slept, stabbing each woman multiple times in the chest. Margaret Whitman had also been shot in the head. He annotated the margin of the lengthy letter he had typed out, noting that by 3 A.M., both of the women were dead. He now had literally nothing left to live for.

After the sun came up, Whitman went to purchase a few last-minute supplies, including more ammunition and weaponry. It was a little after 11:30 when he arrived at the U.T. campus. Bluffing his way into the elevator without being seriously challenged, he went up to the 27th floor, from which the observation deck could be accessed via a flight of stairs. There was a single receptionist on duty, Edna Elizabeth Townsley. Whitman smashed the butt of one of his weapons into her head, then moved her body until it was out of plain view. He would shortly go on to shoot her at point-blank range.

A family, the Gabours, happened to be ascending the staircase and heading for the observation deck themselves. Completely unsuspecting, the two teenage sons reached the top of the staircase first and walked straight into an ambush. Probably anticipating a close-range shootout with police officers, Charles Whitman had brought a pump-action shotgun along with him. He opened fire on the two young men before they had a chance to react.

Sixteen-year-old Mark Gabour was hit in the head, while his brother Mike, 19, suffered a shoulder wound from which he would subsequently recover. Mark Gabour died of his injuries at the scene. Pumping another shell into the chamber of the shotgun, Whitman then went to the head of the staircase and started firing down as the Gabours were coming up. The father, M. J., and his brother-in-law, William Lamport, both managed to get away and sound the alarm. Both of their wives were shot. William's wife, Marguerite, was hit in the chest and was killed instantly.

With the surviving members of the Gabour family now gone from the tower (Whitman had no idea that M. J. Gabour's wife, Mary, was only pretending to be dead), Whitman began to carefully stage his rifles and ammunition on the balcony overlooking the rest of the campus. He had also brought knives and a hand-axe, though for what purpose it is difficult to say.

The U.S. Marine Corps has a well-deserved reputation for training some of the most proficient marksmen in the world. Whitman was a competent shot. After selecting and loading a rifle, he fired at his first target. Eighteen-year-old Claire Wilson, a student at U.T., was shot in the abdomen, just above her left hip. It knocked her to the ground, stunned, but it was not a killing shot—for her, at least. Tragically, the bullet did take the life of her unborn child. Claire was eight months pregnant. She would survive the shooting.

Wilson's companion, Thomas Eckman, was hit next. He was fatally shot in the chest. The sniper was reloading and firing as quickly as he could manage.

At first, nobody was sure what was going on. Some passers-by jumped to the conclusion that this was an anti-Vietnam War protest. But as more victims fell, the horror of what was happening began to sink in. People took cover wherever they could or tried to put as much distance as possible between themselves and the shooter.

Whitman had already shot a lot of people, but there were also many misses. Bullets ricocheted from the asphalt, breaking windows. Some victims played dead, lying on ground that was becoming burning hot in the noonday sun. Others were incapable of moving. Despite the best efforts of the police, there seemed to be no easy way of stopping the killing.

People were shot while helping others, trying to carry or drag the wounded out of the line of fire, displays of pure selflessness and courage. In addition to students, tradesmen, and teachers, one victim was police officer Billy Paul Speed, 24, who was shot and killed while taking cover.

The tower at the University of Texas at Austin, where Whitman took his time shooting down at people on the ground.

Being a sniper firing from an elevated position, it was almost too easy for Charles Whitman to pick off targets whenever one moved from cover and exposed a part of their body. Police officers did what they could to try to pin him down, with limited success. Victims lay either dead or bleeding in a hemispherical arc around the tower's frontage. Because this was Texas, a state in which most of the citizens own guns and are not afraid to use them, rifle-toting members of the public began to appear at the scene. Finding what cover they could, they started to return fire, taking pot shots back up at Whitman's position on top of the tower.

Approaching the base of the tower over open ground would have been nothing short of suicide, but the frustrated police officers knew that they had to do *something,* and they had to do it fast, before even more lives were lost. A light aircraft was sent up, carrying a police officer who hoped to take out the shooter with a rifle—this was hardly the most stable platform from which to make a clean shot, and return fire from Whitman forced the pilot to back off before he or the officer was killed.

Somebody even floated the idea of getting the army involved, asking them to bring in an artillery piece and using it to blast the top of the U.T. Tower to pieces. In the end, cooler heads prevailed.

In a brilliant piece of lateral thinking, a small group of officers went down into the tunnels beneath the campus. There was an exit at the base of the tower that allowed them to climb up to the observation deck. Interviewed years later, Officer Houston McCoy recalled that they had no idea only one man was responsible for the day's carnage. The amount of damage inflicted led them to believe that it could have been a group of shooters, taking turns to open fire while others reloaded.

Although he had done his best to block the doors behind him, Whitman was taken by surprise when the handful of police officers suddenly appeared. Despite the danger of stray rounds coming up at them from their fellow officers on the ground, who were keeping up a hail of suppressing fire to give them cover, none of them hesitated. They also didn't bother to issue a warning. Officers McCoy and Ramiro Martinez both opened up on Whitman from close range. One cop took a shot at the shooter's face, while the other used his shotgun. Their combined efforts took him down. Taking no chances, the officers shot Whitman again after he had hit the floor, just to make sure.

Charles Whitman's roughly 90-minute killing spree was finally over. The aftereffects, however, would echo for many years after.

Fifty years after the shooting, on August 1, 2016, a stone memorial was erected close to the scene of the tragedy. Upon it are carved the names of seventeen dead victims. Thirteen were killed by Charles Whitman on August 1, 1966. One man, David Gunby, died in 2001 but had been shot by Whitman, and it was determined that he had ultimately died of complications from the gunshot wound he had sustained decades before.

> Charles Whitman's roughly 90-minute killing spree was finally over. The aftereffects, however, would echo for many years after.

The names of Kathleen and Margaret Whitman, murdered before the shooting spree began, appear at the bottom of the list, followed by one final, tragic entry: Baby Boy Wilson, the unnamed son of Claire Wilson, who had died as a direct consequence of his mother being shot.

In the aftermath of the shooting, Texas governor John Connally set up a committee to study the tragedy to better understand its causes, with the hope of preventing such a thing from ever happening again. On August 2, an autopsy was performed on the body of Charles Whitman, and a physical abnormality was located deep inside his skull. The pathologist who carried out the procedure had discovered a malignant tumor in the recesses of Whitman's brain, where it had been putting pressure on his amygdala. Although it could not be proven definitively, the doctor concluded that the tumor may indeed have been responsible for the violent emotional swings and highly irrational thoughts to which Whitman had become increasingly prone over the few months prior to the shooting.

There were no huge red flags during his upbringing to suggest that Charles Whitman would one day go on such a killing spree. He was not a violent or unusually angry child or young man. Although trained to kill by the Marine Corps, many thousands of young men received the same training and did not go on to do anything so heinous as Whitman did. Nor can combat service in Vietnam be blamed, for Marine Whitman never served there.

We know from the letter Whitman typed on the night of July 31 that he was suffering from violent and irrational thought patterns. In the aftermath of the shooting, a review of his recent history showed that Whitman had not been psychologically or emotionally stable. He had made threatening gestures and comments to people who got on his bad side for relatively minor infractions, such as sitting in what he considered to be his personal chair inside a classroom.

A closer look at his USMC service record shows that Whitman was once busted down in rank and sentenced to jail time for physically threatening another Marine that he had loaned money to.

Could it be that the mass growing inside his brain was the last straw, finally pushing him over the edge into committing an act of mass homicide? The tumor was malignant, it was expanding, and doctors believed it may well have eventually killed him. But was it the reason Charles Whitman finally snapped? Some people believe that it may have contributed in some minor way, but it's considered highly unlikely that the tumor alone drove Whitman to kill.

In his book *The Anatomy of Motive* (cowritten with Mark Olshaker), FBI criminal profiler John Douglas posited that Whitman possessed what he terms the "assassin personality," two characteristics of which are a sense of deep insecurity and the paranoid compulsion to believe that everybody is out to get you. Such personalities sometimes lash out to "get their retribution in first." Could this be what happened with Charles Whitman? The speculation on Whitman's motives has been endless, with people blaming the tumor, drugs, a psychotic episode, or some other form of mental illness, to name just a few. The answer is likely more complex than any single factor.

THE CENTURY 16 MASS SHOOTING: JAMES HOLMES

My own personal experience with a spree killing began in the early morning hours of Friday, July 20, 2012, although I would not know it until later that morning. I was working as the assistant clinical chief for a private ambulance company in my adopted state of Colorado. My responsibilities were primarily administrative, overseeing the education and training of EMTs and paramedics; I'd get out in an ambulance when I could but never often enough for my liking. My primary focus was teaching.

As I climbed into bed on the night of July 19, a deeply disturbed young man named James Holmes was putting a plan into effect that would scar the city of Aurora forever. The big new Hollywood summer blockbuster was opening that night at a midnight show: *The Dark Knight Rises*, the third and final film in director Christopher Nolan's Batman trilogy. The most recent movie in the series, *The Dark Knight*, was a huge hit. Audiences seemed to like Christian Bale in the role of Batman, but it was Heath Ledger's turn as the Joker that had gotten everybody talking.

Anticipation was high for *The Dark Knight Rises*. At the Century 16 movie theater in Aurora, the parking lots were packed full of cars. This was the main reason why 24-year-old James Holmes had chosen this particular time slot—it had nothing to do with which specific movie was playing. He was one of the 400 ticket holders for the midnight screening. Holmes was wearing a T-shirt, a skull cap, and pants that sagged at the back, though he would soon change into something entirely different.

Holmes walked into Theater 9 and took his seat, which was as close to the screen as it was possible for him to get. He had deliberately chosen a spot

The Century 16 movie theater in Aurora, Colorado, was the site where James Holmes shot 12 random people to death on July 20, 2012.

in the front row because of its proximity to the exit door that opened out into the parking lot.

The Dark Knight Rises opens with a bang. It's a fast-paced movie, and a very loud one. Holmes wasn't there to see it begin. He had waited for the movie trailers to start and then ducked out through the exit, taking care to prop the door open behind him. If anybody paid attention to his leaving, nothing was done about it.

Holmes had parked his car close to that exit and didn't have very far to walk. The trunk was full of firearms and tactical clothing, which he changed into right there in the parking lot. The vest he donned would not stop bullets, but it contained enough pockets, pouches, and attachments to store potentially hundreds of rounds of ammunition. Extra protective armor was applied to two particularly vulnerable areas: his throat and crotch.

He put on a gas mask, cinching the straps down firmly. He slipped on a set of headphones and cranked up the volume on some techno music, effectively drowning out all external sounds. Lastly, a ballistic helmet of the sort used by S.W.A.T. teams went on his head. To the casual eye, Holmes would have looked like a member of just such a team.

He had purchased a variety of weapons prior to what was about to unfold. He had a semiautomatic rifle and a tactical shotgun. Both could put out a significant amount of firepower in a very short amount of time, and their effects could be devastating, particularly at close range. As if that wasn't enough, he also had a pistol and a pair of knives.

Holmes had fitted a high-capacity ammunition drum to the rifle in advance. Picking the weapon up, he made his way back into Theater 9. This drum model was capable of holding 100 rounds but often had a tendency to jam. The door was still propped slightly open, exactly as he had left it.

One would expect mass panic to have swept the auditorium at the sight of a heavily armed man wearing body armor entering the theater, but it is important to remember that in the summer of 2012, the idea of an active shooter in a movie theater had not yet entered the public mass consciousness. On July 20, audiences around the world would see things very differently. There was also the fact that some members of the audience had worn costumes to the screening. In interviews afterward, survivors recalled that the shooter at first appeared to be nothing more than another fan who had dressed up for the event.

They were disabused of that notion when the first shots rang out. He emptied the tactical shotgun into the crowded auditorium first, then let it drop to the floor. Holmes then walked up the aisle, slowly and methodically shooting at people with the semiautomatic rifle. He had thrown a tear gas canister out into the auditorium first, filling it with smoke and adding to the confusion and sense of disorientation that people felt. It was also the reason he had purchased a gas mask and put it on in advance.

According to several eyewitnesses, a sense of panic immediately enveloped the audience. All of them turned to run, heading for the exits. Holmes climbed the stairs and seemed to be picking his targets without any apparent rhyme or reason. He would reveal afterward that there was actually a perverse type of logic at work inside his brain. His intention was to shoot those who were running for the exits, preventing them from getting away, and only then would he go after those who had taken cover instead of running.

> His intention was to shoot those who were running for the exits, preventing them from getting away, and only then would he go after those who had taken cover instead of running.

After emptying more than half the drum magazine, it jammed. Holmes stepped to one side and attempted to clear the weapon, ejecting the drum and trying to get a different magazine to seat. Thankfully, he was unsuccessful; had he been able to do so, the death and casualty toll would almost certainly have been much higher. His efforts to get the semiautomatic rifle back into service frustrated, Holmes made for the exit and left the theater, ditching the now-useless rifle along the way. At some point, he also fired off a few rounds from the Glock pistol.

The 911 dispatchers sent out emergency tones to police units as soon as their switchboards were flooded with calls from terrified moviegoers. The instant they got outside the auditorium, people pulled out their cell phones and called for help.

In all, a total of 70 people sustained gunshot wounds. Of those 70, 12 were fatal. A paramedic performed triage inside Theater 9, pronouncing ten people dead of their injuries. The remaining two victims died shortly after arriving at the hospital emergency room.

A pair of police officers caught Holmes in the parking lot. He was standing placidly next to a car, slowly pulling off the various pieces of equipment and ballistic armor from his body. He seemed so nonchalant, in fact, that they at first took him to be a member of their department, possibly a S.W.A.T.-trained officer who was also responding to the reported shooting at Century 16. But cops have a keen instinct for when something isn't quite right, and the way in which James Holmes was carrying himself seemed a little off somehow.

The officers both drew their pistols and yelled at Holmes to put his hands up. Now that he was being held at gunpoint and ordered to surrender, Holmes obeyed the shouted orders immediately and without question. Unlike many other spree killers, he was not determined to go out in a case of "death by cop."

His almost unnaturally calm demeanor may have been at least partly influenced by the narcotic medication he had taken prior to leaving his apartment for the last time that night. The officers handcuffed him and dragged him away from the car, looking for a clear spot in which they could safely search him. Somebody capable of carrying out an act like this might be wearing a suicide vest or might have a death wish that involved taking others with him in a final act of desperation.

Holmes smirked when the police asked where he had an accomplice, so there were valid concerns about the possibility of a second shooter, lying in wait somewhere inside the theater to ambush the first wave of emergency responders.

Cutting his chest rig and ballistic protection armor away, the police didn't find anything worrisome, but Holmes told them that he had left a surprise back at his apartment: improvised explosive devices (IEDs).

Although the shootings at the theater were tragic enough, a second disaster was only narrowly averted just a short distance away at Holmes's apartment building on Paris Street.

Before setting out for the theater that night, Holmes had booby-trapped his apartment with an elaborate setup of what he hoped were going to be explosives. The idea was that when police officers and other first responders came to his apartment, this homemade bomb would go off and kill as many of them as possible. Ideally (for Holmes, that is), this would take place before he started shooting. In that way, the police, fire, and EMS response to Century 16 would be delayed while they dealt with the incident in his apartment building.

So went the theory. But James Holmes wasn't quite as smart as he liked to think he was. The floor of his apartment was covered with trails of ammonium nitrate powder, plastic bottles of gasoline, and containers full of chemicals. His main source of information was the internet, not necessarily the most reliable place for the amateur bomber to learn how to construct explosives and the detonators to trigger them, but there was so much combustible material crammed into one single room that it did have the potential to blow sky high, with the

Holmes's apartment was in this building on Paris Street. He booby-trapped his place in the hope that it would delay police and EMS responders to the shooting.

gasoline-filled bottles meant to set everything on fire. The detonators were also homemade. Holmes had bought his materials from a mix of scientific supply and chain retail stores. He had experimented with trying to make a form of napalm.

The last piece of his intended deathtrap was the large quantity of unused ammunition left over from his target practice sessions. Holmes placed them around the apartment and then dumped gasoline onto the floor, working on the premise that once it either went up in flames or exploded, the rounds would start to cook off, inflicting further damage on the first responders who had come to his door, not to mention the unsuspecting residents of the building.

A tripwire ran across the inside of the front doorway, intended to trigger the booby trap once somebody broke the wire. This would, Holmes hoped, be members of the Aurora Police Department, who he expected would soon arrive to investigate a noise complaint that a neighbor was going to call in. The CD player was set to kick in at a deafening volume shortly before he arrived at the Century 16 movie theater.

Holmes had also left a remote-controlled child's toy outside the building, along with a radio playing loud music. The remote control did not actually work on the toy, however; if pushed, it would set off the contents of his apartment. James Holmes was nothing if not imaginative, but neither of these lures worked in the way that he expected them to.

Nobody took the bait when it came to the remote control. The loud music screaming out through the walls of his apartment came close to achieving what Holmes had intended; a neighbor did indeed call in a noise complaint to 911. The time was a few minutes after midnight, and the Aurora Police Department would soon have their hands full with more pressing matters.

I woke up early the following morning and switched on the news. What I saw was horrifying. Twelve innocent people had been killed and many more wounded during a senseless act of violence in Aurora. After I showered quickly and threw on a uniform, I drove straight to the ambulance operations station.

The mood there was somber but determined. There was a definite pall about the place. I began to hear more about what had happened at the Century 16 theater.

The emergency services tend to attract a specific type of personality; many of us are Type-A individuals who are hard-wired to want to help, no matter what the situation. Because of the difficulties gaining access to the Century 16 multiplex earlier that morning, a lot of the ambulances had sat at a staging post, their engines idling and their crews itching to get in there and help. EMS crews from multiple fire districts and ambulance services had lined up to help, but only a relative few had been able to contribute. It was extremely frustrating for them to stand by and be unable to put their skills to good use.

> **What I saw was horrifying. Twelve innocent people had been killed and many more wounded during a senseless act of violence in Aurora.**

The police officers, firefighters, and EMTs who were first on the scene were confronted by a huge crowd of panicking moviegoers, most of whom descended on them in a swarm and begged for help. Some had been shot. Others had been hit by shrapnel. The medically trained responders did their best to start triaging this swarm of patients in the jam-packed parking lot, separating them into different groups depending on the severity of their wounds.

Due to a multitude of different factors, there was a delay in getting EMS units into position at the back of the theater, so some police cruisers drove a number of critically injured victims straight to the closest hospital. The parking lots were full of cars, shooting victims, and fleeing moviegoers. The official after-incident report stated that "at least 27" patients were transported in police cars, and that if this had not taken place, a number of them would have died before reaching the hospital in a later-arriving ambulance. Amid the high-energy penetrating trauma, this out-of-the-norm behavior on the part of the police officers led to many lives being saved. My hat goes off to the cops who made that brave decision on the spot, under immense pressure. People who would otherwise have bled to death survived because of it.

The EMS crews would ultimately transport 20 patients to hospitals, and many went straight back to the theater. Access was even more difficult because of a traffic jam that occurred because moviegoers were driving away from the scene.

With the perpetrator now in custody and the survivors receiving much-needed medical attention, the focus now shifted to securing the apartment building on Paris Street. Officers evacuated all the residents and cordoned off the building, taking Holmes's IED threat seriously. By now, the FBI, ATF (Bureau of Alcohol, Tobacco, Firearms and Explosives), and a host of other agencies had descended on Aurora, offering their support and expertise wherever needed.

There was no desire to put more human life at risk, so the first thing through the door of James Holmes's apartment was a remotely operated robot. The operator spotted the tripwire booby trap and made sure not to trigger it. It was obvious even to the untrained eye that the apartment was rigged to cause harm.

Working from the long arm of the fire department's ladder truck, an explosive ordnance technician broke out the apartment window and put another camera inside. So complex was the mess of wiring, ammunition, gasoline, and chemicals inside that little progress was made for the remainder of Friday. Responders worked overnight and into Saturday morning, planning the best way to render the apartment safe once more.

The Aurora Fire Department worked with FBI and ATF agents at the scene of Holmes's apartment to defuse the complex array of wiring and explosives in Holmes's apartment.

Back at ambulance operations, there was a request for a paramedic crew to go out and stage at the scene. If all went well with the disposal efforts, there wouldn't be much for the EMS providers to do. If all *didn't* go well, then things would have gone very badly indeed.

I volunteered to go and staff the ambulance early on Saturday morning. A little after sunrise, we parked next to an Aurora Fire Department engine and waited. Staging in a parking lot across the street from the apartment building were vehicles from a wide range of emergency and law enforcement organizations from the federal, state, and municipal levels. Everybody was doing their part, and it was good to see so many people all working on the same team. TV camera crews had set up beyond the black-and-yellow crime-scene tape and were broadcasting the proceedings to news channels around the world.

> To me, the interior of James Holmes's apartment looked like the sort of thing a mad scientist or criminal mastermind would set up to trap the hero in some old-style superhero movie.

One of the things that impressed me most was the sense of calm that pervaded the scene. There were no raised voices, no sense of great urgency—just a determination to do the job right, no matter how long it took, and prevent further senseless loss of life.

The operators of the robot were kind enough to let me watch over their shoulder for a short while as they went about their business, scanning the interior of the apartment. On the monitor screen, I could see what appeared to be clear plastic jars filled with bullets, round black containers that looked like cannon balls, and lots of wires. A bike was propped up against one wall, and it too was draped in wires. I could also make out bottles filled with some kind of liquid (I would only learn what this was later on).

To me, the interior of James Holmes's apartment looked like the sort of thing a mad scientist or criminal mastermind would set up to trap the hero in some old-style superhero movie. I was glad the bomb disposal experts were on hand to take care of this mess. These quiet, heroic professionals donned their protective suits and went into the apartment. If things had gone the way Holmes had planned, there's no way those suits would have kept them alive. Their sheer courage left me in awe.

As the day wore on, we could only watch and wait. Inside the apartment building, the bomb technicians were slowly and methodically dismantling the death trap set by James Holmes. Ultimately, the technicians successfully disarmed all of the explosive material, bundled it up, and loaded it into their vehicles. My EMT partner took the wheel, and our ambulance fell into position at the back of a long convoy that headed out to the nearby town of Bennett.

We waited for a short while longer, staring out across a flat and empty expanse of land. Finally, there came a series of loud crumps, and a column of dirty black smoke started to rise above the far horizon. The controlled detonations represented the last remnants of James Holmes's ability to harm others.

James Holmes did not make any attempt to deny having committed the atrocity. He was a prime candidate for the death penalty, which the state of Colorado still has on the books. The nature of his crime meant that there was a huge groundswell of public support for having him executed if he was found guilty.

Holmes's attorneys tried to cut a deal with the prosecutor, offering up a plea of guilty in exchange for their client not being sentenced to death. The deal was turned down, so Holmes's legal team entered a plea of not guilty by reason of insanity on his behalf. It was up to the jury to decide whether he had been criminally insane when he had walked into Theater 9 and opened fire.

In the courtroom, he was tethered to the floor. Much was made in the global media of his bright orange hair and perpetually bug-eyed facial expression. Thanks to the *Dark Knight* movie connection, it was stated publicly (and wrongly) that Holmes had taken his inspiration from the character of the Joker, Batman's long-term arch nemesis (though the Joker has green hair, not orange). In reality, James Holmes had dyed his hair out of a simple desire to be more memorable, to stand out—and because a friend of his had recently dyed his own hair blue.

In the days before the attack, Holmes had spent time practicing his marksmanship both on a shooting range and out in a canyon. His clothing, ballistic protection, weapons, and ammunition were all purchased legitimately, the bulk of it shipped by mail order from online retailers. Much would be made of this later when the shooting sparked a furious public outcry about gun control. He had broken no laws in purchasing either the guns or the small mountain of ammunition.

Considering the amount of preparation, Holmes knew there could be no argument about the attack having been premeditated. In addition to stocking up on firearms, he had spent hours carrying out reconnaissance at the Century 16 theater. He drew sketch maps of the building's layout, narrowing down the choice of auditorium to number 9—the one he thought would allow him to kill the maximum number of people in a short amount of time.

During the three-month trial, the defendant showed no signs of apparent remorse, guilt, or regret for what he had done, even when pictures of bodies of the shooting victims were shown to the jury. Holmes waived his right to speak to the jury or send them a written statement, offering nothing in his own defense. Members of the jury were visibly moved to tears when family members of the victims spoke about the irreparable damage the loss of their loved ones had caused them.

Unsurprisingly, the jury voted in favor of the death penalty being permitted, although the final sentencing was still to be determined. Ultimately, there would have to be a unanimous finding by the jury for Holmes to be eligible to be put to death.

At the trial's conclusion, the prosecuting district attorney pushed strongly for Holmes to be executed. Holmes's attorney, on the other hand, argued every bit as forcefully that he should *not* be put to death, primarily because he was severely mentally ill and therefore not responsible for his actions.

> Many hoped that James Holmes would be executed. I counted myself among them.

Many hoped that James Holmes would be executed. I counted myself among them. Leaving him alive to grow old within the relatively safe confines of a secure institution seemed to me like a slight against those families who had already lost so much. How would the families ever get any closure if the state of Colorado allowed the murderer of their loved ones to keep on breathing the same air as the rest of us?

James Holmes was found guilty on all of the charges brought against him, but there was no unanimous verdict on whether he should be given the death penalty—which meant that he could not be executed.

Three years and one month after the mass shooting at the Century 16, James Holmes was given the longest custodial sentence that the judge could impose upon him: a staggering 3,318 years. He will never be eligible for parole.

In the weeks after the Century 16 shooting, the people of Aurora did their best to heal. There would be no forgetting the tragedy, and many of those involved struggled to come to terms with the loss of so many innocent lives. The subject of what would happen to the movie theater itself was the subject of dispute. Some wanted it demolished, with the hope that the biggest lingering reminder of the darkest night in Aurora's history would be swept away by bulldozers and wrecking balls. Others wanted the theater to be reopened, adopting an attitude of "You're not going to beat us with terror tactics." Both perspectives are completely understandable.

Those who wanted the theater to survive eventually got what they wanted. The chain that owned Century 16 invested more than a million dollars into refurbishing the building, converting Theater 9 and its neighboring theater into one big auditorium. In doing so, they altered the original layout completely and removed all traces of the massacre.

In January 2013, six months after the shooting, the theater reopened under the new name of Century Aurora. The first movie shown there was another big-budget Hollywood epic, *The Hobbit: An Unexpected Journey*. Invita-

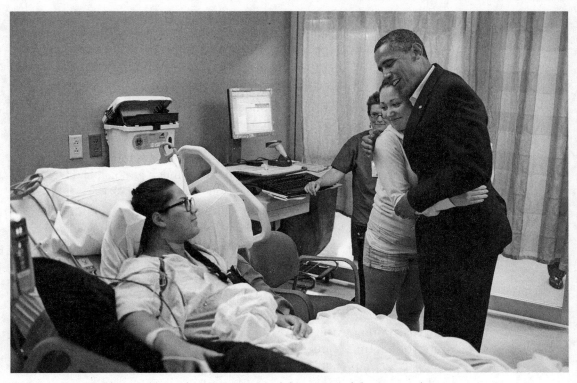

President Barack Obama is shown here visiting one of the victims of the Aurora shooting.

tions were sent to family members, survivors, and members of the emergency services who had responded to the shooting. Some accepted; others were shocked at what they saw as an insensitive response by the movie theater chain.

An official memorial was commissioned and sculpted by Kentucky-based artist Duowe Blumberg. It truly is a thing of beauty. The memorial, which was officially unveiled in July 2018 and is titled *Ascenciate,* is comprised of 70 white cranes with outstretched wings, each one representing a person wounded during the shooting. They are flying inward toward thirteen silver cranes, one for every person who was killed. Sealed within each crane are some of the handwritten messages of love and compassion that poured into Aurora from well-wishers.

It goes without saying that somebody who took as many innocent lives as James Holmes did was not going to be popular while behind bars. There is a strict hierarchy and pecking order in all prisons, and still some semblance of "honor among thieves." Rapists, sexual predators, and child abusers are considered to be the lowest of the low. Mass murderers such as James Holmes are not far above them. There is also a degree of infamy to be obtained from harming or killing a high-profile prisoner, and infamy is its own form of currency in the correctional system. Little wonder that one of Holmes's fellow inmates went for him when he saw his chance.

While it was known that Holmes would make an attractive target, and he was therefore prevented from interacting with the other prisoners, all it takes is one simple slip-up, such as momentarily leaving a gate open that should have been kept locked. Corrections officers therefore did their best to keep the location of James Holmes off the grid as much as possible. He was the only occupant of an entire 16-person section of the cell block.

On October 8, 2016, four years after the shooting, Holmes was an inmate of the Colorado State Penitentiary in Canon City. As he was emerging from the office of his case manager, another prisoner, 27-year-old Mark "Slim" Daniels, recognized him and went on the attack, raining blows down on Holmes's head and neck.

After the attack, which left Holmes with a few bruises but no serious injuries, Daniels wrote to the *Denver Post* and Denver's *Westword* newspaper to explain his actions. After expressing his condolences for the victims of the Century 16 shooting, Daniels wrote:

> I'm so sorry I couldn't wipe him out and sent[sic] him to Satan's lake of fire. It was just impossible to do by myself with so many cops. I did get him six or seven good ones....

Although Daniels ended up locked down in solitary confinement as a punishment and lost his privileges for a while, he also gained public supporters. Money and letters of encouragement came in after word of his attack on Holmes got out. Many viewed the attack as an act of public service.

After the assault, James Holmes was quietly transferred out of state, to serve out the remainder of his lifelong sentence at a maximum-security facility. At the time of writing, he is currently incarcerated at the federal penitentiary in Allenwood, Pennsylvania, where he has more than 1,300 years left to serve on his sentence.

> At the time of writing, he is incarcerated at the federal penitentiary in Allenwood, Pennsylvania, where he has more than 1,300 years left to serve on his sentence.

In the summer of 2017, the mother of James Holmes, Arlene Holmes, shared her thoughts with the *San Diego Tribune*. She bemoaned the fact that assessments of her son's mental health were only carried out "all too late to prevent his deterioration, all too late to stop him from carrying out a horrible act driven by psychosis, obsession and delusion."

Holmes's mother clearly feels guilt and a sense of helplessness at the fact that she did not see her son's descent into mental illness coming and will probably never get over the events of July 20, 2012. It is hard not to feel compassion for her. Far from some of the individuals we have studied in this book, the childhood of James Holmes was a safe and normal one. He was not beaten, abused, or tormented. Nor was there any indication that he was capable of going on to do something so monstrous.

As a boy, James Holmes had "a few friends" but did not do much in the way of socializing outside of school hours. He was a quiet child who studied hard and liked to keep to himself. Arlene Holmes described her family as introverted, which is one reason why her son's affect didn't set off any alarm bells.

The teenage Holmes could be irritable at times, but what teenager isn't? With hindsight, she believes that her son suffered from adolescent depression, which was never diagnosed or treated. As he grew to adulthood, he began to develop homicidal ideation, thoughts centered around wanting to kill other human beings. A psychiatrist assessed him and concluded that he may well be psychotic and offered antipsychotic medications—but Holmes turned them down.

During the lead-up to the Aurora shooting, James Holmes had called a mental health helpline, but after he was disconnected, he did not try again to get help.

In his superbly detailed study of the events surrounding the Century 16 shootings (and required reading for those seeking insight into the case), *A Dark Night in Aurora: Inside James Holmes and the Colorado Mass Shootings*, author and forensic psychiatrist William H. Reid produces unique insight into what motivated James Holmes to do what he did. Reid had unprecedented access to Holmes after the incident and recorded hours of interview material between himself and the killer. He determined that Holmes came to believe that his suicidal urges and mental health issues could only be assuaged by him taking other human lives.

There can be no doubt that James Holmes suffered from significant mental illness at the time of the shooting and almost certainly still does to this day. It is extremely unlikely that he can ever be cured or treated to the point where it would be safe to walk the streets again—nor, of course, should he.

In the aftermath of the shootings, gun sales throughout Colorado and across the United States skyrocketed. One of the burning topics of conversation was that of gun control and concealed carry, something that now comes up with the all-too-familiar mass shootings that occur regularly in the United States.

Movie theaters are usually "no carry" zones, meaning that even with a valid concealed carry permit, patrons are not allowed to go onto the premises armed. Some gun owners obey that law, while others do not. No armed citizen confronted James Holmes and returned fire during his shooting spree; if one had, it is impossible to say what the results would have been. Would the mass

One result of the Aurora—and other—shootings is that gun sales in the United States have gone up. Some have speculated that profits are why gun manufacturers oppose laws that might lower gun violence in America.

shooting have been cut short, with lives saved and wounds prevented? Or would a firefight in a crowded movie theater, played out against the backdrop of a loud and frenetic Batman movie, only have resulted in more deaths as innocent moviegoers became caught in the crossfire? We will hopefully never have to find out.

I grew up with a deep, abiding love of movies and of going to the movie theater, which began when I first saw *Star Wars* at the age of five. There is something very therapeutic and cathartic about sitting in the dark with a crowd of strangers, enjoying (if the movie's good) a shared experience for a couple of hours and escaping from the real world. Until July 20, 2012, movie theaters were safe places, marred by no more than the occasional drunk patron at the late show.

Now, all of that was gone. Some immediate changes took place after the tragedy. Rather than lounge back easily in their chairs and relax, members of the audience waiting for a movie to start had their heads on a swivel, anxiously looking around at their fellow human beings in the near-darkness. Who was carrying a gun? Was anybody acting suspiciously? One moviegoer made a bad-taste joke about "going Colorado" only to find himself hauled out of the theater by police officers and taken to jail. He ended up serving several months behind bars. Jokes about shooting up movie theaters just weren't funny.

At every single screening, staff members patrolled the exit doors, making sure that they were closed and secured. Sometimes, it happened multiple times throughout each screening. As a moviegoing public, we had lost our sense of trust and comfort. To a certain extent, it still hasn't come back.

In 2019, actor Joaquin Phoenix appeared in *Joker*, a dark and offbeat story set in Gotham City that provides an alternate origin story for Batman's nemesis. The false rumor concerning the character of the Joker being an inspiration for James Holmes came back with full force.

The movie theater in Aurora announced that it would not screen *Joker*. The families of some of the victims banded together and wrote to the studio that made the movie, Warner Bros., expressing their feelings about it. They expressed sincerely held concerns that *Joker* might inspire or influence a viewer with mental issues to commit a violent atrocity. The letter asked Warner Bros. to stop making payments to politicians who accepted money from the National Rifle Association (NRA) and who also voted against gun legislation.

Warner Bros., for its part, replied that its parent company donated money to the victims of gun violence and were supporting initiatives to try to control it, but it was standing behind its movie.

It's not difficult to see both sides of the argument. For the families of the deceased, the movie was another reminder of the tragedy that took the lives of their loved ones. For the filmmakers, there was the desire to tell a story

Mourners place flowers and other tributes to the dead outside the Aurora movie theater shortly after the 2012 shooting. Such memorials are an all-too-common sight in America.

whose subject matter, while deeply unsettling for many viewers, had something to say about mental illness and its potentially violent consequences.

Whether you love it, hate it, or are indifferent, there is no denying that *Joker* is at least a well-crafted movie, and one that has only the most tenuous connection to the Century 16 shooting. The same cannot be said of the ultra-low budget *Joker's Poltergeist: The Aurora Massacre* (2016). The title alone is insensitive. The movie begins with a mass shooting in a movie theater, carried out by a man with bright orange hair wearing a clown mask. The link to James Holmes is both blatantly obvious and extremely ill-conceived. In a surreal turn of events, the shooter is stopped by an armed moviegoer who also happens to be wearing a clown mask. Just in case the viewer happens to miss the subtle point that the director is trying to sledgehammer home, the protagonist of *Joker's Poltergeist* is a young woman named Aurora. It's nothing but a shameless cash grab, trading on the name and iconography of a genuine tragedy to try to sell a few DVDs.

Eight years after the tragedy in Aurora, mass shootings are now more commonplace than at any other time in American history.

Joker went on to be a great success, both at the box office and at the Oscars, receiving plaudits and critical acclaim. *Joker's Poltergeist* sank without a trace and went straight into the bargain bin. That's about as close to poetic justice as the movie business gets.

Eight years after the tragedy in Aurora, mass shootings are now more commonplace than at any other time in American history. They show no signs of slowing down. Holmes's actions represent the very worst behavior of human beings. I am not willing to give this sick and twisted individual the last words in this chapter. Instead, I choose to highlight the very best of human nature, by recounting some acts of pure goodness and heroism that took place as a direct consequence.

Navy veteran Jon Blunk, 26, reacted instantly when the shooting began. "He laid up against me and had the other side of my body against the concrete seating," Blunk's girlfriend, Jansen Young, recounted to CNN's Anderson Cooper. In using himself as a human shield, Blunk saved her life but paid the ultimate price for doing so. Jon Blunk's name should be remembered.

Alex Teves, 24, made the same sacrifice, shielding his girlfriend from gunfire. As a direct consequence, his girlfriend, Amanda Lindgren, lived. He did not. Alex Teves's name should be remembered.

So should the name of 27-year-old Matt McQuinn, who also acted selflessly. Matt used his body to protect his girlfriend, Samantha Yowler, from Holmes's bullets. He was killed in doing so. Samantha was wounded but survived. Matt McQuinn's name should be remembered.

FURTHER READING

Amirante, Sam L. (with Danny Broderick). *John Wayne Gacy: Defending a Monster*. New York: Skyhorse, 2011.

Brady, Ian. *The Gates of Janus: An Analysis of Serial Murder by England's Most Hated Criminal*. Port Townsend, WA: Feral House, 2015.

Brown, Robert. *The Candy Cards: The Shocking Story of Dean Corll*. privately printed, 2012.

Cahill, Tim. *Buried Dreams: Inside the Mind of John Wayne Gacy*. New York: Open Road Media, 2014.

Carlo, Philip. *The Night Stalker: The Life and Crimes of One of America's Deadliest Killers*. New York: Kensington, 2016.

Clarkson, Wensley. *Evil Beyond Belief: The True Story of Harold Shipman, Britain's Most Prolific Serial Killer*. London: John Blake, 2019.

Coffey, Russ. *Dennis Nilsen: Conversations with Britain's Most Evil Serial Killer*. London: John Blake Publishing, 2013.

Conradi, Peter. *The Red Ripper: Inside the Mind of Russia's Most Brutal Serial Killer*. New York: Dell, 1992.

Cornwell, Patricia. *Portrait of a Killer: Jack the Ripper—Case Closed*. New York: G. P. Putnam's Sons, 2002.

Cullen, Robert. *The Killer Department: Detective Viktor Burakov's Eight-Year Hunt for the Most Savage Serial Killer in Russian History*. New York: Pantheon, 1993.

Douglas, John (with Mark Olshaker). *The Anatomy of Motive: The F.B.I.'s Legendary Mindhunter Explores the Key to Understanding and Catching Violent Criminals*. New York: Scribner, 1999.

Estep, Richard (with Robert Graves). *The Horrors of Fox Hollow Farm: Unraveling the History and Hauntings of a Serial Killer's Home*. Woodbury: Llewellyn Worldwide, 2019.

Frank, Gerold. *The Boston Strangler*. New York: New American Library, 1966.

Gottlieb, Daphne, and Lisa Kester. *Dear Dawn: Aileen Wuornos in Her Own Words*. New York: Soft Skull Press, 2011.

Graysmith, Robert. *Zodiac*. New York: St. Martin, 1986.

———. *Zodiac Unmasked: The Identity of America's Most Elusive Serial Killer Revealed*. New York: Berkley, 2002.

James, Bill (with Rachel McCarthy James). *The Man from the Train: The Solving of a Century-Old Serial Killer Mystery*. New York: Simon & Schuster, 2017.

Junger, Sebastian. *A Death in Belmont*. New York: W.W. Norton & Company, 2006.

Keightley, Alan. *Ian Brady: The Untold Story of the Moors Murders*. London: Pavilion, 2017.

Kelleher, Michael D. & C. L. *Murder Most Rare—The Female Serial Killer*. Westport, CT: Praeger Press, 1998.

Kelly, Susan. *The Boston Stranglers*. New York: Pinnacle, 2013.

Krivich, Mikhail. *Comrade Chikatilo: Russia's Most Notorious Serial Killer*. Graymalkin Media, 2015.

Larsen, Richard W. *Bundy: The Deliberate Stranger*. Englewood Cliffs, NJ: Prentice Hall, 1980.

Larson, Erik. *The Devil in the White City: A Saga of Magic and Murder at the Fair That Changed America*. New York: Crown, 2003.

Manners, Terry. *Deadlier Than the Male*. London: Pan Books, 1995.

Masters, Brian: *Killing for Company*. Arrow, 1985.

Nash, Jay Robert. *Bloodletters and Badmen*. New York: M. Evans, 1995.

Olson, Jack. *The Man with the Candy: The Story of the Houston Mass Murders*. New York: Simon & Schuster, 2000.

Reid, William H. *A Dark Night in Aurora: Inside James Holmes and the Colorado Mass Shootings*. New York: Skyhorse, 2018.

Ressler, Robert, and Tom Shachtman. *Whoever Fights Monsters: My Twenty Years Tracking Serial Killers for the FBI*. New York: St Martin's Press, 1992.

Rosner, Lisa. *The Anatomy Murders: Being the True and Spectacular History of Edinburgh's Notorious Burke and Hare and the Man of Science Who Abetted Them in the Commission of Their Most Heinous Crimes*. Philadelphia: University of Pennsylvania Press, 2011.

Rule, Ann. *The Stranger Beside Me: The Inside Story of Serial Killer Ted Bundy.* London: Sphere, 1994.

Russell, Sue. *Lethal Intent.* New York: Pinnacle Books, 2002.

Sands, Stella. *The Dating Game Killer: The True Story of a TV Dating Show, a Violent Sociopath, and a Series of Brutal Murders.* New York: St. Martin's Press, 2011.

Selzer, Adam S. *H. H. Holmes: The True History of the White City Devil.* New York: Skyhorse, 2017.

Skinner, Keith, and Stewart Evans. *The Ultimate Jack the Ripper Sourcebook.* London: Robinson Publishing, 2002.

Sounes, Howard. *Fred and Rose: The Full Story of Fred and Rose West and the Gloucester House of Horrors.* London: Sphere, 1995.

Stapley, Rhonda: *I Survived Ted Bundy: The Attack, Escape, and PTSD That Changed My Life.* Seattle: Galaxy-44, 2016.

Sullivan, Terry (with Peter T. Maiken). *Killer Clown: The John Wayne Gacy Murders.* New York: Kensington, 2000.

Taylor, Troy. *Murder by Gaslight: A True Story.* Decatur: Whitechapel Press, 2013.

Vronsky, Peter. *Female Serial Killers: How and Why Women Become Monsters.* New York: Berkley Books, 2007.

Weinstein, Fannie, and Melinda Wilson. *Where the Bodies are Buried.* New York: St. Martin's Press, 1998.

West, Mae (with Neil McKay). *Love as Always, Mum XXX: The True and Terrible Story of Surviving a Childhood with Fred and Rose West.* London: Seven Dials, 2019.

Whittle, Brian, and Jean Ritchie. *Prescription for Murder: The True Story of Dr. Harold Frederick Shipman.* Boston: Little, Brown, 2004.

Wuornos, Aileen (with Christopher Berry-Dee). *Monster: My True Story* London: John Blake, 2004.

Yallop, David. *Deliver Us from Evil.* London: Constable, 2014.

INDEX

Note: (ill.) indicates photos and illustrations.

Albert DeSalvo, 286
Andrei Chikatilo, 214–15, 217
Anthony Sowell, 256–57
Carl Panzram, 114
Dean Corll, 319
Dennis Rader, 268
Edmund Kemper, 143
H. H. Holmes, 239–42
James Holmes, 351–52
Jeffrey Dahmer, 180
John Christie, 301–3
John George Haigh, 295–96
John Wayne Gacy, 20–21
Lonnie Franklin, 230
Nannie Doss, 207
rampage and spree killers, 321
Richard Ramirez, 81, 83, 91–92
Rodney Alcala, 201–2
Samuel Little, 273
Sawney Bean, 219, 222
Ted Bundy, 66–68
Tsutomu Miyazaki, 166–67
William Burke and William Hare, 224–26
decapitation
Anthony Sowell, 255
Dennis Nilsen, 78
Edmund Kemper, 132–33, 137–43
Fred and Rosemary West, 10
Jack the Ripper, 307
Jeffrey Dahmer, 169, 173–75, 178–79
Peter Sutcliffe, 154
Richard Ramirez, 83
Tsutomu Miyazaki, 165
Denver, Colorado, 63, 109, 236, 354
Denver Post, 354
depression, 50, 52, 162, 326, 355
Des Plaines River, 19
DeSalvo, Albert, 275–90, 276 (ill.)
DeSalvo, Frank, 275
DeSalvo, Richard, 283–84
Dirty Harry, 191, 194
disappearances. See abductions

disembowelment, murder by. See evisceration, murder by
dismemberment
Andrei Chikatilo, 209–10
Anthony Sowell, 255
Dean Corll, 315
Dennis Nilsen, 77–78
Edmund Kemper, 132–33, 137–38, 141
Fred and Rosemary West, 8, 10
H. H. Holmes, 234, 238
Herbert Baumeister, 26, 29
Jeffrey Dahmer, 171, 173–79
Peter Sutcliffe, 145
Richard Ramirez, 87, 89, 91
Sawney Bean, 220–22
Tsutomu Miyazaki, 162, 165–66
DNA evidence
Albert DeSalvo, 276, 283, 289
Dennis Rader, 264, 267
Herbert Baumeister, 30
Lonnie Franklin, 229
Richard Ramirez, 85
Rodney Alcala, 201
Samuel Little, 272
Ted Bundy, 56, 61
Doctor Death. See Shipman, Harold Jr.
Doi, Bill, 87
Doi, Lillian, 87
Donneybrook Medical Centre, 98
Dookhran, Celine, 295–96
Doss, Nannie, 203–7, 204 (ill.), 207 (ill.)
Doss, Samuel, 206
Dostoevsky, Fyodor, 35, 35 (ill.)
Douglas, "Black" Agnes, 219–22, 220 (ill.)
Douglas, John, 131, 342
Downey, Lesley Ann, 40–41, 43–45
Doxtator, James, 173–74
Dozier, Crystal, 257
Dr. Phil, 58
drowning, murder by, 12, 68, 74–76
drug abuse. See abuse, drug

drugs, murder by, 21, 176–78, 237
Duffey, Martyn, 76
Duffields Yard, 309
Dunblane, Scotland, 332
Dupree, Daryn, 231
Durand-Deacon, Olive, 294
Dynasty, 30

E

Eady, Muriel, 299–300
East Cleveland, Ohio, 251
East Grand Forks, Minnesota, 103
Eastwood, Clint, 191
Eckman, Thomas, 339
Eddowes, Catherine, 309–10, 310 (ill.)
Edinburgh, Scotland, 222–25
Edmond, Oklahoma, 328
Edwards, Diane, 52–54, 67
Edwards, Tracy, 179
Efron, Zac, 49, 69
El Dorado Correctional Facility, 268
El Paso, Texas, 83
Elizabeth Lund Home for Unwed Mothers, 50
Elwes, Cary, 49
emotional abuse. See abuse, emotional
England
Carl Panzram, 110
Dennis Nilsen, 73, 76–77, 80
Fred and Rosemary West, 1–4, 6–8, 9 (ill.), 12–13
Harold Shipman, 94–96, 98
Ian Brady and Myra Hindley, 33, 35–37, 44–47
Jack the Ripper, 305–12
John Christie, 297–303
John George Haigh, 291–95
Peter Sutcliffe, 145–48, 150–59
rampage and spree killers, 329–32
Sawney Bean, 219
Englewood, Illinois, 235
Ermey, R. Lee, 335
Evans, Beryl, 299–301, 303

ALSO FROM VISIBLE INK PRESS

The Alien Book: A Guide to Extraterrestrial Beings on Earth
by Nick Redfern
ISBN: 978-1-57859-687-4

Alien Mysteries, Conspiracies, and Cover-Ups
by Kevin D. Randle
ISBN: 978-1-57859-418-4

American Murder: Criminals, Crime and the Media
Mike Mayo
ISBN: 978-1-57859-191-6

Ancient Gods: Lost Histories, Hidden Truths, and the Conspiracy of Silence
by Jim Willis
ISBN: 978-1-57859-614-0

Angels A to Z, 2nd edition
by Evelyn Dorothy Oliver, Ph.D., and James R Lewis, Ph.D.
ISBN: 978-1-57859-212-8

Area 51: The Revealing Truth of UFOs, Secret Aircraft, Cover-ups & Conspiracies
by Nick Redfern
ISBN 978-1-57859-672-0

Armageddon Now: The End of the World A to Z
by Jim Willis and Barbara Willis
ISBN: 978-1-57859-168-8

Assassinations: The Plots, Politics, and Powers behind History-changing Murders
by Nick Redfern
ISBN: 978-1-57859-690-4

The Astrology Book: The Encyclopedia of Heavenly Influences, 2nd edition
by James R. Lewis
ISBN: 978-1-57859-144-2

The Bigfoot Book: The Encyclopedia of Sasquatch, Yeti, and Cryptid Primates
by Nick Redfern
ISBN: 978-1-57859-561-7

Celebrity Ghosts and Notorious Hauntings
by Marie D Jones
ISBN: 978-1-57859-689-8

Conspiracies and Secret Societies: The Complete Dossier, 2nd edition
by Brad Steiger and Sherry Hansen Steiger
ISBN: 978-1-57859-368-2

Control: MKUltra, Chemtrails, and the Conspiracy to Suppress the Masses
by Nick Redfern
ISBN: 978-1-57859-638-6

Cover-Ups & Secrets: The Complete Guide to Government Conspiracies, Manipulations & Deceptions
by Nick Redfern
ISBN: 978-1-57859-679-9

Demons, the Devil, and Fallen Angels
by Marie D. Jones and Larry Flaxman
ISBN: 978-1-57859-613-3

The Dream Encyclopedia, 2nd edition
by James R Lewis, Ph.D., and Evelyn Dorothy Oliver, Ph.D.
ISBN: 978-1-57859-216-6

The Dream Interpretation Dictionary: Symbols, Signs, and Meanings
By J. M. DeBord
ISBN: 978-1-57859-637-9

The Encyclopedia of Religious Phenomena
by J. Gordon Melton
ISBN: 978-1-57859-209-8

The Fortune-Telling Book: The Encyclopedia of Divination and Soothsaying
by Raymond Buckland
ISBN: 978-1-57859-147-3

The Government UFO Files: The Conspiracy of Cover-Up
By Kevin D. Randle
ISBN: 978-1-57859-477-1

Haunted: Malevolent Ghosts, Night Terrors, and Threatening Phantoms
by Brad Steiger
ISBN: 978-1-57859-620-1

Hidden Realms, Lost Civilizations, and Beings from Other Worlds
by Jerome Clark
ISBN: 978-1-57859-175-6

The Horror Show Guide: The Ultimate Frightfest of Movies
By Mike May
ISBN: 978-1-57859-420-7

The Illuminati: The Secret Society That Hijacked the World
By Jim Marrs
ISBN: 978-1-57859-619-5

Lost Civilizations: The Secret Histories and Suppressed Technologies of the Ancients
by Jim Willis
ISBN: 978-1-57859-706-2

The Monster Book: Creatures, Beasts, and Fiends of Nature
by Nick Redfern
ISBN: 978-1-57859-575-4

The New World Order Book
by Nick Redfern
ISBN: 978-1-57859-615-7

Plagues, Pandemics and Viruses: From the Plague of Athens to Covid 19
by Heather E Quinlan
ISBN: 978-1-57859-704-8

Real Aliens, Space Beings, and Creatures from Other Worlds,
by Brad Steiger and Sherry Hansen Steiger
ISBN: 978-1-57859-333-0

Real Encounters, Different Dimensions, and Otherworldly Beings
by Brad Steiger with Sherry Hansen Steiger
ISBN: 978-1-57859-455-9

Real Ghosts, Restless
Spirits, and Haunted
Places, 2nd edition
by Brad Steiger
ISBN: 978-1-57859-401-6

Real Miracles, Divine
Intervention, and Feats of
Incredible Survival
by Brad Steiger and Sher-
ry Hansen Steiger
ISBN: 978-1-57859-214-2

Real Monsters, Gruesome
Critters, and Beasts from
the Darkside
by Brad Steiger and Sher-
ry Hansen Steiger
ISBN: 978-1-57859-220-3

Real Vampires, Night
Stalkers, and Creatures
from the Darkside
by Brad Steiger
ISBN: 978-1-57859-255-5

Real Zombies, the Living
Dead, and Creatures of
the Apocalypse
by Brad Steiger
ISBN: 978-1-57859-296-8

The Sci-Fi Movie Guide:
The Universe of Film
from Alien to Zardoz
By Chris Barsanti
ISBN: 978-1-57859-503-7

Secret History: Conspiracies
from Ancient Aliens to the
New World Order
by Nick Redfern
ISBN: 978-1-57859-479-5

Secret Societies: The
Complete Guide to
Histories, Rites, and
Rituals
by Nick Redfern
ISBN: 978-1-57859-483-2

The Spirit Book: The
Encyclopedia of
Clairvoyance,
Channeling, and Spirit
Communication
by Raymond Buckland
ISBN: 978-1-57859-172-5

Supernatural Gods:
Spiritual Mysteries,
Psychic Experiences, and
Scientific Truths
by Jim Willis
ISBN: 978-1-57859-660-7

UFO Dossier: 100 Years of
Government Secrets,
Conspiracies, and Cover-
Ups
By Kevin D. Randle
ISBN: 978-1-57859-564-8

Unexplained! Strange
Sightings, Incredible
Occurrences, and
Puzzling Physical
Phenomena, 3rd edition
by Jerome Clark

ISBN: 978-1-57859-344-6

The Vampire Book: The
Encyclopedia of the
Undead, 3rd edition
by J. Gordon Melton
ISBN: 978-1-57859-281-4

The Werewolf Book: The
Encyclopedia of Shape-
Shifting Beings, 2nd
edition
by Brad Steiger
ISBN: 978-1-57859-367-5

The Witch Book: The
Encyclopedia of
Witchcraft, Wicca, and
Neo-Paganism
by Raymond Buckland
ISBN: 978-1-57859-114-5

The Zombie Book: The
Encyclopedia of the Living
Dead
With Brad Steiger
ISBN: 978-1-57859-504-4

"REAL NIGHTMARES" E-BOOKS BY BRAD STEIGER

Book 1: *True and Truly Scary Unexplained Phenomenon*

Book 2: *The Unexplained Phenomena and Tales of the Unknown*

Book 3: *Things That Go Bump in the Night*

Book 4: *Things That Prowl and Growl in the Night*

Book 5: *Fiends That Want Your Blood*

Book 6: *Unexpected Visitors and Unwanted Guests*

Book 7: *Dark and Deadly Demons*

Book 8: *Phantoms, Apparitions, and Ghosts*

Book 9: *Alien Strangers and Foreign Worlds*

Book 10: *Ghastly and Grisly Spooks*

Book 11: *Secret Schemes and Conspiring Cabals*

Book 12: *Freaks, Fiends, and Evil Spirits*

PLEASE VISIT US AT VISIBLEINKPRESS.COM